Five Minutes A
by Mary Virginia Ma...

Loved ones will weep o'er my silent face,
Dear ones will clasp me in sad embrace
Shadows and darkness will fill the place,
Five minutes after I die.

Faces that sorrow I will not see,
Voices that murmur will not reach me
But where, oh where will my spirit be?
Five minutes after I die.

Here I have rested and roved and ranged
Here I have cherished and grown estranged
There and then it will all be changed,
Five minutes after I die.

Naught to repair the good I lack
Fixed to the goal of my chosen track,
No room to repent, no turning back
Five minutes after I die.

Mated for aye with my chosen throng
Long is eternity, O so long
Then woe is me if my soul be wrong,
Five minutes after I die.

Oh what a fool, hard the word but true,
Passing the Savior with Death in view,
Doing a deed I can never undo,
Five minutes after I die.

If I am flinging a fortune away
If I am wasting salvations day
Just is my sentence, my soul shall say
Five minutes after I die

Oh how marvelous grace that rescued me
Oh joyous moment when Jesus I see,
Oh happy day when like him I'll be,
Five minutes after I die.

Publisher
Reverend Tim Jones

Printed by:
Thomson-Shore, Inc.
7300 W. Joy Road
Dexter, MI 48130

First Edition - 2012

All rights reserved.
No part of this book may be reproduced in any form,
except for brief reviews,
without the written permission of the publisher.

ISBN
0-0000000-0-0

Editor
Mark Jones

A Note From the Editor

    I was honored when I was chosen to be the first to read the story you are about to read. My mission was simple.....correct the misspelled words and get it to the publisher. That was three years ago.

    I read the entire book within a week of receiving it, and completed the second edit shortly thereafter. It is difficult to explain why I dwelt so long on the third and final edit. I could chalk it up to the fact that I was extremely busy, but even I know better than that. Perhaps it is because I didn't want to read the last chapter of an autobiography written by my Pastor, the most influential man in my life; or the last chapter of an autobiography written by my best friend in the world; or that written by the man to whom I owe my all; strength, spiritual direction, wisdom, and guidance. As if publishing the final chapter would somehow be accepting the fact that there were no new chapters to be written.

    I bought some time by asking him to continue writing, which led to the prelude; and then to the final words that he most recently added. He kept writing, I kept enjoying what he produced. If I thought I could get away with requesting another few chapters, I would have, because as much as I personally enjoyed the journey he shares in the chapters ahead, I anticipate the continued blessings and memories that would make up the next chapters were I to continue to delay publishing. I guess I don't want it to end.

    Because I took so long, I also decided to forego asking for assistance. Like anything else, if I were to seek additional literary guidance, I am certain it would be available. That would add even more time, and I could tell by the tone of each extra chapter I requested that the author's patience was wearing thin. Therefore, if you find errors, I take full responsibility. Lord knows, I had ample time to correct them. As you read this, refrain from being too critical of the fact that the author jumps frequently from past to present tense, and sometimes fails to use complete sentences. Rather than correct them, I realized that is exactly how he speaks when telling a story aloud, so to change them just didn't feel right. I encourage the reader to sit back and listen as the author tells you his story.

    But again, I am so enjoying his autobiography playing out in real life, that I am not overanxious to close it out. Souls continue to be saved weekly, and the political landscape he references continues to change.

    How do we add what's coming next to the book once it's published? Maybe he will have to write a sequel.........I sincerely hope you enjoy getting to know a little about the man I have been blessed to call 'Pop'.

Table of Contents

~Prelude 1

Chapter 28
~The End 9

Chapter 1
~The Beginning of Discovery 25

Chapter 2
~Civilian Life 41

Chapter 3
~Call to the Ministry 53

Chapter 4
~The Man with the Holes in his Shoes 67

Chapter 5
~False Start 77

Chapter 6
~The Ride Begins 89

Chapter 7
~Preparing for Fights and Flights 101

Chapter 8
~Sharp Contention 117

Chapter 9
~A Change of Countenance 129

Chapter 10
~In the Caves of Obadiah 143

Chapter 11
~The Call to Japan 159

Chapter 12
~The Campaign Begins 177

Chapter 13
~The Race is On 193

Chapter 14
~Louisiana and Our Final Sweep 209
~Photo's 226

Chapter 15
~West for the Clean Up 247

Chapter 16
~77777.7 265

Chapter 17
~I Can't Read 283

Chapter 18
~Sports, Little Children, and Memories 299

Chapter 19
~Working Without a Net 315

Chapter 20
~The Winds of Change 331

Chapter 21
~Reunions 349

Chapter 22
~Round Two 367

Chapter 23
~Finding the Way Back 383

Chapter 24
~Laying Foundations 401

Chapter 25
~And Then There Were Two 419

Chapter 26
~What A Ride 435

Chapter 27
~Final Words 451

Epilogue
~Final Words, One Year Later 461

Prelude

Abe Lincoln said "If I take time to answer my many critics, we might as well shut the shop down for any other business. I'm doing the best I can and I will continue until the end. If things turn out for the good, the criticism won't amount to much. If things turn out for the worse, then ten angels swearing that I was right won't amount to much either." Amidst a hailstorm of anti-war liberal media attacks, he put this nation back together. He won the Civil War and freed the slaves. Had he tried to appease the naysayers, as seems to be the trend today, nothing would have been accomplished. Might I suggest, after forty years in the ministry, that old Abe could as easily have been talking about Christianity? Old Reverend Clark preached here in the Goldfield Saloon a hundred years ago. Today, he'd be ostracized from the modern New Testament for such a thing.

People say if you would have moved out of that old west resort in the middle of the desert, you would have a thousand people in your congregation by now. Some people drive fifty miles because they enjoy solid messages with a jovial delivery (I think I heard my wife say 'amen'). Heck, I've run that many off in the past five years. There have been a few serious hanger-ons that I've had to sternly recommend find a church more their style. There are a lot of good works around here with much better pastors than me. East Mesa Baptist is a good one. Valley, I think is another one close by. They're all over, God love them. I'm glad I've got good places to send people.

I've got a few dozen I can't get rid of though. This book will probably get a couple of them. They deserve better than the likes of me. I envy them. I spent twenty years trying to be half as good as them. I failed miserably. Several said they are impressed with my humility. This record of my life will prove that just the opposite is true. I'm just intimidated by their holiness. I should probably ban this book from them; I've really gotten used to having them around. Except for a couple of our ladies, I'm even getting to where I can look them in the eye. The only thing that will ultimately impress them is how God used me at all. He did though, and he did so mightily. He worked miracles for me. Some of them he did just for my personal blessings. I am evidence of the unsearchable goodness of a loving God.

It's strictly by the grace of God that our church is also the greatest little mission I've ever seen. We have influenced souls from all fifty seven states and many foreign countries. I'm sorry for the little pun there. This is not a political book, if you can get past the first chapter. I get it all out of my system, then the rest is just a fun ride. It's unbelievable what God can do with a man that has nothing going for him beyond his begrudging willingness to give it one more shot. It's a miracle I'm even preaching. I came from what is called the back side of this business. I wasn't employed for my spiritual gifts. What most of us never knew or paid any attention to is the fact that a religious organization lives or dies by competition. They compete for pastors to get the churches. They need the churches to get the students. They need them to keep their colleges alive. It is life and death when you're in the founding stages. That's the ministry I cut my teeth on.

~ Forced to Pastor ~

Who? Not me. God can't call me. A Baptist minister once explained it. The qualification of blameless cannot be met by everyone you know. He was quite clear. Well, good; my wife is pregnant and I'm leading my area in sales and making too much money to just walk off. Besides, most people think I'm nuts for even thinking about uprooting the family. My boss said it would destroy their opportunity for a decent education as well as deprive them of a normal childhood. 'Anyway', he added, 'you can serve God right here doing what you're doing'. That was 1969. In 1986, seventeen years later, I visited my old boss. He had retired and was still living in Milford, Delaware. He was the most influential voice that had almost delayed my decision to leave for Bible college. In the end he was the main reason I went. He told me he had run across a couple mutual acquaintances over the years. He said from what he'd learned about my experiences, I ought to write a book. It has been another twenty years since he made that recommendation. This is the prelude to that book.

At the time, standing in my old boss' driveway, I thought I could write a book. I had been featured in Christian publications regularly over the years. I had written "The Bear, Giant or Teddy" where I had predicted the economical collapse of the U.S.S.R., and "The Modern Dark Ages", which now sounds like an outline from modern A.M. radio. I didn't know that when I wrote them. Rush Limbaugh wasn't very big yet and no one had ever heard of the rest of them. "The Lie" had already been republished by request. This publication revealed the possibility that the Biblical prophesy of 'the lie' might not just be some profound statement made by the Anti-Christ. It may well be the result of rejecting the truth so long that you will believe any lie. Sounds like modern times, doesn't it?

Two of us were once chosen to feature an article on "Dispelling the Myths of Heaven". Dr. Henry Morris of Creation Science Institute and I were chosen by a leading magazine in our field. This led to opportunities to work with some other big names. Therein was the problem. I didn't have one (a name). Who would publish me? The editor and founder of a first class publication, the Pillar, once told me he likened my style to C. S. Lewis. Now there is a name! Wonder if they could leave off my name and just say, 'authored after the style of C.S. Lewis'?

I once picked up a book in a yard sale (or somewhere, I don't really remember). It was written by some unknown pastor. He said he felt like he should write it, even though he couldn't take credit for any major accomplishments, but hoped someone might get something out of it. It held the reader to the last page waiting for the point. This brought me to ponder an honest question at the onset of this endeavor. Could the time required to write this book be rewarded with more than the simple accomplishment of publishing a book? Twenty years ago, it would have been questionable. Old Mack (my old boss), was impressed with how one of his underlings had succeeded in a whole new career. I was just a kid, but a pretty good salesman. Then he heard I was a chief pilot and field representative working for my first college after completing phase one of my education. Upon hearing of my travels throughout the Pacific Rim, it started to sound rather exciting to a guy that rarely got out of town.

In retrospect, it just didn't seem like the accomplishments outweighed the failures. One of my old publishers tracked me down while I was recovering from losing the institute in Florida that had contracted me to help build it. He said he had been approached to fill the position of pastor of the church that owned the institute. He came to the conclusion on his own that I had raised so much money for the effort and had gained so much influence in the process that I was a threat to the ruling elders. They had just fired the pastor that had hired me, and he believed they wanted me to leave because of my loyalty to the pastor, and that they wanted to close the institute and redirect the moneys I had raised. He was also familiar with the history of a very popular college in Pennsylvania that I and my staff had fought so hard to save from moral and financial corruption. We ultimately failed after a long and bitter struggle, after which he offered me a place in his work in North Carolina. He said he had never before known anyone that had been involved in such intense spiritual battles, and he felt led to give us a place to serve and a time for healing. We'll go into a little more detail about the battles.....

The popularity of some of the characters in this book may surprise you. To best understand, you'll have to be old enough to remember the ones that have passed on. I was a young man when much of what you might call my successful times took place. Back in those days, I could walk into almost any pastor's office I desired to meet with. Like Paul said, unknown, but well known. The people didn't know me, but the pastors sure did. I'd been described as the Mafioso of New Testament Christianity, and one whose pen you prayed never mentioned your name. I never attacked anyone in print that I was sent to question. I wrote favorably of them if their actions were defendable in the light of New Testament policies.

I know I will someday answer for the hurtful means in which I conducted myself at times and for how I influenced others under my direction. I was ruthless and proud because I was right, and I could prove it. It was common knowledge that in the discipline of ecclesiology, there were few willing to confront me. When I questioned their actions concerning the New Testament Church or missions, I was on solid ground. This was the area of concern for which I was sent or summoned to resolve. It was my calling. I never could figure out, while it was so plain to some of us, why some just couldn't figure it out. I mean it's not eschatology which is to come. It's the church, which is plainly laid out in scripture.

We're going to talk a little about what went on behind closed doors in the work of the ministry. I'm not talking about immorality in particular, although I will mention it where it applies. It will shock you, as it should. Some might wonder what could be edifying about revealing such activities. I've asked myself that same question. The only answer I can come up with is that I believe I was supposed to write this book, and if I failed to include such activities, then a major portion of my ministry would forever remain a mystery.

Don't get me wrong, I don't think my experiences should be classified as the norm. I like to believe God spared a lot of good men from things that would have destroyed them, by using a few men like me to deal with the dirt none of us should have had to deal with. I can think of a lot of wonderful people that never had to get involved, or were never exposed to the unpleasant activities, because there was someone like me to handle it. As Ruth said, 'maybe that was my purpose'. I also like to think that maybe it's why the Lord has given me such a wonderful ending. He has, as I like to think of it, taken up the slack, pulled me out of the mire, and cleaned me up as if I'd never been in the swamp.

There are only two men from my past that still communicate with me willingly, but somehow God preserved my family. It was them He used to recover me. More than recover me; He restored me to more than I ever was. They are the ones that God used to force me to pastor. A calling I answered forty years ago but thought I was disqualified from ever realizing. After so many years behind the scenes, learning more than most of us ever need to know, He set me a hundred years back in time and gave me a fitting end.

You know what I am? Did you ever read about the Raggedy Ass Marines? Sorry, but that's the name someone chose for them. It's been years since I read the book, and I can't remember exactly, but they were a bunch of officer candidates nearing the end of WWII, and the need for what they had been trained to do had gone away. They were all given N.C.O. grades and stationed somewhere until the end of the war. They were not the young officers they were trained to be, yet they didn't feel deserving of the high enlisted rank they had been granted. They were not intentionally assigned to any meaningful task. They just turned into a ragtag bunch looking for anything to contribute to the war effort. By some accident, they became the best problem solvers the service has ever known. They were comfortable dealing with officers and enlisted alike. They spoke officer from an enlisted platform. As go-betweens for the enlisted, they accomplished seemingly irresolvable reconciliations. High ranking officers eventually figured it out and started using them in the reverse as well. They were assigned as trouble shooters throughout the division.

That same thing happened to me. I didn't have the commission of ordination, yet was better educated and trained in Ecclesiology than nine out of ten pastors I had ever dealt with. Without intending to do so, I became a go-between.....a trouble shooter, a comforter, and companion to many New Testament pastors, missionaries, deacons, Christian school administrators, and teachers. Ministers I had never heard of would request the college send me out to give them a presentation of our ministry. That was seldom what they really wanted to see me about. It was really about something they just didn't have anyone else to whom they could talk to about. They weren't afraid to share most anything with me, even though I was mildly published even back then. My appearance and stature was always as impressive as I could afford. Some called me a mobster. My personal conversation, however, was self demeaning. I let them see my flesh. It was clear to them; they were better than me spiritually. I just had a much easier grasp on Ecclesiology. I was just like the ragtags..... not commissioned, but a crude N.C.O. that would never seek promotion in their ranks.

Not until I was ordained did everything change. It was as though they suddenly felt I would blackmail them to support my work or something. The shields came up. Even the big shots that are still living and preaching will take my calls, but it's plain to me that it is only to appease me, and to avoid ruffling my feathers. If I miss anything of my early life, it's the relationships I shared with so many.

Let me clarify something, in the event you're thinking about reading this just to see some well known people exposed...don't waste your time. Only two popular men ever invited me to sleep with them. If I write this properly, only the most experienced pastors will figure out who they are. Mostly it was New Testament practices I was invited to discuss. They needed someone they didn't think would hurt their ministry. If they related it with one of their regular fellowship, they risked being ostracized. Today, however, their questionable practices have become universally accepted and others have gone on to fame and fortune. The once major issues are no longer a threat to any of them these days. I honestly doubt they will even mind me using them as examples. True New Testament practice is a dinosaur... not even a debate. Most pastors wouldn't even know what we're talking about. That's why I'm forced to pastor.

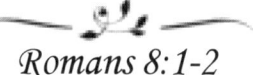
Romans 8:1-2
There is therefore now no condemnation to them which are in Christ Jesus, who walk not after the flesh but after the spirit. For the law of the Spirit of life in Christ Jesus hath made me free from the law of sin and death.

Chapter 28
The End

We're sitting out here in the desert, about 30 miles East of Phoenix. As I write this, I have cactus in my hand that I haven't been able to get out. I touched something I shouldn't have. Everything out here says 'look at me, but don't touch'. My daughter-in-law just brought a shovel out and sat it by me here on the veranda on her way to bed. She said, "You know the snakes are coming out at night now." It's that time of the year. I can remember over twenty-five years ago, I brought the family through here while we were on deputation on our way to the mission field. The last church we had preached in was in California, and we were headed to the next one, which was in Texas. For hundreds of years, this was the Bad Lands. Even in the California gold rush days, they didn't come through here. They went north of us or dropped south into Mexico 'til they got to California. Heat, snakes, and the last of the meanest Apaches that ever lived, made this place no place for white men or brown. Some Mexicans will tell you they lived here long before we got here. What they mean is they died here long before our Cavalry made it so anyone could live here. I live two miles from Massacre Grounds, where the last of the Mexican miners perished. Not even other Red Men came around here. It was truly the Bad Lands.

It's appropriate, I guess; I spent much of my ministry in the wilderness. I finally make it into the promised land of my life, and it's a desert. For the first time in my forty-plus years in the ministry, I've accepted the position of pastor. I'm the pastor of a church in a hundred-year old ghost town. I wouldn't trade it for any other pulpit in the world. I surrendered to be a pastor, but went off to school and got sidetracked into Christian Education. From there, it's real easy to get involved in religious politics. Most people don't even know such a thing exists, let alone how wicked it can be. I tried to break out of that and ended up on the mission field. Missionaries are still very much involved in the political game, but not as bad as the schools they're associated with. I might be one of the last people that ever broke all political ties and still made it to *the field.* *You* won't find this book in many college bookstores. I'm an outcast from every religious organization in the world.

This morning, I'm standing here at the kitchen counter, waiting for the computer to come up, and the sun. Until this line was written, I wasn't sure which one was going to win. This old computer is like the sun; you can't hurry it, you can't stop it. Now that's a thought.... an old man like me calling a computer old. I saw my first one about twenty years ago in the Ryukyu Islands, just south of mainland Japan. It still seems like yesterday when I sat at a park bench, pounding out some of my best stuff on my new portable typewriter. The sun isn't quite up yet. I didn't want to let the dogs out yet; there might be a mountain lion out there. One put my neighbor's horses up into the fence not long ago. They come down here when it gets really dry up in the hills. The sun is still not up, but the deep pink has turned a promising silver. I can see a little more than the outline of the Superstitions and the tops of the tallest Saguaro cactus on the hill between here and the mountain. It looks like it's going to be a nice day out here in the desert. We moved out here just north of Apache Junction a few years ago. We've been around this old globe east to west, but I intend to die right here if I ever get this book done.

I just started chapter twenty-three last week, but I'm getting so bored, I'm starting to write about my writing. There's something repetitious in writing about your past. I don't care how adventurous it may have been. When you're determined to recount every bit of it, you find out you spent a lot of time not doing much worth talking about. At my age, it's more fun talking about your kids. I've been working on this thing for over two years now. Since I started, my oldest daughter published her first book. She went all over doing book signings and started her second one already. My youngest boy preached his first message last Sunday. My oldest boy preaches for me when I'm sick or out of town. I guess if nothing else really great comes of this work, that alone was worth the effort.

Boy the sun is really up now. It was daylight for about twenty minutes, but now it's out from behind the mountain. The guy that built this big old place really liked glass. The whole front of this place, as well as a lot more of it, is lined with floor to ceiling glass. I'm about to go into my end of this place and get in my third set of clothing. Fall is funny in the desert. The mornings are chilly; then it warms up to T-shirt weather; then by nightfall, you're sitting by the fire, wrapped up in an Indian blanket. At least the rattlesnakes aren't around for a few months. You don't have to worry so much when the grandkids are playing around the property yet. They like to roll stones over and capture scorpions while they are sleeping. Even if they do uncover a snake, it will be sleeping as well.

My end of this place is a really rustic A-frame. Thirty years ago, it was all there was for miles around. The mailman wouldn't even come up here until enough people settled in to justify maintaining the road. I first passed through this area about the time the rest of this house was being built. I-10 was a rather new highway when I first came through Phoenix. We were headed for Texas to pack up for the mission field. We could have bought this whole hill for less than a couple hundred an acre. Now it's running for a couple hundred thousand an acre. I met an old guy that moved out here in the forties. There weren't a hundred people from Goldfield to Florence, including Florence. Goldfield was an undiscovered ghost town when he had bought his five acres that now borders the Ghost town resort. That's what we're doing here. We built the church at the top of the hill four years ago come December, 2008.

I was preaching to about four families in a living room in Gilbert when my company told me I was being transferred to L.A. When I took my severance, our little group told me to find some land out here and we'd build a church. That's when I remembered the Ghost Town. Remember, I first visited it on the now infamous nine-eleven, 2001. My sister's family had come out from Pennsylvania to visit us the day before. We had planned to go to the Grand Canyon, but we heard that all national parks were closed. We took them out to the lakes and stopped at the ghost town on our way back. We sat on the patio of the saloon enjoying the view of Superstition Mountain and trying to put aside the horrible events of the morning. I had no idea I'd ever build anything in the town, but I remembered all the undeveloped land around it. When I was looking for some affordable land out here, the area came to mind.

The mayor was up in the old bordello when I found him. I wanted to ask him who owned the land behind his town where I wanted to build a church. He said, "Build it right here, I'll help you." We discussed the details there in the old bordello, and six months later, signed the papers in the saloon. After it was a done deal, we all went out to the town to hold our first wedding. I married my daughter to JT. He is now our head deacon. Then we went to the saloon patio to celebrate. We were standing there with our celebratory glasses in hand when JT made a prophetic statement. He said, "You realize there will never be any more than the eight of us in our church?" He had been raised in a legalistic family. He couldn't fathom normal people wanting to be a part of a serious church. Except for us, only religious people go to church every Sunday morning, is what he was thinking. We'll have to support the work with weddings. He couldn't imagine normal folks loving the Word the way we do. This conversation came back to me the day he had to shut the door and tell people we were too full to let anyone else in.

At JT and Tonia's reception there on the saloon patio, there was a truck driver sitting at a table just behind us. We were talking about how we could afford to build the building, even if no one else wanted to be a part of it, when he interrupted us. "I'm not eaves dropping," he said. "I can't help but hear you." As he laid a ten dollar bill on the table in front of us, he said, "I want to be the first contributor." I thought if this guy wanted to help, probably a lot of others may want to help. We found out there were not as many as I thought there might be. I put out a letter to all the churches in the area, plus up in Flagstaff. I told them if they wanted to help us, we'd build them a youth camp for their use down behind the church. These guys all belong to some group or another; we're outsiders. Now I'm glad no one responded. I had forgotten what it was like being a missionary. You answer, as you should, to every one of your supporters. God didn't want us living a phony lifestyle to please anyone. We have led so many people to Christ that later told us they would never have gone to church anywhere else. They only visited our little church because they were visiting the ghost town.

Our attendance goes down in the summer. The first summer was scary. The winter visitors went home and all of the sudden, we were nearly as JT had predicted. The next year we had baptized ten or fifteen more into the work. We still seldom ran much over the twenties. The third summer wasn't much better. We ran into the thirties, but they were regular and generous. Last year, we seldom fell out of the forties. (I started writing this chapter last fall. It is now summer of 2008. I'm updating as I go along.) I thought we'd be running two services, at least in the winter, but we're only running in the sixties. (This year we ran in the eighties in season and our summer crowd is hanging in the fifties.) By the time the rest of the winter people get here, I think we'll only be a full house again. The great thing about the work is that at every service, there are at least as many visitors as there are members. Half of them are new people just passing through. We don't advertise, and we still get new visitors from somewhere.

A pastor from Pennsylvania visited one Sunday and saw our track rack in the back of the church. We stock it with fifteen different languages. During the week, in season, we leave our door open. The town is so well advertised that people come from all around the world. We only use Chick tracks and only one subject, "This was your life." I told the visiting pastor that we go through so many, it's hard to keep them in stock. I've walked through town and checked the trash barrels to see if they were being thrown away. I find flyers from all over town, but never a Chick track; they're taking them home. The pastor envisioned a man on his way back to Communist China reading it on the airplane. He went home and led his church to send us a month's supply. That's about three hundred dollars worth. I told him up front that we were not a religious bunch. We have bikers, bartenders, roughnecks, and ranchers. They don't slink down the alleys to pull out their tobacco. He didn't care. It's still a wonderful mission opportunity.

I almost never ask for a show of hands after the invitation is given. I don't invite them down front. I invite them to pray right there in their seats. One day, I just felt led to ask. We had a full house that morning. One of the most influential men I knew was in the back pew. I counted a dozen hands before his hand went up. I was so flabbergasted, I quit counting. One morning an Indian fellow showed up to ask if he could rent the building for a union ceremony. That's not a marriage. My deacon told him to have a seat, and after the services, he would introduce him to me. He didn't have to. After services he told me he wouldn't need it; he had found Jesus that morning. We had another Native American that came regularly because my head deacon was helping him beat alcoholism. You're more than welcome with us if you drink, but not if you're a drunk. We have two rules in our family; no idolatry and no immorality of any kind. Otherwise, don't blow your smoke in my face and I won't spit on your shoes.

This is campaign season, and I'm a news junkie. I'm better than I used to be. I used to listen to talk radio while I had Fox News on. I would turn down the sound on the TV and read the headlines as they came across the bottom of the screen. At the same time, I would be working on my computer. I don't know how I went so many years paying no attention to what's going on in the world. As a child, my father used to say we don't talk politics or religion. That left baseball. Then I went into the ministry, and for years I never paid any attention to anything else. The rest of the Christian world was the same. The government came along and closed most of our Christian schools. They made it so hard to operate a Christian college that many of them had to close. All we did was bitch. Meanwhile, more liberal judges were appointed to the courts and we lost even more of our Christian rights. Yet we sat on our hands until the President of the United States was performing elicit sex acts in the highest office in the land.

Now don't get me wrong. We're not a Trinity United outfit. If you're just looking for some place to charge up your political ideals, it's not us. The only time politics is mentioned is when it gets into theology. In the first place, there is no such thing as a separation of church and state. If you bought into that, then you don't know your history. All I'm saying is, if there is a separation, then both sides need to know it. They stand on the floor of congress and bash Christianity, but we can't say anything about it in church.

We preach whatever God puts on our hearts. How can you live in this world and ignore what's going on? God ordained government. He didn't tell his people to stay out of it. Oh, yes, he said not to get entangled with the things of this world. I'm sorry, but government is not of this world. Israel was a government, and when God used another government to judge them, Israel became a government within a government. The Pharisees were the ruling party when Christ was here. God ruled with judges and then against his will, with kings. Who does the Bible call the god of this earth? Who offered the nations to Jesus? Are we to ignore the work of Satan? Satan wants us to. God said if His people, called by His name, would humble themselves and pray, and repent, He would heal their land. Whose fault is it that He can't bless our land like He did when it was formed? Worldly living has to do with Satan's people, not God's people. How can you hand everything God blessed us with over to Satan's people and call it scriptural? When Jesus told his disciples to render unto Caesar what is Caesar's, it included a lot more than just paying taxes. We have a spiritual responsibility and a civic responsibility.

I didn't want to get on politics. There are a lot of good people from both parties that love to visit the old church. They've just been so deceived for so many years, bless their hearts, they don't have a clue. One Godly old lady and her husband visited us one Sunday. I'll never forget her. After the first service, as she shook my hand, she whispered in my ear that she didn't think she'd ever come back. Her husband had other ideas. He brought her back every Sunday. A couple weeks later, she whispered in my ear again. She said she heard from God today and she loved coming to our services. I thought maybe there is hope for her. These old gals sit around in their little AARP groups and hear nothing but negatives about conservative leaders. This could cost her friends. Only I was wrong. The Sunday after '06 elections, the mid term election when the Christians didn't go to the polls, she said she was glad JD Hayworth had been voted out. She said she only wished Kyle had been voted out as well. These are both solid Christian men and she wanted their opponents to win.

It isn't a secret that I'm a conservative. I had to face the fact when we built the church. They tell us if we preach anything political, that they will take our tax free status away. We decided from the first that we would not file for a 501c3. If they want to tax us, we'll pay. They still have to figure a way around the constitution to tax a church, even if they take your 501. We are not going to build a church that can't talk about what Satan is doing. When you got saved, you were not disenfranchised from the world. You were saved to impact the world for Christ.

I'll tell you how plain a message from my pulpit is. My sister-in-law came down for a wedding that I did for my nephew, and she came to services. She is a very boisterous liberal. My wife said, "Don't talk politics around her." That evening after services, she was sitting on the porch with me. She said, "I get the idea you believe you can't be a liberal and also be a Christian." She said "I'm a liberal, and I'm a Christian." I answered, "Penny, you don't fully understand one or the other. How can you support a party that supports taking God out of every part of our society that they can. How can you support a party that appoints judges that keep abortion legal, even though the majority of Americans are against it? How can you say you support Christ as a Christian?" She never said another word. I think she is a Christian.

You know the Bible says that if you reject the truth, you'll believe a lie? Most theologians teach that that means you will believe the Anti-Christ when he lies. I believe it means any lie. An atheist isn't a person that believes in nothing; they'll believe anything but the truth. God said he will send them strong delusion. This means that they are supernaturally stupid. I listen to Sean Hannity on talk radio. The poor man gets so frustrated. I once heard him tell a Clinton supporter that he could show them a film of the Clintons robbing a bank, and they would make some excuse as to why that bank had to be robbed for the overall good of the people. He doesn't understand what happened to him. He's a Christian. Jesus said that if you accept Him, he will save your soul. The Greek word used for soul in that verse is SUKA. This is the word from which we get our English word Psyche. What he is saying is that He'll save our sanity. You are supernaturally intelligent when you accept Him. The brain is just an organ we use to think with. The soul tells it what to think. When you become a Christian, God gives you a living spirit. That's what Christ meant when he said 'I give you life'. This enlightens the soul with the ability to know the difference between true and false. Christ said 'Let this mind be in you'. That's the only way you change a blind mind. These poor people are spiritually insane. You can't reason with them, and you can't scold them for their blindness.

Now that all the liberals have slammed my book shut, we'll go back to talking about normal life in the desert. Today, I'm not at the kitchen counter. I'm standing at the barbeque outside, looking up at the Goldfield Mountains. November here in the desert is like December in Florida, without the mosquitoes, and unfortunately, without the rain. Yesterday, I thought I woke up back east somewhere. My windows were dark. It looked like it was about five in the morning, but I had gone to bed late the night before and it was more like eight. I hadn't read about an eclipse of the sun or anything. I got up, and sure enough, it was totally overcast. We have what we call the monsoon season out here. It doesn't mean that it rains all the time; it just means that the humidity is much higher than the rest of the year. It's the only time of the year we have to run the AC.

For most of the hot season, we run a swamp cooler. That's a machine that runs water down over a bank of fins, with a blower that pushes the moist air into the house. It gets colder than an AC unit can make it, and for a fraction of the cost. Anyway, in the monsoon season, we get clouds. When we're really blessed, they have rain in them. We had lightning, thunder and wind; it was really a fun day. I even saw a few rain spots on the glass table beside the barbeque. It started out a really good day. It ended up my worst day in Arizona.

I wrote the previous paragraph last November. It is now the following June, and well into the heat of summer. The swamper won't work now for a couple months, because it is useless when the humidity is high. I'm trapped in my A-frame with the AC on. I'm working from my portable desk that I carry from place to place in the house. I use it so I don't have to sit down. Except for breakfast, I don't sit down until supper. My book is finally done. I'm just updating this part that I started to write one morning when I was bored with trying to remember my former life. Lately, the present has been most dominating. We had six or seven bad months, but my wife's final test came back inconclusive, but cancer free. It probably never was cancer, but who knows. God is still in the miracle business. It was a miracle that started everything I'm writing about in the first place. You'll find it in the book in its proper chronological order. People from all over the world visit our church, over a hundred thousand a year. We have the most photographed New Testament Church in the world, without a doubt.

I titled this chapter 'The End'. That may sound a little weird, but the following twenty-six chapters of this book will end with the beginning. This is the end result of the following recorded lifetime of experiences that brought about this beginning. So in effect, this is the end. The question is this: Is it the end of the beginning, or the beginning of the end? The Bible teaches that some will answer for their actions now, and some will answer later. It's more like some sins will be revealed now or covered until later. I'm in the latter group, I guess. That doesn't, however, change what I know. When I first began to grow in the knowledge and understanding of God's Word, I used to pray everyday for God to give me the heart of David. I didn't know that it might come with his weaknesses as well. God called David one that seeks the very heart of God. I got that request. God also called him a bloody man. I got that too. I lived the Christian life carelessly, and served some Christian organizations ruthlessly. For one outfit, I was both the eraser and the terminator.

Because of my careless lifestyle, God has allowed physical life to be terminated. Because of my ruthlessness in service to some big cause, both pastors and missionaries have been erased. I felt the power of God, but I never thought about the consequences of mishandling it. When I was flying for the college in Concordville, I would justify some of my assignments as the work of the Christian underground. In retrospect, I think Pastor White of Aberdeen, Maryland, better defined it as the Christian Mafia. Most of you blessed saints can't imagine the necessity of a Tim Jones. That's why there was a Tim Jones; so you didn't have to deal with it. When you're dealing with a godless government official, don't think God won't send them a lying spirit. Could you stand in an office in the capital building, looking in the face of a high official, and tell a bold face lie? It kept a Christian school open when hundreds of others were being shut down.

You've heard the Bible say to be cunning as a fox and harmless as a dove. Unless you're a really strong person, it's very easy to get that turned around. After years of success in the ministry, and seeking God's will, you can start to believe that He shows you his will through your will. You would not believe the number of pastors that came to believe it's so. Without even knowing it, and with all good intentions, your fleshly desires are interpreted as God's will. This philosophy was fully ingrained in me by my last year on the mission field. I cannot believe what I passed off as the will, or at least the sanction, of God. That's why you'll read about some bad decisions from the time we came off the mission field.

If you read the story, you'll make several useful discoveries about serving God. One is how normal, fun loving people, learn to love the Lord and his New Testament Church like they never imagined possible. I'm talking about normal people......not religious people. Most people have never been around church-going people that didn't base their fellowship on some degree of self-righteousness; a self-righteousness to which they could not attain. The most important thing you'll learn is how God can take a down and out servant, and remake him, despite his past. I don't know any preacher that destroyed his ministry and ever recovered. Let me tell you the greatest lesson I learned from this book. You don't recover. You start over. I tried to revive the old me several times. I was an arrogant, powerfully influential, administrator of once great works that are mostly gone. I served organizations and associations that I no longer respect as New Testament authorized works. What possible use would God have for that person if he revived him? A hundred year old blacksmith in modern Detroit would produce little, regardless of his once useful talent.

This is the case in all secular fields. You constantly advance, or you fall behind. There is, however, one field of practice that has never been outdated. It's been modernized, but never improved upon. In spite of all its innovators, reformers, and promoters, it only remains solid, because you can go back to the foundations and start over. That's what we did. We couldn't find a place to worship that preached the word with nothing added. We found some good works, but not one that was not a part of something beyond the New Testament Church; some organization started by a well meaning innovator, centuries after the foundation of the original church. To the average church member, such ties mean little or nothing. Coming from my background, it's another ball game. No matter what outfit it was, I knew someone in it. Worse yet, they knew me, or at least knew of me. I had a local pastor friend that was trying to become an influential part of one of these outfits. When he found out that more of them knew me than knew him, he became very defensive. It ruined our fellowship. If God wanted these outfits to exist, Jesus would have started one.

I have three friends left in full time ministry. I may still be able to call the office of some big name preachers, and they'll take my call, but I'm no friend. Last year, I was working on my qualifications for an officer's commission. I got my commission. I'm qualifying as a volunteer pilot for the Air Force Auxiliary, working with Homeland Security. I had to do it the hard way, though. My colleges are all gone. I needed someone on the Air Force higher education list to accept my degrees so that they could make me a captain and let me serve as a chaplain. I called several big colleges where I knew the big shots on a first name basis. I called one who is now the number two guy in maybe the biggest Christian university in America. I knew this guy back when he was writing his first book. I palled around with him when I was in college, before he was even a Baptist. As soon as they were sure I was no longer in any position to cause them any grief, they told me to go pound sand. I had to join the Auxiliary as a safety officer, and settle for 2nd Lt. I can't go and visit the boys in the VA hospital in my uniform as I wanted, but I can still fly.

I'm no longer a member of any religious party. I don't even qualify as an independent. That's what most Baptist colleges call themselves. If you're not a part of some man-made denomination, you're just not recognized by the government. All you have in this world is God. It took me years to get back to that, and I'm never leaving it again. A whole lot of people need to get out of their religion, and turn to Jesus. When people ask what denomination we are, I tell them we are pre-denominational. I feel sorry for a lot of young men serving in these mission outfits. They'll never know the real power of God, because they don't need it. All they have to do is call their mission director with their problems. I'm not saying they're bad people. They're just limited to whom they can serve. One guy wanted to help me so badly, he pleaded for me to sign our church up with their organization. I explained, and he understood. He just didn't know it was even possible to have a ministry today that operated only by the Book.

If you care enough to read this record, you will see that it is not only possible, but totally liberating. We didn't set out to build liberal religious organizations, but that's the natural order of things. You may say your outfit is not liberal. Well, you may not vote that way, but that's how you serve. Liberalism depends on making people dependent on them. That's how they maintain power. You say you just can't get to the field without the help of some organization beyond the church. You're wrong. I did, and I know many others that did it as well. If a church won't take on the command to reach the world, they are trading their blessing to some other organization for a pot of porrage. It's clear that God is blessing some of these organizations, but the blessings were supposed to belong to the church. You may think your church isn't big enough. The church that authorized and sent me was tiny. You'll read about how great a job they did.

I hope you didn't buy this book because you attended one of our services, and found that along with the solid word you received, you were also entertained. I add a lot of humor to the messages, because it is stimulating to the mind. In five years, no one has ever gone to sleep during services. Writing is a different thing; I'm no Erma Bombeck who wrote 'The Grass Is Always Greener Over the Septic Tank'. Humor is not spontaneous for me. It's hard work. It takes me as long to include proper humor as it takes me to build the entire message. It has to be properly placed to illustrate, emphasize, or clarify a point. Otherwise, it's just material for a stand-up comedian. Give the book to someone that wants to travel, but can't leave home. It would also be a good book for someone that got out of the ministry, or a church, for any reason, particularly if they think they screwed up. Failure is never final.

At age fifty-one, I started over with absolutely nothing. Only that time, I had no goals beyond living a normal life. I gave up on trying to be a good person. I had never lived up to my standards, and I never will. I was going to worship Him the way I was. I hoped He could accept it; it's the best I could do. I remember the day I made that decision like it was yesterday. I decided I was going to live a normal moral life, and make no plans for my life ever again. I had wasted the last couple years putting programs together that went nowhere. God may have been using them to keep my brain alive, but He didn't bless any of them. I quit; all I was planning on was working hard until I retired. That was the beginning of a wild ride. It began right there as a content trucker, and ended in a top corporate position in record time. How could that happen with no experience in that career field? God started it all one rainy day in a truck yard in Cincinnati with an old leather hat. You can follow how he did it in the last two chapters.

You'll see how God used the events of 9-11 to show us where he wanted the church to be built. You'll see how he took me from the office and put a hammer in my hand. Under the direction of the mayor, construction began July 23rd at 3:30 AM. It ends with the last line of the last chapter of this book. To keep us alive until we got on our feet, God began to bless my wife's part time work. She was doing hair at one of her friend's beauty shop. To make a little more, she took a job in a salon in a Wal-Mart. I owe her more than I could ever repay, because she never enjoyed her work. She only learned how by cutting my hair in our first year of college. Most of us couldn't afford a professional haircut, so she ended up learning on more heads than just mine. You'll find her real calling, besides being Mom, was always a church and Christian College secretary. However several times in our life she ends up back in the hair business. Over the years she managed to complete beauty school, and even won a serious beauty competition.

When we put our priorities in order and built the church first, God let the big house in Gilbert sell. The first place out here in the desert we looked at was just before that sale. We had to turn down a house on four acres right at the foot of Superstition. They were only asking $250,000. Two years later, that property would value around two million. I tell everyone this house is worth more than that. It's only on an acre and a quarter, and we paid more than we were asked for the four acre home we looked at. There are thousands of homes out here, but this was the first one. It was built by some master builder. After we bought it, a couple contractors stopped and asked if they could go up in the attic and try to figure out how he had built it. We didn't let them investigate, but when the mayor asked, we grabbed a ladder and headed for the master bedroom. He came down shaking his head. He said he thought he would find all kinds of short work up there that made our roof look like it did. He said it was an optical illusion. Everything was straight as a dye. It looks like an upside down boat, with all its bends and curves.

I told everyone that we had found Noah's Ark. Everything was broken but the view. We replaced the floors; tore out walls; remodeled the bathrooms; and commenced painting, just for starters. The view, however, is priceless. The front of the main house is built like a Swiss chalet. It faces the famous Superstition Mountain, home of the Lost Dutchman Mine. After dark, we overlook the entire Valley of the Sun. My A-frame has the same beautiful board ceiling as our church. I couldn't afford to rent a place like this for a weekend getaway. We lucked into the place because of a sad situation. It turns out that before the land values went crazy, this was known as Meth Hill. Our place was party central. The Boeing engineer that owned it told me his wife had gotten hooked years before, and he tried for five years to recover her, but couldn't do it. He said he made her a deal; the house proceeds for the teenage daughters. It's been over four years now, and still an old van or something shows up looking for a place to party. They just got back in state or out of prison.

Things are getting better every year. There are still parties about every weekend, except in mid summer. The only difference is that the crowd sitting around the fire ring at night, or throwing horseshoes in the daytime, are Godly men and women. We've met some good neighbors, and we've made some good friends. The occasional stranger still shows up, but it doesn't take him long to realize he's out of place. None of our guests have a record, so if they please, they wear a pistol on their belt. I never take mine off except to preach on Sunday. I'm not worried though. A number of our members are armed and certified to carry concealed. This is Apache Junction, AZ. If I was a thief, I'd move to Massachusetts or Toledo, OH; someplace where law abiding citizens are easy victims by law. We have some real bad guys from south of the border that even manage to kill our enforcement officers. Just think of the hey-day they'll have when they find Toledo.

Where do we go from here? I don't know. What am I planning? I don't make plans. When I told the boys I'd do this, I told them two things. Number one, I wasn't building any programs or promotions. God was in charge. The doors He opened, we would go through. Number two, if I was going to be a pastor, my major concern would not be that of the overwhelming majority of the pastors I'd worked with. Attendance, attendance, attendance..... it consumes their thoughts, their conversations, their writings, and their prayers. 'So and so wasn't there this morning', or 'so and so missed Wednesday night'. If so and so doesn't want to worship with us today, that's his business, not mine. We're not a church for weak Christians. The Bible says assemble on the first day of the week, and that's what we do. I've heard people say, "I can't make it through the week without midweek services." Don't you have a twenty-four seven relationship with God? You'll read why we only meet on the first day of the week, and why it's such a blessing for us.

If God had asked me to write a list of things I wanted Him to do for me in my old age, I would have missed some great stuff compared to what he did. I'm poor; I've always been poor. You'll read of our adventures across America and around the Pacific Rim. I only missed preaching one Sunday a year for the past four years. One day, I was sick. One day, my mother was dying. One day, I was standing on the Great Wall of China. One day, I was standing on Mars Hill, and I walked the streets of ancient Corinth where Paul preached. Mom and I may be struggling to meet the bills today, but that doesn't take any of this away. Oh, I told you she got a little job at Wal-Mart hair salon to help out for a couple of years. God made her a manager, the second highest producing manager in the state of Arizona, before she got sick. Her company sent her to these incredible destinations, and she paid to take me along. 'What a fitting end', as the Psalmist calls it, 'if it is THE END'.

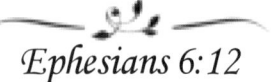

Ephesians 6:12

For we wrestle not against flesh and blood, but against principalities, acgainst powers, against the rulers of the darkness of this world, against spiritual wickedness in high places.

Chapter 1
The Beginning of Discovery

A young Airman stepped off the plane in a foreign country forty-five years ago. My, how time flies, particularly when you're looking back on it. There were many times over the course of my life that I wish I could have wound back time to that very moment and done it all over again. Now I don't have the energy to re-do the last forty-five minutes. In those days, however, I didn't have the patience to wait forty-five minutes. It had only been months since I had gotten out of boot camp and was assigned to my first station, Dover Air Force Base, Delaware. When I first arrived at Dover, we were welcomed, and told to prepare for this assignment to be our last one until separation from the service. That didn't set well, as I bored easily. High school just about finished me off. The day I turned sixteen, finally old enough to walk out the door without the truant officer in pursuit, out I went. I did not so much as slow down until I had left Punxsutawney, PA and was working in Maryland. Most kids that age can't fathom ever looking forward to as many boring days as you can schedule. No wonder my family couldn't keep up with me.

My father and mother lived in the same little town, in the same house they had bought as newlyweds. He was working the same job, and as it was in those days, expected me to step into his shoes when he retired. Man, I could never slow down that much. He had reached the top of the ladder many years ago. He held records in his profession, but the thrill had turned to the mundane. I think he drank to slow his mind down enough to cope with his current lack of challenge. A whole year dragged past and on my seventeenth birthday, I joined the Air Force. *(Just for the record, my first year on my own was the least edifying year of my life. Not worth mentioning, but what am I going to hold against a lost sixteen year old punk? At least he was smart enough, or desperate enough, to look for a new beginning.) Today, you're not allowed to take the G.E.D. in advance of when you would earn it by staying in school. I finished boot, went on to graduate eight months of technical training, and came home on leave with my diploma. My old classmates were still trying to stay awake long enough to get theirs.

A few months on Dover A.F.B. and I had finished all the required on the job training and all the extracurricular certifications I could qualify for. I discovered learning was fun, duty was boring. All you had to do was get your plane in commission, which meant ready to fly, and go home. I sat on the barracks steps waiting for my plane to be assigned a mission. When it left, I'd hitchhike about four hundred miles to my home town in PA and wait. Sometimes it was a week or so before I got an inbound call and had to head back to meet it. All you needed to do in those days to get a ride in any direction you wanted was to put on your uniform and stick out your thumb. This was before the Jane Fondas and John Kerrys ruined all that. We old Vets can remember what it meant to support the troops. It was natural; no one ever said it... they just did it. People would go fifty miles out of their way to get you to a good spot for your next pick up. One day during deer season, I even carried my deer rifle with me. Every hunter on the road picked me up. Try that today!

One day I was sitting on the barracks steps and a neighbor pulled up on a little red motor bike. I had never seen anything like it. It was not a Harley, an old Indian, a Triumph, or a B.S.A. He told me he had found a guy down the road in a little block building that was selling them like hot cakes for about a week's pay. I bummed a ride out there, and sure enough, it was true. That very week, he had received his first big bike. The biggest bike Japan exported. It was a black 305 Honda Dream. It was going to cost a couple of pay-days, but I wanted it. He was putting it together and told me that he was contacted by his distributor and told to offer a franchise to anyone from out of state. He really tried to talk me into taking one to PA and working it when I got discharged. He told me it wouldn't cost me anything, but I'd have to sign an agreement to start a little shop like his to get started. I was eighteen; I didn't want to work in a garage..... besides this Honda thing would probably fade out before I got out of the service anyway. I decided I would just take my bike and go, thank you. I saw the same tall, skinny, greasy young man about ten years later. Only he wasn't sitting on the floor of a one car block garage on a side road out by the Air Base. His dealership filled two city blocks. He had become one of the hard working young men with foresight that today's liberal politicians want to punish for their success. Boy, I'm glad I didn't get sucked into that world!

You didn't need a helmet to ride in Delaware back then, but you couldn't ride on Base without one. One day I forgot my helmet somewhere, and I was pushing my bike through the main gate when I saw a cartoon someone had taped on the guard shack. It was a picture of two gate guards in Confederate uniforms with white beards down to their knees, and the caption read, 'once on Dover, forever on Dover'. Just the week before, two of my fellow crew members went up to Punxsutawney with me to wait for our inbound call. We were having a beer in a little café in Rossiter, a tiny village about three miles from Punxsy, when our world changed. President Johnson came on the TV and announced that we were now active in Vietnam and all leaves had been canceled; we were to return to our duty stations immediately. We were the only three in the place and we were in uniform (that was about the only way you got served under-age in those days). The owner looked at us as we stood up and said, 'drinks are the house'. The only thing I could imagine worse than being stuck on Dover Air Base was being stuck on Dover Air Base without leave. I pushed my bike right over to personnel and volunteered for Vietnam!

Ever since I had left school, I'd had a plan. The plan was, as best as I can remember, was that whatever plan anyone had for me, I'd chance it. See where the new one went. Only with age and experience comes wisdom. Wisdom to recognize that change without thoughtful cause is an escape mechanism to avoid the responsibility of making any plans. Continual change will eventually out run preparation. Until then, change was working well for me. I got my new orders within two weeks. Now all that needed to change was a relationship I had made with a young girl the week before on the beach. Over the last couple months, I'd been trying to get in the circle of guys I really respected. Seemed like any party I showed up at, this group stood out. They were fun, but not a rowdy bunch. Only the week before, I decided I didn't want to be a part of any group....I was going to get out of here.

I shaved my head and rode my bike down to the beach, and there they were. Davenport was the leaders name. As soon as he saw me, he left the boys and walked over. I was impressed. He pointed down the beach to a spot where two girls were sunbathing. He asked me which one I wanted? I didn't want either, but this was the first personal attention I'd ever received from this guy. I told him I'd take the little one. Now, I knew the test for membership in this gang would be to leave this beach with that girl on the back of my motorcycle. I would have tried my best, even if she had been uglier than a mud fence, but when we got in good viewing range, that wasn't the case. When I got a good look, I started to wonder if I could pull this one off. They were congenial. They knew from our hair we were Air Force guys, yet they smiled and let us introduce ourselves.

At this point, I'm not allowing myself to examine the girl with any personal interest. All I want to do is whatever it takes for her to let me take her home. I knew I had my hands full, but I got lucky...seems I reminded her of someone she had great affection for. She really wasn't seeing me. She wasn't even really talking to me. It was all about this other guy that I looked like. She wasn't hard to look at, but I decided if I was lucky enough to leave here with her, I'd leave her wherever she wanted to be left. The last thing I was looking for right now was a relationship beyond the gang leader that I was out to impress. At that age, I was still in the high school mode when it came to girls. They never let me chew my tobacco. As soon as her sister pulled out and I was certain she was stuck with me, I pulled out my snuff can and took a chew right in front of her. I figured that would put the nail in the coffin. All she did was climb on the back of my bike and hug up tight. Now I was really impressed. I was even a little interested. What would it be like to have a girl like this? I knew I had never had one like her.

She had me take her to her sister's house in Smyrna, about ten miles north of Dover. She said she was staying there so she could walk to the Dairy Queen where she was working. Remember, I said I intended to leave her there? I think the only thing I left there was my heart. I had never been so intrigued by anyone in my life. There wasn't a phony bone in her body. The fact that she didn't try to play hard to get was what really threw me. It's like she had graduated from more than high school. There was no high school girl left in this woman. She was all business. She said, 'if you want to see me again, call me at this number'. Now tell me how you say that and convey a whole different message? I looked into her piercing green eyes and heard her clearly say that she wasn't fooling around. She wasn't looking for a date.....she wasn't looking for a boyfriend either. I heard her say, 'if you want me, call me; if you don't want me, then don't bother me'.

When I rode off, I swore I'd never make that call. I felt like a judge had just acquitted me from a life sentence. I didn't even kiss the girl and she had her hooks in me deep. I knew they'd leave scars, too. Thank you Davenport.... just days before, I had said no more girls. I had just broken up with Pat Sweeny back in Punxsy and swore I didn't need this shit. I was footloose and fancy-free. I was going to war. I'd figure the rest out when I got back. I felt like the rebellious young boy that was so tired of being told what to do that he decided to join the Marines! I understood what he was feeling. When you get fed up with the way you're running your life, or the way your life is running you, change it... put yourself in a situation where you're not making the decisions. I'd done that when I joined the service. I furthered it when I volunteered for Vietnam. I didn't know there was a third and final step coming.

Yeah, I made the call. What could I do? Every woman I saw with platinum hair was her. I went back home and dated an old girlfriend, but when I held her I called her Cheryl. It's a good thing her name was Cheryl, too, but I knew what I was saying. For the first time in our long time relationship she wanted to get intimate and I couldn't. What the heck was wrong with me? When I went back to the base, I asked my friend Mike Beasley what was wrong with me. I told him what had happened in Punxsy and added that I had tried to light a stick of gum just after I dropped Cheryl off at her house a few minutes ago. He said this is going to sound funny between a couple of guys like us, but you're in love. He said the same thing had happened to him with Margaret. Wow! This love thing must be real. But I had to face reality. For me, it came a little bit under-developed, and a little bit too late to develop it. I was on my way out of there.

A week later, I got my new orders. Tell me you can't get off this base. All I have to do is ride out and tell her goodbye. Somehow I resolved to do this. Partly because of what I was now facing, and partly because I just couldn't separate what was happening with us from a dream. She didn't want to hear it. I said I'm not having a girlfriend waiting on me, for God knows how long. It's either goodbye, or what, we get married? I tell everyone I told her this at a Chinese restaurant. I asked how she wanted her rice, fried or plain... she said thrown. That's not true, but two weeks after the first sighting on the beach, we were married. Now there I was, nine thousand miles away in a strange country, with the first thing in my life that change didn't wipe away.

I was assured I would either be assigned to Tonsonute Air Base, Saigon or Cameron Bay, Danang. I got the main support base to South East Asia located in mainland Japan, called Tachikawa. It suited my training. It was the only other Air Force base bigger than the one I'd left. I was qualified to crew anything they had. That very thought scares me now. I was a teenager! Most of us were not sure we could handle anything, let alone everything. Now that I'm old and looking back, I see for the first time, we could, and did handle everything. Kids handle the matters of war. Things had not heated up yet down South. They were in the midst of a massive build up and everything had to be supported from here. No one was sure where to put me. I was Shanghaied because I was qualified to crew bigger stuff than what was based down there where I was headed. During in-processing, they just said to check in every once in a while and they'd place me where they needed me most. They were initiating so many new programs, this decision took weeks. Meanwhile, I was discovering a new world.

When they sent me to Delaware, I'd never seen the ocean. Now I was clear across the other ocean. I was in a land that saw the U.S. serviceman as a mighty conqueror. Japan was nothing like the John Wayne movies. These people held us in the deepest respect. Remember again, this was before Jane Fonda and John Kerry's finished work. I wish all of you were old enough to have experienced a time the world held us in awe. It was not the world that changed this; it was the American media. When the world hears our news, telling them only how bad we are, they do what they have always done. They follow our lead. If it's popular to run America down, then that's what they do. Germany picked up on it and their politicians ran on anti-American platforms and got elected. France did the same, but they didn't have to make much of a change of policy. It wasn't the world that turned on us. It's the new anti-American movement that began right here in the good old U.S of A., while thousands of us were nine thousand miles away.

There we were in all our glory. We couldn't walk down the street without being touched and admired. The admiration exceeded what we experienced back home. Now think a second, we were kids. We couldn't even buy a drink in a bar back home. Now we were men of the world. Cock of the walk. No kid can handle that. Now I've got too much time on my hands and the little bit of money I've got is worth about five times what it was back home. I could go to town with a dollar, get drunk and go home with change in my pocket. That was because I didn't buy colored water, supposedly drinks, for the hustlers working for the bars. I got bored with that very quickly. I realized what was going on. Most of the boys in the bars were in Japan on R&R. That meant they'd been sent up from the battlefield on one of our supply planes for a week of rest and recuperation.

I put a copy of my permanent station orders in my pocket the next time I went to town. Only now I don't go to bar alley by the base. I go seven train stops away from the base to a small town called Fusa. They still hit on you because there was a new jet base being built not far away and R&R boys still found their way here from time to time. The girls weren't the hardened professionals and I even found another permanently based airman that had just come down to have a few drinks. Once they knew we weren't just here for the week they pretty much left us alone. In a couple days I went back. I sat at a table because I didn't see the guy I'd hoped to run into again. One of the hustlers slid in beside me and grabbed my thigh and asked me to buy her a drink. I said I don't buy colored water. She left. I lost the hand too. I won't lie to you, it felt pretty good. I hadn't seen my woman in weeks and she was nine thousands miles away. I wasn't a Christian but I was still a little too proud to be hustled. I'm still amazed at the fortitude I had as a young man.

A woman came over to my table. She didn't slide in on my bench and she didn't ask me for a drink. She said "you new here, you stay here long time." That wasn't a question, so I didn't have an answer. Don't forget, I was eighteen years old. You could write my total resume on your thumbnail at that time. I was about to get involved in a real misunderstanding. "I need long time GI", she said. "I need partner. My place, you give some, I give some, that good deal." I'm thinking business. I bring GIs, I get a commission. Boy was I screwed up. She ordered me a drink. She didn't ask me what I wanted to drink. Even as a kid I didn't drink the real stuff. I couldn't even handle the beer I drank. I don't remember much more after that. I vaguely remember being escorted down an alley in the dark. I remember the next morning. I woke up looking at the woman I remembered sitting at my table. She was standing over me cleaning my face. Oh shit, it was blood. I was looking for the door and she was pulling on me. "You long time man now", she reminded me. I found the door and she let go and hit her knees on the floor with her hands extended toward me. "You no pay, you stay, I pay" she said.

I was married! A realization I'd forgotten somehow in that distant world. This was not going to work. I had to get some help or I was really going to get into trouble over here. I may already be in trouble. Whatever this deal was, it wasn't for a night with a whore. You can buy that anywhere, and there's no blood and bruises included. I'd figure it out later, but right then, there was a restraining force on my heart like I'd never felt before. I had made some serious vows just a few weeks before, and now they were weighing heavily on my young heart. I had always believed in God; I had just never sincerely sought to know Him. It was afternoon when I made it back to Tachi. I walked straight to the Chaplain's office. All three major faiths were represented in the same compound. I didn't know anything about religion. All I knew was that left to my own devices, I might not see maturity. This wasn't Kansas anymore.

The first office was that of a Catholic Priest. Well, they must be the oldest Christian thing going, I thought. If I'm going to get religion, I want the real McCoy, I'm not doing this out of boredom. I want to know God and no nonsense. I can't remember the conversation. What I remember was a bunch of stuff I had to do, even to get to the point where I could start looking for what I went in there to find. I walked next door to the Rabbi's office. It would not be fair to comment on this visit, as I don't remember any of it. All I knew was I still had no answers. The last office was the Protestant office. They wanted to sign me up to some assistant Chaplain program is all I remember about that. God, I know it's not this hard. I've met some real dimwits in my life that have told me more about what I'm looking for than any of these professionals have been able to share. I wish I had given any one of them this kind of serious time. Where do you find one of these nuts when you need one? I walked around for hours looking for one. The only advice I got was to go see a Chaplain.

I went to chow and then to the club, but it didn't go away. Now I'm back at the barracks and it's late. There was an old sergeant, maybe in his early twenties, standing outside waiting for something. I walked up to him and asked him who the most religious man he knew was. 'Why, Deacon Gray', he answered without hesitation. He's right up there on the third floor, at the top of the steps, first door on the left. I beat on the door. This skinny, bulgy eyed guy opened the door and asked what was going on? Incidentally, about twenty years later, I was speaking at his church in Kansas. He informed the congregation that we met one morning about three-thirty in the morning! Airman Gray worked in the parachute shop. When I told him what I wanted to know, we went straight into the word. By now it was getting twilight. He advised we get some chow and then he took me to work with him. This went on day and night. I moved into the room across from his. I still didn't have a job assignment, so I spent all my time with him.

He took me out to a little mission just off the base. We were helping to build on an addition to the building. He looked down from the ladder and said something I remember as clear as if he had just said it. He said, "I'm not getting a single spiritual blessing for this work." "Why", I asked. Deacon Gray explained, "This is not a true New Testament work". God had made it very clear to this young saint that I was not interested in religious activity. He knew that I wanted the church that Jesus built or I'd put my membership in the V.F.W. He knew I did not want to waste my time with anything less or more. He went on to say, "There is only one around here that is what you're looking for, but it's not an English work like this one. I brought you here so at least you'd get the Word." He wouldn't tell me where the church was; he just indicated that it was too far away.

I finally got my first assignment on Tachi, but I continued to hammer him every night with questions on the church. About a month later he asked if I was off duty Saturday. He told me he'd taught me all he could and that we were going on a trip to meet the man I was looking for. I asked him if we were going to the church? "No", he said, "the church is in Tokyo, we are going to his house." In the mid sixties, the Japanese must not have discovered vitamins yet. From the sixties to the eighties the average height of a teenager must have increased a foot. When us two six foot G.I.s got on a bus it was no less a sight than the giant show at the circus. Little children couldn't take their eyes off us. In all innocence, they would just point at you with their mouths wide open. I didn't understand why their mothers would cover their eyes and turn them away from us. I later learned it was not polite to point.

No one spoke to you unless you spoke first. As a matter of fact, almost no one spoke to anybody. There could be five people standing at a bus stop and not a word uttered among them. It would be many years before I would learn Japanese culture and realize they were just being polite. You learn these things as you learn the language. There are appropriate greetings, but you must know the social standing of the one you are addressing. They don't speak on a social level as do most Occidentals. They speak up to you or down to you. At first this sounded rude to me, but I later learned that it's just as offensive to speak up to one that considers himself in a lower station of society than the one speaking. To avoid this embarrassment either way, they just didn't speak. When it becomes necessary to speak, they face each other with their business card in hand. They bow and exchange cards without a word. Only after each of their social standings are determined will they address each other accordingly. Times have changed a lot, but this remains a common practice among business men.

In today's Japan, if you're not a business type, you're probably not wearing a suit and tie. In the sixties that was not the case. Everyone wore a suit and carried a briefcase. Only the peasant farmer or pauper was clad in traditional wear. The only one that seemed to be able to speak without offence was the G.I. We didn't know any better, therefore it was acceptable. It took a while to figure out where the working type went. All you saw was hundreds of bicycles going up and down the streets, everyone wearing suits and carrying briefcases. I thought there must be a secret underground tunnel or something for the working man. Then one day I walked into the changing room where our Japanese civilians that worked in our shops would emerge from every morning and retire to every night. There in the lockers hung the suits and the briefcases containing their lunch bags and personal papers. Mystery solved. About the only contact the average G.I. ever had with the Nationals was on Bar Ally, and that was not much of a learning experience. I had met a couple of guys that had a regular girl. This was rare, but these were the guys that could tell you anything culturally useful. I would not need one. I was about to meet the most culturally informed American in the entire country.

The farther away from base we got, the older the buses got, along with everything else. We got off the last bus and set foot on very strange territory. Most of these people had not seen an American since the wars end. Back then all they saw were armed, uniformed soldiers bringing food to their villages, and M.P.s patrolling the roadways. You had to be at least twenty-five years old to remember that. We started out on foot, on not so much a road, as a path between rice patties. We came to a small compound of rural homes. The only people I remember seeing would look at us, bow, and point to a small wood-sided house ahead of us. Now here's where things get sketchy. I don't think Airman Gray went a step farther once the house came clearly into sight.

There was some bad blood between these guys over something. Whatever it was, it's long since resolved. If it was anything serious, I was well protected from it in my tender searching years, and to this day, as far as that goes. All I know is this guy dropped off the edge of my earth for about twenty years. Nevertheless, he served his purpose in my life. My life was about to change forever. *(I had just written these words, Dec. 9th 2005, when my wife walked in with a letter in her hand. It's from the man we are just about to meet. He is requesting a picture of my wife and I standing on the Great Wall of China. I'd never have seen China or any of the many countries we lived and worked in if I had not made these steps in this strange land some forty years ago. So, changed my life forever, was an appropriate choice of words.)

I walked up to the little house and stopped at the boarded fence. There was a mean, ugly black dog tied to the house. The door opened and a big man walked out. Suddenly, there were two mean, ugly things standing inside that fence. This guy's head was used by Marlin Brando in the movie "Godfather." He must also have used it in "Apocalypse Now", because it had a big round hole in the forehead. Even from where I was standing, you could see the skin over the hole pulsating with every heart beat. His hands could have been used by Shrek, but they weren't animating anything in those days beyond Bugs and Mickey. But now I know where they got the idea for the hands. I must have looked quite puzzled. I was expecting Lawrence of Arabia crossed with an Einstein of New Testament Theology. That was not what I was looking at! I don't think I uttered a word. Then a deep resounding sound emitted from the head. "You must be Airman Jones", followed by a smile you could hardly discern from laughter.

The whole face reflected what you would call a belly-laugh. This told me that he had done this before. 'Brother Gray said you were looking for me and I'm looking for the man that's looking for me, so come on in', he said. 'That dog won't bother you. He seems to know if people mean well or not'. That stinking dog tried to take my leg off. So much for the dog test.... we never did make up. 'You're just in time for lunch. Will you join us?' he added, then turning to his wife, 'Neva, set another plate, we have company'. Now I was eighteen years old, two hundred and ten pounds with a thirty-three inch waist. I was an eating machine. It had been nearly two months since I'd had home cooking. I hadn't even seen a female cook since I'd landed. We exchanged pleasantries, made the minimum family introductions with Neva and two children, and sat down to a delicious bowl of beans. Great start, I thought. While I was wondering what the main course was going to be, Neva started to clear the table! It never crossed my mind that we were done until I saw her at the sink doing the dishes. Now, I was just a kid, but I knew a man that size didn't exist on a small bowl of beans and not even a slice of bread. At that point, I was thinking that Airman Gray refused to come the rest of the way with me because he knew a lot more about the situation than I did. As young as I was, it didn't take long to figure it out. Not long before that, I shot rabbits in the ditch with the light from the headlamps, and killed numerous groundhogs, pheasants, and deer. It didn't matter what was in season, it went in the pot. These people didn't have anything to eat.

Maybe God had set this all up. The lesson I was about to learn could not be bought. It could not even be articulated in the best lesson plan you ever made. In the next couple of weeks I was going to learn the meaning, the power, and the result of faith in action. It would forever change my life. It would put power in my future ministry like nothing else could ever do. Many times I've been asked how I could have exercised such faith in my life. I could always say that I'd seen real faith, my friend. If I had never gone on to college, never learned another thing about faith and true New Testament Missions, it wouldn't have mattered. I was forever ruined on second best methods of service. Many years after learning what I was about to learn, I would become one of several missionaries that lost their sending church. I would someday be the only one that went to the field the New Testament way. These were good men. They had just never seen true New Testament Missions work. They all ended up in one group or another, practicing something that even they believed to be second best.

A natural pearl and a cultured pearl are both real pearls. You miss so much when you let someone else do for you what God wants you to experience through the work of His people and His churches, without any other assistance. They told me they just couldn't put it all on the line without some outfit backing them. It's just the opposite when you've witnessed it working the only way you can find it in the Bible. There is indescribable confidence in knowing that if you get it done, God did it. But what is even more comforting is what I was witnessing out there in the rice patties. Eddy had no idea why his support checks had just quit showing up a few weeks before.

I couldn't get it through my head that any family could even be there without some big organization sending them and helping to sustain them. That, he said, would worry him. 'I wouldn't know if God put me here or man put me here', he said. Then added, 'but I know who put me here. No way could we be here if God didn't do it. I have a lot more faith in God than all the organizations in the world. We'll be just fine'. What was so convincing was that he meant it. They remembered back when they didn't have enough money for a ticket to Japan, but they had enough to make it to Hawaii. They lived in the back of a church and worked to feed themselves until the money was provided for the rest of the voyage. God was in it all. Many of the small missions in Hawaii ultimately became churches. They would become a great help to his ministry in Japan over the next twenty years.

Meanwhile, I couldn't help much. I made eighty-four dollars every two weeks and most of that went back to my wife in the states. I was broke when I found this guy and it had been nearly a week now. At least I could eat at the chow hall. I'd get paid in a couple days and I couldn't wait to show up with some milk and bread. For now, we're both on the short end. He gave me a little scooter he said was too small for him. Closer to the truth, looking back, was the fact that I could get it registered on base, while he couldn't afford to register it along with the car he needed. In reality, I also think he wanted to keep teaching me, yet he couldn't afford the gas to come see me.

That first week flew by. Before I knew it, it was Saturday and I was motoring up the little path to his house. 'Look what I found' he said, as he walked to the small refrigerator, almost as if he was sneaking up on a rabbit, or was about to uncover some hidden treasure. 'The little shop down the street got this somewhere', he says. Cradling a small bundle in his hands wrapped in butcher paper, he says, 'I don't think the shopkeeper was even sure what it was, but I recognized it and talked him out of it for a song'. He set it gently on a saucer in the middle of the table. He'd been waiting to share this treat with me. I'd brought over a small bag of dried bread that the night cook let me have. It was a match made in heaven. Fresh beef tongue sandwiches! I've never forgotten the gleam in his eye as he sliced it up and handed me my portion. *Some twenty years later, down in the South China Sea, we'd share some exotic dishes together. Nothing, however, came up to this mysteriously affordable find of fresh tongue.

This man's faith was so contagious, I wasn't even worried about him anymore. In fact, I was looking with anticipation as to how the Lord was going to provide for him the next day. 'There's got to be more cow where that tongue came from.... we just have to find it'. *(I wrote this in 2005, it's now Saturday June 28th, 2008 and this is the first edit. The message God gave me for tomorrow is titled "How to pray for our daily bread". I'd forgotten about this. How appropriate I should find it today. Every Christian should write an autobiography even if they don't intend to publish it. It will strengthen the confidence of your calling.)

Incidentally, my expected pay had not yet come. In fact, my orders were messed up and they were not sure when it would find me.

I couldn't just give the wife a call. I had to reserve a sound booth. When my turn came, I had to yell as loud as I could at the party on the other end of the line. Pacific Cable Communications....that's a long wire under a lot of water. Even a letter was about a week away. I had left my young wife with my folks. Now, imagine as my new wife gets the first batch of mail from me. She was not religious when I married her and, remember, neither was I. Now she's wondering who's writing these letters. She's never heard this terminology before. Not in Kansas any more, Dorothy. She's not sure where she is now, and she's not got a clue where it is that I've gone. All she knows for sure is that she can't go home. That was clear from the onset. When I asked her to marry me, she said I'd have to ask her Daddy. When I met her, she had just finished school and was working at the Dairy Queen down the street from her sister's house where she was living. Ask her Daddy?

I had never heard an adult use that word before. All I could think was that he must be a Teddy bear sort of guy. 'He'll see you now', was what I remember next. I was about to enter into another world of family....totally different than anything I'd ever experienced. Daddy would be translated "Don" in my world, as in Corleone, only Greek instead of Italian. I was standing outside in the long circle drive when this message was solemnly delivered. I walked in through the outer porch. There were a lot of people standing around; some big guys with their hands in their pockets who just gave me a nod towards the office. Women were whispering in each others ears, 'he's going in'. His back was towards me. I sat down in the only chair. It was behind Daddy. A two-hundred sixty pound, six foot six figure, sitting at his desk, never looked up or turned to look at me.

I don't remember anything I said. I only remember what he said. He grunted, then laid down his pen and spoke loudly and clearly enough for the entire adjoining room to hear. 'Don't bring her back'. There never was a question in her mind. Daddy spoke it, she's never going back. Wasn't much question in my mind either, at that point! He'd hunt me down and kill me if he ever saw her walking on the property with a suitcase in her hand. I'd be part of the Baklava in the back of some

Greek restaurant. We weren't leaving each other if it kills us. But now she had to find a way to get to me before it was too late; before I joined the monastery and she never saw me again.

Her sister agreed. She agreed to lend her the eight hundred dollars for the flight to Tokyo. I got the news and ran straight to Eddy. I told him, "My wife is coming, and they won't let us live on base. I have to find a place off base, but my paycheck is still MIA and I don't know how I'm going to do it." 'No worry lad," he said, "mine found me. I got all we need". Here I am praying for him to get through tomorrow and he's suddenly taking care of me? Turns out, a guy in a little church in Oregon was collecting his support checks and mailing them to him regularly. He had up and died. Eddy got a letter from some other church that just figured out why their checks came back and they put two and two together. 'We hear you're in some straits over there, so here's a check to hold you over until we get it all back together' was the communication from the church. Word spread throughout the country. Almost every day, another letter would come with more offerings.

Not only had I seen the clearest demonstration of faith I had ever witnessed, but I saw God working through His churches like I could never have learned if I had not witnessed it first hand. My wife came over and our lives of discovery began. It started right there at the Tokyo airport when she found the restrooms but couldn't find a toilet. Nothing in there but a porcelain ring around a hole in the floor was her first discovery. Eddy only had a Japanese work in Tokyo, but we didn't speak Japanese, so we built an English work at Eddy's house. We watched it grow to a source of enlightenment that reached many generations to come. At least three preachers came out of that little work that I know of, and we've heard rumors of others.

At the time it never crossed my mind that I'd be one of them, but the seeds were planted. Never again would I be satisfied with second best. I would become one of the main figures in the field of ecclesiastical apologetics. I would speak in hundreds of churches in defense of New Testament Missions. I would be involved in some of the biggest church and college battles in the country. By the mid 1980s, I would see more losses than victories. I thought it was all over, but I guess not. Here I am, 'Forced to Pastor'.

Chapter 2
Civilian Life

We could leave a lot out right here. Our military career did not end well. As a matter of fact, it wouldn't have ended until I was thirty-seven years old if things had gone as I had planned. This military thing was pretty cool. Remember, I walked out of high school and got a whiff of civilian life before I enlisted in the service. I remember those few months on my own. There was no door I could walk through and yell, "It's me Mom, what's for dinner?" Oh, I was pretty good at taking care of myself, because I knew how to work. When I was only eleven or twelve, I left my family home in town and moved to my uncle's farm. My mother would send up bags of groceries every Friday. My aunt loved it, because they were really poor. My uncle's mother had died and left no will. The estate auction had left them with nothing but a mortgage they could barely make.

In those days, banks were family owned. The one that held their mortgage was owned by the family that owned the adjacent farm. Old Red Eberhart, President of the Big Run Bank, kept them from losing it right up until the day old Red died. The weekly groceries dried up eventually, but by then, my Uncle Ray had learned that I could work. Too poor to replace fencing, we tied the few cows we had to large tent stakes. They had to be led to the well twice a day and water needed to be dipped to fill the old bathtub for them, and then we re-tied them in higher grass. The boarding horses needed to be fed and watered, and their stalls needed cleaned. In return, I was allowed to ride old Buck, and Uncle Ray would bring me home three beers every Friday night. He taught me to hunt rabbits, pheasants, groundhogs, and deer. We seemed to bring in enough food. For some reason, my Aunt just couldn't part with enough of it at meal time for me to ever leave the table having had enough.

In junior high, I would meet this blonde headed guy every day at noon in the hall and we would have our daily pushing match. Nothing serious, just a challenging jest we both enjoyed. A small crowd would form every day to watch. I think we were the only ones that knew we had no intention of hurting each other. It's really strange, but for that whole school year, we never even introduced ourselves.

In the summer, the wells dried up. The underground mines had taken the water before I was born. One day I was riding old Buck and decided to visit Tuck's spring to see how it was running. It was nearing the time I would have to take the water wagon out there and fill it a couple times a week. When I rode up, there was a John Deere tractor hooking up to a water wagon that had been parked there the day before. I looked down at the boy fastening the tongue to the drawbar and made some kind of address. He looked up, saw me, and jerked his head into the hitch so hard it drew blood. It was the blonde headed kid from the hall. I asked him if he was an Ishman. I knew the Ishmans had John Deeres; I could hear them working the fields on a clear day. They had their own sound in the old days. We had known each other for over a year and finally, Mike Ishman and I met for the first time.

Their farm joined ours on the west end of the heaviest wooded part of our hundred and eighty acres. It was too thick to ride through, and besides, it was common knowledge that you didn't wander on to Fat's land without good reason. They were bigger moon-lighters than we were. They had a big family of big boys and Mrs. Ishman didn't ration their moonlight harvest. In addition to the deer and rabbits, they had pigs and beef cattle. The first time I sat at their table, she set a huge wash bowl on it, heaped with mashed potatoes. I was embarrassed when she chided me for not being able to eat as much as their littlest boy before my tummy was full up. I still helped out around my uncle's farm, but I had found someone that paid a whole lot better every meal.

Mike got me to enroll in the Agriculture class. Tenth grade was the first year you could enroll. His older brother Dave was the biggest man in school. He was twenty-one years old. His dad never let him go to school during harvest or planting season so he failed most every year, but he never quit. The three of us did everything together for the next two years. They were the brothers I never had. We worked hard and we played hard. As long as we got our work done, old Fat didn't seem to mind me being around. He only came home on weekends. He worked away, drilling for the gas company. Mike and I shared a room. We were inseparable. These were the greatest memories of my entire childhood, but we went our separate ways.

Not long after my new missionary friend helped find us a place out in the rice patties, not far from the back gate to the base, I got word from my mother that Mike had been called up. She said he had come to town to say goodbye. He had told her he wasn't coming home. Mom said she had just let it go and as he walked down our walk, she told him to just keep his head down. War wasn't real to many in our little town. No one we knew had been killed in war. Things changed fast; the first Tet offensive had just happened. We went from normal duty to twelve hour shifts, seven days a week. From then on, we would get one day off a year…Christmas if you were married and New Years if you were single. Everything going to the war effort came through us. If we didn't fly it, they didn't get it.

Somewhere in this madness I received an official notice that I had been chosen to escort Michel Raymond Ishman's body home to his parents at their request. There was to be a very involved ceremony and they wanted me to be the representative pallbearer from the Air Force. My wife was the only American out where we lived at the time, and she was pregnant. We had just been assigned a bunch of trainees, and I knew if I left, there would be flights that wouldn't get off on schedule. We were flying boys in, by that time, by the hundreds, and seeing our share of body bags coming back. They were laid on the cargo floor in long, neatly spaced rows. I would see more than my share before I got out of there. I would never equate Mike to just another black bag, but for some reason, I felt an equal responsibility to each one of them.

There would be ceremonies waiting for them, too, and I believed it was my duty to get them to their parents as well. *I've since been granted a service disability, many years later; I've spent a lot of time at the V.A. hospital. Not fulfilling that one mission request torments me more every time I go. It is the second most grievous regret of my military experience.

Little did I know, there was an even more grievous escort duty coming my way. I couldn't pass it off to another Airman even if I had wanted to. One night some months later (why is it always at night?), my wife said, "Get up Tim, it's time". Sometime during the next day, my first son was born. George Thomas Jones III had his father's and grandfather's nose, so we gave him our name to go with it. There was no guessing about this kid's family tree. The very night I brought my wife home from the hospital, it happened again. "Get up Tim, I'm in labor", and back we went for another delivery. The military doctor had not delivered the afterbirth when he had delivered my son. That was back in the days when you took what life gave you and never thought about seeking retribution for much of anything. Anyway, the baby was healthy.

My closest friend in the military at that time was a short Buck Sergeant from Colorado with a Texas drawl. We got him and his wife going to church with us, and we spent what little free time we had at each others homes. He was under four years service time like me, and the Air Force wouldn't let him live on base either. He was always bragging how rich his daddy was and how large their ranch was. Off base, we were the best of friends, but at work he spent most of his time with the superior N.C.O.s. He had them mesmerized. I never thought anything about it. I trusted him with my life; he was my Christian brother. I never got suspicious until I was promoted and an N.C.O. from a flight other than mine came out to inform me.

That was not his responsibility, but for some reason he wanted to get to know me. My short friend had always told me this guy was not to be trusted, but I found him quite honorable. Jack, another Buck Sergeant, transferred in to take the night shift. I'd worked with him a month or so in the shops before I got my transfer to the line. We would talk at shift change debriefings every day. My short friend told me not to trust him either. Now what I didn't know was going to cost me my career in the service. For months, I had been giving my daily reports to my good friend that had convinced me he would go over them with the supers when he took his in. "If there is ever a question or a problem I can't handle for you, I'll call you in," he had told me. That saved me about an hour a shift. Besides my friend had these guys in the palm of his hand; I figured he could take care of me better than I could.

On the worst day of my life, I bumped into Jack down at personnel getting some paper work done. He pulled me aside and told me I needed to listen to him. He said he could get into a lot of trouble just talking to me, and he informed me that the old N.C.O. that informed me of my promotion was my only friend in the squadron. He said "The two of us have been fighting to keep you from being busted, but I'm afraid it's gone beyond that. That short shit you call a friend and trust with your daily report meetings has convinced the supers that he carries you on every assignment. When it came up that your reports are better than his he told them you were fudging them and he just can't keep covering for you. Last week they asked for evidence and he brought one of your new trainees in to testify against you. The same trainee he had been borrowing from you now wants your position."

He went on to say, "Your N.C.O. friend thinks he found evidence that you're so-called friend's rich daddy is a used car salesman working out of a trailer in a small town, I forget where. He doesn't have enough time to do anything about it at this point. The reason I'm telling you is because the E-9 said busting you wasn't enough. He is going to write your next evaluation. He said it will be the last one you'll ever get. My wife and I like you guys and she said I've got to warn you to get you're wife and kid back to the states."

I said, "Thank you Jack." Then I said, "I have only recently begun to think something was wrong, but none of it matters anymore. I'm here at personnel getting a power of attorney that I was going to give to Lyle (the short shit) to oversee getting my house packed and shipped home. I lost my son this morning. Just weeks after his three month examination had declared him a healthy baby, I found him dead in his crib this morning. Would you consider taking care of this for me?" I handed him the power of attorney. He said nothing. He nodded his head and took the power of attorney and I walked out. He kept his word and handled things very well. About seven or eight years later, his family visited us in Punxsy, while on vacation from Michigan, or maybe it was Wisconsin. Unless he killed somebody, he should be long retired from the U.S. Postal Department, where he worked since he was discharged from the service.

I had extended my overseas tour so that I would be over four years service when it was time to return home. The Air Force would then be obligated to transport my family home when my assignment was completed. The Red Cross notified me that this would be handled immediately, regardless of my time in service. The Air Force offered me an immediate curtailment of my enlistment, or the relocation to the base of my choice until discharge or reenlistment. I went to see the only one of the Supers I thought might not be totally deceived concerning my service. We had a pretty good relationship in the past, but lately he had begun to grow cold towards my wife and I at social gatherings. I asked him what he thought I should do. Tech Sgt. Sipplini looked at me with sympathy and said, "Get out of here as fast as you can." I called the Red Cross and told them I would relocate to Dover Air Force Base. They said they would handle it and offered me internment for my son at either Arlington or Gettysburg National Cemetery. I was from PA, so I chose Gettysburg. They asked me if I wanted them to handle notification of the families or if I wanted to handle it. "Handle it", I replied. "Handle everything please. I'm occupied with my wife".

I didn't want a hardship discharge. I'd served well and had always intended to make a career of the service. Except for this near catastrophe, orchestrated by my most trusted Christian brother, I had an exceptional record. I was well decorated for my service, and had maintained an appearance that stood out in every assembly. This performance may well be the only thing that had slowed action against me long enough for me to get back to the states unblemished. I didn't look the part of the willful screw up. I was sharp. I was military to the core. It was going to take more than lies from a fellow crew chief and a low grade trainee to destroy me. It would take a disastrous evaluation by an E-9 to make my career a dead end, or even a dishonorable discharge.

If God hadn't taken my son when He did, that's exactly what would have happened. I wouldn't be sitting here right now thinking that I shouldn't be writing too late into the night because I have lab work in the morning at the V.A. Clinic. I've been in and out of the ministry all my life. If it wasn't for the V.A., I'd have no hospitalization at all in my old age. Would I rather have my son? *Of course*. Was God in all this? *Of course*. All I know is, it was like it was.

The head Line Chief met our plane when we landed at Dover Air Force Base. He offered me a very respectable position, which I would fill until I was discharged. I was still gung-ho. He said he didn't have anyone that could recover a C-133 and he had one stranded at Tinker Air Force Base in Oklahoma. If I would go get it, he would give me thirty days to bury my boy. He told me I'd have a nice assignment when I got back. He kept his word, but it didn't really matter to me anymore. It seemed about everyone stateside had lost their will to fight. Discipline was lacking at every level and they looked like they slept in their uniforms. It was all over. This wasn't the America I had left just a couple long years before. For the first time in four years, and the first time in my married life, I decided I was going to be a civilian.

The crew bus picked us up and took us to the terminal. It had never snowed the last time I was stationed there, but there were large piles of snow everywhere. I thought that might be why my wife's family was not there to meet us. I remember calling Cheryl's house up the road in Smyrna to find out where they were. Her dad answered and was shocked to hear that we were back in the states. No one had been notified. I called my undertaker friend up in Punxsutawney and told him what was going on. He said he would take care of everything. I went through my duffel, packed a small bag, and jumped a C-124 for Oklahoma City.

When the line chief saw me, he saw a junior N.C.O. listed as a crew chief on 130s. He didn't see the airman second class that worked on 133s years ago. I knew I'd have to do a run up and the closest I'd ever got to running up four engines of a 133 was standing outside on fire watch. Now I was on my way to some place I'd never been to recover the largest airplane in the Air Force. No sweat. I was a crew chief then, and I knew how it was done. It's like any other management job; you find the guy that can find the problem, and then you find the guy that can fix the problem. The Air Force is a pretty big outfit, but ex-133 crew chiefs stood out. It took me less than an hour to track one down. He was working in the engine shop. We ran it up and called fuel cell people out for the repairs. I signed it off and notified the flight crew. We were back in two days time. If civilian life was this easy, I figured I better start out in management.

We had a nice military ceremony at Gettysburg National Cemetery, right on the grave sight. I waived the gun salute. My plot is just behind the left wheel of the left cannon looking at the Gettysburg Address Memorial. The Red Cross screwed up again. The marker has my boy's middle name as his last name, George Thomas. It's still like that today. If anybody bothers flying my bones clear out East just to put me in that same hole, they can fix it then. I didn't worry about it then. I had to find a place to live. I sure couldn't put my wife up with her parents while I finished up this Air Force thing. I had started this military looking like an Airman was supposed to look, and I was going to finish it the same way. I knew I couldn't turn my whole squadron around, but my flight would know that compared to me, they looked like shit.

My crew learned quickly that you were an Airman first... you were an aircraft ground-crew member second. Why do you think they had taught us to march and shoot? Gen. Curtis E. Lammae, General of the Air Force tells this story. "One day I was boarding an aircraft with my customary cigar in my mouth. Some crewman dared to say, 'Sir your cigar'. I thought this guy must be looking for a way out of this man's Air Force and I'll just give it to him. Only when I turned and saw him standing at attention in a salute, his uniform said otherwise. He was as sharp as a tack. I flipped him a return and yelled to the Base Commander, 'If I blow this thing up, give this boy another one'."

That was my boss; a man I held in the highest respect. It was only a matter of weeks and I heard other crew chiefs complaining to the supers about my tactics. You know, Ansel, (the short shit) was a pretty sloppy Airman now that I think about it. I never looked at him beyond the fact that he was my closest Christian friend in uniform. I overlooked the uniform. When some officer wanted to show off a 130, they came out to mine with their friends. That's no reason to try and destroy a person, but that and the fact that I was close enough to him and his wife to doubt his role as the rich rancher's son is all I can get for possible reasons. Anyway, I was going to spend my last days in this kite club getting even with the sloppy part. No super dare tell me to back off being military. None of them did. In fact, it was quite the opposite.

One of the more popular crew chiefs, known for his turnaround time, walked out of the ops room and popped me a salute. (N.C.O.s do not salute each other). Then he called me Captain Jones. Although we were the same rank, I addressed him as sir. I said, "You, Sir, are in no way a disgrace to your uniform, but your uniform is a disgrace to the military." With the line chief sitting in his truck right beside us, I never would have said such a thing before. This guy was one of his star players, but I was wearing my short timers ribbon on my lapel. What did I care? I was nearly a civilian.

Dover, Delaware was not half bad, looking at it from the outside. It was clean, not at all hard to get around in, and a lot of ex-Air Force lived and worked there. Two of them were visiting my in-laws one night. One was married to my wife's cousin and one to a friend of the family. Referring to me, one of them said to the other, "What do you say we put him in the family business?" Neither of them were Greek, and only one of them Italian, so I knew it wasn't that business. Besides Pop had sold out of the restaurant business and was doing very well back in the insurance business. Nonetheless, it was his acceptance of me that had fostered their offer. What they were talking about was International Latex. At that point, I was thinking of Dustin Hoffman and the Graduate. They were talking retrofit. A secret little enterprise comprised of past and current Air Force people working in DuPont's Apollo 13 Space division. I was learning real fast about the part of the civilian world that I had never seen. It was a lot like the service; it was who you knew....at least at the entry level.

They put me to work in a tiny little room about the size of the average kitchen in an old house. You had your own code to get in and there were no windows. I learned to assemble cryogenic equipment and install them on space suits. I could tell you more about the other gear and the men I worked with, but then I'd have to kill you. I said that once to a group and some fellow yelled out, "Would you tell my mother in law?!" Time Magazine came in once and made a cover shot with all the original astronauts in their gear. In the picture were the only two civilians still working on the project. I had left the team less than a week earlier to start a new career. But I have been assured that my work had made it to the moon. When my grandkids look up at the moon, they can say, 'There's junk laying up there my Pop-Pop built'.

With that experience and a couple of dollars, I can get a cup of coffee most anywhere. I'm grateful for having had a part in the mission, but I'm an outdoors sort of guy. It didn't take much persuading for my brother-in-law to get me in the co-drivers seat of an eighteen-wheeler. That move would help me throughout my life. In between colleges and ministry work, I could always find a decent income behind the wheel. Things are seldom as they appear in the movies. One night, many years later, a little guy I had gone to elementary school with was sitting by my campfire. Of the four original designers of the B-1 Bomber, Mike Lelock was the only surviving member. His whole resume reads, "If I told you, I'd have to kill you." Suddenly, he was sitting beside me wishing he had a job. So I gave him one. He had a twin Cessna he couldn't afford to fly, and I needed somebody picked up in Texas. We scraped together enough for fuel and off we went.

Had I remained in the space industry, I'd probably been worse off than Mike, but I jumped in the truck with Smokey and off we went. It was really nice to be in the outdoors. That is until one night near Riviera Duluth, just north of Quebec, when we broke down. It was 22 degrees below zero. The last thing I remember was the two of us climbing into the same sleeping bag and passing out. We woke up in the loft of a log cabin. The man of the house couldn't speak English, but we got the point. We were to wait there for someone that could communicate with us. Twenty-one year olds think they are owed life. We never even got the man's name that pulled us out of that sleeper and saved our lives.

A few months after that happened, I was sleeping in the same sleeper when I was awakened by the sound of my brother-in-law dropping the trailer in a truck yard north of Prescott, Maine. He was headed down an icy hill into town to get a drink. I was just climbing out of the bunk and taking my seat when I saw the car in front of us applying his brakes. In those days, there was no such thing as anti-lock systems. With no trailer, as soon as you touched the air brakes, the wheels locked up and you were riding a multi-ton sled. We slid 188 feet, went through the guard rail, and rolled three times. We didn't use seatbelts back then, unless we were on an airplane. I can still hear the tire chains we stored under the seats, banging and slapping with each roll. I can remember saying with each roll, 'If it stops now, we're still alive'. It came to rest at an angle. My side was up in the air. I was still in my seat, but the driver and his door were gone. I wondered what was holding me, and I wanted out of there in case of fire. I wiggled myself free, slid out of my seat, across the dog box and the drivers' seat, and into the snow.

The only thing I didn't think about was all the glass from the broken windows that was imbedded in those leather seats. If I could have got my hands on Little Smokey when the nurse hit my back side with whatever was in that spray bottle, I would have killed him. They subsequently fired my brother-in-law. I stuck around for a few more harrowing events, common to those old timers that drove back in the day... the days before the CDL training and engineering we have today. The U.S. Department of Transportation didn't even exist.

When I was a kid in the Future Farmers of America, I had raised calves and sold them at the auction, but I had never sold anything face to face. When Pat McCann knocked on my door and asked if he could talk to me about selling insurance, he might as well have been speaking Greek. I ran him off. When my wife came home, I told her about it. She said she had gone to school with the guy and that he worked with her uncle at Home Beneficial Life. It wasn't a big outfit like New York Life that her Pop had worked for, but if her Uncle George could work there, she assured me I could qualify. That sounded a little like a challenge. I could do better than that. I went down to the office of Prudential Life and applied. They called me in a few days later and said they had chosen an older guy that had just retired from the Air Force. He said they used the same meeting room as Home Beneficial though, and he thought they were looking for someone.

Well that's twice that name had come up. As soon as I got out of that cast I was wearing, I decided I was going to call that McCann guy. Driving rigs in the old days was hazardous, to say the least. I can't tell you how easy selling this stuff was. Unlike the big guys, they had what you call a weekly premium police. They called it a 'book'. My Father-in-Law said he had worked for a little company like that once and had a book. He told me I wouldn't be selling any million dollar policies, and that I would be working mostly with the poor. But if you had a book, you already had a hundred or so families that welcomed you every time you came to collect, and they wouldn't buy from anyone else. He taught me to fill my bag with cash on the 1st and the 3rd of each month, social security and welfare days. I became the guy that cashed the checks, collected a month of premiums, and wrote the newborn in the communities. Back in those days, there were welfare communities you didn't go into day or night. But if you were the man with the book, no one dared touch you. They would have to answer to everybody.

I wouldn't try that today, but in the late sixties it was the safest place on earth. After a couple years of that, I ran into a man that worked for

Civilian Life • 51

Prudential Life. Remember, they used the same room as we did for our weekly meetings. They could see our numbers. They could see the trips to the Bahamas and elsewhere that we were earning by those numbers. He said his manager pointed my numbers out every time they talked about recruiting agents. He said, 'I turned this young man down for an older man with more experience. The older man never made the grade and this kid is number two in the state of Delaware every year'. The only guy I couldn't catch was Doug Emory. Doug could write the big and more sophisticated policies. He didn't waste his efforts on weekly premiums. To qualify for the annual trip, you had to have some sort of a balance of whole life and weekly premiums. So he would write the whole life I needed to qualify and I would write the weekly premiums he needed to qualify.

I never unseated him as number one, but together we were an unbeatable team. I named my next son after him. In my third year with the company, I exceeded my father's income. He was the senior conductor for the Baltimore and Ohio Railroad between Pittsburgh and Erie. I was a hick from the sticks with no schooling in business, and I had just made four grand more than the lead man in his railroad career. I once made three hundred dollars in one week! That was real money when you had an eighty dollar mortgage payment. That might help you appreciate the level of confrontation my next decision brought upon us.

Romans 8:28

And we know that all things work together for good to them that love God, to them who are the called according to His purpose.

Chapter 3
Call to the Ministry

My military life had ended in disarray and my civilian life had had a few false starts. However, things looked pretty rosy for this small town boy and his fancy bride. I was renting out a couple of places, while buying another one from Doug Emory, and I had just bought the biggest and sharpest convertible on the market. I was living out a childhood dream. As a little boy, I remember hitchhiking from town to the farm one time when a fancy convertible with a beautiful blonde in the passenger seat passed me by. I thought to myself, that's living. All we hoped for in those days was to make ten grand a year and live in a twenty thousand dollar home. I was thinking I had arrived, including the beautiful blonde in my convertible. I had it all by the age of twenty three. I really enjoyed my job, I wanted very little, and I needed nothing.

Looking back, there were warning signs that I should have recognized. I was living for Thursdays, my office day. That was the day we turned in the policies we had written and figured our percentage of collections from our weekly premium book. We figured out what our paychecks would be all morning and we celebrated our success all afternoon. We would always meet in some bar for lunch, and then play pool and shuffleboard until supper time. It used to be I'd get home shortly after my wife had picked up the kids and was making supper. I'd come home, share my good numbers, have supper, and watch Star Trek with the family. I can still hear my little girl yelling "Star Trek's coming on."

Thursday was about the only weekday that I didn't go back out on calls after we ate. We'd watch TV until bedtime, and then the wife and I would go to bed and celebrate a successful week. Over breakfast, we'd plan out our Friday night. Every weekend was planned in advance. The guys and their wives would have it all figured out, where we would meet and where we would go. It was the crowning of the week. Whether we went dancing, bowling, or someplace else, we always did it together. We had been accepted into this tight knit group after a few months on the job for two reasons: I was a producer, a real competitor; and second, we maintained the utmost respect for one another and one another's wives. We were the group that would make the annual company trip each year. We planned our week in Florida and then our trip to the Bahamas. I don't remember a cross word in two years.

The third year, however, things began to slip. The tranquility level was increasingly ruffled. Thursday's supper with the family was no longer a sure thing. Sometimes, Thursday afternoon spilled over to Thursday evening, and it wasn't uncommon for our wives to go on the hunt until they had tracked us down in some bar and drove us home. Our wives didn't like it, but they put up with it, because they had it pretty good. It was only one night a week that we went astray, and we were never in some bar alone. Nevertheless, it was the first sign that my lifestyle was slipping. Every Wednesday night, my wife and I would go through my collection book in preparation for office day Thursday. We would add up what I had spent out of the collection bag through the week and make out a check to cover it. This in itself was a violation of insurance code, but so long as it was always there on Thursday morning, all was well. To the best producers, it was seldom mentioned, and then always overlooked. The amount to settle my book each week had grown to about forty dollars, and I can remember the first time my wife commented that forty dollars was just about out of hand.

I had slowly developed the habit of a mid-afternoon stop at the zoo, so called because of the animal heads all over the walls in the restaurant and behind the bar. Since I had started drinking again, I had not drank on a weekday, and never during the day, but I agreed that I'd been taking my liberties a little too far. We needed to find a church and get our lifestyle back in order. We had left Dover and taken over a territory about thirty miles or so to the east. Harrington, Delaware was the center of my territory, but the rest of my staff lived about fifteen miles from there in the slightly larger town of Milford; though in those days, one wouldn't call Milford big. I knew where everything was located, and I knew there was a Baptist Church just a block from the kid's day school, so we decided to visit it the following Sunday. In the Baptist realm, if you drank beer at all, you didn't go to church. If you went to church, you didn't drink anything but coffee. So I knew it meant a total change of lifestyle and friends.

The two groups never mixed. Either the non-church group would shun you or the church group would shun you. That's just the opposite of the way it should be, but that's how it was. As a matter of fact, I thought I better rethink this church thing, because it would separate us from every friend and social activity we had. I would even have to alienate some pretty big customers and their activities. I really missed talking about spiritual matters and studying the Bible, but no one in my business knew I was a Christian, and I figured I'd better leave it that way for the time being. God had other plans. On my way home from work one day shortly thereafter, I ran off the road, glanced off a telephone pole, then woke up and drove home. Not a week went by before the same thing happened again! I ran off the other side of the road and glanced off a different pole. A few inches off either time, and I could have been killed. By that time I was thinking, 'God, if you're trying to tell me something, I need to know before I kill myself'.

Both sides of my car were beaten in and the top Sergeant of the police department was after me. It was a small town, and he knew I had hit the pole in the middle of town. I was going downhill fast. I'd probably have been arrested if my wife weren't the chief's personal secretary at the time. I had just been chosen by the staff to organize a weekly poker night, and since I loved poker, I was looking forward to it. I had just had my car fixed, and it was the night before the first poker event. I picked up my car and headed home. The next thing I remember were two officers standing over me saying, "It's Tim, call an ambulance". This time I had caught the pole right in the center of my car and broke the pole in half. I was in pretty bad shape. To this day, I carry scars on my forehead and have several false teeth to help me remember that night. All right, I'm stupid, but I'm not suicidal. I decided I'd be in church Sunday.

If you have had any dealings with the Lord, it really isn't that hard to figure out. It all started when I decided it wasn't time for me to start back to church. When you give yourself to the Lord, and mean it, like I did that morning in the rice patties in Japan, a plan for your life is put into motion. One might think he can alter it, and death may even try. The authorities might even get involved with legitimate intentions, but it's God that is ruling in the matters. He'll even overrule the circumstances when the matters go against His plans. The morning staff meeting after my accident, I informed them that I would not be handling the poker event. This was way back when I thought that poker was one of the filthy five sins. It was many years before we learned that cards were a great avenue for winning fellow game lovers to the Lord.

We fit in church really well. We had been taught by the most educated New Testament Church builders you'd ever want to meet, so we put the good life behind us and started our church career again at the Milford Baptist Church. Larry Cornel, a skinny young kid from New Castle, Delaware, had just been called as pastor. This was our first New Testament Church, and in those days, they put 'Independent Fundamental' on their signs. Up until then, we had only attended overseas missions. I was baptized in the Tamakawa River by a missionary that had come to Japan to help Brother Eddie. That added me to his sending church that was located in Denver, though I had never even been to Colorado. The new pastor was as unfamiliar with proper transfer procedures as I was, so he said he would baptize my wife into membership and accept me by statement. A letter should have been sent to the Denver church, I would learn years later, but I don't think it made me any less a member at Milford.

We went full steam ahead. We were there every time the doors opened, visitation nights included. When we joined, the membership was involved in debate. The new pastor had accepted the position contingent on the congregation voting to remove their affiliation with the American Baptist Convention. After we had been solid members for a few weeks, the pastor called me into his office and filled me in. I didn't know a lot, but I knew a New Testament Church was supposed to be independent. You couldn't put it on your sign if you belonged to a convention. The old members didn't want to cut ties, figuring we could still do what we wanted to do, regardless of our convention affiliation. They knew that if we became independent, we wouldn't get the Sunday School materials sent to us anymore. True New Testament church had never been taught there before. The building was financed by the convention and the convention still held the paper on it. They could potentially close the doors, and they certainly would have if they could have. It was going to be a fight and the pastor told me he was going to need my support. Well, I figured I was a pretty good salesman. When vote night came, our family was on the road to PA to visit my parents, so we had to stop and phone our votes in. I don't remember the count, but we won, and we pulled the church out of the convention.

Things weren't like they should have been, meaning we should have been responsible to Jesus alone. The pastor began teaching us about a fellowship made up of independent churches for the express purpose of fellowship. It wasn't a convention; the fellowship held nothing over the churches, so I figured I could support that, and we did. For the first time since I had gotten out of the Air Force, my job was not number one in my life. I only saw the guys that I had run and played with for the past three years at staff meetings. We would argue about religion. I can't remember exactly what subjects, but I just knew I needed to know more about the faith I practiced. Leading someone to the Lord was simple; you really didn't have to know much more than the basics. But when dealing with men that are not seeking, you had to know a whole lot more, as you were defending your faith, not just sharing it. I studied as much as I could, but my job was consuming. It wasn't fun anymore. I soon found myself in the pastor's office in the middle of the day, when I should have been working.

I had begun to wonder if God was calling me to the ministry. I remember standing in my bathroom looking in the mirror and telling God that I would think seriously about it when I turned thirty-three. That was the age at which Jesus began his earthly ministry. At that point, I was only twenty-three. My wife was pregnant and I was making a lot of money. In ten years, I figured I'd be in good shape if I worked really hard. The next thing I remember, I was laying on my back in the hospital looking at the ceiling wondering if I was ever going to work again. I couldn't move without immense pain. I wasn't getting any better and no one knew what was wrong with me. I had a joint-related ailment and an unknown virus. I obviously didn't know it at the time, but I would have it again almost forty years later, when I refused to finish this book, because I couldn't figure out why anyone would want to read it. I didn't know what my illness was back then, but I got rid of it the same way I got rid of it the second time I got it. I said, "Okay God, I won't fight you". I walked out of that hospital three days later. The next time it happened, it didn't take more than three hours to get rid of it, and it shouldn't have taken me three days the first time to realize what was going on. Just a few days before I had gotten sick, an old black guy was kidding with me about women. He told me that if they didn't listen, you needed to beat them around the joints, so that every time they moved, they'd remember that they didn't listen. Don't tell me God has no sense of humor.

I can't remember what caused my boss to go into his office and get a Bible, but I remember what he did with it. He threw it on the table in front of me and opened it to the Old Testament. He randomly placed his finger on a verse and asked me what it meant.

Mack wasn't a godly man, so why do you think he had a Bible in his office? But when invited to his home, he always said grace. It was God behind what happened there. I don't remember what verse it was that he read, but I remember the one God laid on my heart at that moment: Psalms 119:72 'Thy hands have made me and fashioned me: give me understanding, that I may learn thy commandments'. From that day on, nothing else mattered. Nothing at all. No matter what it cost.

I was making more money than my dad ever had, and he was at the top of his career field. I had taken my wife to the Bahamas twice and to The Fountain Blue at Hollywood Beach. Boy, that was a trip. There was a large fountain in the lobby that turned pink when it rained. Waiters brought out cups and we tried to drink it dry, but all it did was put us in bed. That's where they wanted us to go so we wouldn't care that it was raining. How could I think about leaving the best job a young man could ever get? I had just bought a new house. Many times in the following years, young prospective ministers would ask me how one could know if God was calling them into the ministry. All I could say was if you can do anything else, do it. If you could do it, then God likely wasn't dealing with you about full time service. Even for the sake of your family, if you can't recite Psalms 119, and mean it, then forget it. Verse [127] says 'I love thy commandments above gold; yea, above fine gold'.

Sunday came and the pastor wasn't there. Some very talented speaker from New Castle was filling in. At the invitation, I walked forward with my wife and surrendered for the ministry. Others came forward also, but I didn't know what for. As it turned out, three families had surrendered that day. When the pastor returned, he acted overjoyed. Now that

I'm in his shoes, I know better. We had built the church back up to about a hundred and fifty people. Suddenly three of his faithful, tithing, working families were going at the same time. He had to be in shock. I got a little shock of my own that week when the missionary that had baptized me showed up at our house. I eagerly announced our recent decision, expecting him to rejoice as well. That didn't happen. I had a very tangled past, and I'd done things I had never even shared with my immediate family. One night as a young service man, stationed in Japan, I had shared all of it with him. Now he was sitting on my couch doing his dead level best to convince us that we were not qualified to ever serve God in the pastorate. He told me I might be able to serve as a missionary, but not a pastor.

We were talking about things that happened before either one of us had ever accepted Christ. I thought the Word of God said all things are passed away and all things become new. I didn't know any better than to believe that. I wasn't studied enough in the Word to know that God didn't mean 'all things' when He said 'all things'. Let me warn you while on this subject....... If God is calling you, follow. If He is not calling you, though you think he is, don't worry, you won't make it. Ten years after this event, after having been in the ministry for ten years, God called me to the mission field. The pastor I was working with at that time tried his best to convince us we were not qualified to be missionaries. I am here to tell you that the only one that can disqualify you from the ministry is you, and I'm not even sure about that. We have quit the ministry several times and went into other fields, but God wouldn't accept our resignation. Each time it turned out to be only a leave of absence. When God has a plan for your life, He will not let you alone. If you are sincere, you will end up doing the only thing you can do, and that will be what He has planned for your life. If you are sincere with God, and put your life in His hands, there are no mistakes. Your ministry and the subsequent blessings will leave no doubt about it.

But who was I and what did I know? A very schooled missionary, supposedly a very intelligent man, was telling me God hadn't called me. Looking back from a fairly blessed life in the ministry, it baffles me that I ever believed him. The Lord had made it so clear that He was dealing with me at every turn, yet that short surprise visit changed everything. It never dawned on me that perhaps it wasn't God that had sent him to assist me in my time of decision, and I went to my pastor for clarification. After decisive counsel on the subject of airing my dirty laundry for no good reason, he called his favorite college and put me on with the administrator. Between the two of them, I was reassured of my calling, and somehow ended up talking with the director of their missions training department. He talked me into registering as a missionary, at least to get started.

I know now that God was not leading me to the mission field, nor did he want me tied down in a pastorate. The third choice was Christian Education, but that was not even in the realm of consideration at the time. I now know why. There were several already in that field whose first jobs would be working with me. I didn't need that experience, as it would be readily available to me. He wanted me to have an understanding of how the most successful missions operations of our times functioned. When making those types of decisions as a young man, it's a lot more about discovering what God has planned for you than it is about education. I can look back at the early days of my path to the ministry and see clearly that He wanted me in Springfield, Missouri. It wouldn't matter if I went there for school or to pick cotton. God had some people there whose hearts he'd prepared for our arrival.

I was about to be sucked into the machine. I was soon convinced that the independent type that had led me to Christ overseas were a dying little group of stick in the mud's that refused to progress in any form of evangelism. I was now with the elite. No one could touch us. We led the world in church building and missions. Now don't get me wrong; I wouldn't shut one of these places down if I had the power to do it. The reason they were there was because too many churches had gladly passed their responsibilities on to them. They had sold their birth rights for a pot of porridge. God doesn't have to bless the individual church to train and send out missionaries. He doesn't, because they aren't going to do it anyway. I would have to say the greatest blessing I've ever seen was watching God bless a church with the ability to train and send men to the field because they were heart-set to do just that. Those are the people I was led there to meet.

I temporarily forgot that the Great Commission was given to the church. But there I was, my first semester in Bible College, and I was overwhelmed. Over two-thousand of us sat in assembly and listened to really talented speakers. I was ready to charge hell with a squirt gun. I can remember thinking that anyone that wasn't a member of this Fellowship was missing the boat. I loved it!....and learning what you love is a high in and of itself. Not to mention, I was still turned on by achievement. I was on the Deans list. Only problem was, I was running out of money. I had sold everything we owned and split a U-Haul with one of the guys that had surrendered for the ministry the same night we did. He also chose to go to Baptist Bible College. His name was Ken Huffman and his wife was Tanna. He drove a truck delivering home heating oil.

When we arrived in Springfield, we found places to rent. My wife and I found a little hut in a field behind a liquor store about ten miles outside the city limits. Ken and Tanna found an apartment in town. He got a night job inspecting potato chips as they came off the line. God was already teaching me before I even got to school. There were never two more different personalities than Ken and I. I was a hustler, leading in sales, and Ken was as reserved as they came. My wife used to kid me when it came time to make a big decision. She would say "now let's sit down and think about this." That was the most outstanding thing we remember about our relationship with Ken. I don't know how he ever made the decision to surrender to the ministry, but he did, and he stuck to it. I wish I knew what became of him. All I know is that he went straight into a pastorate somewhere.

At this time, our son Mark was three weeks old. My wife was a waitress before we had come out here and had been collecting silver coins ever since the first copper was added to them. If we had them today, we could retire. But by that point, everything we had had run out. She traded them for face value to the liquor store owner to purchase food and milk for the baby. I saw her once walking the highway, looking for pop bottles to turn in at the store for the two cents deposit. Things were getting tougher by the day just to eat. My tuition was paid and I was putting every ounce of my energy into learning. My wife was trusting God, never burdening me with the truth about our financial situation. I didn't pay much attention to it until the day I came home for supper and found it consisted of a few small bags of potato chips. Ken was allowed to keep the rejects from work, and he and Tanna had shared their bounty with us.

For breakfast, we opened our last box of cereal. For supper that night, we finished the box. I mixed some peanut butter and some honey into it because the only milk we had was babies milk, and I couldn't use that. I got sick. I had already sold everything that was worth anything. I had dropped my insurance, which was the only retirement plan we'd ever have. Ten years later, as I mentioned earlier, I was sitting in the cafeteria at the hospital where my father was dying, and I remember seeing my old dentist who was there for some reason. He asked what we were doing these days. We told him we were about to hit the road visiting New Testament churches and raising support to go overseas and work a mission. He asked a lot of questions, as people that don't understand trusting the Lord often do. The one that broke the camel's back, though, was when he asked who was providing our insurance? We told him that ever since we had gone into the ministry, we couldn't afford insurance. He stood up and yelled, 'You can't do that. You have got to forget about this stupid idea and get a job with an insurance program'. He was mad, as he gave me a disgusting look and walked off. That was the last time we ever saw him.

Well, about the third day of eating potato chips, reality began to set in. I was just starting the second semester. I'd tried a selling job, but couldn't divide my interests and didn't do very well. There were several major colleges in Springfield, and no jobs available that paid more than minimum wage, which was $1.60 an hour, and even they were rare. I remember sitting in my bathtub in that little shack behind the liquor store (we didn't have a shower). I can remember asking God, as sincere as I have ever been, to take me home. I didn't want to live another day. Today, I just ask Him for another day. That was the first brick wall in my ministry. I failed. I couldn't feed my family and that was a major sin. If I couldn't stay in school, I had no reason to live. I had left a fantastic career, so I figured I must not have been following the Lord. He would not have led me to do this to my family. I had dropped my insurance, but it wouldn't lapse for thirty days, so if He'd take me home, I figured my wife would be in good shape to feed the babies and get back out East. Fifty-thousand dollars in those days would be like a million today. Only the wealthy had that kind of coverage, and mine was about to go away.

I don't remember where we went the next day. I think it might have been Sunday, so we would have been in church. I remember thinking that that was it, I had failed. When we got home from wherever we had been, we saw an amazing sight. Our front porch, which was as large as our living room, was stacked several feet high with groceries. I tear up today as I recall our reaction. No one in the world could have convinced me that within a few short years, I would witness God providing millions in ministry needs. That was our first such provision out of virtually nowhere. Our pride had prohibited us from sharing our situation with anyone. We had called several government agencies, only to discover they were not out there to help you on a temporary basis, and that was before we knew anything about politics. Those outfits were there to generate permanent dependents upon whom they could rely upon to vote for continued entitlements. I was a student in a conservative college, for goodness sake, yet there was no one out there interested in helping us.

To this day we have no idea who bought the groceries. No one we knew could have done it, but it was like Christmas morning. There was even meat in bags of ice. You might be thinking, 'that is fine, but who's going to feed you next month?' When you're hungry, your thoughts are not focused on next month; they're focused on the next meal. Our babies were going to have food for weeks. A months worth of our daily bread was what we were looking at. The death wish had been suspended. Now I just had to figure out how I was going to stay in school? I had to find a job that wouldn't dominate me. I had to shed what professional pride I had left, and find something that would pay for groceries. The G.I. Bill was just barely making the tuition. That's another miracle in and of itself. Remember, that was long before George Bush. The G.I. Bill would never have given us a dime to go to a Christian College. Just before we surrendered to go to school, I signed up for a correspondence business course. The paperwork was completed and the checks were sent directly to me, not to the business school. They would continue until my total GI education allotment was diminished. That would be just enough. God is good.

We knew that if we couldn't find a decent job by the time it ran out, we would be back to zero. The $1.60 per hour wouldn't make tuition and the rent. Facing that dilemma, each day was a faith builder. When the last check was gone, it was now or never. I went home in our old car, which by that time was smoking, and there was the wife standing on the porch waiting for me. "I got a job!" she proclaimed, while jumping up and down, "a real job!" Not being able to contain herself any longer, she added, "And so do you".

I had finally taken one of the minimum wage jobs. A guard company had hired me. I was breathing when I had applied, so I had qualified. They handed me a gun and sent me into the night. I had to call in every evening to see where to report. One day my dispatcher said "Congratulations, you've earned a decent assignment." I guess that's because I had shown up somewhere on time for a whole week straight. He said, "Watch how you dress, it's a tie factory". I thought he meant to dress well, you know, shiny shoes. I remember when I found the location. The driveway was dirt and after awhile it started to turn to mud. I found the only building on the property that had lights on. Something was stacked up over ten feet high everywhere I looked. I stepped out of my car and was hit with the strongest odor of creosote I had ever smelled. It was a railroad tie processing plant and a mud hole. I sat in a little building with a bare light bulb that they called a guard shack. It was there in the dark that I read Mural F Unger's entire research on Demonology. Then I had to walk the rounds in the darkness.

Tri-city Tupperware distribution was owned by Frank and Ilene Sharp. Already working for them was a man and wife from a church back in Delaware. Somehow my wife had run across the wife. Because of them, we were both hired. My wife ran bookkeeping and I was put in the warehouse. She worked all day and I came in after college until five or six. Frank and Ilene were the most generous people in the world. They supported many missionaries on a regular basis, but what they loved the most was meeting the missionary's personal needs. Years later they showed up on our mission field in the South Pacific and asked us what we wanted. Our little mission building was full. People were standing around the walls on Sunday morning. I said I'd like to add on a little to that building. That was not going to happen.

We were the only missionaries they helped that were not a part of the

B.B.F. (Baptist Bible Fellowship). They made it clear that they had come to help us personally. They were not interested in helping any work independent of the B.B.F. They bought us a really nice van and went home. Such was their ministry. The work could not go on without those with the gift of giving. When they were first married, they had lived and worked on a chicken farm. They had just made ends meet. The church they went to had started a drive to help support missionaries. She told the Lord that if He would give her a way to earn anything extra, she would give it to the program. The next day someone invited her to sell Tupperware. She said she would do it to make money for missions. The next thing you know, those two chicken farm workers were now running sales and distribution for three states and donating about fifty percent of the profits to missions. God had these wonderful people prepared for us. We couldn't have made it without them.

Ephesians 1:11
In whom also we have obtained an inheritance, being predestinated according to the purpose of Him who worketh all things after the council of His own will.

Chapter 4
The Man with the Holes in his Shoes

The last time we communicated, I owed Ilene about ten-thousand dollars. She had loaned it to me upon our return to the states from the field so that we could buy a van and a travel trailer. After letting us meet our agreed upon payment schedule for about a year, she found a way to make it impossible for me to continue our payments. She had her lawyer send me an official notification instructing me to remit the entire balance immediately or have no further communication with his client. She knew we couldn't do that. It took me years to figure out what she had done. She had found the only legal way to break our contract that gave me no recourse. Her husband had died. I was the only missionary she supported that was not in her fellowship group. I was the only missionary chosen by her husband. She was just cleaning house. I understand now.

I was in my last year of school and things were going well. I was only worried about my graduation thesis; I was more concerned with it than which ministry offer should be entertained. I'd had a bad history in writing. When I was in sixth grade, they brought in an expert to analyze handwriting styles. He had passed our papers back in the order of his approval. He praised the first group, encouraged the next, and so on. After they were all returned, he had one left. That genius thoroughly humiliated me in front of my classmates. I was a well-mannered child and had been raised to respect my elders. I took it humbly, but I never forgot it. I'd love to send him a copy of the reprint requests I've received over the years for articles I have since written. But at that time, I had no idea I could write anything.

Mrs. Watford was my senior literature professor and was preparing us for the most important paper any of us had ever written. She gave us an outline on basic article building. I think it may have been the most valuable academic contribution I'd ever receive. It made writing fun and easy. I used every point as I prepared my practice paper. To my lacking,

I've never used it again, but it was what I needed to overcome the writing inferiority I'd carried from grade school. I suddenly realized that I could do this. We were all given the same assignment. We were to read Beowulf and comment as to why the writing was rooted in ancient Christian philosophy. The class following ours having completed the assignment already, she began handing them back in a manner that was eerily reminiscent of my sixth grade experience; praising the first group, commenting on the following group, and so on.

She was all finished except for one paper, which she held up above her head while looking right at me. I wasn't in sixth grade anymore. I was turning red and just about to overrule my embarrassment with a resounding analysis of my own when she began to speak. She said of my paper, "This is the only paper that took an opposing view to our theme. It is the most convincing argument that Beowulf not only was not influenced by Christian Philosophy, but indeed could not have been so. I would like permission to add this to my teaching curriculum".

There was a young man present in the classroom that day that would eventually use me to build a newspaper. Maybe that was what motivated him to show up on my doorstep…..I don't know. I do know that is why I went to Springfield, MO. I belonged to High Street Baptist Church and attended the same Sunday school class Jerry Falwell had attended while he was there in college. I wasn't looking for another church. I was in pretty tight with their new assistant pastor, Bob, from Texas. I'd been elevated to the inner circle that consisted of three of us that would show up for Thursday night visitation. We would organize the visitors, pass out the prospect cards for them to visit, and then spend the evening at Denny's Restaurant drinking coffee and making plans to elevate ourselves in the B.B.F. That in itself is not a bad endeavor, when you believe the Fellowship is the greatest thing God ever built to reach the world, and we did.

Bob went on to become the head of the Fellowships' missions department. That's probably the most influential position you can attain in modern Christendom. Thousands of churches look to you to approve and recommend men to them for the mission field. Hundreds of missionary families look to you for such recommendations. You're pretty much the Holy Spirit of modern missions. Had I hung onto his coattail, who knows where I'd be today? But events surrounding this kid from South Africa were about to remind me where I came from. He showed up at my door one evening for a visit. He was testing the waters for men to join him in a church building effort. I'll never forget our first meeting. Thanks to the Tupperware shipping job we'd recently been blessed with, we had been able to move into a much nicer place. It was a newly remodeled duplex, just a few miles from the college.

He came in and began to praise an old lamp we had picked up somewhere. I, too, had read "How to Win Friends and Influence People", so in the spirit of the old missionary in Japan, when he left our home, he turned to see me carrying the lamp to his car. He tried to refuse the gift, but in the words of Brother Eddy Sullivan, I explained that if he took it, I would get a better one in the millennium. During his visit, he noticed that the other half of our duplex was unoccupied. They later became our neighbors, but oddly enough, I don't recall ever seeing that lamp again. He was Fred to us, but a few months later, he would secure a degree from a school in California and for evermore, become Dr. Drummond. Up until then, our house was frequented by other college students with roots in the Delaware B.B.F. churches. We played cards with Ted and Dreama Lilly, plus several others who desired to become Fellowship preachers. Those wonderful friendships, along with our jobs, were all about to go away for evermore as well.

Many scriptural questions began to arise concerning New Testament Church authority. If I realized my goal of becoming a big shot in the college and the fellowship, what church would be authorizing my ministry? I discussed these concerns with my colleges to no avail. They had never been in a local church that was not sold out to the college and the fellowship. To them, the fellowship was the ultimate authority. How could I possibly give up everything? It was no secret that I was on the fast track in the Fellowship. I was of no further use to them. I went from the favored son to an outcast, literally overnight. What meant more to me? My passion to become a player in the largest group of churches in the world, or being one of six men bent on building a scriptural New Testament Church? Once again, we were in a position that only God could handle. Our lifestyle had elevated above the minimum wage level. If God was not in this, we would be on the streets long before we could find another shack behind a liquor store with a porch full of groceries.

They didn't fire me from the Tupperware shipping job, but they put their druggy son, just returned from who-knows-where, over me. The radio station in my shop was changed to heavy metal and the moral people that had worked for me were quickly replaced with the baser sort. I had to work extra hours to get the job done, and I didn't have many extra hours. I felt obligated to serve. Just before all this happened, Frank (my boss) noticed my car was smoking and he sent me to his Cadillac dealer to pick out any used car we wanted. These were really good people. Not long before this they had ordered our duplex totally carpeted. They didn't want to see our babies crawling around on hardwood floors. As I told you before, years after this they would become the only Fellowship people to support our ministry. I think one of the reasons they did that was because they remembered the day I walked into their office and told them in tears that I couldn't work there anymore.

My wife didn't last much longer either. Her best friend, Dreama, wouldn't even speak to her. She was moved to a room by herself and they wouldn't even ask her to lunch anymore. I once asked an old preacher friend why he was mad at me for leaving the B.B.F. and he told me that I had caused disunity. Think about it. If we all belonged to N.T. churches that did not belong to any man-made organization, we would all be united in the Spirit just like the early churches. Man-made organizations divide God's churches, they don't unite us. If Jesus wanted an organization beyond the institution of the local church, He would have built one. Now what were we going to do? We had a decent car and a decent place to live, but if you don't know somebody, $1.60 an hour was the best you could earn in a college town. Illegal immigrants didn't even come there. It was going to be fun to see how God worked that out. There was no one else interested in helping us out.

Our assignments had to be typed. One day a fellow student asked me who I used to do my typing. He said his typist had reached her quota for the month and he was in a fix. I didn't realize that was a real business. My sister had given me an old Underwood typewriter when we had left for school, and my wife could pound out my papers in about an hour the night before they were due. I never thought about charging him. I just suggested that maybe my wife could get him out of his fix. I gave him my address and told him to come out after supper and ask her. He showed up with such a sense of urgency that she took compassion on him and completed his papers while he waited. While he waited, we talked. He was even older than me, about mid-twenties. There weren't many of us that old in Bible College. He insisted on paying her for the favor. That told me he had a real job. I explained how mine had gone away and how we were in a fix worse than his. He said he could use another man on his security team. I told him that I had once worked security and that kind of money wasn't an option. He said he wasn't talking about a security guard. He was talking about a deputy sheriff placement program. He said he could get me on the Sheriffs department if I could give him all the mandatory hours.

That meant I would have to do some department work off duty that they wouldn't pay me for. "Don't tell the Sheriff that you're not still going to High Street Baptist Church and we can make this work," he told me. "I'll call you and we'll meet in his office". I thought it would never happen, but sure enough, I got the call. I walked into his office and there sat a big man behind a desk. He had a waste paper can sitting in the corner with newspapers taped to the walls on all sides and a big chew in his cheek. He asked if I was a college student and if went to High Street. He said, "I have a security team that will take one of my deputies full time and he wants you. If you qualify, you work for me... you do everything in my name. You are a full time court-commissioned deputy sheriff... always on call. You will never go unarmed. You are authorized to generate any income you desire while off duty".

He leaned towards the corner, spit a mouthful at the waste can and said, "Raise your right hand". I agreed that any time I was not working for the security team, I was his. Within a week, the St. Johns Hospital contracted me as their #2 security officer. I had a real job. It only got too real a few times, but I was young and strong. Only a few times was I required to assist other officers, and then it was only because I was on or near location. I only had a couple serious physical confrontations and only drew my weapon once as a commissioned officer. I owe Sheriff Owens a great debt of gratitude. He not only gave me an opportunity to make a living wage but kept me out of harms way more than putting me in it. When my contract was completed at the hospital and we were ready to move on to our first ministry attempt, I learned that I was required to report to the Sheriffs office and resign or I would be A.W.O.L. from the Green County Sheriffs Department. When I reported, my boss reported at the same time. Mickey Owens pulled two cards from his desk. He said, "You two have proven to be loyal deputies, so I'm making you honorary deputies for life unless you commit a felony. Promise me you will carry your weapons and uphold the law at all times. We need your kind these days. Keep your badges; put these cards with your commissions, and as far as this office is concerned, nothing has changed".

He meant it. Ten years ago, I was stopped for a traffic infraction, (of course I was innocent); the Ohio patrolman saw my badge and asked for an I.D. I gave him my honorary commission and he came back from his car and said, "Have a nice day Sheriff". A similar incident occurred only months ago. That would be thirty years later, and it ended with the same result. That didn't take place until I had left the college. In the meantime, I had gotten a real job again, but the hours took their toll. I couldn't get five hours rest most nights. My grades took a hit as well. Worst of all, my wife got almost no help from me with the children. My number two daughter had been really hard to control. My wife just couldn't handle her without my support.

Tonia was so rebellious; it was embarrassing for someone training for the ministry. One of the scriptural requirements for a minister is that he has his own home in order. My wife is my strength; if she loses it, I can't function. I prayed about it and God dropped a book in my hands from somewhere that was written by a lady Doctor. She taught me that I had a strong willed child and instructed me how to handle her in one application. She said put the child between my legs and bend her over and hold her down with my hand on her back. She said paddle the child until I could hardly stand it and then let her go. If she runs away as usual, then do it again, and again, until when you turn her loose, she doesn't run but curls up in your arms and hugs your neck while she cries, instead of screaming and struggling to get free.

I did it out of desperation. The third time I put her back between my legs, she did just what the author said she would do. Her will was broken, just like breaking a wild horse. She hugged my neck and sobbed until she fell asleep. That was the last time I ever remember having to paddle her. She became my girl and still is. It broke my heart. What's really heart breaking is to think about the thousands of children that grow up unbroken. They grow up hating their parents and run away as soon as they can. All it took was breaking her will one time and she was my girl....she'd give her life for the family. Today's public school teacher would make us put her on drugs. We would have raised a zombie and she would still maintain her rebellion. We are seeing today that many who grow up that way end up hurting themselves or someone else. It's consistent with the Bible. Follow its direction, and handle a lifetime of misery in ten minutes. I think the only hint of lasting negatives was that she never asked me to buy her another one of those paddles with a ball attached to it by a rubber band. I never thought about that until right now, but that could be one of the major accomplishments of my life. Children who are allowed to rebel against their parents unchecked, seldom ever humble themselves to their Saviour and grow up to raise a Christian family of their own.

Many a night, the ambulance brought in a couple of guys all cut up from some kind of a fight. Within minutes, family members of each of the victims would show up in the waiting room and the fight would continue. It didn't take me long to figure out why only commissioned officers worked this job. I learned to use a slapper, a little leather thing about the size of a small sock filled with bb's. A well placed tap on the forehead and the argument was over.

The worst part of the job was getting used to death. The first time they called me to assist with an accident, we pulled two G.I.s in uniform from a mangled sports car. The guy I was attending to was laid on a trauma table and the curtains were drawn. There I stood at his side, all alone in the dimly lit end of the emergency room of Saint Johns Hospital around midnight. The guy they laid on the table next to him was now surrounded by doctors and nurses working frantically. Surely they were going to get over here to my guy, because he looked really bad. Finally, a single Doctor stepped in through the curtains with nothing in his hand but a tape recorder. 'Facial lacerations', he began, 'broken neck' and so on. Then it dawned on me. My guy was dead on his first night back from Vietnam and still in his dress uniform. Visions rushed through my mind. I had only been discharged a few years before. My plane flew a lot of boys in and out of that hell hole. Many have found themselves in a mess and made a deal with God. 'Get me through this and when I get home I'll do this and that'. I had made those promises; once as a young boy hiding under a garage, and once as a young Airman. I don't know but it made me think. God said if you make a vow, you better keep it. I kept mine, but God gave me more than a day or two to honor it.

Fred was now settled in the other half of my duplex. We rode to college together and we held church in the front room of an old warehouse. There were six of us men when Fred called us together and made his first presentation I can remember. He began, "There are twenty-eight independent Baptist Churches in this city, and I don't know why God would lead us to build another one. You five men have filled this little room with a respectable group of people. Now let's see if it's God or us. Lets step out on faith and build a building and a work for God or finish it all right here where no one gets hurt." That may not be exactly what he said, but that's what I heard. Why not? Within weeks we ordered nine-thousands dollars worth of laminated beams, with dollars we didn't have. They were to be delivered to a piece of property we didn't even own.

When they were delivered, we had the money and we owned the land. We all built it. Very little outside help was required. God was adding to us daily. There were contractors from all fields, businessmen, and even a banker. My wife was the first secretary. I'd learned so much in a few months from this kid that moved in next to us with a car that hardly ran. He had one double-breasted suit, and holes in his shoes. Now when you see him as the big time T.V. preacher that he is today, it's hard to see us out on the James River, wallowing in the mud catching crawdads. It's tough to place us siphoning gas out of one of our cars to put in the other so we can go visit a widow in some ransacked apartment. We did that kind of stuff back in the days before we had built anything. She needed everything and we had nothing to give her but our visit.

Years later, this same guy would send me clear across the country in our own airplane to meet with the most influential Christian leaders in America. We would spend time together in some of the most elegant places in the country, not to mention on the yacht we purchased from the founder of McDonalds. But if I could meet with him again in any time period of our relationship, it would be back then. Back when we couldn't cross our legs for fear of exposing the holes in the soles of our highly polished shoes.

Matthew 6:26
Behold the fowls of the air, for they sow not, neither do they reap, nor gather into barns; yet your Heavenly Father feedeth them. Are ye not much better than they?

Chapter 5
False Start

Elmer Towns came to town back when I was working at the Tupperware distributor. Ever hear of him? As far as I knew, he was Jerry Falwell's number one guy in his college. When we first met, he was a Presbyterian. He was in town doing research for a book he titled, "The Ten Largest Churches in America". High Street Baptist Church had a way of turning interesting people like Elmer over to the Sharps to entertain. They invited him over for lunch. By that point in his research, Elmer had figured out most of the objects of his study were in some way connected to the college I was attending. He was looking at High Street Baptist Church, and when High Street had someone that fit the bill, and they didn't really care how he may be influenced, they would put them together with the Sharps. Don't get me wrong, the Sharps were two of the most generous people you would ever want to meet, but like a lot of us, they needed to be recognized for it from time to time.

That day they invited me to go along with them, as they often did. After lunch, they took us to a men's store and bought us each our first ever Double Knit suit. I wish they still made the stuff, but it would probably put dry cleaners out of business. You could not wrinkle them. You could just throw them in the washer. Anyway, I got to meet a lot of interesting people that someone didn't have time for, didn't want to stroke, and didn't really want to ignore either. I'd never met Elmer Towns, but if there had been any clue as to who this guy was to become, he would have been having lunch with the big shots in the churches and the colleges. He would not have been hooked up with a chicken farmer turned wealthy Tupperware person and a second or third year college student. So I got lucky once in awhile. I don't remember how our relationship was maintained. Somehow, after his remarkable writing success and his becoming a Baptist in the process, we hooked up again. He was going to start a college for a church in Virginia, and invited me....or recruited me, I'm not sure which. But it was serious enough for me to pack up the family and head to Manassas, VA.

Virginia was a disaster, but I would learn some years later that, again, God was in it. What was about to take place would most likely have destroyed me. Maybe it wouldn't have destroyed me, but it would have made what God had in mind for me much harder to accomplish. I don't recall much about that move except a townhouse and a mansion. The townhouse had a basement and two stories above it. Those things could catch on. They were much nicer than the average apartment. What didn't catch on was the college. The church helped us get a job, but the cost of living was outrageous. We were just outside of D.C. I went out into the countryside looking for something affordable. I didn't find anything to live in, but what I found, I'll never forget. I turned off onto a dirt road that was really an old country lane. I drove through at least a mile of corn fields. It ended in the courtyard of a long-abandoned mansion in the middle of the cornfield. It was more like an overgrown orchard than a courtyard, but you could see what it had been a hundred years before. There was no sign of life. I shut off the car and just let my imagination run wild.

That place was right out of "Gone with the Wind". The slave quarters behind the main house were intact. The brick ovens were two stories high. They must have fed hundreds. I could see the remains of barns and stables, but I wanted to explore the main house. The doors were all open, or missing in most cases. It was remarkably solid in construction. Someone must have been keeping a roof on the place, but no one had lived there but hippies. The walls were covered with hippie stuff. I was about to learn a lesson in the law of diminishing returns. I heard a tractor and went out to meet the land owner. I couldn't believe this guy owned the place and worked his own corn. I was thinking the place was worth millions. I asked him why he didn't fix the place up and live in it. His response was, "Are you kidding? It took a house staff of at least thirty or forty to run this place when the paint was still wet. If I could afford to maintain this house, I wouldn't be farming". I thought, oh Lord, I can't afford a decent place to live and here this place sits empty.....but then I returned to reality.

When the Jews got away from the Lord and keeping the law, the Levites had to leave off keeping the temple and turn to farming just to stay alive. The temple, which would qualify as one of the wonders of the world, sat empty just like this place. Not even a king could afford to maintain it without the entire Leviticus population. One day a few years from this time, I would find an abandoned convent on ten acres in similar condition as this place. I would, however, get to see it revived, just as Hezekiah revived the temple. Because of this lesson at the mansion in the corn, I realized the cost and the dedication it would require to re-open and maintain it from the onset.

I guessed God wasn't in this Virginia thing. I was only a few hours from my hometown in PA, and I could survive there a lot easier than here until I figured out what God was doing. That was the first time since I had surrendered to the ministry that I would take the family back to Punxsutawney for more than a visit. I truly wanted God's will for my life, so I had to accept that He was in it. But Punxsutawney was my Egypt. My uncle Ray gave me eight acres of the farm, and we put a nice doublewide on it. I walked into Mean's Brother's office, and they put me to work the next day. I worked every day building the new sewage plant, and every evening, I worked on our place. I got a road built and a well drilled, but try as I might, I couldn't get a septic system in. I was coming apart inside and was too proud to ask for help. I was a failure, and Satan took over where I left off.

I knew I wasn't going to make it, no matter how I tried. We were living on venison. When I shot the first one, I thought my wife was going to have a heart attack. It came out of the woods below our house and I got my rifle out. I dressed it out and took it down to the old milk house and processed it. My Aunt and Cheryl wrapped it. My Aunt also taught her how to prepare it. Most people think wild meat is just that....wild. Those are the people that try to treat it like beef. When you learn how to prepare it, you can't tell it from beef. I'm not talking about the steaks, of course.....I'm talking about the roast. We ate it for every meal, and she even packed it in my lunch box. That's all it took to corrupt her. A couple weeks later, I was sleeping on the floor in the living room when I felt someone kicking me. I looked up and Cheryl was standing there with my 30.06 rifle in her hand, whispering "There's a deer right out there in the lane".

When a man is really down, he is at his weakest. When he's really tired physically and mentally, he is most vulnerable. Satan sets him up for a fall. Everyone that knows you knows you're a failure. He runs people across your path that you can look good to. When you have an outrageous ego like mine, it's like a drug. I never did drugs, but I know how they work. You know it's wrong, you know it's harmful, you know it's temporary, but oh what a high. Just for a little respect, you'll risk everything you really love. As a matter of fact, you'll drive everything real in your life away..... and I did. I lost everything. My wife got a place in Delaware at the promise that I would join her when I got my life back together. I enlisted in a trucking school in New Jersey.

I passed my New Jersey road test and leased a tractor from National Freight based in Vineland. They assigned me to their terminal nearest to Punxsy. I retrieved my faithful wife that wouldn't give up on me. We started over again in a rental house just outside of town. I drove Sunday to Sunday. God honored her faith and pulled me out of a life I thought I could never have sunk to, nor ever rise out of. God used the trucking school to revive my self respect, at least to a functional level. Then the independent truck strike happened. People were hanging railroad spikes from overpasses until the National Guard was dispatched to patrol the overpasses. On my last trip, a car pulled up beside me and the passenger rolled down the window. There was something shiny in his hand. I forced him into the median and kept going. I spotted a state trooper and started flashing my lights, but he wouldn't stop. I chased him to the next overpass, where he bailed out and ran up to where the guard troops where stationed. It got so bad, I called the terminal and told them to come pick up their tractor.

I got a job the next day driving a cement truck for an old friend that was then part owner of a lumber mill. Soon thereafter, I got into an argument with one of the other owners and walked down the street and signed up with Means Brothers again. I worked with them until one cold winter morning, when my fingers nearly froze while we were building a steel building. I walked over to the field office and said, 'Thanks again, but I can't do this anymore'. The oldest of the Means brothers was in the office that day. He was a high ranking mason from the temple in Altoona. I'll never forget the off-the-wall question he asked me. He asked, "Have you ever been out East?" I told him I had met my wife in Delaware. What

I didn't know at the time was that this was how a mason inquired as to whether you were a brother mason. If I had been one, he would have put me to work in that nice warm office.

I wasn't sure what I was going to do next, but I knew that at least until spring, it would be something inside. Somehow, I learned the Eagle's club was looking for a bartender. I knew it was no money, but it would make the rent and keep food on the table until spring, so I asked for the job. The number two guy said 'no chance'. There had never been a non-Italian behind that bar or on the board. The head bartender then broke into the conversation. He said, "Have you lost your mind?" George, my Dad, was the oldest living member of the club and about half of the members were railroaders that either worked with him or worked for him. Gil Carney was visiting from out east, sitting at the bar, and was close enough to hear the conversation. He used to be the chief engineer of our local radio station. When I was a young boy, he had boarded his horses at the farm. He was always kind to me. He joked a lot about the calves I had raised for my FFA project. He called me cow face Jones, but he also made sure I had full use of one of his horses. He even called it Tim's horse. He asked the manager if the president was in the office. The answer was yes. Gil told me to wait a minute if I wanted the job, and that he would be right back. He came back in ten minutes and told me the job was mine. It would be a while before I found out that Gil and the manager were lovers.

I made eighty bucks a week, but didn't care. Spring was coming. I had no idea what was going on until one night the manager came in, opened the safe, and left. The next day, I heard the number two guy yelling at him in the back room. He was saying things like, 'Noone has ever taken that much at one time'. The manager told him to forget about it and shut up. I never figured it out until I left. They were robbing hundreds of dollars a day from the safe, and I was expected to do the same. Many years later, the club was taken over by an honest man. He expanded the club and made it the nicest place in town. I'm ashamed I ever worked there. I have to be suspect, even though I never took a dime.

The only Baptist Church in town was an American Convention outfit that had long since quit preaching the gospel. The only church that did preach the gospel was an Assembly of God, so we didn't go anywhere. A few months later, while visiting with my uncle in his favorite pub, I quit refusing the many offers and had a beer. That led to another, and I spent the night hugging the porcelain god. In those days, if I drank a beer, I didn't witness or do anything else spiritual, so church was out of the question. As most legalists, I lived by the list. If I did any of the no-nos, I put myself in Baptist Purgatory until things would get so bad I'd stop everything and go back to the list of do's and don'ts. I flip-flopped back and forth, changing friends and activities, depending on which mode I was in. Legalism either drives you away from God or drives the lost away from you. It just depends on whether you're on the flip or on the flop.

One thing I will never forgive myself for is when I was on the flop once, and I ran into an old friend in a bar on my way home from work. He knew I would live the religious life most of the time and he had a spiritual question and seriously needed help. I told him that was not the place for such a discussion; I'd talk to him later. He took his own life before we talked. It was over the subject he wanted to discuss. I have blood on my hands, and I blame my legalistic practice. I had not learned that every one was not a hypocrite if he didn't live up to my standard of a Christian lifestyle. After living in my purgatory for a while longer, I decided I couldn't live like that, and that I needed a church. So my wife and I began praying for God to send someone we could help build a New Testament Church. About a week later, I met a man that was trying to build a church in Brookville, about seventeen miles away. He came to town and we had a group waiting for him. I had even found a building.

Spring came and it was time to get a real job. I called my old friend, Bill Pyles, and asked if he could get me on at the mines. He said he'd pick me up in the morning....they needed a D-9 operator. He figured if I could run a tractor trailer, I could run a bulldozer. He introduced me to the owner and took me out to a location where they were back-filling. He climbed up on the 9, pointed to the clutches, and said, "Never touch those. You steer these things with the joystick that operates the blade unless your blade is up. If you're going downhill backwards, remember, they work backwards. The gas pedal is not an accelerator, it's a decelerator. You only push it when you want to slow down. Just follow the grade". He'd learned to run these things in the army corps of engineers. I'll bet he had a little bit better training program than he had just given me.

The next day they put me on ripping rock. You raised your blade and dropped your ripper and dug all the way up the mountain. Then you raised your ripper, floored the decelerator, and let her roll back down the mountain, using your blade as your brake and steering with the clutches in reverse.....piece of cake. Don't let the size and power of the equipment you're operating intimidate you; just concentrate on the controls and you can run anything. Lunch time came and I saw the owner standing by his truck watching us work. Actually, he was waiting to talk to us. When we shut down, he called us over to the truck. 'Guys, I need a tri-axle driver for a couple of days. Can any of you drive one?', he asked. I really didn't want to give up the 9, but he said he was desperate for a driver for the next couple days. I told him I could drive it. He said, 'Good, but if you break my springs, you're fired'. That was a nice thank you.....but then that was mining. There were only two cant's out there.......can't do it and can't stay.

I never got off the tri-axle. I was hauling coal from the mines to the railroad tipple, but Sunday was just another day. You hauled when the coal was uncovered and got some time off between diggings. I ran into an old friend that managed the unemployment office, and he asked me if I was looking for a good job. I said, 'Thanks Bob, but I'm good'. Then he told me that Swift Meat Co. was coming to town and needed about fifteen people. Sundays off, I thought. I filled out an application he gave me, but just forgot about it, because he said there were over a hundred turned in already. Meanwhile I made a deal with the mines. If I could stay off the D-9 and only run the coal truck, I could work around my Sundays somehow. So when Swift called, I told them I wasn't interested. Then another guy called and I told him the same thing. Then the corporate office called. The District Manager asked if I would at least meet with him when he came to town. At that point, I figured I'd better think about it. Three times they had called me, and Bob informed me that over two-hundred applicants were now waiting for such a call. Okay, I decided. I was happy doing what I was doing, but I agreed to meet with them.

There were twenty of us at the meeting. They only needed five for driver positions and I wasn't on that list. I said, "I came here to drive".

The plant manager told me they had decided on their drivers. He advised I work the freezers for awhile and maybe I'd get an opportunity down the road. I said, "I've got a truck waiting for me. I'm sorry we wasted each others time". The district manager leaned over to the manager and said something to him. "Okay, Jones, we'll try you on a truck", he said. I said, "Excuse me sir. I respect the dog out of you guys for including me in this select group when you had so many to choose from. The fact is, I have a good job. I came at your request; I didn't come here to try out on one of those little things parked out there". The district manager then spoke up. He said, "You're a driver... period". I never saw that guy again. It's unfathomable how God works. When man rules, God overrules. He had brought this plant to Punxsy for a purpose.

My life was back on track. I was out of purgatory again and enjoying life just working and building our new church. They only gave me forty-five hours a week. Within a month, I had worked myself up to the second driver position. I just couldn't beat George, the lead driver, until he had a heart attack. I got his new diesel and suddenly I was the lead driver. In three days, my time for the week was in, and I was off until the next week. We had horses we boarded at the Punxsutawney Saddle Club. I had so much time, they asked me to be Barn Boss. That led to Vice President. Membership at the time was down to seven members. Old George McGowan suggested we just close it down and keep it for a hunting camp for the seven of us. If I had it to do over again, I would have agreed with him. But I remembered as a child helping my cousin build the very clubhouse we were meeting in. I remembered the many weekend horse shows I had enjoyed growing up. I thought it would be a little selfish to shut it all down. I told them to give me thirty days to boost the membership. If I couldn't do it, we would close. Walter Graffus agreed. By the next meeting, we had over twenty new members and an agreement to build a new show ring.

The club thrived long after I went back to college. About ten years later, a friend from Pittsburgh wanted some counseling and asked me to meet him at the old saddle club. We were sitting there talking when a state trooper came and told us we had been reported as intruders and asked us to leave. It hurt deeply. I had built that place, saved it for the public, and now I was being run off without anyone even inquiring as to who I was. That's all water under the bridge of time. If I had taken old George's suggestion to close it down, I would have been the only living owner by now. Well, although no one alive knows it, many young people are reliving the joys of my childhood to this day at my loss. That's worth something. This is minutely how Jesus must feel. He started the church, bought it on the cross, nurtured it through the Spirit, and yet today, He would not be welcome in most of them. The National Council of Churches just voted to remove the cross from their churches to make them less culturally offensive. But if He had it to do over again, He would.

The church was doing well. Cheryl and I were able to incorporate many of the people we worked with. My mother joined us and that brought another group from her many years of associations. We were doing better than we had in a long time. It's amazing how smooth things go when you just live a life that God can bless. It was one of the few times in my life that I had no aspirations of anything beyond what I was doing. When your self respect is at the proper level, and all your needs are provided for, it's just a good life. A pizza pie cost a buck and a quarter. We enjoyed life and still put away about five hundred bucks a week. We had two nice horses that we rode often, and we held positions in several respectable organizations. I think God gives his people times like those to stabilize them, and give them some reference to normal life.

One day, while all was going well for us, a knock came on my door. It was the man with the holes in his shoes. There he stood at my door, all the way from Missouri. Only now it was clear that worn out shoes were no longer in either of our closets. He began to brief me on all I'd missed and praised God for sparing us. He explained the need to relocate the church and schools somewhere away from Springfield. Since we had left on our venture to Virginia, a lot had happened. Fred was a very charismatic individual with a heavy South African accent. Many students from Baptist Bible College visited the church we had built just before I left. The theme developed of church authority as opposed to college authority in one's ministry. This is a really hot subject if your part of an organization that depends on local churches sending you the cream of their crop. The program is to train them to go out and build works that will send their cream back to the college.

The argument is based on who is responsible for those men's ministries. The only Bible prototype is the local church. If after they were trained, the schools would send the men and women back to their churches for the proper authorization and oversite, there would be no problem. That is not how it works. In essence, what was happening was the church was handing over their responsibilities, along with their blessings, to an organization totally outside the protection of a New Testament Church. You may ask what the big deal is? Who cares if some local church starts making traction in pointing out these questionable procedures? What's the reason for concern? The answer is hundreds of millions of reasons, or should I say dollars. The college brings all its influence to bear. City officials with their inspectors, zoning officials, tax people...... and you thought the religion business was all warm and fuzzy.

The carnage of the battle wouldn't go away, and his students deserved more friendly surroundings. He wanted me to look at an abandoned convent a couple hundred miles east of us, not far from Philadelphia. In his mind, I was still one of the six men in that warehouse. I shared with him the peril I had brought on my family during our absence from church. My actions were probably responsible for a couple untimely deaths. There was a suicide I could have prevented and a fatal accident I had prophesied. I gave him all the details and he agreed. It only reinforced his efforts to convince me that God had a great plan for my life. Nothing was going to be allowed to stop it, not even my bloody hands.

Turns out he wanted a little more than my looking into a new campus location. I listened to what he had to say, but the wife and I had stable lives for the first time since we had left the insurance business years ago. We were major players in building a New Testament work that was growing and changing many lives. I would need a clear leading from the Lord to consider another family relocation. Think about it. I didn't have a lot of successful Christian service under my belt at that time. Why would God want me for anything more than what we were doing right then? He'd have to make it pretty clear. I'm afraid I didn't have the faith I had in '69. I couldn't risk another period of flip- flopping. It was a miracle that I hadn't lost my family. Would God really put me back in the game as if I had never missed a play?

I kept an open mind. I hadn't forgotten everything God had done. I was one of the six that had witnessed some real accomplishments. I wasn't, however, going to go out of the way to do any more than help investigate the properties out east that Dr. Drummond wanted for a college campus. What a place. On route 1, between Philadelphia and the Delaware State line, there was a hill, totally fenced in by a beautiful stone wall that was covered with thick ivy vines. From the road you couldn't see anything but the tops of large oak trees and part of the third story of a building constructed of the same stone you could see in the walls behind the ivy. I found a road leaving route 1 bordering the east side of the property. There was a long abandoned Quaker church building where I could park. Just south of the dirt parking lot, along a narrow paved road, was a large iron gate across the small road leading into the property. Through the gate, I could see a large brick building that resembled a barn. There was a two-story wooden house to the right of it with a road between them. Squeezing between the gate and a stone pillar, I gained access to ten acres lost in time.

Thoughts of the mansion I had found in the cornfield in VA passed through my mind. I walked the road between the brick building and the wooden house. Down a gradual sloping stretch about a hundred yards away was the three story stone convent. Two full stories of stone, with elegant large windows, and a third story protruding out of the center of the structure that covered half of the roof of the second floor. It resembled a fort with ramparts fencing in the flat rooftops. There were at least five acres of lawn between the convent and the stone wall running along route 1. Behind it was a valley with at least two acres of an old paved parking lot with weeds growing up through the many cracks. The lawn was a hayfield dotted with huge oak trees. The convent was the size of a football field. It was going to take more than thirty slaves to maintain this place. I didn't know it, but I was prophesying again.

"Fred", I said, "I don't know if the faith of the six men in that warehouse is going to extend this far. If it happens, it's God. This place has to be at least a million dollar property". I didn't realize that I wasn't standing in a field outside Punxsutawney anymore. I was standing in a field outside Philadelphia. The settlement was only ten times my estimate. I have to admit I felt something. I just didn't think I was ready to do this again. Boy was I wrong.

A few years later, not only would my office be up there on the second floor, but I would find another mansion on a back road, just a few miles away from this place. I would drive down an old driveway surrounded by foliage, and would find poorly kept grounds and a luxury home in the middle of it, surrounded by life sized statues. A middle-aged man would saunter over to meet me, as I would introduce myself to one of the famous DuPonts that you're not supposed to be able to find, even if you are looking for one. I'd get the place for the asking. The last time I would speak to Dr. Drummond face to face, I would pull down that same driveway, and he would saunter over. What fitting closure it would provide to a very important chapter of my life that had begun with six of us standing in a warehouse with holes in our shoes. But I am getting ahead of myself.

Luke 2:25
And, behold, (that means, pay attention) there was a man in Jerusalem, whose name was Simeon; and the same man was just and devout, waiting for the consolation of Israel; and the Holy Ghost was upon him.

Chapter 6
The Ride Begins

Fred visited us again in Punxsutawney on his return to Springfield. He had found a place near the convent property to live in while he went to work securing the property and moving the college. I told him I was impressed, but at that point had no clear direction regarding relocating. He was patient. God was in the lead. Things were not getting better for him back in Missouri. I gave him a .25 caliber automatic pistol to take with him. That would be the last time I ever saw that thing. Many years later, while I was preparing for the mission field, I would get a call from a Sheriff's department in Colorado telling me that someone had stolen it from Dr. Drummond's house and had used it in a robbery. If I wanted it, I'd have to go claim it in person. Yeah, right. Whether God would lead me to work with Fred again or not, I didn't want him hurt, and I knew he didn't own a gun. The next time I would see him would be after the exodus. This was a move that rivaled Brigham Young's move to Utah. Fred was now convinced the convent was sewed up. I didn't know all the details, but I knew he had found the title holders and had sent Monty Miller to meet with them.

Monty was a young man from Texas. He was one of two heirs of the Adobe Oil Company. He would inherit twenty million dollars on his twenty-first birthday. Fred would have a lot of that spent by the time he came of age. Good thing Monty's word was reliable; because it turned out we were dealing with the Mafia. We didn't miss any payments on our earnest money before Monty came of age is all I can figure. Dealing with those people was like dealing with the top Jewish diamond marketers. Everything was done on just a hand shake, and the knowledge of whose hand you shook. You renege on diamond dealers and you're out of the diamond business for ever. You renege on these guys and you might get the business.

Fred announced that we had a new place where we could make a beautiful and peaceful campus. Those who felt led to join us could assemble at the church for departure. Two hundred people showed up. I hear it was a Chinese fire drill. People were discarding furniture on the spot to make space for other people's necessities. Whatever it took, we had found a true New Testament church with a scripturally authorized school and there was no turning back for second best. We'd lost friends and family in the fight, but what we found, we weren't going to lose. Those people had come to the same conclusion I came to the day I was saved. We either do it exactly as it is laid out in the New Testament or we don't want to do it at all. I didn't want to make it on the power and ingenuity of even the best of man-made methods. If I made it to the ministry, it would be God's way or I didn't care to make it at all.

That's how I had found the New Testament church, and now these kids had made the same decision. I tell my congregation often that I did not choose the ministry. If I had, it would have been one with a whole lot less struggle and a whole lot more money. If God puts you in the ministry, then it's His responsibility to keep you in it. You don't worry about self elevation, promotions, or downsizing. There is no competition in God's work. Promotion is of the Lord. If God throws a big beautiful orange in the fruit basket you're working in, that doesn't make you any less an apple. This is, and always was my modus operandi. When I think of all the works we were involved in, I can't think of one time I wanted to be the pastor.

If I had any desire to pastor, I would have exercised it in the church at Punxsutawney. Up until the day Pastor Hoover announced that he wanted to associate our church with the Baptist Bible Fellowship, I had made no clear direction on relocating. I went to church, as always on Sunday, with no intention of making a decision to leave, or to pastor. But that was the choice I was given, and had only seconds to make it. Brother Hoover asked for a show of hands as a yes vote to join the BBF. I naturally could not participate in any action to affiliate a New Testament Church with anything other than another New Testament church. I decided in the first second that I would not publicly oppose the desire, though. I would just sit quietly and deal with it privately, but I was not given that luxury. God was looking for a decision one way or the other from me. When I didn't raise my hand, several people spoke up after they had raised theirs, and said 'wait a minute'. One of the men stood up and pointed to me. He said, "Before we vote, we want to know why Tim didn't".

If I had any desire to pastor a church, that would have been the ideal opportunity. The man that was standing pointing at me was the business manager of Swift Meat Company, and a very influential leader in the church. I would learn to recognize crucial moments like that as part of my career, and deal with them. That becomes a lot of my ministry. But at that point, it wasn't my ministry. It was my career decision. By then, the rest of the congregation had put their hands down as well, and were all looking at me. I don't think there was a founder there, nor any of their followers that would not have followed me. There was a group that would follow the pastor, but they were those he had brought in by bus from the retirement home. If I wanted that work, then was the time to take it. The leaders and those that supported it would have followed me. Question was, 'Did I want to split that church?' If I didn't defuse that thing immediately, it was over. By then, more were standing. The pastor was trying to say something. I think he was trying to postpone the vote, but no one was paying much attention to him at that point. They wanted some information, and they wanted it right then.

They knew Brother Hoover had a year or two of night school, but I'd had years in Bible College. It had now been a long period of absolute silence. God help me. We finally had a New Testament church in this town that at least preached the gospel. My mother and my aunts even came regularly, and they hadn't been to church in years. I'd settle for that. What they were doing was wrong, but I wasn't splitting a church. Then my business manager put his hand up and said, "Well brother?" I stood up and spoke. "You are forcing me to make an announcement I wasn't quite ready to make. None of this matters to me (that was a lie). I've been called to work with a church in Concordville. Vote any way you want." At that, a very relieved pastor said, "Oh, the vote carried, but sorry to hear you're leaving us brother." God knew I wouldn't split that church. He wanted me to make that decision, and I did, and I had peace about it. So here we go again.

The drivers that came to Punxsy with Swift Meat were union. The drivers hired in Punxsy were open shop. They had convinced several of us that we needed the union. I gave my view on the subject and a couple of them changed their minds, but not enough. Over half of the cooler workers had been won over. One of the reasons they had moved here was to be near Interstate 80. When management saw that I was clearly open shop, they admitted that maybe a bigger reason for coming here was to break the union. With our help, they could. The strike began unannounced, but we were ready. The office personnel put on aprons and worked the coolers, making up orders and helping to load the trucks. This was the first time I didn't come back from my deliveries with product overage. I realized then why the union boys didn't like me. Someone had to get the overage off my truck in the mornings before management found it. Someone loading the trucks was a thief. I was supposed to sell the overage and share the money with them. When a few of the local hires realized that they couldn't shut us down, they came back to work. Then the union drivers were given an ultimatum, and it was over.

The office manager had told the other managers of my announcement at church. I was invited to meet them down the hill at the Moose Club. Over a pool game, the big boss looked up at me and told me he wasn't going to fight God. He said he could get me transferred to our Newark plant if that would help me. Now you see why the corporate office wouldn't take no for an answer. God is never out of play as long as you stay in the game. Fred was overjoyed to hear of my decision, but asked me to keep my job for now. Fred liked men with good jobs. He wanted my wife back as secretary right away, however. That was good, because it meant no tuition for my kids schooling. I knew God wanted me to work there, but Fred wanted me to finish my degree first. I agreed, but God had other plans. I took a truck at the Newark Swift Plant, but only had it for a few weeks. They promoted me to sales. That was fine, too, but that didn't force the issue God wanted dealt with. I was still working.

In another couple of weeks the plant manager came into my office and told me I had been selected for manager training. I would be sent to Chicago in a week and then to my own plant after that. I told him I was not interested. He told me I would go, because it was too good to pass up. Other managers and sales people told me how easy the job was and how good the money would be. They, too, said I would go. They were right, I'd go.....but not to Chicago. Friday came, and I was to report to corporate on Monday. The boss made his final pitch. He came in my office and pitched his company car keys on my desk. He said, "Here, take my car and put your wife up in the nicest motel you can find. I'll see you when you come back to move your stuff". I opened my desk and scooped them in and shut the drawer. The paper work and company credit card were already in there. He said, "Have a good time", as he walked out and shut my door. That's the last time I saw him.

I unchained my motorcycle, rode it to a Pontiac Dealership near the campus, and started as a salesman that afternoon. That wasn't good enough either. God did the same thing in less than a week. The owner met me one morning and told me he was sending me to the GM Training Program in Detroit. I can't remember what I said, or if I said anything. The next thing I remember, I was walking around the campus property after everyone had gone home. Dr. Drummond walked up to me, put his arm around me, and asked me what was wrong. "All I know, sir, is God won't let me work anywhere else. You know what happened at Swift....it happened again today. I'm going to work for you now I guess". He told me, "Brother Robinson is putting the academy together for now, but he wants to get started with deputation. He needs to raise enough support to get on the field within two years. I gave him the office across from your wife. Tell him I want him to train you to take over. I'll put you in a nicer place to live and pay your living expenses. Build yourself a good school". He shook my hand, hugged me, and said goodnight.

Many times in my life, I've been unsure about what God wanted me to do. But this was not one of them. My heart is aching right now because I know how this ride ends. I know this was the beginning of what was going to be the greatest New Testament work since Pentecost and the Jerusalem Church. Liberty Baptist Church and College in Lynchburg, VA, Pensacola Christian Schools and College in Florida, Independent Baptist College in Texas, and a great work up in Michigan, were all just getting started. There is no doubt in my mind that we would have matched or surpassed any one of these great works. Now, keep in mind that I have been out of the loop for twenty years. I do not believe God has directed me, at my age, to research anything that has developed since then. Many people have recommended that I write a book. Except for isolated periods, I never saw any way for my past experience to bring glory to God. There is much more failure involved than success. I mentioned there were many times that I was not sure what God wanted me to do. When God began my ministry in Concordville, it was not one of those times. Writing this book is not one of them either.

I don't think I slept much that night. I was backtracking the events of my life that had led up to this appointment. There were a couple hundred other people involved in this startup. I only knew a few of them. How were they going to react? I was the guy that just conveniently showed up when everything was coming together. What I didn't realize was that they all knew me. I didn't know about the founders' plaque that had been hanging in their hall of training at the church and Johns College. To them, I was one of those responsible for the very establishment of the institution that had changed their lives. An institution they believed in so fervently that they had cut ties with most of their friends and families just to become a part of it. And of course, Dr. Drummond, whom they all held in great esteem, had been informing them of his communications with me and his desire to reincorporate the Jones'. When my wife took the main office as *resistor* and personal secretary to the president, she was accepted as one having returned to the position she originally created. No one dared challenge her right to the office. She was honored as Dr. Drummond's first choice. Those that came after her were second choice.

The next morning I walked in the main entrance opening into a large marble floored lobby. To the right, behind a glass front was the office of *the resistor* where my wife was busy getting things opened up and running. To the left was an office with no glass, but just as large. I walked in the unlocked door and found a stack of books lying on the large desk in the center of the office, but no Brother Robinson. I just stood there in amazement. I had a high school GED, a business associates degree, and a little over three years of Bible college. What did I know about becoming a school principal, or administrator, as was the current term? Brother Robinson walked in rubbing the sleep out of his eyes. His family had been given an apartment in the east wing of the convent, so I knew this was a pretty established guy. We introduced ourselves, exchanged pleasantries, and got right down to business. He said Dr. Drummond had informed him that I was taking over. He said he had to get on the road.

He had been preaching in sister churches to raise support for his mission tour in the Philippines. He now had to load up the RV and broaden his outreach. He had got the word about me the night before and was so excited about getting started, that he, too, was up most of the night. Isn't God's work great? I was standing there, so thankful for this appointment, and he was standing next to me, just as thankful to get out of it. To me, at the time, what I had was a much higher position than a missionary. To him, a missionary was a much higher position than an administrator. You think God's man has any problem figuring out what He wants him to do? If you're not doing what you know you were born to do, no matter how many times God may change it, then maybe you haven't found it yet. Almost in a state of boredom, he explained that he was only filling in until the right guy took over. "Thank you so much, Brother Jones, and again, it's a pleasure finally meeting you," he said. I countered, "But wait a minute, Dr. Drummond said you'd train me". He replied, "Just read those books I put out for you; you won't have any problems. Let's get together before I leave for Ohio. Have Cheryl get with my wife and set it up. They talk a lot. Good luck and thanks again".

I had been standing there amazed when he had come in; now I was standing there dazed. I was thinking, 'I read these five books and I'm qualified to build an academy K-4 through 12?' Now, I don't want to burst your conception of education bubble. If you have never been an administrator, you would not believe it. At this point, you might say something like I've heard numerous times before....."Oh, you're not talking about a real school. You're talking about one of those uncertified outfits they start in people's homes and in some churches". No. I'm talking about the only Christian school in the state of Pennsylvania ever granted the same exemptions, rights, and privileges given to the best Catholic and certified non-public schools. I learned, first of all, with regards to an administrator, that a background in education is the least of the requirements needed to build a successful institution of education.

I don't remember opening one of those books that had been left on my desk. If I needed what was in those books, I knew I couldn't get it together in the time remaining to open this school on schedule. Remember me? I'm the non-commissioned officer in charge of millions of dollars of U.S Air force equipment. I'm the crew chief that could recover aircraft I didn't really know how to operate. I just knew how to find the people that did. What's changed? I needed a qualified teaching staff and the best Christian curriculum we could afford. The rest is all politics and management. It didn't take me long to get on the phone. I found the nearest large Christian school and made an appointment. He turned out to be the first president of the newly formed Keystone Chapter of the National Association of Christian Schools. They were just building the association.

The Pennsylvania Chapter was brand new. I got in on the ground floor of what was to become the largest Christian Association in the world. They were putting together their first national meeting to be held in Washington D.C. I don't think there were more than fifty of us in a hotel conference room. At the time, there were a few large traditional style Christian schools that had been around for years, but this was the beginning of the new movement of mostly non-traditional schools. This meant a church could start a school in one class room of the church consisting of all grades and taught by only one teacher. Each child had his own cubicle and his own curriculum, which he worked at his own pace. These were called A.C.E. schools, because that was who developed the material. I wasn't interested in that program. I had enough students and plenty of rooms in the convent that were not going to be used by the Bible College.

I learned more in two days about Christian administration than any one of the teachers I'd been interviewing had learned in the course of their entire education. I had not yet learned that teachers learn teaching, not administration. A good teaching staff can be successfully directed by someone with managing skills in any field. In fact, managers in most fields would be way over qualified. One day, when I was completing my Masters in Christian Education Administration, my class was addressed by a teacher. He was introduced as the best teacher in the State of Florida. He told us that many teachers, including himself, could never be an administrator. He also shared with us that no administrator he has ever met would make it as a teacher below college level. I should have listened to him more closely. One day I would try to replace myself with the best of my teaching staff, only to be turned down flat. He told me that no matter how good the teachers were, he needed to know there was an administrator down the hall with a fine pastel hanging on his wall.

The next time the association met was in Roanoke, Virginia. Although it was only a short time later, there were over three hundred administrators in attendance. At that point, I'd been in the career only months, yet I was an old veteran. Even better, I had a traditional school with a sizable staff. Invitations to speak in their school assemblies and churches were numerous. I accepted a couple, but by then my interest had surpassed building the academy. I was teaching a course in Geopolitics in the college, and I was interested in building the college. I was busy lining them up to speak in our assemblies to expose them to our total package. I wanted their graduates. Things were happening so fast that that part of my life was a blur. Our next meeting consisted of over three thousand administrators. We were starting schools at the rate of three per day. Public schools were losing students at an alarming rate.

If we would have had a Reagan or a George Bush in office at the time, we would have emptied those institutions of liberal indoctrination. There was no one to help us and the courts were packed with Democrat presidential appointees. We didn't have a chance. A young lawyer I met back when we were only beginning was trying to build a Christian Legal Association. He was doing the best he could. He'd win one battle, and they'd hit us with another attack before we could recover from the last one. At first, they never could get us on academic issues. They would get a local ordinance passed that required all schools to have an elaborate fence that cost more than the building that was housing most schools. That was about all the meetings consisted of then..... how to fight the current battle. I'll never forget the illustration one pastor gave about compromising with the government. He said it is like a bear making a deal with a bear hunter. He said all the bear wants is lunch and all the hunter wants is a bear skin coat. They work it out so both get what they want.

Something I didn't notice at first was that this school association was religiously bipartisan. It didn't matter what group your church was a part of. If you had a Christian school, you were there. For your school to belong to the association, that meant you had a state and a national accreditation you couldn't get anywhere else. An exemption was something else. An accreditation got you students, but no exemption, and you lost your teachers. That is how they finally got us. If you didn't have an exemption, you had to pay into unemployment and social security for your staff. Eighty percent of the schools couldn't afford it. They didn't even have to pay it for their pastors. For a while, we got by just saying that the school was a ministry of the church, which it was. While I was overseas later, the courts somehow managed to break that. Those that stood on that premise went to jail. Lester Roleof was the first to go. When he got out, he went right back to running his girls schools. He mysteriously blew up flying somewhere in his airplane.

They couldn't get our school, however. When this exemption thing first started, I went to West Chester and met with the highest bureaucrat this side of Harrisburg. I laid it all out. The Nuns lived in the convent and taught as their ministry....our teachers lived in the convent and taught as their ministry. If they didn't give us an exemption, then they couldn't give it to the Catholic churches either. Most church schools were not able to comply with these measures. After I left the school, I don't think they were able to maintain the exemption, even though I tried to relate the process. Nonetheless, we had a four or five year ride and some survived, but only the most blessed and influential churches. Hundreds of thousands of children got off on the right foot. They can't take that from us. Anyway, for some mutual reason, it didn't make any difference what your religious persuasion was.

Once I was sitting in the cafeteria between meetings, and a man walked to my table and asked if he could join me. It was the founder of the Association, Dr. Al Janney. A few years before, he was the president of the Baptist Bible Fellowship. He was in the heart of the Springfield fray. Knowing where I came from, I couldn't have got into his office if he had the plague and I had the only anecdote. God used this meeting well. I shared with him the fact that before I had surrendered to the ministry, I had belonged to a Fellowship church in Delaware. The pastor there had told me to stop and see Dr. Janney on my way to the Bahamas. It was Sunday morning and I had asked one of his deacons if I could meet with him. The deacon led me to Dr. Janney's office, where he was just putting the finishing touches on his message. He ran us out of there rather abruptly. We laughed about it there in the cafeteria, while I told him about our work. He was very impressed with what the Lord had built out of us before I ever revealed who I was. He admitted he had thought long and hard over the position we took in Springfield. Although he regretted the whole affair, he said he could not condemn our stand scripturally. This opened an avenue of communication and healing between us and the B.B.F. pastors in years to come.

I cannot yet comprehend the volume of information, programs, and stats that were made available to me at these meetings. There was no question about the quality of the material or the expertise of the speakers. These meetings enabled me to match wits with anyone in any area of private education. If I hadn't tried it, I had at least studied it. Forget public education. I learned that stuff thirty years ago. There is not a single program in the public sector today that can hold a candle to the least successful of the methods we employed back then. As a matter of fact, they can't compete with themselves. They've gotten even less effective ever since. Well, that is they are less effective in the field of education. I don't think educating people is their goal. At least it hasn't been from the early fifties, when government bureaucracies took over.

Back when Sputnik was all over the front pages, you could find the rest of the papers full of reasons and warnings to the nation. We the public must give our schools to the government or we will fall behind the Russians in education and technology. My wife and I met the launch foreman from Cape Canaveral in church many years after the event. He told us that he was ready to put our satellite up long before that Russian satellite, but he was ordered to postpone the launch. He's not sure that Sputnik really ever existed. The beeps recorded came only from the Atlantic Ocean. He thought they were originating from sea going vessels. The more I studied the matter, the more I noticed the change of agenda in our schools.

The appreciation of the history of our great country soon began to subside. Nationalism disappeared, discipline declined, and with it, the learning process. The absolutes like the three R's were replaced with variables like social studies. These ever-changing philosophies replaced the solid disciplines until the Arts, as we knew them, ceased to exist. Today, they even teach a thing called social geography; only expressing world politics and having nothing to do with world geography. Ninety percent of high school students could not locate New Orleans on the map in 2006. They could tell you, though, that whatever part of the world they were studying hated America. They learned that our only hope for the future was to vote for liberal democrats. What a waste of twelve years of our children's lives. They should be able to just register as democrats and receive their diplomas. There are no other definable goals in public education today.

Acts 17:16
Now while Paul waited for them at Athens, his spirit was stirred in him, when he saw the city wholly given to idolatry.

Chapter 7
Preparing for Fights and Flights

There is no teaching done until learning has taken place. I had a real good teaching staff. They soaked everything up like sponges. We took the most successful programs from all over the nation and applied them to our program. ABeka was the best curriculum being developed anywhere in the world. When we began our first school year, it was only available through the third grade. It was being developed by Dr. and Mrs. Horton, founders of the Pensacola Christian School, located in the Florida panhandle. They were in their fourth year of the development when we discovered them. They built their school and developed the curriculum one year at a time. I seem to remember them having classes up into high school, but the ABeka program was only completed and tested through third grade, at the time. It would be another year before I could incorporate the fourth grade program into our academia. By the time each grade was available, there was nothing you could add to improve it.

These two were masters in the field of education. They opened their schools to us and proved first hand that they had the best in the nation. There were no back walls to the classrooms. The teachers faced each other in opposite sides of the building. It was amazing. They spoke with a soft voice as they taught and you could not hear either one of them if you stood in the hall between the last rows of the opposite classes. Administrators from across the nation were invited annually for these demonstrations. These weeks of instruction soon developed into an administrator training program. This grew into the most respected administrators master degree program in the industry. I feel privileged to have participated from year one. My fellow administrators turned out to be the most successful men in the field of Christian education. The first couple of years, we had no idea how great and coveted an experience this would become. All we knew was we were getting exposure to what we needed to build great schools of our own. The first couple years, all we received were certificates of completion. We had no idea they would accumulate to the most sought after Masters degrees in our profession.

It was at one of these annual trainings that I was reunited with an old friend. One of the guys that had surrendered to the ministry during the same service I had surrendered was also in class. I had not seen him since we had left the little church in Milford, Delaware. He was a tall blonde fellow, though I can't recall his name. It would be the last time we ever spoke, though we would still wave to each other in passing at future meetings. I once heard him referenced as a man I should consider when I was looking for a replacement. You've heard the Apostle Paul refer to us as well known, but unknown. I didn't realize it at the time, as I was busy with my own agenda, but our work was gaining national notoriety. I was turning down more invitations to speak than I was offering to others. Our national meetings had grown into the thousands. Someone was always introducing me to some big shot from Bob Jones or a similar school. I enjoyed meeting them, but I had no aspirations beyond my present passion.

Those guys were my competition. I truly believed God was building the greatest college on the East coast, and nothing could entice me to give up my dream. One of my graduates took a position on Jack Van Impe's staff and hinted that I would be happy working with him. I saw that kid on T.V. many years later and wondered 'what if?', but never even thought about it early on. I was on the books as the administrator of the academy, assistant professor of Geo-politics, chief pilot, and field representative for the college. My corresponding salaries were impressive. Only problem was, I never took a dime more than living expenses. I was a member of the original church staff; I was not an employee. We had an understanding. Take what we absolutely needed to survive and whatever else came in went to the work. The way God was blessing the work, we knew we'd all be just fine, and would none grow old with nothing to live on. We used everything for the work, except that which came in for our missionaries in the field.

The speaking invitations I did accept always dealt with matters concerning our work. Someone I had never personally met would ask me if he could introduce me to a pastor that was very interested in our history. At first, I made these appointments hoping to present our college as an alternative to those run by big organizations. Over time, however, these invitations became more of an interest in New Testament church practices than an interest in our particular school. Once, a very respected founder of a college in Michigan was speaking at our national meeting, and I bumped into him in the hall between meetings. He stepped out of the crowd he was addressing and gestured towards me, and said, "So you're the guy whose work was built the Bible way." Another time, I was greeted with, "Your work's reputation precedes you brother". As hard as I was working in those early days, it still startled me to be recognized without an introduction. Everything was coming together.

God was so present when I was on these missions, that I would go back to my room, lock the door, and undress to my underwear. The only reason I was in nice accommodations was because it came with the conference reservations. When I was doing this by car, I slept in truck stops and used the driver's showers. I knew how to do it, having a background as a trucker. I would get on my knees at the side of the bed. In those days, I even took off my jewelry, and God would strengthen me through prayer. I was out of my league. I had just left Dr. somebody and was to share a table with Dr. somebody else at dinner! God was growing me into my place. I had nothing beyond my understanding of the New Testament Church. I wasn't even one of our church's ministers, and yet I was dealing with some of God's most prominent ministers. I had titles, but who was I really but a truck driver, or a salesman? I had been a pretty good N.C.O., but I knew I had bluffed my way through most of those military accomplishments. I had been pretty successful in the business world, but that had been all mouth. You know what N.C.O. stands for? It stands for Non-Commissioned Officer. That's what I still was, yet I was dealing with high ranking officers in the Lord's army.

I didn't know it at the time, but it was going to get a lot more involved than it already was. Pastors were requesting I visit their churches, but I didn't preach. If they wanted me to deliver an instructive presentation to their student body or to their teaching staff, that was no problem. But I was getting calls from pastors that didn't even have a school. They wanted me to explain to their deacons and other leaders of their church how God can bless a church that wasn't involved with any outside organization. Sort of reminds me of the first church I joined after retuning home from the service, when we took the Milford church out of the A.B.A. Others had been ostracized from one group or another and they just needed some reassurance that the New Testament still worked. They needed to be hooked up with some sister churches, and they needed to know when and where independents met for fellowship and missions conferences.

They needed to find independent missionaries to support. That led to what I believe God was planning all along. The only way a church can fulfill the great commission is to train, send, or support missionaries. If you really desire to pattern your church after the New Testament, and sincere pastors really do, then you can't give your God-called men to some organization. They need a place equipped to train them, that won't steal them. We believe a church must recognize and ordain and authorize a missionary and his work. This authority is not given to a college. If God called one of your men, we would train him and send him back to build missions for your church. In the process of this new effort, I found myself working with God-called missionaries that were looking for independent churches as well as churches that were looking for God-called missionaries.

Fred was an authoritarian to the core, and he believed in pastoral authority to a fault. But during one of our first senior staff meetings, he made it clear to me how it worked. He said, "Any of you have the right to my office at anytime, and you may dress me down in private 'til I bleed, but only in here. If we are going to work together tomorrow, it happens only in here. It will fit in our rules of exclusion for senior staff only. Nothing said in anger will be dealt with by any of us until after morning prayer, and if it isn't brought up the following morning, then it never happened". Sometimes we reminded me of a bunch of drunks. My father used to stagger in the door, fly off the handle, cuss me all the way to bed, yet be sitting smiling at the table waiting breakfast on me the next morning. Nothing had happened. One night after hours, I walked unannounced into the boss's office and found the college president standing on top of Fred's desk with his finger in his face. "Pardon me", I said, as I left. Many years later in completely different surroundings, I asked Brother Eitelman, the college president at the time, what that was all about. He told me simply that it had been justified.

I had been heading in to his office to blow off a little steam myself. I was just tired. My schedule at the time dictated that I hit the road Monday morning and arrive back home no later than Saturday night. I was on fire for that college and my energy level was through the roof. I slept five hours a night, either in a cheap motel or in my car parked behind a truck stop. Driving home one night from Kentucky or Ohio, I don't remember which, I was struck with a weird idea. My Olds 88 had just rolled over 90,000 miles. A couple years prior, when we were just getting started, that car had been the newest and nicest one on campus. Dr. Drummond would borrow it if he had a high profile meeting that he couldn't get out of. Now he was driving a Mark IV that Monty had given to him. My car was now one of the oldest in the staff parking lot. I thought to myself that if I could take a big airplane apart and put it back together, then there really couldn't be that much to driving one. I wouldn't have to bother learning all that navigation stuff; I could just fly these same routes without having to stop!

I got in late that night and Fred had left to spend the night on his boat. I don't know what got into me, but I drove right down to the docks. Those were the days before cell phones, so when I showed up with no warning, he was rather startled. I was the main contact this college had with the rest of the world, and the only times I had ever gone out of my way to talk to him, it had been over a serious matter. I hadn't planned on becoming the guy that showed up unannounced and caused panic. Fred hadn't planned it either, but it just happened. My name was associated with everything he read about concerning our work, and just about everyone that contacted us from anywhere for anything referenced their association with me. That included about thirty new students that had recently enrolled for the next semester.

The effort to build the Baptist Record had been in the works for months. Fred called me in and asked if I could help. He told me that Ed was so caught up in the details, that he'd never get it into print. I knew nothing about it, but I knew men that did. I asked Ed to make a visit to lower Delaware with me. I took him to a church that put out a pretty impressive publication. Ed made note of everything he needed and within a week, we had it. He had the first copy ready in no time. I then introduced him to the Punxsutawney Spirit, the paper from my hometown where my oldest sister worked. That's how we got things rolling. At first

I delivered them to churches throughout Ohio and Kentucky, all by car. That was one of the reasons I was thinking about an airplane.

I can't define what the relationship between Fred and I had evolved into. My office had become, for all intents and purposes, the missions' office. If Fred feared the influence of anyone in our church led organization, it was our missionaries. They were men's men. They, like him, had broken the bonds of the big missionary organizations and gained enormous recognition in hundreds of churches, as well as our own. When they called from the states or from the field, they asked for me, and that was fine with Fred. He was not comfortable dealing with anyone he considered an equal, and I think he associated equality with a man's ability to preach. I was not a preacher. I once heard him tell another preacher that I couldn't preach my way out of a paper bag. In his mind, I was definitely inferior to him, and he was overjoyed that I maintained my influence in the ranks of those he felt to be equally talented.

You might think there's no way I could be referencing one of the most powerful preachers I think had ever been heard, but I was. One day I walked into the main building and several managers ran up to me like I was their savior. No one could find me that day because I had been out at the airport. They explained that there was a real big shot preacher from Virginia waiting in the lobby, and Fred had locked himself in his office, trembling like a baby bird that just fell out of the nest. The only communication that had come out of his office for the past hour was to 'Find Tim'. The number two guy was in his office and the college president was in the building, so I couldn't understand what the big deal was! I was just told that they were all busy. It was the middle of the day, but I said, "You get them out of whatever classes they are teaching and tell them to get in their offices and be prepared to meet a dignitary."

"Well, Doctor Stone, I had no idea you were in the area," I said as I greeted our guest. "Please come with me, I'll show you around. I'm sorry, I just arrived," I told him. I then whispered to him, "We're having one of those emergencies that only people in your profession could appreciate." I took him into Carl's office, which was no slum area, and then I took him into the office of the president, which was really impressive. He said he'd like to say hi to Fred, but he didn't refer to him as Dr. Drummond. That might give you a clue as to why Fred was locked up in

106 • *Preparing for Flights and Fights*

his office. Fred was not facing anyone that he felt inferior to...that was my job. He didn't trust Carl or Ed, and no one had ever really heard of them, but I was his safety valve. That day, I scared the pants off him. I led Dr. Stone right into his office. I told him I needed to handle a situation for a few minutes, and that I would give them enough time to exchange pleasantries.

Five minutes later I returned and said, "Sir, I hate to interrupt you, but maybe I could take Brother Stone to the Inn in your stead". Fred was cowering behind his desk like I'd never seen before. He said the appropriate words of departure and sent us off with a smile of great relief. I made sure that Doctor Stone was not snubbed. I got Fred out of every question that followed their short reunion.

It was late that evening before I saw Fred again. He was walking through the lobby with two new men he'd brought into our work while I was gone. One was to be our new office manager, and the other was a big shot from Georgia whom he had chosen to head our seven church ministers. There I was in all my glory. I was on my hands and knees, polishing the tile at the main entrance. My heart had never left the beginnings of this endeavor, back when we all shined floors if it looked like it was needed. He didn't introduce us. He just shook his head and started to walk on by. Then he turned and said something I'll never forget. He said, "I can't imagine running this place without you." Where did that come from?

The next morning, I was standing in my wife's office when he brought the new head minister in. He instructed my wife to secure housing for the new minister and his family. He explained to my wife that the new minister would have charge over the seven ministers and told her what her responsibilities would be relative to the new minister. All I was to this new guy was the person he had seen cleaning the tile in the entrance the night before. That morning, however, he realized I wasn't the janitor. Fred told him I was in charge of all education below college level, mission relations, publication distributions, recruiting activities, and then some. While his hand was still in mine, the minister turned to Fred and asked, "Where does this brother fit in the chain of my ministerial responsibilities?"

Fred didn't answer. I would have liked to have known the answer to

Preparing for Flights and Fights • 107

that question myself. Fred hadn't given me a direct order in over a year. The number two guy and the college president never asked me anything except whether I wanted to have lunch with them. Now we were all looking at Fred for an answer. He turned to walk out of the office, put his arm around me, and looked at the new minister. He said "You have a lot of ministers answering to you, but this brother answers to no one." Then he put the icing on the cake by saying, "If he answers to anyone, it's to me. Is that clear brother?" Jesse got the message. He pushed the guys a little, but was always careful if they were with me.

Maybe I was forgetting who I was. I was really a high school drop-out. Oh, I had found a way to close the gap by getting my GED and earning some other credits here and there, but I was working with the best in their fields. They were accepting me, even requesting me, as though I were someone that I wasn't. I really hadn't earned anything. I just had a vision of what a New Testament work could do if it was put in the Lord's hands and believed that if you had enough faith, it would work for us like it had worked for the founders. I even had people calling me to talk to other people about what we were doing. They would tell me how they just couldn't do it because they were hopelessly locked into one outfit or another. But I would tell them that I knew someone in Ohio that could put them on the right track, because he was at the right stage of his ministry, and he could realize all the tremendous blessings available for a work that was willing to operate according to the New Testament. I kid you not. I have driven hundreds of miles to talk to people that were excited about the possibility of building a work that wasn't dependent on anything outside the scriptures. Why? Because we were doing it; and it was working. That's another reason I needed faster transportation.

All of this sort of rushed through my mind as I watched Fred sigh in relief as I told him my visit to the dock was not pressing business. He insisted I come aboard, but I told him I had to get home. I told him I wanted him to think about an airplane, and that was the reason I had come down to the boat before going home. My car was done, I told him, but I was just getting started. "We'll get you another car", he said with additional relief in his voice. "Go home and make love to your wife. I'll see you in the morning". I just turned around and walked back to my car. I was tired. I was getting in the car when Fred walked over to my window. He said, "Tell Brother Durham I think providing us a plane for field work might be a good project for his Sunday school class. See what he thinks about it". I had worked with this guy long enough to know what that meant. It meant find a plane and get started. The next morning before class, I took care of the cosmetics. I mean the 'What do you think about it?' part that Fred had told me to ask Carl. Carl said, "What does Dr. Drummond think?" I told him he thought it was a good idea. Carl said, "What do you need to get started?" I didn't have a clue, but told him I would get back to him by the next Sunday.

If I was going to do this thing, it wasn't going to be a part time effort. I didn't have the time. I'd been getting the Baptist Record printed monthly at the Punxsutawney Spirit. The last time I was up there, I had some hats made at the Big Run Pennant factory. I knew the owner was a pilot and a friend of a friend that flew for a local drilling company. I'd ask him about a plane. If I could get something started up there in the hills, I could stay with my parents during training. Everything down here was too hectic. Vietnam was just winding down and the Air Force pilots could see the writing on the wall. All the flight training places around were full of young officers from Dover Air Base transitioning from military to commercial.

The little county airport was about three miles from town, where my parents lived, and it bordered my uncle's farm where I had grown up. This little town played a large part in my life even after I had become rather successful in college. I would use my parent's home as a staging location. Most of my road trips took me into Ohio and Kentucky, and this was right on the way. I would stop at home and refresh on my way out and back. I often brought staff members, even the boss, up here in the hills to unwind for a day. This would be a perfect place to train if I could find what I needed for the task. God had it all set up. He had been working in my life like that since I had started with the school. It was no wonder I was becoming so arrogant. I had begun to think that God was working in my life because I was someone special. There was almost nothing I couldn't get done.

When I drove out to the little county airstrip, it looked abandoned. There were a couple run-down hangers and only one plane tied down by the ramp. There was a single wide trailer next to the ramp that served as the F.B.O., but there was nobody in it. Everything was just as it was when I was a kid. The sun was shining and there was just enough air moving to give a little life to the sock hanging by the runway to show the wind direction. I thought back through time when I would ride old Buck over here from my uncle's farm. I used to ride right across the runway with little thought. You only saw a plane once in a blue moon. I couldn't believe what I had experienced from then until now. Yet standing there in dead silence, it was like nothing had ever changed. That was the first time since the morning I had walked into my office in the convent, three years prior, that I didn't have my week planned. That was the first time in at least two years that I hadn't committed to be in Ohio or Kentucky, or at a missions meeting somewhere in the country. The boss told me when I left to take all the time I needed. He asked me to call in a couple times a week and to return for Sunday services as usual.

I had learned years ago that he trusted me with my time. When I first started building the academy, I would start my day in my wife's office for coffee. Fred didn't usually come in that early, but a few times he did. He walked in and found me sitting on her desk. I'd jump up and start half stepping around like I had something important to do. After the second time that happened, he told me he wanted to talk to me about something. He asked me to wait in his office and he would be in shortly. That happened twice in a row. He would walk in and catch me drinking coffee. I would jump up and start half stepping around. He would ask me to wait in his office, telling me he would be in as soon as he could. He never came into his office. The next time he walked into my wife's office and found me sitting on the desk with my coffee, I didn't budge. He exchanged pleasantries, asked me how things were going, and went to his office. I got the message.

That was years ago. There wasn't any question about my productivity since I had gone on the road. I had brought thirty-three new students in that year, and that meant pastors that welcomed our missionaries in to present their missions to their churches. I knew we had made it. The school was doing well. The teaching staff was superb. I was going to slow down and upgrade my constant road time to air time. I just couldn't believe I was standing there. Two WWII carrier pilots had their little planes in those rundown tin hangers. Well, I was used to being out of my league. I sat there in the grass and in the quiet for hours. I told God I was ready for this, and asked Him to show me how to do it.

Back in the sixties, there had been a flood in Northeastern PA. Piper Aircraft, located alongside the river, took a major hit. All the dyes that made up the assembly line of what some people call the best single engine six-place ever made were destroyed. That was the end of the Apache. If you can find one today, you have found a jewel in General Aviation aircraft. The next morning, I visited the Big Run Pennant Co. to order more hats. One of the Neil brothers of the once great Neil Coal Co. owned the factory. He informed me that he and his airplane partner, a local dentist, had just located an Apache. This meant that their very well equipped four-place Cherokee would be on the market as soon as they were able to sew up their new found prize. If I was interested, he told me to talk to his partner, to see if he'd give me a ride.

I can't remember the dentist's name, but the last time I spoke with him, he was the campus dentist at Liberty Baptist College in Lynchburg VA. At that time, he had a small practice in his home a couple miles out of town. We met at one of his old hangers. I said "Save the ride; give me a price and a couple of days". I rubbed my hand across the engine cowling and down the fuselage, effectively claiming it for the Lord's work. We settled on eleven-thousand dollars. The church cut the check and I was sitting in the Cherokee the next week, asking the Lord how I was going to learn to fly it. It didn't scare me like one might think. I was familiar with airplanes. I had just never been in anything this small. I thoroughly understood the operation of the flight controls, the radios, and the engine instrumentation. The avionics, however, were another story. I needed flight training material.

Within a couple of days I located a Cessna training package. The whole thing fit in a large plastic zip open folder. The flight training center that sold me the package informed me that with this material and an instructor, I would be ready for my F.A.A. exam in fifteen months. The F.A.A. exam consisted of four parts: flight components, communication, navigation, and weather. Flight components and communications would be elementary. The weather thing couldn't be all that hard. The only tough nut was going to be navigation. Since you learn navigation as you learn to fly, I figured I'd be able to reduce those fifteen months considerably. The problem was finding an instructor that would go along with my revisions to the training program.

It probably isn't the same today, but back in the seventies, we had a lot more liberties in aviation than we have today. I was amazed at how loosely regulated general aviation was. I was constantly struggling with increasing regulations as a school administrator. I thought aviation would be a nightmare. It was just the opposite. I found an instructor at a little county airport in Clearfield, about a fifteen minute flight from Punxsy. I drove over to Clearfield and took his discovery flight in a Cessna 172. That was a four-place high wing, about twice the performance as the average trainer. I started it and taxied it to position. I had done this with the largest cargo planes in the world back in the late sixties. I did it with such ease, he allowed me to take if off with only verbal instruction.

Suddenly, I was in a whole new element. This third axis, up and down, was all new to me. The up part was easy. It was the down part that would determine if I would become a pilot. I hit the books. Ground schools were just becoming popular and most everyone I talked to recommended I take one if I planned on passing the FAA exam on the first try. Everything, however, was very familiar to me. Most of it was like a refresher course. Many mornings, the sun came up on me as I sat at my parent's table studying navigation. I had another real advantage over the average student..... I could go to my plane and do almost everything hands on.

The day finally came. I was tired of begging this guy to fly over and give me a flight lesson. He would say the wind was too high, the clouds were too low, or that I was going too fast. It was like pulling teeth to get him to fly his old Aironka Champ over and take me up for an hour. My plane was much better equipped than his and a little harder to handle. The first six and a half hours, he was teaching me......the last six and a half, I was teaching him. He'd get us lost and I'd figure out where we were. In those days, you could be a commercial pilot without having your instrument ticket. That's what he had done. He was an instructor, but had never flown a totally instrument-equipped ship like mine. He was having too much fun. I was in a hurry. Next thing you know, it's my thirteenth hour of flight training and he realizes I'm getting impatient. He told me to stop on the end of the runway and let him out. He told me to do three full stop landings, no touch and goes. That wasn't normal at this stage, but I didn't care....I just wanted to solo.

Now all you have to do after you solo is log three cross country flights. One of them has to be a controlled field. That means one airstrip with a tower directing your approach and departure. Your instructor would sign each flight off in your log book. Then you had to log forty solo hours, with some night flights, and you could schedule an FAA flight exam. If you were renting a trainer, these cross country flights would take you an average of three or four weeks to accomplish. I however, had a plane. I flew my solo and he signed me off. He cut off my shirt tail, jumped in his Champ, and flew back to Clearfield. It was early in the morning when I did my solo flight. He liked to fly before the winds picked up around 10:00 AM. I didn't go home. I went into the trailer and planned my cross country flights, with my three-hundred miler, and my controlled landing being Wilkesboro. I landed at each field, got someone to sign me off, and landed in Clearfield about 4:00 PM that afternoon.

I walked into his office and handed him my log book. He said, "What, you mean you flew your first cross country already?" After closer examination, he realized I had completed all three. He signed me off, and that's the last time I ever saw him. Now that I could fly solo, I flew to Altoona and took my FAA written exam. Then I got a hanger in a little county airport near my office and I went back to work....only now I wasn't driving. It used to be that when I made an appointment with a pastor I had never met, he would often squeeze me in to his regular schedule. Sometimes I sat and waited, and sometimes I got very little time. From then on, I would ask them to meet at the little airstrip near their church, and they would set aside a much larger block of time. We weren't interrupted nearly as often as we might be in his office. Wasn't life great before cell phones?

It didn't take long before I had my forty solo hours. I could now schedule my FAA flight exam. The old guy that flew for the drilling company told me that he could set me up with an examiner in Ebensburg, Pa. She was a personal friend of his. In those days it didn't cost you a dime. Today, they are all third party examiners and it costs a lot. One day I ran into that old guy when I was passing through, and I asked him if he had time to take a ride with me. In one short flight, he taught me how to do a full stall landing, and from that time on, I hardly ever needed my brakes. I asked him as we were walking back to the FBO if there was any other advice he could give me. That was when he told me how to become a pilot that no one was afraid to fly with. He said, "Touch your plane everyday." That's what I did. On my way to my office, I would pull my plane out of the hanger, fly it once around the pattern, put it back, and go to my office. Whether I had to fly that day or not, I already had. It wasn't long after that that I became more comfortable flying than driving. Believe me, passengers pick up on that from the second they climb on board, and their calmness reflects it.

I showed up in Ebensburg on the date he set up for me and was met there by the examiner, just as promised. She put me through the paces and then said, "Give me the controls, shut your eyes, and put your head down 'til I tell you to sit up". She flew around awhile and then said it was okay to sit up. She was about six thousand feet over a little town. She said, "Tell me where we are". She knew I wasn't from around Ebensburg, but what she didn't know was that I had worked in that very town that was now just below us. I could see the golf course I used to play and the RR tracks I used to walk down with a friend I had recruited for college not long before. I didn't say anything. I reached for the chart, tuned in the nearest VOR, and acted like I was locating us. Then I put my finger on Cherry Tree, and said, "We're right here".

She said, "I think I'll give you your ticket today, let's go home". Then I got nervous. She was already sold on my abilities. I doubt many pilots had found Cherry Tree any faster than I did. Suddenly I was thinking that I could blow the landing! I couldn't blow the landing. God blessed, she wrote me a ticket, and I flew off as a certified private pilot. I was a graduate student of a very good program. The Cessna fifteen month flight training program that I had purchased just three months before.

As a result, I was suddenly used for just about everything that needed dealt with off campus. Most of the time it was exciting, not always successful, but always challenging. We had five missionaries in the field from our church. David Isabel was in South Africa when I reunited with the work. I had known him from the early days. We were not close personal friends, as I was with our other missionaries. I don't know how it all came about, but I was called in for a briefing concerning David. For some reason, he began to indicate a desire to have his authority transferred to a church in Texas. Now this is like one of your children wanting to be adopted into another family. If there were some reason for such an agreement, or if it was going to advance the mission work in some way, God might bless it. There was, however, no Biblical precedent for such an action that I knew of. If another church wanted to help you and build a really close relationship with your ministry, there was nothing wrong with that. But to approach him with an offer to switch his membership for no reason was unprecedented.

My part would be to confront the pastor of the church in Texas. I was to let him know where we stood on such an intrusion into another indigenous work. I did not know this pastor, but I knew of him. Brother Thomas was probably the most influential pastor in the group of independent sister churches in his state. If you believe you have the authority from the scriptures to face a pastor, you better do it right. You can't do it alone. I had been walking on eggs for the last year. Many times, pastors would approach me at various meetings. They knew who I was, and the work I represented. I could only state our practice and extend an invitation for them to meet with my pastor. I wasn't in a position for a scriptural debate with a pastor. That defused the efforts of even those most determined to put me in my place.

It also built a level of respect that would out-live my position as college representative. Do things right, regardless of the opportunity or invitation to engage, even in a casual manner, and God would honor it down the road. But this was not going to be a casual meeting. I would need another brother to accompany me. To comply with Matthew 18, it would take at least two. For this job, I also needed the most reputable man possible. I can't remember if I was given a choice, but it was settled that the president of the college would be the man. Brother Eitelman was a good choice. He was well published in the field of New Testament Missions and the editor of The Baptist Record, our growing publication.

His brother was a Southern Baptist missionary, home on leave and living in Arkansas. His father lived in Dallas-Fort Worth, and we were headed for Dallas. That meant we wouldn't need a place to stay on the way or while we were there. In those days, AV-gas was only about a buck.

For two of us in a private plane, it would be as cheap as two tickets on a commercial flight. I planned the trip in two legs. The first leg would take us to his brother's place, and the second leg to his dads, with refuel stops in between. I was about to engage in a fight that very few pastors have ever experienced. I was also about to embark on a flight that very few private pilots have ever experienced.

Zechariah 13:6
And one shall say unto Him, "What are these wounds in thine hands?" Then he shall answer, "Those with which I was wounded in the house of my friends."

Chapter 8
Sharp Contention

When I was doing field work by car, I planned my meetings so I would make it home for the weekends. Most of my speaking took place in the school assembly periods, after which I would head home. About as far away as I could make that work was Delaware, Pennsylvania, Ohio, Kentucky, and Tennessee. It used to take me at least five hours to get from the college to my parents' place in Punxsy, which I used as my field office. With the plane, however, depending on winds aloft, the commute was an average of an hour and forty-five minutes. That took me from the extreme southeastern corner of Pennsylvania to the opposite corner. Only problem was, that put me just under Lake Erie. I would soon learn what lake-effect meant. Northwestern Pennsylvania has less days of sun than Seattle. I have lost a lot of time sitting on the ground because of it. But when I would get a couple of good days, I would more than make up for it with the opportunities that having a plane provided.

Suddenly, the pastors would receive me more readily, and often give me the whole day. When the pastor would meet me at the airport, I would ask if he'd like to go up and show me his area and his properties from the air. Very few turned me down. Working from my field location gave me a good three and half hours start on my day. I could get well into Ohio, and while flying the pastor around his town, I could make him another offer. I'd tell him, "If you like, I can take you down and show you around the campus and have you back for supper". If I only got a couple preachers a month to take me up on it, it was a couple more than I'd ever get by car. Also, our paper was printed in Punxsy, and I would store a couple thousand at the airport. I'd throw a bundle in the plane each time I passed through. All had been working very well for many months when the Texas trip came up. I believed my navigation skills were ready for a trip anywhere.

It took most of the day to get the college president out of his routine, getting our final briefing from Dr. Drummond, and getting out to the airplane. I planned the trip as normal, as if I was going west. The plan was to layover at my parents and head for our first stop at sun-up. The weather looked good, but the lake-effect had the temperature dew point spread less than five-degrees. I had called Flight Service at Dubois airport, about a nine minute's flight from Punxsy, and they reported no fog, even with the poor spread. I called a pilot friend from Punxsy and reminded him to leave the runway lights on for me. Ground fog met us about ten minutes out from landing. I could see patches lying in the valleys. I could see the runway lights clearly from traffic pattern altitude, but right at touch-down, my landing lights blinded us.

You could see straight down through the stuff……you just couldn't see through it length-wise. There was about a three-foot layer across the runway. I pulled up and called Flight Service in Dubois. They assured me they were clear and encouraged me to land there. I said I was going to try it again with my lights out. I just couldn't see well enough to stay between the lights, even with my landing lights turned off. "One-six-whiskey", Dubois radio came through my headset as I was climbing back to pattern altitude. All the controllers in their small Flight Service Station knew my plane as well as they did the locals. Understand, a controller is not allowed to advise, only to inform. We talked on the phone so often, we were on a first name basis. "One-six-whiskey, it's still clear Dubois, please advise intention." Before I could reach my mike, I heard, "One-six-whiskey, please advise me your breaking off, my coffee's fresh."

My car was in Dubois, twenty miles by road from Punxsy. I was going to give it one more try, but this was a personal plea from the closest officials I had in aviation. I radioed, "Dubois radio, one-six-whiskey inbound for landing." With a notable sigh, he came back with the active runway, wind and altimeter. I explained to Ed, as I set up for Dubois, how uncommon the communication he had just witnessed was. For example, the month before, I was flying over Washington, DC. Don't try that today. In those days, the ATP had an eight thousand foot ceiling. What that meant was if your altitude was over eight thousand feet, you did not have to contact Central or Regional Control. You were flying above their airspace. I looked on my chart and tuned in their frequency just in case they wanted to ask me my altitude as I passed over.

I was squawking 1200 on my transponder. The flight controllers knew

I was flying VFR (visual flight rules), not IFR (instrument flight rules), and they wouldn't inform me unless I requested them to. My transponder was not equipped with altitude encoding, which meant they could track me clearly on their screen, but they would not know my altitude. I was listening to normal traffic conversations when one really got my attention. I didn't pay a lot of attention to it at first, but it was building intensity with every transmission. It began like this:

"Navy 751, control" (I really don't remember the numbers).

"751 go ahead control."

"751, traffic your heading 20 knots, altitude unknown."

The Navy pilot came back with a tenseness of voice I've only heard from student pilots. "Control, 751 can you advise?"

The controller's voice came back calm, almost mundane.

"751, control, traffic 10 knots."

The young Navy pilot's voice, even more tense replied.

"Control 751 no joy." That means I do not see the traffic.

By then, I was thinking I was the traffic. Just as I reached for the mike, a beautiful blue fighter passed under me, so close I could see the pilot's bright white helmet through the canopy. It looked like only feet separated us, but the air is really clear at eight thousand five-hundred feet. I was flying visual and he was flying instrument, which meant if we were both on altitude, we were separated by five hundred feet. The second he passed under me control said "Navy 751, clear traffic." "Thank you control, 751," the relieved Navy pilot responded. "751, control, for future reference, control does not advise you how to fly your airplane." A much more relaxed voice came back, "Understood sir, 751."

Ed had just witnessed the opposite emotion with the communication between us and Dubois flight control. He had witnessed a controller frantically desiring to advice. It would be on tape for ever, but he was talking to a familiar voice on a dark lonely night. His humanity had briefly overruled his profession. We walked in the door of FFS and his professionalism had fully returned. He wasn't that nice and his coffee wasn't that fresh. We slept on his benches, had breakfast in the terminal at sun-up, and headed west. We most likely stopped at Cincinnati, as I usually did. Many a night, on my way back from Kentucky, I would land there. After touchdown, if you would ask ground control to direct you to the oyster bar, they would tell you when to turn 90 degrees off the runway and proceed over the grass until you saw a fence. You would shut down, go through a gate in the fence, cross the road, and enjoy the best seafood you could find by airplane.

Before I go into what happened in Memphis, I have a word of advice for any of you that may get involved in general aviation. First of all, unless you're just wasting money and don't really intend to fly anything useful, don't start out in a little two place trainer. Spend the extra money from the get go and learn how to fly something your going to have to learn to fly anyway. If you get your license in a little trainer, you're going to have to hire someone to bring you up to speed on something your going to want to rent to really go somewhere. Then even after you do that, and pass your check flight, you'll fly it like a Nervous Nelly. You won't enjoy it, nor will anyone that happens to be flying with you. I'm not talking high performance adjustable speed prop and retractable gear. That's for wealthy people or those working their way towards commercial endeavors. I'm talking about a genuine four place, constant speed engine, and fixed gear. It's as easy to fly as a trainer, maybe easier. It has twice the lift, performance, and payload. It is safer in any conditions and you can actually take people and go somewhere.

You can always go back the other way if you just want to stay current, but you won't believe the difference. The first trainer I ever flew was to take my biannual review a couple years after I had left the college. It was like flying a kite. I couldn't get it to go up, and it took me two go-rounds to get it to go down. If that's all you want to fly, buy a remote control airplane and save yourself a bunch of time and money. Secondly, if you have a choice, don't start out in a ship that exceeds your abilities unless you're going to keep upgrading from the onset. I never intended to progress to an instrument and commercial rating, but I had bought a fully instrument ship. I bought instrument training manuals and taught myself how to use everything I had. I nearly killed myself and a friend in the process. One night I was showing him how to use the ILS (instrument landing system). I read it backwards as I descended on final. I would have flown it into the ground if there was any there. Off the end of the runway was a strip mine. I flew right down into it. My buddy said, "That's the boom of a dragline we just passed, pull up!" I threw full throttle and pulled up hard as she'd go. When I climbed out of the mine pit I was even with the end of the runway. We cleared the high wall by a few feet and just about stalled onto the runway.

What I was about to do in Memphis was just as dangerous. My safe flight range was about five hours. I could lean it out and get about nine gallons an hour, but three hours a leg is a lot more comfortable. You never know who had too much coffee and I didn't carry a trip extender, even when I flew alone. That put us at Memphis for fuel and lunch. While we were eating, a soiled overcast moved in. I didn't have an instrument ticket, which meant we'd be stuck for who knows how long. I went over to flight service and checked the tops and to see how it looked over our next stop. The tops were only a few thousand feet and it was scattered over Arkansas. I knew I could fly on top, so I decided to give it a try. I decided to play dumb and just go. I pulled to the taxi way and ground cleared me for departure. They said 'One six whiskey, do you wish to file IFR for departure? I can get you in right now." He meant in the system. I had never tried to depart a controlled airport under instrument conditions. I didn't know that you could file a flight plan from the cockpit. Sticking to my play dumb plan I said, 'Roger Memphis." "One six whisky, cleared for departure runway two-seven, maintain three-thousand, contact Regional 27.5," were the provided instructions. So I replied, "Roger Memphis; maintain three-thousand, contact Regional 27.5, one six whisky."

Well that was it. I had climbed up through this stuff before, which was really stupid. This was the first time ever while in the system. I thought if I just maintained my professionalism and followed instructions, we'd be alright. That is, however, the cause of most pilot deaths. They take off even when the birds are walking. I never went into weather unless I was absolutely sure I was going to clear it right away. I reached three thousand, leveled, tuned in 27.5 and said, "Regional, one six whisky, outbound Memphis maintaining three thousand, heading (what ever it was)." Then the problem; I was at three thousand, but there was no top! I couldn't see any top! I couldn't see anything. All vision stopped dead with the windscreen about a foot from my nose.

Then I had a flashback. I remembered back when I was in college and had got a job selling mobile homes. The manufacture of a particular home built in Haleyville, Alabama had invited us to tour their plant. They picked us up at the airport in a little twin turboprop and off we went. I didn't know anything about general aviation aircraft, so I couldn't identify it by name. I said something to the pilot as we walked out to board. I think I simply stated that it was a turboprop; jet engines powering propellers. He invited me to sit right seat. I was familiar with all the instrumentation concerning engines, props, VHF, gear, everything except avionics, of course. What I never forgot was being stuck in a holding pattern and not being able to see past the windows. He tried to tell me how he knew where we were. He explained outer markers and all that jargon, way too much for me. I thought, 'This part, I'll never figure out'. There I was years later, and my vision stopped with the windscreen. It's an eerie feeling, but now I know exactly what that pilot in Alabama had been trying to tell me. I wasn't going to try and explain it to Ed.

I would have liked to climb right up into the clear blue. I thought 'That's what I am going to do', but that wasn't going to happen. The radio interrupted me, "One six whisky, regional." "One six whisky go ahead regional," I responded. "Squawk 4271 and ident," came the order. That meant change my transponder frequency and push the identification button. Regional control was now following me on the code they just requested. When I pushed the identification button, my blip on their screen would flash brighter than the rest of the blips. Then they would know for sure they were talking to the right blip. Then they continued, "Maintain three thousand, come to nine zero."

This was a new page in my IFR system instructions. While locked in a solid shroud of darkness, with only the dim illumination of my instruments, we had to change headings. We had to come to straight and level flight until regional released us to climb out of this stuff. I had to remind myself that I was in the center of God's will, doing God's will, therefore at the hand of God's will. 'I can do this', I kept thinking, but my flashback reminded me what my passenger might be feeling. When in public, he was Mr. Eitelman, and when he referenced me, I was Brother or Mr. Jones. But we had been through a lot together. We had fought together, prayed together, and on the tennis court we had played together. So when alone, I was Tim and he was Ed, and we were both very comfortable with it. If you understood the level of respect between the leaders of our work, you could better appreciate this casualness in our relationship. Among the leaders, you were fortunate to have three or four brothers with whom you could relax your protocol. Open respect among leaders generates respect from followers, which in turn, garners respect from outsiders. I have witnessed this practice. It produces results tenfold that accomplished by a bunch of buds.

"Hey Ed", I said, "I remember once when I was sitting in the seat you're sitting in". Then I reiterated my experience about holding for landing on my way to Haleyville. The major comforting factor that that pilot used on me was his experience. He had accumulated thousands of flying hours in the Air Force. The only reason he was flying a little private plane was because of the surplus of Vietnam-era military pilots. The major airlines really didn't want guys whose experience included fighters. I guess they thought they were hot dogs that would be hard to transition to commercial regulations and procedures. That gave me all the assurance I needed. I couldn't relate any such a record to Ed. All I could say was "Pray Brother, pray". I'm only kidding. Later, I'll tell you about the time I was caught in a storm off the coast of Florida and the brother driving the boat yelled that to me.....and he was not kidding. That was not reassuring to me at the time. All I could do was remain calm and professional in my radio communications.

What I had learned from past experience was that the pilot's voice reflected his competence. The controller's voice reflected their concern. If the pilot's voice was at all tense, this was very rare, the controller's voice reflected an abnormal tone of concern and assurance. On the other hand, the more competent and relaxed communication from the pilot, the lighter and less concerned response emitted from the controllers. I maintained a very calm voice in my response; "Roger Regional, maintain three thousand, come to two nine zero, one six whisky." I carried out my instructions slowly, deliberately. I caught Ed's concern as I gave a glance toward him. I managed a competent smile which was returned with a notable look of renewed confidence. Control held us in the soup at that altitude and heading for about ten years. Then finally, "One six whisky, regional," came over my headset. "One six whisky, roger" I replied. "Clear to climb to desired altitude and heading, have a nice day." It was like hearing Saint Peter say, "Come on in Brother." "Roger, one six whisky" I replied.

I pulled up through the darkness at about a thousand feet per second, my max climb rate. After another ten years, the darkness began to lighten, and then mixed with flashes of brilliant sunlight. We suddenly broke into a crystal clear sky. Below us were now the gleaming white tops of the dark abyss from which we had just victoriously emerged. I did it by the book. I maintained a level of professionalism that had assured my passenger he was in good hands. That confidence would never have been questioned had I not roared out an uncontrollable "Yahoo!!" and looked over at him with a broad smile when we emerged from the clouds. His startled face turned to a gleaming smile.

Ed's brother was a missionary for the Southern Baptist Convention. He was home on leave from his field and was staying in west Arkansas. We set a heading for the little county airstrip nearest his place. The little port was an uncontrolled station, so I couldn't call them and make sure the overcast had not reached them. All we could do was stay on course and hope to outrun it. We were getting close, but the tops were still solid. I grabbed the chart and started looking for some alternates that I could contact. All of the sudden we spotted some breaks in the clouds. I chose the nearest one, cut the throttle and started working us down through about five hundred foot of the mean looking stuff. It was hard to see the ground because it was dark down there under the clouds. It was really dark in contrast to the brilliance we had just left. We got under and still had about fifteen hundred feet of altitude to work with. One last look at the chart and we headed to the strip where his brother was waiting for us.

Today, I welcome fellowship with Southern Baptists, but back in the day, I had no time for anybody involved in anything but a New Testament church. I was congenial, for Ed's sake. He put us up for the night. I don't remember much about it. The next morning we left for DFW International in Fort Worth, Texas. I remember how smooth Air Control handled us. It was dark, and I could see both Dallas International and DFW all lit up. When the VOR that we were tracking read twenty DME (distance measuring equipment) from station, I contacted regional. They took me straight across Dallas International and handed us over to Fort Worth approach. Fort Worth landed us and transferred us to ground that then parked us on the General Aviation ramp. Many years later, an old school buddy would fly me to the same place in his twin. I couldn't get over how nervous he was about it, and it was daytime. It all goes back to what an old pilot that flew for the drillers taught me long ago. Touch your plane everyday. My buddy was an aeronautical engineer with greater qualifications than I ever had, but he seldom flew his twin, and he never flew at night. A lot of people won't fly a single engine like mine after dark in case of engine trouble. I enjoyed nights because it was so much smoother. There were fewer updrafts when the sun went down. I just flew at higher altitude at night so I could see alternative runways in case I ever needed one.

We picked up a rental car and headed for Ed's father's place. He had a moderate home in the hills about fifteen or twenty miles outside of the city. It had been a ranch when Ed grew up. Now it was just an urban development with one old house in the middle of it where Ed had grown up. The old man was crippled up from his cowboy days, but his mind was sound. He had finished his working days working in the stockyards. He could remember when Fort Worth was not much more than a huge stockyard to accommodate the cattle works for Dallas. The city had grown up around it. That had left one of our country's largest packing houses in the center of a massive city. I think it's still there, but I'm not sure. It was there when he retired anyway. Few people complained. Most of them just said it smelled like money. In the old days, the main breed was Texas Longhorns. Ed's Dad would bring the best of the horns home to his ranch and dry them out. He saved the best trophies and had them mounted around the walls of his house. It was unbelievable for someone like me that had never seen these things. One set of horns filled the wall of the largest room in the house. One tip starting at one wall and the other tip against the opposite wall. They had been sanded and polished, resulting in beautiful multi-colors like marble. That meant if you put the large head between those two horns, that steer could not fit in the biggest room of his house. I still can't imagine a herd of those things being moved around from horse back. That was an interesting evening. It took our thoughts off why we had come to Texas. The next day we would meet with the most influential preacher in the state, and we weren't there for fellowship.

I'll never forget the directions the old man gave us when we left. He didn't tell us what route to take to the Interstate or what exit to look for. He said, "When you run out of these hills to your south, head for the giant rock to your west, and that's the road you need". We said our good-byes and got into the car. We didn't speak for several minutes. Then I burst out laughing and asked Ed if he had any idea where we were going. He started laughing, and told me Dad still navigated by landscapes. Years later, I stood outside a restaurant in Phoenix waiting for my reservations. An old man was beside me looking down at the city lights. He told me his son had brought him there for a company thing. He said, "I remember this hill where we are standing. I used to stay just east of it when driving cattle through here". He told me he'd leave the McCormick Ranch and come through Scottsdale where he'd have to deal with maybe two or three cars on his trail. Then he pointed to the center of the fifth largest city in the US, and told me he'd bring them right through there and herd them into the McDowell Ranch. I don't care where you live in America; you're still in a young country. If you live here in Arizona, it's not hard to find some people still navigating our interstates by the nearest mountains.

The church we visited was a really big church, but after you walked out of the receptionist's office into the pastor's office, the walls closed in on you. Behind the large desk, in a big leather chair, sat the man. Either we were not offered to sit, or we didn't accept....I can't remember which. I knew never to take a lower seat than the one I was confronting, so I either never sat down or I stood when the heart of the matter was being debated. The exact conversation escapes me, but the dialogue engaged in just minutes. All I can remember was stating our objection to any church, either initiating or entertaining the takeover of a mission of another local New Testament church, without mutual agreement. Why people like me were called to the ministry was to handle matters like these. The average Christian must be sheltered from the realization that confrontations like this ever happen.

My president was now seated, maintaining his dignity. I was leaning over the desk of the most popular pastor in the west. He was clapping his hands together just centimeters from my nose. He wanted to hit me so badly, I don't know how he restrained himself. The thought crossed my mind that the only pastor to ever shoot and kill a man in his office was in Texas. You might think God can't be in any of this. Let me remind you that the scriptures tell us of the Jerusalem counsel where the Apostle Paul faced down the Apostles Peter and James over a similar matter of church authority. The scriptures also tell us of a later debate between Paul and Barnabas that is described as sharp contention.

One confrontation between the Apostles resulted in scriptural cooperation between sister churches. Another one resulted in the restoration of John Mark to the ministry, and eventually to the Apostle Paul. From a human standpoint, we have about twenty-seven books of the Bible, thanks to Barnabas and his confrontations with the disciples over Paul. I am no such wonderful person as these disciples, but let me tell you, this situation was resolved scripturally because of this confrontational encounter. The results would reverberate around the world. I will also remind you that this same pastor and I would communicate in years to come for the good of missions. The college president accompanying me would become a pastor, in Texas no less, and he would also work with him on missions. But for the present time, it certainly fit the Biblical description of sharp contention.

I lost the starter on my plane and had to prop it to get it started. In the old days, that was the only way they started their planes. Only problem was, they had about thirty six horses to turn over. I had to turn over a hundred and eighty of those prop spinning steeds. When that iron windmill comes to life a foot from your face, your weight better be on your back foot. I remember asking someone in the engine shop if it would even work. He said he had never seen a four cylinder propped before. He said, "If you can keep the plane on its chocks and stay out of the prop when it turns, it should work". He told me if I was going to try it, I should pull it through a couple times before powering the magnetos. That meant leave the key off and let the first couple spins pump in the fuel. I had Ed hold the brakes and I did the deed. A Lycoming one-eighty might be a considerable power plant to the average private pilot, but remember where I had come from in aviation. You couldn't pick your teeth with this little thing next to four J-36 jets turning three-bladed Curtis electric props. Each one of them was as long as Mr. Eitelman's best set of trophy horns. I spoke to the Lord about it on my way back to the ramp. Corporate credit cards were a thing of the future. I had enough cash for fuel and food for the trip home. We also had a very important appointment waiting for us in Oklahoma. It was like God telling me, "What other choice have I given you? You survived the smacking palms of one of my best pastors.... what's a spinning piece of steel in your face?"

I John 4:4
Ye are of God, little children, and have overcome them; because greater is He that is in you than he that is in the world.

Chapter 9
A Change of Countenance

On the way home, we experienced a couple of events that I can only describe as prophetic. I can't recall exactly why I did what I am about to tell you. Now that I think about it, there wasn't any logical reason. What I can recall is locating a small county airport in Kentucky, and circling it just to assure myself that I was where I thought I was. I had never felt the need to do that before or since. It was Paducah County, Nowhere-Ville to me, way out in western Kentucky. I don't know if it is true today, but in 1978, the nearest building to that airstrip was West Paducah Baptist Church. A few years later, Ed would become the pastor of that church, and in that building, I would be officially ordained to the ministry. Nothing in our lives would have changed had I not gone a little off course that night, so why did I do it? As you will see in a later chapter, my ministry comes to a breaking point almost before it begins.

Another night in my future, I'd be sitting outside my R.V., parked behind that little building we had just circled. I'd be making the biggest decision of my life when the silence would be broken by a small plane circling the airstrip. He didn't land. I watched his nav lights going off into the darkness. I guess he was just checking his direction. I had begun to wonder if God was in any of what was going on at that time. After seeing that plane, God impressed me with an old memory. Like He was telling me, "Why do you think I let you go off course and circle this place out here in the middle of nowhere? You weren't really off course. You just needed the assurance that you were headed in the right direction. What was the chance of that happening?" That place was a tiny little speck on my chart somewhere between Dallas and Philadelphia. The chance of it having a non-directional radio beacon on-field was probably one in ten-thousand. It had to be the Lord. I got the message.

On our way home from Texas that night, neither Ed nor I thought there would ever be other places of service in our lives. I had never put it together until that moment alone outside my R.V. Then came the memory of the stop we had made earlier that day at Norman, OK. The man we had met with was probably the most influential New Testament pastor in OK at that time. He agreed to meet with us because he supported one of our missionaries. I thought he came to hear what we might have to say to him, but it was the other way around. He had left his big office and was waiting in the little restaurant on the county airport just outside Norman. I have to admit that I was a little intimidated when he requested a moment in private with me before we departed. The president of the college and the editor of the paper he subscribed to was sitting right there with us, and he wanted to talk privately with me.

He told me an absurd story of monies his church had sent to our missions department. It had been earmarked for a special need of one of our missionaries. The missionary said that he had never received it. I wasted no time informing him that such an event was impossible, and that my wife was in charge of all missionary support checks. He said he would not abandon our man, nor pursue the matter any further, if I would make him a promise before God to look into it. I made that promise against all my unquestionable loyalty to my position and my leadership, but I made it.

How did he know who to ask to investigate this matter? He didn't know my wife was the only one that would know if such a thing were true. I had just that minute told him she was in charge of every dime. That meant everything that came in or went out of every department, period. I blew it off as impossible, but I did promise I would look into it. He took my hand, looked into my eyes, and said, "As a brother in Christ, promise me you will look into this matter". I had to force myself to show some degree of sincerity. "Brother, I promise I will". I knew there was a mistake somewhere. He ran a big place, and I figured he had mixed us up with someone else or our missionary was mistaking. I filed it in the back of my mind, exchanged pleasantries, and departed.

I thought the reason I was so concerned about our location was because our next stop was Calvert, Kentucky. It was also in the middle of nowhere as cross country flights go. Once we circled Paducah, I knew I was dead on for Calvert. I introduced Ed to the very pastor God would later use to get Ed the church we had circled the night before. Around noon we left for Cincinnati, our final stop before home....or so we thought. Skies were scattered, variable to broken. That meant not solid overcast. I could fly above the stuff and get back down whenever I was ready. Cincinnati radio said they had good high ceilings. I figured I could get above this stuff and get back down under safely when we reached Cincy. We were going merrily along on top, but the tops kept pushing us up. When I got to eight thousand feet, I saw buildups much higher. I realized I couldn't get up there.

I picked a hole and went back under. Only problem was that the ceiling was falling as fast as the tops were rising. Suddenly we were pushed down below three thousand and falling. I grabbed the chart. The closest thing was Knox Air Station, right in front of us. I grabbed the radio: "Knox radio, seven niner one six Whisky." "Knox radio, go ahead one six whisky," came the reply. I related our dilemma. They could read our transponder which was transmitting VFR (visual flight rules). They had to take for granted that we could not file IFR (instrument flight rules) and go into the clouds. They knew we had to get down pretty quick. They asked for type, speed, and altitude. They put me in their system and brought us in. As soon as we put down, I knew something was different. I detected old military terms I hadn't heard in over ten years. They directed us to a position on the ramp. I heard "One six whisky, be advised, Apache in your proximity turning down." That told me there was a gun ship near me that had just shut off his engines and his rotors would be spinning for a while. I wasn't in Kansas any more. I was in the middle of an attack aircraft ramp. I was on a military facility, better known as Fort Knox.

Our first two stops were forever prophetic; I wish this one had been. You know it's the gold storage of the country. I never thought about this until right now as I am writing this, but I'm the pastor at Goldfield, the only real gold town in AZ. There is probably more gold under us than there is in Fort Knox today. Do you suppose, God? Nah. That would mean that on that single trip, God had prophesied my leaving the very ministry that had started my life. Then he had showed me the place that would authorize the missionary ministry of my life. If I threw this final stop in the mix, He prophesied where I would complete the church ministry of my life. We had one more stop to make. We had to eat and fuel up at Cincinnati. I have referred to this prophetic flight over the years. The West Paducah thing was nothing short of a miracle. That was sufficient for me. I had no idea that twenty years after that flight, my life would be miraculously changed forever. It would happen in a living room in a house in Cincinnati!

The weather broke and we flew over to Cincinnati. When we were taxiing out to the active runway for departure, I had the only run in with air traffic control I've ever had. We were directed to cross a taxiway as a large airliner was approaching the crossing. The taxi lights on his nose gear filled our cabin with blinding brilliance. I knew the controller had clearly told us to proceed. I had just entered the crossing when those lights began to flash off and on. It was most likely a signal telling me that he saw me, but we were not in voice communication. I pushed the left rudder petal to the firewall as well as the throttle. We did a three sixty and stopped until he passed. From his lights I could not judge his speed, and I could not be sure if the ground controller was actually observing my progress, so I took control. Ground turned us over to departure which advised us to our desired heading and altitude. He radioed that we had reached the limit of his airspace and we could return to VFR configuration. Instead of the normal pleasantry he voiced his opinion of my three sixty.

I told him we were on the last leg of our return flight from Dallas to Philly. He probably never met a private pilot of a single engine General Aviation aircraft that had ever made such a flight. I said, "I think we can complete this flight safely, please advise." He wasn't speaking to a student on his first night flight. He realized he'd strayed from his advisory position. It's not that way today. All airports are now controlled airspace. The controllers have become very bold. In my day, it was hard to find a controller you could trust beyond advice. I knew one left over from the pre-Reagan administration. When they went on strike and would not negotiate, Reagan fired every one of them that refused to return to work. This old guy was one of the few that didn't get the axe. He was the only one that many pilots would take a forecast from by phone or radio. If he wasn't on duty, we would land and examine the progs for ourselves. Most of his replacements could not read them accurately. The tightness of the pressure radiances (gradience) lines on the printouts tells you more than these guys have ever figured out. When you found one of those old timers, you had a real tool for flight planning. I called this guy from my home or office before any flight in his direction.

I wish I could have read Dr. Drummond as well as I could read a forecast. My wife was not only in charge of admissions; she was as she had been from Springfield, his personal secretary. She ran the books, everything in and everything out, finance and communication. For months she had been trying to tell me something. At first, it was just an effort to receive assurance from me. She knew too much to talk to anyone but me, but I wasn't listening. Whatever was bothering her was becoming increasingly serious. I finally had to talk to her about her attitude. I was a big shot in the institution that was her life. Myself, like most of us that had built this thing from the ground, never took anything out of it for ourselves. We all believed we would never hurt for anything. Our loyalty was unshakeable. Our houses were owned by the church; our cars were owned by the church; everything we had was owned by the church. God has given woman a much greater concern for security than most men. They have a better perception of these things and therefore recognize events that could affect them before most of us guys do. Modern science tells us from a study of the cortex of the brain, that women use both sides of their brain. It may surprise some wives that they are following a man with only half a brain, but that's about all we use. Don't try to figure her out; you don't have the brains for it. You better, however, listen to her. They pick up on things we totally miss.

We topped off at Dubois as we finished the last leg of our journey. With good winds, we'd be touching down in less than two hours. I just marveled every time I remembered how many times I had driven that leg in six hours. People have the idea that light planes are expensive toys and cost more to maintain than they are useful. We paid less for that 1965 airplane than you would pay for a good car. Leaned out, I could get nine gallons an hour. That would be about 15 gallons for this last leg. You'd burn more gas in a car. Yes, avgas cost more, but the longer the flight, the more you saved over driving. The more you use a plane, the less they break.....ask anyone that owns one. I spent less on repairs than I used to spend on tires for my car. Add to that the time savings and the preferential treatment you were given, and you were way ahead flying your own plane, as long as you kept it busy.

We pulled the car out of the hangar, pushed the plane in, and drove to the campus just about the time my wife was locking up for the day. This was in the day before cell phones. I didn't call her when we landed. By the time you dialed in your endless codes on your phone card, you could drive the ten miles to the office. She didn't know we were coming so early, so she hadn't told anybody to stick around, and she was the only one in the office when I walked in. We talked about some of the highlights of the trip and then I remembered the promise I had made to check the books. She looked me in the eye and said something to the effect of, 'Do you know what you're getting into?' You could have knocked me over with a feather. She told me it was worse than I could ever have believed.

One thing I knew for sure; you didn't touch mission money for any reason. It was getting late and we had to get the kids home and feed them. "Let's check this out in the morning", she said. I still thought I would get a perfectly good explanation in the morning and it would all be straightened out. That's not exactly what happened. We arrived at her office the next morning to find the books had been removed from her desk. Just about that time, David Durham arrived with a blank look on his face. "What's going on?" he asked. But before I could answer, he continued. "I got a call about midnight from Dr. Drummond. He told me to unlock the office, get the books, and put them in my safe. He said to open it for no one. Are we going to be audited or something?" I told him not to worry about it; I'd take care of it.

Fred walked in just as jovial as ever and invited me into his office. He said he couldn't wait to find out how things had turned out in Texas, so he had had Ed debrief him late the night before. He explained that the missing mission money had been loaned to him personally by Nick, the missionary in question. He said it was a misunderstanding between Nick and the pastor in Oklahoma that Nick had promised to straighten out. The money was for a bush plane. He told Nick that if he could borrow it until he came back a few months later, he'd have me fly him to the factory in Georgia. I don't remember all the ins and outs of the conversation, but he said he wanted it kept secret that he had had a personal need. I think he told me that it was not the first time, and it really wasn't anyone else's business. He said he wanted to clear it up before anyone that didn't know about the arrangement had access to the records. "Tell your wife to give her books to David to lock up every night. You call the pastor in Oklahoma and tell him there is no problem and Nick will explain it all to him."

"You tell Cheryl everything is fine, but it's not anyone's business but Nicks and mine." Then he said, "You and Cheryl take my Gold Wing up in the mountains for a couple days, you need a rest". The last time he told me to do that, I had taken her up to the Pennsylvania Grand Canyon, and we had brought our youngest son back with us. Nine months and a day later he was laying in his little crib in her office. But no worry, the doctor had said it was time to shut down the factory. Brandon was her fifth and hardest, so we had agreed. Cheryl seemed to be satisfied with the outcome of my explanations, but there was more to it than I knew about. This was about our missionary in the Yukon. We had several others she kept records for and she knew things she had kept quiet about right to the end.

I kept bringing in pastors to speak to our assembly. I liked to time it so that when I would walk them through the college, the classes were just starting their next hour. He would hear them singing before class. I've had them say that their entire choir couldn't hold a candle to our students singing. This was true because most of our students were in our church choir. They had to practice eight hours a week or they didn't get to sing. They held concerts in some pretty impressive places. We were on top of the world. It was nothing to come home and find my office being renovated. The talent God had given our college, I have never seen matched. The last man that did my office walls is now a famous artist.

A preacher friend told me that a few years back, and I told him you have to be dead to be a famous artist, and he agreed. I have a large painting on my wall that he did in the early days. Fred gave it to me when he remodeled his office once and had too many on his wall. I never took a man to our campus that was not greatly impressed with every facet of our ministry. As a matter of fact, one was over impressed. He had a very nice church in Aberdeen, Maryland when I met him. He was so impressed that he gave us around thirty of his best members as new students in various fields of study. One day I came home and found him living on campus himself. I never really knew what happened. From our short conversation, I gathered that Fred had convinced him that he needed to sit under him for a few years if he ever wanted to be truly successful.

Things were changing every time I came home. The last influx of students I noticed were all of a different cut. Nothing like the personalities of those God had given to me in my recruiting. Something was happening, but I couldn't put my finger on it. Fred was still preaching powerful messages every Sunday. That was about the only time I saw him anymore. I was very slowly waking up. I think I really started to wake up when Ron Patterson came to my office one afternoon when I wasn't traveling. He had built the most impressive college class I had ever seen. He was about to graduate the missions course and start rounding up support for a mission endeavor in South America. But on this particular day, he was sitting there crying like a baby because of what had happened while I was on the road. Fred had put him down in a style I did not believe. Then Fred had elevated a young preacher boy to his position. I really wish I'd listened better. If I had, he may have come to me with what he really knew. Instead he took it to The Philadelphia Enquirer.

The same liberal press today would probably applaud him for what he was doing. However in those days, Jones Town was still fresh on people's minds. Fred had been building a whole new something right there under my eyes and I could not bring myself to accept the fact that it was happening. I saw all the indications. I don't know what was wrong with me. I had bought into it a whole lot more than I wanted to admit. My fellow founders were now on the mission field. I was only home on Sundays unless I was speaking for someone on the road. If a missionary had a question they wanted to ask privately, or if they heard a rumor or had a concern, they called me. I was there, right? No, I was as gone as they were. That worked just great for Fred. He was keeping every one of the men that had real influence dumb and happy.

Fred became less and less accessible. He had the founders plaques removed to his private office where they sat faces to the wall. More and more strange faces kept showing up on campus. I couldn't put my finger on it, but these new people were just unsociable. At first I chalked it up to their unfamiliarity with the Christian life, but it was more than that. Sometimes I would walk into the dayroom and just hang out awhile with the second and third year men. These men held me in high regard and looked forward to working with me after graduation. They charged my batteries and made me feel that things were as they always were, and convinced me that I was just over-reacting. There were never any of the new students mixing with these men. This didn't make any sense, since these second and third year guys should have been the role models. It hadn't really bothered me as long as Ron Patterson was their class leader, because he was solid. But suddenly Ron was being pushed out. Something was amiss.

Then it broke. I was up in Punxsy where our paper came off the presses of The Punxsutawney Spirit after they ran their local paper. I loaded the bundles in the car I kept at the county airport, and was ready to take them out and load the plane in the morning. Morning came and so did a phone call from Brother Carl Durham, our official number two man. He said, "You have a lot of old business contacts; I need you to find Dr. Drummond a job right away. Last night, about seventy people gathered in front of his residence and demanded he resign. They accused him of having an affair with some of the new students. He consented to their request and we've got to get him out of here quickly."

Following is the part of the story I never tell. I said, "Carl, is this what you want?" The phone went silent for about a hundred years, and then he said, "Talk to me". I said, "I need some time. The only thing that outrages me more than what he's done, is letting an arrogant mob get away with making our decisions. Did they talk to you before they gathered?" He said no one had talked to him. I agreed that Dr. Drummond may have to go, but not this way. "What would you do if you were in my place?" he asked. "I think I would find some men loyal to the New Testament Church and secure the campus, first of all," I responded, "and then I would bring our Elders in from the field and we would save this work from mass division. This is a hostile takeover and ungodly in nature. Did Dr. Drummond confess to these accusations?" Carl told me he had denied them. "Then tell him we do not accept his resignation made to a mob," I said, "and call me back. I'll wait right here 'til I hear from you."

To this day, I contemplate the way it might have played out if I had not made that snap decision. But such rebellion set my blood on fire, and my anger at Fred had put me in a rage. I felt betrayed. I had suspected he had a problem, but never thought he'd be foolish enough to give in to his flesh in such a careless manner. Maybe I could have settled things down and brought Nick and Pepper in from the field and stabilized things with Fred gone. Brother Sullivan always said, "How do we know what it would have been like if it hadn't been like it was." Whatever, the way it was being handled was wrong, and God could not be in that rebellion. First thing first, I had to stop what was happening and get Nick home.

All I could think to give me peace in the matter at the time was that if those rebels had done things right and sought the Lord's leadership, it would have come out right. There would have been no sides to choose. If those men had come to Carl, Ed, or myself, I would have gone to the elders on the field and it would have been brought before the church. It would have been handled. But I could see no sign of Matthew 18 in action from where I stood. Maybe those men thought they were using the scriptural guidelines. They were some of the best men I'd ever met. But the fact that they went around the senior staff members and showed up at night in a mob left me no choice for the moment. For the moment, I needed to pick a side. I didn't know what those guys had in mind. Had I supported getting Fred off the campus, I'd have probably come back to find my office occupied. All I could think was, 'Guys, you weren't doing this right; there's no rebellion in a church.'

So either way, it was my fault. Within a couple of hours, Carl called me back. The two biggest men in the church, our ushers, and several others had shut down the campus and were manning the gates. My teaching staff and most of the students I had brought in were supporting our decision to retain the Pastor. A lot of my class was supporting us, along with Ed's people. We weren't over the top yet, but we were treading water. Carl asked me, "I need to know this, do we have you?" I couldn't believe he had asked me that. If it weren't for my outrage, they'd be driving the pastor and his family out in a U-haul by then. The only thing I can figure is Carl hadn't told Fred who had instructed him to secure the grounds. Fred wanted to confirm where I stood. Ok, call me a kool-aid drinker, as many have, but you don't pick sides in a New Testament Church.....You deal with problems as a church.

Carl made one more call. He said, "Okay, we're good for now. Those that support us and those who pledge not to join the opposition are in a solid majority." Fred also asked him to tell me not to speak to anyone until after he had met with me. I think he realized I was very much aware that he had been distancing Ed and I for some reason. Now he needed us back in his good graces with every bit of our influence. Ed and I pledged our full support, but it went without saying, the age of innocence was gone forever. We were both acting out of sheer obedience to our understanding of the New Testament Church. Our wives could not figure out why we would do so with such energy. They do now. We are both pastors that understand you will never be called to serve over until you show you can serve under. Regardless of the circumstances, you do things right. David never rebelled against the anointed king...... and he had known the guy was wrong, too.

As soon as the mob realized that the campus was locked down and there was no U-haul being loaded, they made a reckless decision. I can't believe it to this day. These were good men. A lot of them have since built great works, but this was a blunder that hurt only the innocent. Listen, several of these guys were ministers of the church. If they had worked with the leading elders, there is no way they could have been ignored. Quietly, and in order, they would have succeeded in replacing the pastor without destroying the church. Many innocent Christian babies were destroyed forever by what they were about to do. My brother-in-law and sister-in-law and many of my good friends have never recovered. They are in false religions today, or in no religion at all. I know two who lost everything they had. They had sold their houses and invested everything in the work. Several lost their wives and families. If it had been handled scripturally, under whatever new leadership God would have led us to choose, they would have recovered everything, along with their education paid in full in return for their sacrifices.

These rebellious souls could not separate the institution of the church from the pastor. They mistook our efforts to retain Fred and recover the church first, as us being kool-aid drinkers. Only one of the six men that had put this rebellion down would have failed to support them had they followed the scriptures in their efforts. And even that one would have come around in the end. The pastor's own brother would have been supportive, for goodness sake. But we were not given that choice.

I got back home. I flew up to New York and picked Nick up at the airport on his way home from the Yukon. Pepper was on his way from South Africa. The opposition group had regrouped elsewhere. They were good men. It was a real loss, but we had not lost our general congregation which consisted mostly of spiritual babes. We cut our losses; our missions would remain financially unaffected. We worked day and night on damage control, and things were looking up. We were almost to the point of orderly addressing the original problem when the other shoe dropped. I had just flown in from sewing up relations with a couple of churches that had previously associated with some of the dissenters. We knew what we had to do and it would have been done. The good men we lost would have returned eventually. They would have asked forgiveness from the congregation and been reinstated without loss. There is no doubt in my mind that is how it would have ended.

I was sitting in my bathroom. I'll never forget the moment. My wife walked in with the morning paper and handed it to me. I thought that was nice of her; then I looked at the front page. Pictured across the whole front page was our campus. First Baptist Church of Concordville, home of Pennsylvania Baptist Bible School: a Jones Town Cult. I'm not sure what the actual headline read, but that was how it translated. That was The Philadelphia Enquirer as I remember. The next day, the rest of the major papers followed suit. That was just the beginning. All across the nation, stations were picking it off the wire. Our general congregation dwindled, our babies were gone forever. What happened next was the exact opposite of what those misguided souls had hoped to achieve.

Each of the missionaries we sponsored was now totally occupied with their own personal damage control. There was no time for working the local losses. My time was given totally to saving the integrity of our missions. All we had recovered was gone. No one but the true kool-aid drinkers would be seen near the place. News trucks and reporters kept constant vigil at our gates. I cannot begin to describe the endless attacks. After a solid month of national damage control, it was only God that preserved our mission fields. Fred and Carl rallied the locals. They saved over half the general congregation by the time the story wore out. That should give you some idea of the power of this man's gift to preach. When it was all over, no one, except us five, were at all interested in looking into the original accusations. Now it was a cult. Thanks to the very ones that thought they were going to save the church, it was hopelessly lost.

The five of us were suddenly a dangerous liability. There were still a lot of second and third year students that had great respect for us. Not enough, however, to overcome Fred and Carl's influence. Divide and conquer was Fred's method of control. He warned Brother Robinson, our missionary to the Philippines, to be leery of my influence with the bulk of his supporting churches. I don't remember the details, but it was enough to achieve his desired result. We began to grow apart. The same was working between Nick and Pepper as well. None of the once most united leaders trusted each other. It was John Robinson or me that recognized what was going on first. Since it was me that showed up at his campus apartment late one night, I'll take the credit.

We hashed things out in minutes and came to the same conclusion. Together, we were a tremendous influence on the student body. If he could use me against him or him against me, our influence would be measurably reduced. After being less than cordial toward one another since this had all began, the next day we happened to meet on the stairs during change of classes. Fred happened to be coming down the stairs just in time to witness John and I speaking and embracing. The countenance on his face immediately changed. You read what the bible says about a man's countenance. It's the Spirit's way of showing you things about people that cannot be masked.

The end of the line for me was when I was flying Fred, one of his new sissy friends, and Carl, back from Hanover, Md. They were looking at Hammond organs. We got back as far as Lancaster, PA. when we ran into low ceilings. I said, "I have to put it down, Sir". He said, "Go on, you can make it." "I have to make this call, Sir", I told him. As we were taxiing to the ramp, he asked who else in the school might be able to learn to fly. I told him Bud McCartney would be my choice. While sitting at a table in the terminal, he said something very down grading to me. In the old days, if he ever had anything less than elevating to say, he would never say it in public. He'd never say it in the presence of a first year student. I called him on it immediately, something I'd never have done in the past either. His countenance changed even more. I did not know this man. He said, "You amaze me." I got up and went into the men's room, noticeably irate.

Carl walked in behind me and said, "Brother?" I turned on him with a countenance he had never seen on my face before. I said, "Brother, I've spent the last six months cleaning up after this man. Is this my reward?" Carl put his head down and walked out. I don't know what he told Fred. When I walked back out to the table, it was clear that no one wanted to ruffle me any further. God only knows what I might have said next. Carl had never seen the slightest hint of insubordination from me. He was just sitting there like a little puppy. I knew he had been sent in to put me in my place. Now he looked like he was about to cry. I said, "You can call for someone to come get you or rent a car. I'll bring the plane home when the weather clears." I started to walk off when Fred smiled and said, "Leave it here, get us a car. I want you to drive me home." Whatever Carl had told him, it was plain.... he could end it here and now. His call.

If it was me leaving that he wanted, I gave him the best chance he'd ever get. I guess that's not what he wanted right then, and maybe he never did. It all had something to do with his realigning influences or something. Maybe it was as simple as showing his little friend that I wasn't his darling boy, like most everyone thought I was. I don't know, and I don't care. The Fred I had grown up with in the ministry was nowhere in that airport. The only one in this world I had greater loyalty for was the Spirit of God. I could see that Spirit in Fred's face from the day we had met, but it wasn't there anymore. There was a clear change of countenance.

Romans 8:33
Who shall lay anything to the charge of God's elect?

Chapter 10
In the Caves of Obadiah

I knew from that day in the airport in Lancaster that it was over. I just couldn't let myself face it. We had had rough times before and had gotten through them, but this was different. Fred was two people. One was the man I'd worked with all those years, and the other was one I'd never met. I convinced myself we would get through this. I would put my life into recovering and rebuilding this place. We had come from six men in a warehouse to a ten-million dollar campus, and had put nearly that much more into it since we had purchased it. There were little things I should have picked up on a lot sooner than I did. One night, when he was the old friend and spiritual leader I had given my life to follow, we came out of our offices at the same time and met in the hall. He looked at me and smiled. One look at his face and I knew it was my old friend. It was not the new guy that rarely spoke with me. I wouldn't share any of the matters of my ministry in the field with that guy. My list was getting longer every day, and moments like these were becoming less frequent. I chose not to draw him into our pressing business this time. I missed my friend. I prayed daily for these opportunities. It was as if I was running the recruiting, the missionaries field relations, and the teaching staff, totally separate from his office and leadership.

He was the old Fred, but he was talking to me in the past tense. It was as if he was reminiscing. He spoke of all we had accomplished and all we were doing as if it were ancient history. He said, "You know how you kill a snake? You cut his head off. I've lost". He said, "I fought hard but I lost". I assured him of his coming rewards for all this tribulation, as well as the fight for the rebuilding of our reputation. Without going into detail, I assured him we were making good progress in the field. He told me that God would reward me for my efforts, but that his rewards were history. I gave him the impression I was consoling him and that everything was going to work out. He said, "You are going to be surprised my brother". Although the appearance of our working together would continue for some time after, that was the goodbye from my old friend. It probably only happened as a final answer to my constant prayers for those moments. It was the last time I'd ever see him as my old friend.

The man with the holes in his shoes and one old double breasted suit was MIA. I think the reason I had defended him until the end and beyond was in memory of who he once was. Even as much as I despised what had replaced him, I respected the memory to a degree some expressed as inordinate. Brother John Louis was a missionary I respected very much. He was a direct descendent of the Louis of Louis and Clark. I was told his mansion and properties were still there in Virginia. Instead of managing them, at his mother's request, he chose missions. He had followed the whole debacle because he had been involved with us in the Springfield work after I had left Springfield. He was a good friend of Nicks, our missionary to the Yukon. Nick introduced us as fellow bow hunks, referencing the fact that we all three had come from a history of serious hunters; even though I never took a deer with a bow until Nick bought a new one and gave me his old one.

Nick was a real man, so I figured John must be one as well. It's hard to believe Fred surrounded himself with men like us. I can remember one winter turkey camp I was invited to attend. It was Nick's dad's camp, located up in Tionesta, Pa. That was about two years before the trouble started. When I got there, the snow was at least six inches deep. The tents were set up and the camp fire was burning. It was easy to see that I was in my element. First it was just because I had found the place and actually made it in. I climbed out and donned my insulated coveralls as a half dozen surprised faces looked on from their perch around the fire. Nick stood up laughing with his arms open in welcome. "How did you ever get in here in a two wheel drive?" he asked. "We wrote you off when the snow hit, even if you could find it to begin with".

It's hard to share with you how a moment like that feels. Here were men I'd worked with over the years. I knew they were real men. Two of them had been serving in the Yukon for a couple of years. Their tents were certified to seventy degrees below zero. They had heard me talk like a hunter, but they had never seen me outside of a suit and tie, sitting in a comfortable office or restaurant. Now there I was, standing in their circle for real. Their four wheel drive trucks were parked all around, and

I plowed in driving the same car I drove to church. They figured I was either nuts, or really good. They couldn't see that beneath the snow, I was equipped with the greatest set of snow chains ever made. Even back then, chains were a thing of the past. A friend that builds them to get his trucks out of the coal pits had put them together special for his wife. He gave them to me just for that trip or I wouldn't have even thought about going back in the woods in an Oldsmobile. I was introduced to men with names I'd heard, but had never met. I was received with respect. I was properly dressed, and my outer gear showed years of brush wear. It was clear enough that I wasn't a tenderfoot that had found this place by accident and made it in there by a miracle. They were probably relieved that they wouldn't have to worry about my getting lost or shooting one of them by accident. They wouldn't quit marveling, however, of my arrival. I had to tell them.

I still had a couple surprises up my sleeve. My father was the head conductor on the railroad. He ran freight trains, but never put on his heavy work clothes without donning a heavy flannel tie over his flannel shirt. As I warmed by the fire, I unzipped my coveralls revealing the same configuration. I kept my composure as long as I could and then broke into laughter as I untied it. They were woodsmen, but they were gentlemen up to that point. They took it from me and burnt it in the fire. I got them good, but I couldn't stop laughing long enough to ask them not to burn my dad's tie. It seemed like a long time, but that all transpired in minutes. That's all the longer it takes to really fit in, if you fit. Now I was Brother Tim. I wasn't Mr. Jones, whose office maintains Brother Nick's mission relations with the local churches. I also had a double barrel ten gauge with thirty- two inch goose barrels like they had never seen.

I was a pleasant surprise. Nick was glad he would not have to apologize for inviting me, even though they had been prepared to suffer me out of professional courtesy. They had, however, a surprise of their own. There was a bundled up figure at the far edge of the firelight that had not been introduced upon my arrival. "Ok, we have an early morning", Nick announced. Then he turned to the figure in the shadows and asked, "Where do you wish to bunk Brother?" "I'll bunk with Timothy", was the reply. No one called me Timothy. That is, except for Dr. Drummond. It was their way of saying 'figure this out smarty'. I'm sure he had let them know it would be a significant shock. He never got more than walking distance from the campus unless I took him. I had to agree to this arrangement from day one. I don't know what had happened over the passing years. I had heard old stories of him and Nick and John Louis camping out in the Ozark Mountains after I had left the original work in Springfield. This, however, had never been even a possibility since I had rejoined the work in Concordville. As soon as he knew Nick was coming from the field, he would start making plans for me to keep him as far away as possible. This hunting trip was part of such plans.

For the next couple of days, he was manlier than I had ever seen him. He cooked and ate food I know he wouldn't have touched for love nor money. He even stood on ice covered rocks under the small waterfall and showered. I had been in enough meetings with him to recognize this side of him however. Anytime he felt intimidated by other preachers, he could do this act very well. I had watched him cower in his office for hours in anticipation of a meeting with anyone known as a real leader. Normally, I handled those meetings for him, but when he had to participate, this is the guy that would spring out from behind his desk and greet you. Something had happened while I was out in Ohio that had brought all this about. I never would find out what it was, though. I know when we got in my car and drove out of sight, it was over. It was over for good. He said it and he meant it. I never saw that guy again. Fred liked his feminine side, and had determined that I wasn't threatened by it. He was even comfortable with it around my family. He traveled up to my folks place and spent Thanksgiving with us. He carried on with my sisters in the kitchen to the point that after we left, I had to assure them he was straight. Well, at least then, I still thought so.

The day finally came that I had to face the facts, no matter what I believed about his other side. For awhile, I had begun to think if he did have weak moments, they were few and discreet; at least to the point that God must not be overly concerned. I had fallen for a philosophy he had been teaching for years. He used to say, "God doesn't care if you sleep with horses; all that matters is your obedience to his work". For awhile, I thought that whatever peace he had with God in the matter must be mutual. God was truly blessing the work, and the messages were powerful. I look back now and see how devastating that realm of thought really was, and how much harm it caused in my life. I carried some degree of this poison with me for many years after. You can't entertain small possibilities of such perversion in a man's life without it affecting your own. I'm not talking homosexuality, but any form of immorality. One of the ministers we are going to study was a part of the mob we spoke of. He would go on to build a great work, but like me, he had accepted just enough of this poisonous teaching to destroy everything he built.

When God brings something to the forefront, clear and plain, and you ignore it for whatever reason, you are infected. It may not manifest itself in the same manner, but you are infected with some form of the same disease. It may take awhile to incubate, but the culture is still growing. Not long after I had become the field representative, Fred called me into his office. He shut the door. He seldom ever did that in the old days. When he did, you knew he had something to say that was either private or personal. His message was plain. "You're out there a lot and often alone. Satan hates you bringing young men into the ministry. No man is an island in this business. I want you to make me a promise. You won't be that woman, so overwhelmed with guilt that she must confess her infidelity. You get tired, depressed, and you do whatever you believe to be apprehensible. I don't care if you get seduced. If you have to tell someone, you tell no one but me. God will forgive and forget; people won't. The ministry is bigger than you". Well, what he said contained some wisdom. If all the devil has to do to destroy a work is destroy you with one little shot, then you're an easy target. If he finds out that his perfectly placed shot was given only to God to deal with, he wasted a bullet. In fact, your scar tissue probably made you even safer from his next shot. This is, however, a two-edged sword; you're going to get cut badly on either side.

To understand it, you must study the difference between Bathsheba and Delilah. One was the result of a seduction, wrong as it may be. The other was a lifestyle, based on the philosophy that God doesn't really care about it as long as no one gets hurt over it. The difference is simple. With a Bathsheba seduction, Satan gets you involved in sin that you do not want to commit; that's his fault. With Delilah, all Satan has to do is expose you for sins you want to commit; that's your fault. Do you remember how many times God delivered Samson from this woman? He got to thinking it didn't matter, and that philosophy ended his ministry.

God brought it to my attention clear and plain. One day Fred asked me to go riding. We took our bikes up to a Pocono resort. The cabin had only bunk beds. "Do you want the top or the bottom?" I asked. His answer is forever seared in my memory. "You're getting in this one with me." I guess it didn't take me all that much by surprise. I never blinked. I said, "Dr. Drummond, it's never coming to that". As he climbed up into the top bunk, he just looked at me with an expression I couldn't really interpret. It was somewhere between, 'I knew that', and 'I'm a little disappointed, but no big deal'. Anyway, in all our years, it was my first direct invitation. Even though I passed it off as if he was only kidding, and he let it go as if that was all it was, I think we both got clear and plain answers. Ok, he was perverted. But you wouldn't equate it with the same level of perversion practiced by lost people. I guess I didn't either. I was giving him a pass. He would retain my respect and loyalty; I would retain my office and responsibilities. I just wouldn't participate. Even better, I wouldn't even let myself believe I had heard him say it. But I had heard it, and I was infected.

So now all the birds had come home to roost. I fought for him; I as much as lied for him. He tried repeatedly to convince me there was a vast difference between him and my perception of a homosexual. I tried repeatedly to believe it. One day after we had saved the work from total destruction, he met me on the way to my office. I had not seen the Fred I once knew for many months. He put his arm around me and told me that he had been fighting something for as long as he had known me. Today, he said he got the answer he had been praying for all those years. "It's ok. Finally, it's settled, I know I'm ok," he said. I looked into his face. It was not Fred. I said nothing. I walked on toward my office, knowing I had just received the final confirmation of all my fears. Not only was my Fred gone, but he had just proclaimed that God had confirmed it. For the first time, I was facing reality.

All the years I had put into this place, all the effort I had put forward to save it from destruction were wasted. The reality set in; I had not saved the work. I had saved Fred. The work was gone. He was so talented that this place would survive, but it's not what I had set out to save. So many of the really godly men were gone, and in such a way that I could never bring them back. If I would allow myself to accept what my eyes were seeing, I knew it was gone. The dayrooms that used to be full of excited young men headed for the ministry were now occupied by feminine young boys. The spirit was so cold, that when you walked through the place, it gave you a chill. I walked to the third floor and sat out on the same ledge I had sat on years ago. I had sat there before we had opened. You got up there through the dark, in peril of your physical well being. I thought of the hundreds of man hours it had taken to make this old convent into a campus. I could envision my daughter out there on a farm tractor, mowing down brush. Now I was looking at a beautiful five-acre front lawn.

I walked the halls for the last time. The same halls I had walked so many young prospects down the last four years. For some reason, I went down to the basement level. I had not been down there for years. I was shocked. People were living down there. I saw many faces, but two remain forever in my mind. One was a girl I had brought in from a church in Maryland. Her pastor had been so concerned because she was subject to seizures. I assured him she would be living with a caring family. She had been, but now they were gone. She was living in a damp dark basement. I heard she died not long after I left. One other face was that of a younger sister of a man I had found in a church in Butler, PA. She was in a room with a small group of people I did not even recognize. Not long before that, when I spoke to her, she looked back with a gleam in her eyes. She'd also lived with a family that had left when the trouble began. I reached out to her and asked what they were doing down there? She shrunk back with a look of fear on her face that said "Don't hurt me."

I didn't know what was going on, but I wasn't privy to any of it. Ed lived in that building. He'd know what was going on. It was late, but I didn't care. Ed was perplexed to find me at the door. "Well, let me in Brother", I said, which he did almost robotically. I should say dutifully. We used to work together very closely, but for the last few months, we had only exchanged greetings while passing in the halls. "What's going on?" I asked. "What do you mean?" was his response. The sparring went on for about a half an hour before he started to recognize his old friend. "Brother, you are always gone. Your loyalty is often used as a shining example to the congregation, but within upper management, Brother, it is clearly discouraged", he told me. It took him about an hour to say what he could have said before I sat down. "I don't know what side you're on; I don't even know if you have a side. When we saved this school, we didn't save anything that you and I worked to build", he said. I agreed with him and told him why I had been down in the basement. It was my memorial walk. I couldn't kid myself any longer. Things weren't going to get any better. We had lost this place. I didn't know where I was going yet, but I was out of there.

"Don't do anything just yet, Brother", he requested. He informed me that there was a little get together that night. "That just might be why God brought you here", he said. "You wrote a few articles defending Dr. Drummond. None of us knew where you stood. Do you want to go with me?" he asked. About an hour later, we pulled off the highway onto a narrow drive that wound up and around through the trees. You couldn't see anything not directly in the headlights. At the top of the hill, the grassy lane leveled out and came around in a circle. There in the shadows were a couple of vehicles and two men standing at the rear of the nearest one. We pulled up behind the pickup that I recognized as belonging to Nick. The man standing with Nick was John Robinson. There stood our two most influential missionaries. Fred had been trying to put a wedge between these two like he had tried to do with John and I. Only I had thought for some time that he had been successful. It had broken my heart to see these two brothers so cold toward one another over the last few months. I realized immediately that it had been an act. Now it saddened me that they couldn't trust me. These men had too much to lose if my office turned on them. I understood.

Ed opened the car door and the dome light illuminated my face. Nick did a 360 without moving from the spot where he stood. As if to say 'I'd run but it's too late'. Brother John was less upset. We had talked rather candidly. He just couldn't bring himself to ask the serious questions. I don't understand powerful preacher figures. I worked with preachers everyday. Paranoia was their most common characteristic. Nick, being one of the most powerful I've ever known, displayed this character with the best of them. I stepped out to watch him focus his eyes on Ed and begin his display. "Well", he said, "we are meeting in the right place. We can just dig a hole anywhere around here and bury our ministries."

John stepped in, and I don't know exactly what he said to Nick, but it calmed him down. We started over, exchanged pleasantries, and began to stroll through the tombstones in the dark.

Nick made sure I was committed to the purpose of this meeting. All was lost and we were just there to evaluate our situation and examine our options. John was the only one of us that couldn't afford to just load up and leave the campus. When I reached into my wallet and handed John a credit card, Nick was convinced we were unified in this effort. The sparring ended and we began to seriously consider various ideas for our exodus and destinations. Between the four of us, we held more national influence than the rest of the college combined. We're talking about hundreds of ministries and thousands of supporters. We had to find a way to separate ourselves from this institution without severing our relationships with our sister churches and their pastors. We never even considered the influence we might still hold with the remaining students and members of the church.

Recovering the work was not even a consideration at that point. We had to do whatever we could to save the missions. Nick's family was still on the field. The first thing we needed was a New Testament church that would immediately authorize Nick and John's ministries. We needed a quick and smooth transition to a new work. It would have to be capable of convincing the supporting churches that the missions were doctrinally unchanged and sound. We talked about a lot of different works that would fit the bill. We did not have the confidence that any of them could handle the transition with the required expedience to maintain our supporting works. True independent missionaries have no mission board receiving their support checks and doing their accounting. It is all done by a New Testament Church.

Missionaries that go out under some mission board are used to receiving ten or twenty-five dollars a month from a bunch of different churches. Independent missionaries have only a fraction of this number but each church supports their man with one to three-hundred dollars a month. What this means is that an independent can get on the field with far less supporting churches, but he cannot afford to lose a single one of them. These supporting churches are also very interested in the sending church. Churches that support mission boards seldom know what church the missionary came from. They look at the board as the sending authority instead of the New Testament church. So we knew we had to find a solid New Testament work with an administration that these supporting churches would trust. These kind didn't grow on trees and weren't available on any list of affiliates.

I believe Nick had already prepared himself for this meeting. When we realized we would have to start one, he already had the place and plan in mind. We would contact John Louis, who would lead his church to authorize a home mission in Butler, PA. Then we would organize as a New Testament church and select a pastor in our first meeting. We had to really move if we were going to get this all done and documented in time to notify the supporting churches of a new address. That had to be done before the supporting churches sent several thousand dollars that might never make it to the field. We needed a post office box and letterhead right away. Finalizing the details and getting a building and housing in the area could come later. Ed got to work on the printing. Among his many spiritual gifts, Ed was also an accomplished artist and editor.

I got to work building the notification letter. It had to be clear and convincing to generate the level of confidence we needed for a quick and smooth transition. This was back before the days where anyone could get on a computer and generate something that looks legitimate. We didn't want any support checks going to my wife's old office. We definitely didn't want any dialogue created between our supporters and whoever would replace me. We had the letterhead, the address, and the notification letter put together and in the mail within days; long before anyone except John Louis and our families had any idea we were leaving.

We would have to vacate our church-owned residences and clean out my office in unison. We didn't want any of the hassle we witnessed when the original group had loaded up and left. If I had not showed up at the gates when they were trying to exit the campus with their u-hauls, I don't know what would have happened. I told the guards to unlock the gates and let them go. Back then, no one questioned me. They just figured I had spoken to Fred, who wouldn't come out of his house or speak to anyone for days. As we discussed before, the more powerful these leaders become, the more paranoid they become.

We didn't rent a big enough truck. When we had it so full the doors wouldn't close, I still had a bunch of boxes in the basement of our house. I made a big mistake. I listened to Nick when he said, just leave it. To this day, about thirty years later, when my wife can't find something, she says I left it in the basement in Concordville. That now amounts to enough stuff to fill Grand Central Station.

I can't remember where Fred had gone, but he was far away when we agreed on a day to pull out. I had been cleaning out my office, one briefcase at a time. I was down to my certificates on the walls. I also wanted the painting Fred had given me a couple years before. It had been painted by one of our students and could have been sold by that student back when he really needed the money. He wanted it in our work as an offering back when he had little else to give. I vowed to keep it in a place of honor and this place no longer fit the desires of his sacrifice. It now hangs above my desk in our church office here in Arizona. I decided to have it evaluated. I heard he had passed on some years ago. I figured if it was really worth as much as I thought it was, I'd donate it to meet some need that he would appreciate. But how was I going to get it off the campus in the first place? There was no way I could get that picture, let alone my parade saddle and my pistol. They were on display in Doctor Drummond's office. He wasn't in town, but I did not want to risk the fire storm that could erupt if one of the new people saw me hauling that stuff off. Now I was starting to sound paranoid.

We just all knew each other too well. We none wanted to face each other in times like this. God had displayed His power on each one of us and no one wanted any part of it being unleashed on them. I still think that's better than looking for a confrontation. You have to realize the depth of commitment we had placed in each other over the years. We felt like we were leaving our family, even though we knew we could no longer serve God together. Even when a woman has scriptural justification to leave her husband, most of the sincerely loving ladies I know, snuck out like we did. We could have really hurt what was left of the church and schools. We just had no desire to do it.

Many years after we left, I found myself on a back road in Delaware. I was visiting my in-laws and suddenly realized I was very near to the mansion that I had talked one of the DuPont families into donating to Dr. Drummond for a church retreat. All the feelings I had experienced as we were leaving the work many years before were long gone. I very boldly turned into the private drive. The gate was open and everything looked almost as it did when I had originally found the place. The drive wound down into the river bottom through dense Delaware swamp land. As I approached the residence, I slowed to a stop. Believe it or not, I looked over to my right at the hillside garden and walking through the same life size statues was Fred.

I got out and walked over to him. I can't remember anything we said to each other except what he told me about the time we had left. He said the first group that left had called the newspapers and did everything they could do to hurt us. Now I was expecting to hear him say how he appreciated the quiet manner in which we had departed. To my surprise that was not what he said. "When you guys disappeared, it was ten times as devastating" he said.

A woman drove in behind my car and Fred called her over. I recognized her. She was the one that had replaced my wife. When I had made arrangements to go back and pick up my stuff, she was the meanest person I met. Now there she stood in front of me. Fred said, "Welcome this brother with love". She put her arms around me and fondled me with her body. I shook my head and looked at Fred for the last time ever. I walked to my car in silence. He had just offered that woman to me; but my infection was totally cured. The infected thoughts I may have allowed over the years are those I got from him. Now there was not even a hint of contemplation. As I said, you can't justify anyone's activities and not compromise your own. I'm not justifying anyone ever again. How clarifying to have a clear conscience.

Well, I couldn't take my personal stuff from Fred's office, but I wasn't donating it either. I made one last stop before leaving the state. I drove out to the airport and removed the aircraft logs from their holder. I knew they would want to sell it, and they couldn't sell it without the logs. I had learned this from an earlier episode. When I flew up to Ebensburg to take my FAA exam, the logs were not in their holder. The examiner said she couldn't give me my ticket without them. The shop had just completed a hundred hour inspection and had forgotten to replace the logs. They felt so badly about it that they got a pilot to fly them to an airport half way to where I was. I kept the logs, knowing that I had all I needed for a bargaining chip to recover my personal belongings.

All our stuff was loaded but our suitcases. It was late, and we would be pulling out in the morning. A knock came on my door. It was one of the men I had watched being put into positions they could never fulfill. He asked to come in. He looked around as to be sure no one else was there but my family. Then he went to the door and motioned to the car in my drive. Dr. Drummond walked in and sat down. "I know your leaving, and I want to talk to you," he said. Somehow he had found out, and he had returned home in the dead of night. I was determined to be civil, though by then I was thinking my old friend had wrecked my dreams. He offered me a new twin engine airplane if I would remain on as his pilot. I wasn't his pilot. I was the field representative that had used a plane.

I had determined in our last staff meeting that he no longer wanted an outreach program. I didn't know what he was building, but I knew I wasn't called to be his personal pilot in the endeavor. I told him everything was set up and we were starting anew. "If things change in your life and you ever need us, we have enough respect for you", I started to say. He interrupted me and was very offended that I would offer him anything. I can't remember anything else that was said as he huffed off. I had total peace about everything now. We were just building stones to him. I don't know why he would even want to recover me. He told me about a week before that he was only using Carl to build a solid music program. He said he was going to put a really talented music man in his place. Carl was the only original founder still remaining faithful. Carl's dedication to his calling resulted in a music department second only to the Mormon Tabernacle Choir. From that moment on, I never looked back.

We found a house on the outskirts of Butler. The street was still made of red brick. It reminded me of my childhood. My grandmother had had an apartment building in Pittsburgh on Hill Street. Yes, when you see the opening scenes of Hill Street Blues, even though it's filmed in California, that station is in Pittsburgh. The landlord was a young man we met only once. After we moved in, the local bank contacted me and said to do no further business with him. They said the bank owned it now. I asked to whom we should pay the rent. They said they'd be in contact with me. They told me to take good care of the place and they would get in touch with me. We never heard from them again. God was setting us up to be the main financier of this new project and free rent was just the beginning.

My notification letter was blessed of God and the transition went smoothly. Nick and John lost no support. They could make expenses, but had nothing extra to meet the needs of the new work. Ed was like me. We had no supporting churches, and we had just left our paychecks in Concordville. He was a very talented man, but the little mining town in the hills of Western PA had little in the way of employment to offer him. He had two very industrious sons, however. They were painting houses and handy-manning all over town in no time. Now I needed a job.

My parents lived about forty or fifty miles east of Butler and I knew I could find temporary work in Punxsy with one phone call. I could also stay in my old bedroom if I needed to. My folks never changed a thing in either my sisters' rooms or mine. When I was flying for the college, I used my room at least once a week. I made the call. "Hey Bill, where are you working?", I asked my old friend. "We got a pretty good mine going out here on the flats. I'm running a nine (D9), backfilling and bench building", he said. This is the town I had grown up in and had returned to every time I was in transition in my life. Some people hate small towns because everybody knows everybody. There is another side of that. Anybody with a reputation of showing up on time and doing a days work is very glad everybody knows everybody. "I need some work for awhile, can you get me on?" I asked. He said, "You remember that big guy we used to mess with in Rossiter? He's the super on this mine. I'll give him a call. I'll pick you up at your moms at 6:30." We drove to the entrance of the mines and Bill ran into the office trailer. He came out in a couple minutes and handed me some paperwork. He said, "You're an oiler on the 4600 drag. You're on my shift. We work five days, five nights, and five off."

The operator on the dragline was a young man. His father and I had worked construction together years back when I was between colleges. Just about every lunch break, Bill would climb up into the cab with us and we would talk about realities. For about thirty days the young man listened to our conversations, but seldom joined in. Then one night while I was back in the engine room, I felt everything shut down to an idle. Thinking something was wrong, I returned to the cab and found the young operator just sitting there looking out the window. I asked him what had happened? He slowly turned his seat around so he was facing me. He was reading an article I had written in the last paper we had published before I had left Concordville. He said, "I can't read most of the words; I never even heard of most of them. How do I get what you and Bill got?"

You could have knocked me over with a feather. This boy had no frame of spiritual reference to relate to. I had been working with only pastors and church leaders for so long that I had to really work to put the simple plan of salvation into terms he could understand. His past drug use didn't help his thinking, but together, with the Spirit of God, we got the job done. This took place on the last night of the night turn. When my five off was over and we returned to the mines to start our day turn, the place was abandoned. Equipment was just sitting empty, exactly where they were when we had left them five days before. As we approached my drag, we could see a tag had been wired to the door handle. It read 'No trespassing by order of the Sheriffs Department'.

I had just spoken to Brother Ed, who was the last one of us to leave the campus. I related my feelings to him. I told him how empty I felt out here in the world, working at something with no relation to the ministry. The only thing that gave me any satisfaction was the night those mines were forever lost and a soul was forever saved. Ed encouraged me by referencing the seven years David had spent in the caves hiding from King Saul. David knew he was annointed king. He just had to wait it out until his ministry was ready. God would remind me of this many years later as well. When you are called to the ministry, God never repents of His calling. Don't get the idea that when you lose a ministry, you're out of the ministry.

Nick had located a building that had been left empty by some church for some reason. We rented it and called Ed as our official pastor. Nick would remain the preacher, but he couldn't take the pastorate. He was a missionary to the Yukon, and would have to get back at the end of his stateside furlough. I found an ad in the Punxsy paper looking for an operator for a 4600 dragline located just outside Butler. I answered the ad and spoke to the super. He told me I could oil and train as an operator at the same time. He told me when and where to report. Now things were coming together. I was back with my family, not just five days at a time. We had a church to build. I figured I would work the mines until the church was strong enough to build a school. When you're only thirty years old, time is not that important an issue. After all, I was the youngest of the four founders of our new endeavor. I could envision myself back flying and building a college in a year or two. I'd get out of these caves and into my annointed position quicker than David did. Boy, did I have a lot to learn. God was putting things together all right. I just had no idea of the new life he was planning for me and my family. If I had, I would have just got in his way. All I needed to know for now was that whatever it was, it was going through this little town of Butler first.

Psalms 37:3
Trust in the Lord, and do good; so shalt thou dwell in the land, and verily thou shalt be fed.

Chapter 11
The Call to Japan

The call from Concordville was the last call I received before leaving for Butler. It was Carl Durham, speaking very pleasantly. Carl was the number two man, and the man responsible for building the greatest choir east of Salt Lake. If you missed one minute of his mandatory eight hours of practice per week, you didn't sing on Sunday. This was the guy I mentioned that Fred was going to replace as soon as he found a man with real musical talent. Carl told me that when he had confronted Fred about that, Fred had laughed hysterically. He made a point on this call to inform me that he was taking the choir out to sing professionally again. My disappointment had subsided over the last month. I was likewise very pleasant. I knew that for all his years of loyal service, his days were numbered. Bless his heart; he was a really godly man. The last I heard, he was doing carpenter work somewhere up in New Jersey. At the time of this call, he was still living in denial. After exchanging pleasantries, he said, "I have a couple problems I need your help with".

"When you set up the academy, you got us an unemployment exemption," he said. "How did you do that?" he asked. I told him, but had little hope that he could pull it off. Christian schools were being shut down almost as fast as we had been opening them three years before. I knew ours was the only school in the state that had successfully secured an exemption. I had set us up exactly as a Catholic school. Our teachers were not paid, and they lived on campus just like nuns. If they denied me an exemption, they would have to deny Catholic schools one as well. I don't think they ever got it renewed. I don't think they opened the school at all after Ed and I left. "Oh, by the way" he added, "do you know where the logs for the plane got to?"

Aircraft logs are not pilot logs. Everything ever done to that plane from the manufacture to regular maintenance was recorded in those logs, right down to the smallest screw. "Sorry about that Carl", I said, "but I left a couple of things in Fred's office that I really want. My world was upside down, and I didn't want more of a hassle before I left. I figured you would eventually get a hold of me and we could trade belongings." All I wanted was my saddle and my gun. He was relieved. For all he knew, I had pitched them. That would mean they owned a twelve thousand dollar piece of scrap mettle. They must have had a buyer that had discovered the logs were missing.

I can't for the life of me remember how or where we traded belongings, but we did. Compared to the nasty things that took place when the original group left, Carl was almost apologetic that I had to do what I did. I could tell in his voice that he was genuinely impressed when I wanted only what was mine. "I give you my word, Brother, your stuff will be safely returned, and thank you very much," he said. That's the last time I ever heard his voice. We had prayed together over so many things. Many others left over the following months, including Fred's brother. Most of them tracked me down in Butler on their way to wherever they were going. They just wanted to sit with me for a few minutes over a cup of coffee. We had all lost so much. Over a hundred young men in their third year, nearly ready for the ministry, would never graduate. I could have prevented all of this. I'm so sorry guys. I made all the wrong calls.

Busiris-Erie 815-B electric. If you know open pit mining, you know what machine I'm referring to. It was about four times bigger than any dragline I'd ever seen. It didn't even have tracks. It was a walker, kind of like the huge robots in those futuristic sci-fi movies. I was supposed to show up at the mines one week after my telephone interview. I showed up, but the super that hired me was on vacation in Hawaii. The main office didn't know anything about our conversation or my subsequent hiring. They did respect Jim Strange, however. "If he hired you, we will put you to work," they said. I was told to report to the foreman of mine five for the night shift as an oiler on the 815-B. I can't remember the foreman's name, but he was what I had learned to expect as a mine foreman.

When you're running a mine reasonably for about fifty thousand dollars an hour worth of production, you tend to be under considerable stress while keeping it running. This guy was really stressed the night I arrived. It was also the first night a new operator was starting on the big drag. He had already told the foreman that he didn't know if the new operator could handle the thing. I didn't know the guy for five minutes before he told the new operator and I that if we could run it, we could stay; if we couldn't run it, we couldn't stay. The mines are just like the oil fields, and there are only two cant's; can't do it, can't stay. I knew something was awry right off the bat. I had been sent out here from the office to oil something that oiled itself. No wonder the foreman was a little confused when I told him I was his new oiler. He asked me who had hired me and I told him Jim Strange. That name was sort of magical; Jim knew this rig did not require an oiler. He shook his head and handed me a time card.

He was true to his word. When we broke our second cable, he told us one more and we were down the road. That took about an hour. It was a cool night, but the operator was in a heavy sweat when he turned to me and said, "I guess we're done." It didn't take long for the foreman to show up. "Get your shit and get," he said. "Me too?" I asked. "Can you operate this thing?" he answered. Was he kidding? I told him I was hired to oil a thirty-six hundred. "Well, if you can't run it, you'll have to go sign up." I said, "Sign what? Jim hired me. I moved here from Punxsy. I didn't break anything and you're telling me I'm down the road?"

If I was not so close to the Lord in those dark days, I probably would have just left and started looking for another job. I looked that hard man in the eyes and said, "I don't have anywhere to go." I didn't know enough about mining at the time to know that all this guy was thinking about was the fifty thousand dollars an hour his drag was not producing. In real frustration, he turned and headed for his truck. I moved between him and his truck and said, "I was not hired on a trial basis. Where is the 3600?" I didn't know if he was going to hit me, shove me aside, or what. I blocked his advance about three times, and kept my face in his path until he finally stopped. For one brief moment, he saw me, and not just a broken rig. "I don't know what to do with you," he said. "I don't even know why you're here. Go to the office in the morning and ask for Mr. Grisham. Tell him Mr. Strange hired you. That's all I can tell you."

That was all I needed. That statement told me I was not fired for breaking cables or anything else. He just didn't know what to do with me. There was nothing on his mine to oil. As I drove down the deep valley leading to the office, the shop, and the cleaning plant, I had an awesome impression. It was as clear as if God was sitting in the seat next to me. I said "Father, I feel like Joseph. I've been thrown in a pit and left for dead. You took him out of that pit and made him second in the kingdom. You can do that for me." I can remember that as clearly as I can remember asking God to save me. I walked into that office and asked for Mr. Grisham. When seated at his desk, I told him my story. I told him I didn't come to work for him for one night. I was committed from the moment Mr. Strange had said I was hired. "Where is your commitment?" I asked him. He said, "Jim is in Hawaii, but if he hired you, you're hired. Do you know anything about a cleaning plant?" All I knew was the coal went through it for processing and then it was sent over to the power plant. "The chemist and the engineers run the process," he said. "What I'm looking for is someone to coordinate between the plant and the mines. I'll give you an office in the shop and we'll put this idea in motion if you're interested."

I reported to the shop foreman and told him I was going to be trained as some kind of coordinator. He didn't know anything about it, but what he saw was an extra hand. His son worked in the shop office. He kept up with the radio and spare parts. Now he had me. I don't think his boy had ever finished school. He was nice enough, but made a real mess of everything he did. It didn't take me long to figure out that this office was the heartbeat of the five mines. We were in charge of all equipment, maintenance, parts, and transportation. If we didn't have what was needed, we were to find it wherever we had to. All the parts were in piles on the floor. The first thing I did was build an inventory file. They had never had one. Until then, the mine foreman and the mechanics would just rummage through the piles hoping to find what they needed.

It took me about three days to build the inventory file. For the first time, when someone radioed in from the mine asking if we had something, they actually got an answer. They heard me say, 'Yes, we have it', or 'I'll find it and call you'. Every chance the shop foreman got, he would pull me into the shop to clean parts or help a mechanic with something. I would stay late and work on the inventory. I ordered shelves and built a real parts room. One day a short stocky fellow walked into the office. I had vendors coming in several times a day. I figured he was selling something. In a few short weeks, I had developed a full blown mining demeanor. I was short in conversation, and wasted no time when I was in the office. I was doing things to increase the effectiveness of this office that no one had ever thought of. The field mechanics loved me, and the foremen respected me for the organization I had brought to their lives.

"I'm busy man, what do you want?" I asked. "Who the hell are you?" he responded. I didn't get a chance to tell him. He saw the shop foreman through the office window and yelled, "Get your ass in here." The shop foreman was the oldest of all the foremen and just as hard. When I saw him put his tail between his legs and actually run for the office door, I knew this short fellow was no salesman. He didn't speak to me at all that I can remember. He chewed the foreman out for several things and yelled some additional commands and walked out. The foreman looked at me humbly and told me I had just met Jim Strange.

By my third week, I had the foreman's son running parts most of the day. He gladly did so, because he was out of his league, and he knew it. In only two weeks, the vendors were calling and asking to speak with me. For the first time in the history of these mines, I was asking them for prices, not just placing orders. They all knew a new wind was blowing. All the kid and his dad had ever cared about was getting something as fast as possible....no matter what it cost. For the first time, the foreman heard things like, "I can get you one from Cat, but I can get the same thing from the local machine shop for half the price and just as fast." Jim heard these conversations as well. By the next week, I had a gate put up and had locked the foreman out of the parts room. I knew I was pushing it, but I took a stand. "Give me a part number and I'll check in the office to see if we have it," I would tell them. "You're not rummaging through my shelves." They looked at me as if I'd moved into their house and took over their kitchen.

I might have spoken to Jim over the radio once or twice, but it took an event that was about to happen to get his personal attention. One night I was about to leave when he radioed in and informed me the 815 was down. He had called directly to the manufacturer in Chicago and they were flying a part into the local airport. "This thing is costing me thousands of dollars an hour, and I just found out they're sending the wrong damn part," he yelled. "Someone has got to meet that plane before it drops off the part and leaves. Tell them to go back and get the right part. They'll be here in about an hour. Tell them the right part is being delivered to their hangar, and they need to go back and get it!" "Can you give me the telephone number at the factory," I asked. "I'll see if they can turn him around and save a lot of time, sir". He said he had already tried that, and they couldn't.

Now remember, I'd been flying regularly up until about a month and a half before this. Jim didn't know anything about that. All he knew was that I was supposed to be oiling a 3600 and somebody had stuck me in the office. I don't even know if he remembered that much. I said, "I'll take care of it sir." I called flight service in Dubois and got a hold of my old controller friend. He gave me the land line for central that would be covering all flights from Chicago. I told the central controller of our emergency and asked if he could help me out. He found the plane that had filed from the factory through to our county airstrip and gave me the tail number. He told me he was patching me through to regional; they had just entered their air space. Regional said they had him, and asked what my message was.

I radioed the foreman of mine five; remember, he was the guy that had fired me. I told him that flight service had found the plane, patched me through to regional control, and we had turned him around. I had a new ETA of 8:40 into Grove City County, right there on I-80. That was closer to him than anyone else, and I asked if he could have someone pick it up at the HBO? I had called over there and they said someone would be there all night. There was dead silence. The next thing I heard over the speaker was, "Five, did you copy the shop?" It was Jim asking the foreman if he had got my message. The foreman spoke, "The shop said the part will be at Grove City; how the hell they know that? It's still the wrong part isn't it?" Jim spoke next, "Shop, did you say 8:40?" I said, "Roger 8:40". "We'll take it from here," he said. That was all that was ever said about it.

That took place in a space of about 15 minutes. I don't blame the foreman for being confused. Those fifteen minutes, however, changed my life at the shop. Not long after that, Jim walked into the office and I wasn't there. The shop foreman had me working in the shop, elbow deep in grease. Jim walked into the shop. Again, he never spoke to me. He spoke to the foreman. "What the hell is Jones doing out of his office?" he demanded. "He doesn't work for you. This better never happen again." I didn't know who I worked for. One night after dark, I was gassing up the company pickup that I had used to go somewhere that afternoon. Mr. Grisham pulled up to the gas pump and got out. "You're putting in a lot of hours," he said. "If I had one of these trucks, I would have parked it by my house when I passed by it thirty minutes ago," I said. "I'd be home right now." "I'm not buying another truck," he said. That was the only time we had spoke since he had told me to report to the shop office.

I wondered who I worked for. Mr. Grisham didn't talk to me, Strange didn't talk to me, and now the shop foreman didn't talk to me, either. I spent thousands of dollars a day, buying whatever it took to keep five mines in operation. Except for the men requesting I find what they needed, and the vendors I purchased the stuff from, no one talked to me. Someone was paying the bills I signed everyday. I got an idea. I'd make up a boss. I'd keep a daily log, and at the end of each week, I'd compile it into an activity report. The next time I ran into this guy telling me I worked too many hours, I'd give it to him.

The Bible says that whatever you do, do it heartily, as unto the Lord. I worked for God. I had for the last many years in the ministry. What had changed? It dawned on me that night that I'd been there for nearly a year. I had come to this office not knowing what I was doing, and suddenly I was the sole purchasing agent for the entire operation. When I had first come to work here, Loren Green, of Bonanza fame, had owned it. I never talked to him. Then Amcord bought it, whoever that was. Now Gifford Hill, of Dallas, Texas had just bought us. Someone was signing my bills, but I had never met him. I did what I said I was going to. I made that log. In it, I highlighted the savings my comparative shopping was generating. No one had ever done that. There hadn't even been a purchasing agent before me. The shop had just ordered everything from Caterpillar. I had just bought an under-carriage for a set of D-9 twins the week before. I got it complete, delivered and assembled, for over twenty grand less than Cat had quoted me.

When the Cat mechanics that often came out for warranty work saw someone else doing a rebuild on one of our mine sights, I got a visit. Caterpillar sent their top man in the territory to visit me. He had been the undisputed supplier for all our mines for years, yet he had never been here. He didn't even know where to go. Mr. Grisham called me from the main office and told me he wanted to meet me. I lied. I said, "Unless you want me working late tonight, I can't fit him in today. Tell him to give me a call next week." "This man does a lot for us," Grisham said. "Sir, we give them thousands of dollars a week," I said. "He'd better be doing a lot." I had yanked two chains with one pull. I was having way too much fun.

"God, you led me here and blessed everything I've touched, except the church. It hasn't grown beyond the families that built it. You gave me a house with no rent, and the only job that's paying everyone's bills. I don't know what you're doing in these other men's lives, but I don't think you called me here to run a mining operation or a rest home. What do you want me to do?" I asked. The scriptures I got as an answer were, "I want you to start over; back to the rock from which you were hewn." To me that meant Japan. If it hadn't been for an old missionary in Japan, I wouldn't be asking these questions of God. I'd be managing my own insurance staff by now. I'd probably be divorced or dead, but I wouldn't be where I was. My wife wouldn't be a Christian, and I wouldn't have wonderful kids in a Christian school. I would know very little of reality. Me, a missionary? That's what I had lived for these last years, but had never envisioned me as one of them. That's a higher calling.

"I'm a first rate Christian education administrator, thanks to you, Lord, but a missionary calling is for better men than me. I wheel and deal for these guys. If I called any of the many pastors I'd worked with over the last four years and told them I was going to the mission field, they'd think I was joking," I told God. 'You're joking right?' That's what Nick thought when I told him. He showed up at my house the next day and told me he saw red flags everywhere. I told him I was going to present it to the church Sunday and we'd let God take it from there. Sunday morning I got up, got dressed, and threw up all over the place. I told my wife I'd better stay home, but she and the kids should go; I'd be alright. One of the greatest things that provides me assurance is the fact that God gives me scriptures that address what is going to happen, even before it happens. Sometimes I'm too stupid to realize it, but He really does.

Once it was about a real bad mistake I was going to make. I made it, and then the scriptures came back to me like a rock on my head. I said 'God knew I was going to do that, and He had prepared me in advance for the pain I'm going through now'. Why didn't I see it? At least it is comforting to realize that He had forgiven me in advance. Then He used it to begin the healing process. That's what happened this particular Sunday morning. I sat down for my personal time and God gave me the scriptures where David said he was the musing of the drunkards. People that knew nothing of his heart were talking about him in jest. My wife came home from church and asked me how I was feeling. I said I felt like I was the subject of the message she just heard. She smiled and said, "I'm so glad you weren't there." My heart was broken, but it was also on fire. I cried like a baby at the thought of parting with these three Brothers. I believed they were the closest Brothers I'd ever have.

One of our truck drivers came into my office and asked if I knew anyone looking to rent a place. It was small, but much closer to my work. I told him I'd take it. My wife packed everything, but then does what she always does. She had a yard sale. The porch was packed with stuff. How does that happen? First you're trying to put together enough stuff to get by. Then you're trying to get rid of enough of it so that what's left will fit into your moving van. She had to run somewhere, so she asked me to mind the sale until she got back. She had forgotten already that I was the guy that had left all her stuff in the basement when we had packed up to move here. A couple people came and left. Then a van pulled up with a bunch of kids in the back. The guy wanted necessities. I could tell by the questions he asked and the stuff he was picking out. He put together about five dollars worth of stuff and asked me how much. I said, "If you have a ten dollar bill in your billfold, and promise to load every bit of this stuff in your truck, we have a deal." My wife came home right after he had left. The porch was empty. I handed her a ten dollar bill and said we can move now. She reminded me of our last move and said some other stuff I can't remember.....but we moved.

I never saw Nick again. The last thing we did together was go to Ed's house and tell him he was no longer the pastor. Nick had picked me up one morning and told me Ed's wife was openly disrespectful and Ed wouldn't do anything about it. He wanted me to go with him and tell him he couldn't serve with this church. I jumped in his truck, but by the time we got there, I had decided not to do my part. I told Nick to do what he felt led to do, but I wasn't going with him. Ed and I had been working together for years. His wife had been on my teaching staff for years. Ed and I had come to an agreement years ago. There are some things you can change to serve the Lord, and there are some things with which God lets you serve without changing. She had been raised in the home of a surgeon. From the time she had hooked up with a man called for a life in the ministry, her world had changed.

I went through the same thing with my wife. She had grown up fairly well off too. Then she married me. At first we ended up fairly well off. Then God led us to the ministry, and everything changed. God put that need for security in a woman, along with the child raising factor, and it's not easily dealt with. We came to the point that I had to choose between my ministry and my wife. I truly believe if I had chosen my wife, I would have lost both of them. Ed managed to balance the both of them, and didn't do too badly at either. He may never have broken her strong will, but had still molded her into an asset to both family and the ministry. I'm so glad God would not let me face him that day. I had no idea the asset he would become in my brand new calling.

What I needed next was a sending church; a people to authorize our ministry as a missionary. The same thing Nick and John had needed when we had left Concordville. When you decide to run your ministry the New Testament way, you face serious obstacles in today's religious world. Even independent church people have begun to believe that a missionary must be approved by some mission board. The only boards in the New Testament were the ones Paul had floated on to Crete, when his boat to Rome had broken up in a storm.

William Carey formed the first mission board. Even he admitted it was an extra-biblical organization. He blamed the New Testament churches of his day for making it a necessity. I think maybe he was right. I knew I could join one of those things. I could say the same thing William Carey had said. But I had spent too many years proving that God didn't need anything beyond the institution of the church, or he would have started one. I called Brother Louis. He was solid New Testament Church mission's philosophy. He offered to sponsor our mission during our first conversation, so I knew I could begin preparing for deputation. We started looking for a pickup, sufficient to pull something large enough to accommodate the six of us for up to two years on the road. On my way home from work, I saw a pickup sitting in a yard with a for sale sign on it. It didn't look well enough equipped, but I stopped anyway. The owner said it was just way more than he needed and just the day before, he had decided to downgrade. It turned out to be a lot more than met the eye. It was a full one ton with an overload and towing package, and low mileage. We made a deal and I picked it up the next day. Next, we needed a trailer.

My kids were attending a Christian school in the little town down the road from us. I asked my wife to look into setting up a home schooling program with them. The administrator was a little out of his league compared to what she knew about Christian education. He wasn't ready for the questions I had told her to ask him. He put her in contact with a larger school. They said they would certify her to teach the type of curriculum they could provide for us. She started training while I continued working on my list. One day I was picking up some parts at the Clarion Caterpillar distributorship, and I noticed a small RV Sales lot located near the exit to I-80. I stopped and told the owner what I needed. God must have prepared that guy. I didn't have any idea what I needed. I would have bought way too small to begin with. I also would have bought the wrong thing.

I told him that over the next couple of years, I planned to park in church parking lots with other missionaries that did just that. He told me what I needed wasn't there. He'd bring one in next week and call me if I wanted him to help me. I'm so glad I trusted that guy. He brought in a 31 foot fifth-wheel in the price range I had given him. It was the only trailer we looked at. It had room enough for all of us to sleep in comfort. It was a lot bigger than I would have bought, but he convinced me that our rig would handle it just fine. He assured me that I could handle a fifth-wheel mount twice as easy as something I'd pull on a hitch. We put in the paperwork, and I went home wondering if we would qualify for anything that good. You feel bad about your lack of faith when you're shocked because things work out so perfectly. We picked it up the next day and parked it in our yard.

The only thing I was not at peace with was working with a pastor I had never worked with before. I knew a lot of pastors, but I had personally counseled with most of them about one problem or another. There was one man I had worked with for many years, however. Ed had called me shortly after he left Butler. He asked me if I could introduce him to the right pastor to help him find a church that was looking for a pastor. I told him I would call a pastor in Calvert City, Kentucky and get back to him. I think Ed was staying in his brother's house in Arkansas. His brother, as I mentioned before, was a missionary for the Southern Baptist Convention. I called him back and gave him the pastor's number and told him he was interested in helping him find a church.

This Kentucky group of independent preachers was a funny bunch. Every couple years, about a third of the churches changed pastors. I never had to meet a new pastor because they were always the same guys, just shuffled around. They called it shaking up the fruit basket. They were all of different styles and talents, but all really nice guys. It was a click. When you got in with one of them, you were in with about thirty of them. I had forgotten that I had introduced Ed to the leader of this bunch on our way home from Texas. That was where we had landed just after we had circled the West Paducah County airstrip with the little church just off the runway. Sure enough, this brother set Ed up to candidate at that same little church, and they called him as their pastor. I believe in coincidences, but this was too much.

Ed called to tell me that the church had called him. I told him about my lack of peace and told him that I believed God wanted me to work with him. He said he would really like some time to pray about it. "Call me in a week and we'll talk," he said. When I hung up, I told Cheryl we were going to join West Paducah Baptist Church. Ed just didn't know it yet. A heavy burden left me. I knew there was no question about it. We just had to work out the details and get there. I found a little shop on my way home from work that sold kerosene heaters. I miss those days when you could find some guy selling a product out of his garage. That's the way overseas companies found inroads to US markets before Walmart. This guy was hit in the head with the new innovation of a circular wick and round glass mantle that dispersed the heat. He said it would out last me. It's since been around the world with me, and it's sitting in my wood shop. I don't know why I bought it. The trailer had a great heater, but it would really come in handy in the years to come.

The next time Ed and I spoke, it did not go well. I was upset that he was trying to discourage me from choosing his work as our sponsor. This went on for the next several conversations. He said everything negative about our joining with him, just short of saying no. That's how it remained, but I had no doubt that God wanted us there. We were ready to go. Ron Miller had me set up to park at his father-in-law's place in Cincinnati, and had arranged a church for us to give our first presentation to.

Things had really gone well at the mines. I had run a tight ship. The super had instructed the foreman to make every purchase, and to clear all contract work through either him or myself. That didn't mean anything to my wallet, but it literally made me the assistant super. The big wigs from the main office never bothered me anymore about my overtime. One day, the foreman of mine five, the guy that had fired me, and the shop foreman that used to make me clean parts, were both waiting in my office. "We need to talk to you about something," they said. "We made a real mistake last night." They were standing in my office when I got there in the morning before daylight. One worked nights, and the other one worked days. Neither one of them was ever there at that time of the morning. In my mind, these guys were both higher on the totem pole than I was.

I wasn't a foreman, and I sure didn't make foreman wages. I was just overjoyed that they had become quite congenial with me. They even minded their language when speaking with me in person or on the radio. It seems they had had a little emergency the night before. The mine foreman had called the shop. I had left early to meet with the owner of a machine shop to work out a deal on hydraulic hoses. The shop foreman only ever came in my office anymore to do his reports. Number five called in a request for a Cat tech, and wanted to know if they could call him in right then. The shop foreman had looked down at my desk where he was sitting and saw a work order for a tech for number five. He just took for granted that I had made the request to Cat and was waiting for the foreman to call. He keyed the mike and said 'Yeah'.

The work order on my desk had nothing to do with the machine that the foreman of mine five was talking about. The foreman also thought it was me that had said 'yeah'. When the tech finished up, about an hour before this conversation was taking place, he handed the foreman an authorization form for his signature. The foreman told the tech that I had called it in, and it was taken care of. The tech called in and they told him I had not authorized the call. The foreman wouldn't sign it. Jim told them that had better never happen. The whole thing just escalated out of proportion from there. Neither one of them knew what had really happened. The tech knew Jim better than he knew the foreman. When he stopped at the diner for a coffee on his way back to his shop, guess who was there eating breakfast? Jim called Gene, the foreman of five. They figured if I didn't authorize it, then someone in the shop had told him to make the call. So the shop foreman got a call. Now they were afraid that the super thought that they had just decided to do things the old way.

Open pit miners are the hardest men I've ever worked around. It takes a really hard man to be their foreman. You can only imagine what kind of man is hired to handle the foreman. You could go to a mining operation clear across the state, and they would know, or would have heard of Jim Strange. Foreman move around, as do techs and miners. If you went to high school back when I was a kid, you could equate it to telling stories about your principle or head master. It's almost supernatural. Those guys had the ability to put a greater fear into a guy than God. It's like a ship captain, or like that admiral that was over the captains. Even a good foreman had so much responsibility, that no one would hire him without first talking to his past super. Neither one of these guys were clear on exactly what they did. They just knew their lives were about to be changed and they were really desperate. If Jim fired them, they'd never work another mine anywhere.

They really didn't care much for me. Things had run smoother before I had come along. On the other hand, in their eyes, I had earned a respect that superseded friendship. Now they hoped against hope that this respect might pay off in any way possible. It only took a few minutes for me to understand what had transpired that evening. I explained it to them, actually. Then, they at least had some explanation. I was the only one that had nothing to lose if I got involved and things didn't go well. I already had my next job.

The inventory door shut with a slam that rattled my office windows. The fear in those men's eyes almost made me want to run. I raised my voice so Jim could hear me as he stomped towards my door. "Sit down and I'll explain exactly what happened," I said. I kept my back to the door as Jim entered. I pointed to Gene and said, "You called in here and thought you were talking to me…. that's an honest mistake." Then I turned to the old shop foreman and said, "You were doing your daily report at my desk when he called. You looked down, saw a work order for number five, and made a reasonable deduction that that was the order I had called in for the tech." I turned around and said, "Jim, we were confused, but we got it figured out and I'll take care of it with Cat. If you have a minute, Sir, I need to talk to you about something really important."

Jim's face was as red as a beat. His adrenalin was off the scale. He was about to put down a mutiny, and I had just downgraded it to a trivial event. He looked at me like a calf looks at a new gate. His silence was deafening. "What?" he finally asked. "I would really like to share something with you personally, Sir," I told him. There was another eight year silence. Then he looked sternly at the foreman and said, "Are you guys straightened out?" Whatever these guys were to say at that point would be straight from the heart, because their hearts were in their mouths. "Yes Sir," they both responded. Jim just nodded his head toward the door and the foremen were gone, one out my office door and the other out into the shop. Jim looked at me with an inquisition that radiated from his eyes. He never broke eye contact as he slowly rotated his body and sat down. "What?" he asked, this time with a more relaxed tone. I had his full attention.

Ever since I was a child, I had always wanted to talk like the man on the six o'clock news. I found that what you said was superseded by how you said it. For the ten years before that, I'd either been in college, teaching college, or working with colleges. I used words that were not commonly used. I was always careful only to use them in situations where they were self defining. Over the last year, I'd been coordinating these mines mostly by radio communication. One day I was sitting at my desk listening to Jim communicating with his foreman. He said, "I would not say that dogmatically." I smiled. Good English is contagious. This man, as far as I could tell, had never been to college, but he was picking up the words that I used when they fit.

I have long since lost that ability, because I have not been exposed to those that use really good English. I don't mean my friends and associates speak poorly. They're just as I am now; not in a place of constant exposure to it. There is no other way I could have gained this man's respect. I knew nothing about real mining when I got there. This man recognized, many months before, that he had an educated man working for him. He also noted that I showed him great respect. He may have been one of the hardest men I ever met, but my respect meant something to him. He was old school. The college thing was never an option to these guys. They became leaders in their fields through genuine accomplishments. In other words, they came up through the ranks. They earned their respect.

I invented a phrase concerning these old guys. 'Lost in the paper shuffle' is what I called it. I experienced it in every field of endeavor from the seventies to this very day. These old guys had been passed over. Many of them had been replaced by kids fresh out of college with a piece of paper in their hands. That paper said they were geologists, or chemists, or whatever. Their only practical experience was sitting in class for the past four years or so. They couldn't handle real men, whose job it was to handle other real men. What happens after that is they replace these real men with men they can handle. This dominoes on down the ranks until most of the best are gone. Then they have to call in a consultant to tell them how to do what these old guys could have done with their eyes closed.

I worked for one such consultant firm when I left my job as safety manager. These are some of the few companies that still hire according to one's work experience, rather than one's college experience. You still had no paper, but you worked under a company name that did. Jim Strange could tell you where to dig and how much cover you could afford to remove, and still turn a profit. He knew from experience how much you would spend on labor and maintenance, and his expertise was available twenty-four-seven. Many mines lost hundreds of thousands of dollars before the college boys got to their offices the next morning, six or eight hours too late. We'll see this in more detail later, when I get involved in cryogenics.

I now had Jim's full attention. He knew whatever I was going to tell him was more important to me than someone ordering an outside contractor without my approval. "I'm giving you my two weeks notice, Sir," I said. "I believe God has called me to the mission field." We spoke for a few minutes, just long enough for him to determine that my decision was not job-related, and there was no recourse that could be made on his part. He asked for one favor. He requested an outline of my responsibilities, my contacts, and any business I had in the works. That was several hundreds of thousands of dollars of dealings that no one else was involved in at this stage. By today's standards, he may have been uneducated, but he requested information on the only thing I was concerned about walking away from.

The two weeks flew by. Some were sorry I was leaving; others were happy. My last day was a shock. About three o'clock, people started coming into my building and just standing around talking with each other. Even some of my vendors showed up. Then a catering outfit came in and started setting up. The main mining office personnel came in. We never saw these people. They just kept the coal moving from us to the power plants. I hadn't quite figured it out. Then I looked down at my microphone and realized that everyone on the other end of it was now sitting at the caterer's tables in my building.

That was the first time in my entire year there that I had ever seen them all in the same place at the same time. Even the night bosses were there. The truck drivers even came in. I was really impressed. These guys wouldn't even show up at the hospital if I was dying. By then, I thought I'd figured it out. A tall, well dressed man walked in with Mr. Grisham, and everyone stood up. I was still sitting in my office watching all this through the glass. The big guy never sat down; he walked straight into my office and introduced himself as the VP of Gifford Hill, from Dallas, Texas. He represented the third outfit that had owned us since I'd been there and I hadn't met any of them until right then. No one else came in my office. I can't remember the small talk, but then he came to the point. He said, "I came up here to offer you a corporate position in our mining division in Dallas. I've been told that this is not an option for you, but corporate wanted the option delivered in person, and that's why I'm here."

My mind flew back to the day when the manager of Swift Meat Company had thrown the tickets, hotel reservations, and his company car keys on my desk. He had said, "You just can't pass this up and walk out." I passed, not knowing anything except that God was leading me in another direction. What did I get out of that decision? Well it may not have ended just like I would have liked it to, but I had received my BA in Divinity and my MA in Christian Ed Administration. I had earned an associate professorship and served as a field representative and chief pilot for a once great college. Just think, instead of all that, and for a few dollars more, I could be managing a meat locker somewhere. Now my option was an office in Texas, doing God knows what. I don't know if I could be certain God was leading me, if there weren't some fine options to the contrary.

The VP seemed to be a fine Christian man. He shook my hand and said 'Let's eat'. I was cleaning out my office after everyone had gone home or back to work when Jim walked in. It is difficult having a conversation with someone that knows you only for what you do. The only thing I can remember is him telling me that his wife had set this all up, and he wanted me to meet her. He was the last man to shake my hand. It was really just another day in his career, but for me, it was the beginning of my life's greatest challenge.

Romans 8:29
For whom He did foreknow, He also did predestinate to be conformed to the image of His Son.

Chapter 12
The Campaign Begins

We were loaded and ready to hit the road. We decided the twin beds above the fifth-wheel would be given to the girls. In the back of the trailer was a dining table, surrounded with a circular bench like you would find in a restaurant. All six of us could fit just fine for family meals. That converted nicely to a king sized bed for my wife and I. We were stocked to the hilt with everything we could possibly need. I don't know how that truck ever pulled it out of the driveway. God had provided us with exactly what we needed. This thing was the heaviest trailer ever built, eight-thousand pounds empty. It was manufactured in Elgin, Illinois and was ready for any weather conditions we might encounter in North America. It wasn't new, but it looked as good as just about anything out there. Our plan was to spend a couple days with my parents and then head west. As we pulled out of our driveway, my headlights revealed a freshly hit deer on the side of the road. That was not a rare find in Pennsylvania. No less than a couple hundred thousand a year end up like that. I had grown up on venison. Our first year out of college, it was probably the only meat we ate. I even took it to work in my lunch bucket. I didn't think much about loading that deer up and heading for Punxsy.

This was the first time I had ever pulled one of these things. I had driven eighty-thousand pound tractor trailers, so there was no apprehension on my part whatsoever. It was cold and there was some fresh snow coming down. When we got to Punxsy, I realized how hard it would be to park this thing at my parent's house. They lived on a hill, and the spot I was planning to park it would be snowed in. I knew the town had just built a new metro complex with a large parking lot. I pulled into it and walked over to the police station. I told them of my dilemma and asked if I could drop the trailer for the night. An officer told me it was no problem, and walked out the door with me as I headed for the trailer.

I had forgotten about the deer. This was back before it was legal to pick up a road kill. My wife saw us coming and walked to meet us. "Hi dear, deer, deer," she said. I had parked in about the only spot that was not well lit. How I disconnected that trailer without the officer seeing that deer remains a mystery to us. To make things worse, as I was skinning it out I found that someone had dispatched it with a shot to the neck. If the officer would have identified the dark form I was working around as I disconnected the trailer to be a deer, all the time, money, and preparation would have been in vain. The state would have confiscated the entire rig on the spot. My boys today are the age I was then. I tell them frequently how easy it is to put your ministry at risk. If it wasn't for God getting us through some really dumb moments, I don't think we'd had a chance.

There wasn't any doubt in my mind at that time that we were going to Japan. It was many years later that I overheard a conversation and learned that I was about the only one that really believed it. My mother was talking to a friend that told her I would not go 'somewhere' like I'd said I was going. She answered with, "He said he was going to Japan, didn't he?" Almost no one thought you could go to the mission field unless some big organization was sponsoring you. It would be a few months before I would share those same doubts. I called Ed and told him we were speaking at a church in Ohio, and then we would head straight for West Paducah. Ed tried one last time to raise doubts, but he still did not close the door. I was sure God was in our choice as West Paducah being our sending church. I just wished Ed was a little more convinced.

We said our good-byes and took off for Cincinnati. Ron Miller met us and led us to his father-in-law's place. The next Sunday, he took us to the church to which he had arranged for us to make our first field presentation to. It was a bigger church than I had expected, with at least a couple hundred in attendance. I was used to large churches; the only thing I was not used to was being the main speaker. Ron had heard me speak to Sunday school classes, and was very nervous. God blessed wonderfully, though, and he was more thrilled than I was. "You didn't let me down, Brother," he told me. Now don't get me wrong. I was not an accomplished preacher, but as missionaries went, my presentation was just fine. We never heard from that church again. We knew going in that they had only consented to let us speak so that they could help us along in our travels. They were a Baptist Bible Fellowship Church, and wouldn't consider supporting an independent like me.

A couple days later, we called Ed and gave him our approximate time of arrival. That was the first time he spoke positively about our coming to West Paducah. The only time I'd ever been near the place was the night Ed and I had circled it on our way back from Texas in my plane. I don't even think I remembered that night at that point. I'm not sure I ever even mentioned it to Ed. All I knew was that we were going where we were supposed to go. Whatever happened once we got there was in God's hands. I had perfect peace about it. I only wished Ed was half as excited about it as I was.

The place was way out of town on a two lane road, just past the county airstrip. We turned into the parking lot and met one of Ed's sons, who directed us around back. As we pulled in through the yard behind the church, we saw a whole crowd standing there. They were holding a large banner that read 'Welcome Joneses'. Ed was standing in front of them, smiling ear to ear, with arms open in a welcoming jester. We met everyone, and each of them assured us that they had been praying for this moment from the day Ed and I had first spoke about it. Ed was clearly overjoyed. He had been overjoyed since our first discussion about the possibility of us working together again. He had just wanted to make sure it was of God. He had never offered an ounce of encouragement, but had led his people to pray for the success of this union from day one. We felt as though we had known these people for years. They knew each of our children by name, their ages, and even some family stories that only close friends would know. We had definitely made the right choice. We were home.

We decided to use the next couple of weeks to get to know the people and use the church office to schedule speaking engagements. It was rather simple booking the local churches, since I knew all of the pastors. Most of them gave me Sunday or Wednesday evening service. Most of these churches ran about a hundred or so in attendance. The problem we learned about right away was that all of them were supporting missionaries from each others churches. I was an outsider that had just happened to have an 'in' with their pastors. None of them had much of a surplus in their mission's budgets. They didn't take up a separate offering for me when I spoke. They would write us a check out of the mission's account. These checks varied, but seldom added up to enough to meet our bills at the end of the month. Our church was most generous, as were several individual members. But as the weeks went by, it became clear that we were not making any headway financially. After a couple of months, we had depleted all the Western Kentucky churches and we would have to start traveling a lot farther out. We couldn't afford to pull the trailer from church to church. It took just about everything we could get just to run the pickup. This went on for about as long as I could stand it. We were no closer to making it to the field than when we had first pulled out of our driveway on that snowy night months before.

The weather was getting good by then. If I was back East, I could pick up some money doing odd jobs on weekdays and preaching on the weekends. I knew a lot of New Testament churches back there as well. I kept telling myself that many of the churches would eventually vote to support us; they just needed some time. The men and I prayed about it and decided we should give it a try for a few months. We had just enough money to get back to Punxsy at that point, so it was then or not at all. We arrived in town and drove directly to my uncle's farm. We parked in the grass alongside the large circle drive, just between the house and the outhouse. That would be home for the rest of the summer. If my plans worked out, we'd head south for the winter. I had a very close friend pastoring down there. He was one of the original mob, as I call them, that had left the college in Concordville first. He was the only one of the bunch I had tried to follow. He was building a church in Northern Florida. He had heard that we had also left the church, and he had allowed his daughter to communicate with mine. It was through our daughters that we kept up with each other's activities.

I walked down to the neighbor's farm and found old Walter shoeing a horse. Walter had been the president of the Saddle Club back when I had been the Vice President. He was getting up there in age, but was still a strong looking figure for his age. "How are you doing, Jonesey?" he asked through the sweat dripping off his nose. This was a guy that drank at least a gallon of whiskey every day, and had since the day I had met him. He told me he had to lay off it a little these days. He said he needed more time sweating the poison out of him to keep feeling good. Three hot meals a day is all I can figure that kept him going. My dad drank whiskey like that, but wouldn't eat a decent meal. It was really starting to slow him down. Dad would pour a glass of beer and break an egg into it for breakfast. The rest of day, he'd eat like a bird.

"Let me finish this for you, Walt," I said. "After all, you taught me how to do this in the first place." When I finished, he reached up over his head and pulled down a six pack of Budweiser and handed me one. "What's on your mind?" he asked. Well, what was on my mind at that point was what I was going to do with the eighty-five degree beer he had handed me. That was a real show of friendship, coming from Walt. I'd only ever seen him do that once since I was a kid. Many guys had worked for him all day in the July heat and he had given them each just one beer. I had filed and finished just one hoof. I figured that must have been a special home coming celebration.

Walter was a casualty of prohibition. His life taught me something about the temperance movement that you would never learn in Bible College. When I was a young boy, Walt's dad had lived about a mile up the road. Frank was an old man back then. He drove an old forties model Hudson. At that time, it was only about ten or twelve years old, and as clean as the day he had bought it. We were talking about the car one time, and the fact that the old man still drove it once in awhile, and that prompted old Walt to tell me a little story about his own childhood. What I learned was that old Frank had taken the family to church regularly until the temperance movement had reached their small town.

I knew what prohibition was, because I had watched the then-popular TV show about Elliot Ness fighting Al Capone. Robert Stack was the star, if I remember right. I didn't, however, know much about the pre-prohibition temperance thing. Before this thing had come about, it was common for the man of the house to go to church every Sunday morning and never miss a church picnic. They would take the family to the little country park down by the river and have a whole day of fun. The men played horse shoes and moderately enjoyed their homemade beverages. No one ever got drunk. No respectable gentleman ever did so intentionally, in public or in private. But with the temperance movement, everything changed.

That conversation didn't mean much to me at the time. Years later, when I had just started driving, I was taking my father somewhere. As we drove past a church, Dad said, "There's the good people in town." I knew my Dad believed in and respected God. When the preacher would make his regular visit, Dad would sit with him and Mom in the parlor that was never used for anything else. I later asked him if he went to church as a kid. He told me that men went for weddings and baptisms, but regular attendance wasn't common for the average man. Only women and children went for services. It was a strange thing, though, that about the only men that went were the town drunks when they were on the wagon.

Dad told me about the prohibition clubs that had started opening up around town. If you were a solid citizen, you could join one. They were the only places you could have a drink on Sundays. Most guys dropped the family off at church and met at the club. Even though most of them just drank coffee until after church, they still met at the club. If you only had a drink on occasion, you still didn't go to church. If you did, some of the women would start whispering, and you didn't want to embarrass your wife. A lot of guys still went to the Baptist Church for awhile, but he said they used to call them the town hypocrites. It wasn't long before those men quit going as well. By the time I came along, the Baptist Church I attended with the neighbor kid was mostly women and kids.

After I became a teenager, I was welcome to ride horses with the adults. On one of those rides, we rode past a run down farm, not far from Walt's place. He said, "That's where I had my first drink boys. I was just a teenager, but during prohibition, I'd walk over here on a weekend and he'd sell me a Mason jar of homemade shine. Since it was illegal anyway, they'd sell it to you if they knew you lived close by." The revenuers never bothered the little guy that only sold to locals. Many years later, I met a pharmacy student who opened my eyes to the whole prohibition debacle. They taught him that it is common knowledge today that prohibition had been engineered for one purpose. All the news was about the booze; what was suppressed was what happened to the drugs. They always intended to relax the liquor laws as soon as the government had total control of the drug manufacturing and marketing. Believe what you want. I think it was a movement from hell.

For every soul saved during prohibition, and there were many, ten times that number of average men would never darken the door of a church again beyond childhood. Over time, they wouldn't even take the kids. Old Walt said that was the last time he'd been to church. When his Dad dropped out, he had to decide if he was ever going to have a drink. He reminded me of that old run down farm where he could get a jar of moonshine on a weekend. That was where he had made his decision. "I guess I'll never go to church again," he had decided. He wanted me to know that he never had anything against going to church, but he told me he had to make up his mind, like his Dad. He wasn't going to be a hypocrite, so he never went back. You can call it the Temperance Movement; I call it the great American falling away.

After old Walt and I had caught up on everything, he shocked me. He said, "I'll help you out with some gas money. Remember how you and Teddy (his boy) used to lime water those fence posts and tree trunks around the corral?" That meant white wash; a bag of lime mixed in a bucket of water and then painted on the wood. The corral was just a fenced area at the foot of a small hill dotted with apple trees. Walt was the last guy I was looking to earn a few bucks from. I'd worked for him before. However, his assumption was right; all I needed was a little gas and some groceries. I had made arrangements to speak in a church in Pittsburgh the next Sunday, and I only needed a tank of gas to make the ninety mile trip. "Good, I'll see you in the morning," he said. When the wife and I had finished the white wash, he asked us to paint the house. That covered the expenses of getting out and presenting our field to churches a couple times a week. We were making the bills from offerings, but still not one church except ours had taken us on for regular monthly support. It was not looking good.

"God," I said, "You have been orchestrating this from the beginning. You have met every need. You have provided all the basic requirements. Ninety-percent of the men who attempt to reach the mission field without joining some organization outside the local church never get this far. I've had many temptations to pursue other avenues in the ministry, but no inkling that you want me to do anything but continue the course. I need to see your hand in some progress." We were still parked in the edge of the field close enough to plug into my uncle's house. Our mail was going to my parent's house in town. There wasn't much beyond communications with our home church in Kentucky. Just answers from some churches that were receiving our monthly letter that the church put out for us. We got a couple offers from church schools that needed an administrator. We got one from a college that wanted both of us as teachers. But nothing we needed to show us any promise of progression towards our goal.

Then came a letter from a church in Denver, Colorado; Arvada Baptist Church, I think. I had never heard of it. It was a letter informing us that we were being disciplined for non-fellowship. That's what the old-timers called being churched. They said I'd been baptized into their church by their missionary in Japan in 1965. They had recently been informed that I had long since returned to the states, and had made no contact with them. I had not requested a letter of membership transfer to any other local church. I had been baptized fifteen years before. I had to rack my brain to figure out what was going on. I was one of the strongest preachers on church authority in every circle I'd ever run in. Since then, I had started one church and belonged to five other churches. How could I have missed this blatant fact?

I had always credited Brother Eddie Sullivan for bringing me into the fold and teaching me what the New Testament Church was. Why had he never contacted me? Then I remembered, it wasn't Brother Eddie that had baptized me that cold winter day in the Tamagawa River. It had been a new missionary that Eddie was helping to get settled in- country. Brother Elkins was his name. He had visited our home in Milford, Delaware, about three years after we had returned to the states. His visit had come just as we were preparing to leave for Bible College. We even took him to the church we belonged to in Milford. He was the guy that had told me I did not meet the qualifications of a pastor, because he knew my past and I was not blameless. I guess this little church fellowship thing had slipped his mind for the past fifteen years, because he never mentioned it.

I wrote the pastor that had sent the letter and informed him that we had no idea what church we had been baptized into. We had joined the church in Milford by statement of faith that we had accepted Christ and had been scripturally immersed. I brought him up to speed on our past service and apologized for not doing the right thing. A few days later, we got his response. He not only took our letter to the church and secured forgiveness for our lack of fellowship, but expressed their desire to support us regularly. I don't know for sure what that old missionary's motive was for stirring up the past and causing all of this, but it was the blessing we had needed all along. I'm not positive Elkins started all of this, but I can't think of anyone else that would have. For some reason, it had slipped his mind that I was not qualified for the ministry.

How could I have not even thought about trying to contact Brother Eddie? Don't confuse him with our pastor, Brother Ed. Brother Eddie was my total inspiration for serving God in a scriptural manner from the beginning. His teaching was responsible for our being independent church missionaries in the first place. I guess I thought I had a much larger group of churches than he ever had. We had not communicated in so many years that I had no idea how to find him. But I now had contact with a church that had to know where Eddie was.

All of this still hadn't hit home with me. One of the churches from Eddie's circle of influence had expressed interest in helping us. I couldn't imagine that little group making a significant impact on getting us to the field. It was encouraging to have this little addition to our effort, but the thought of asking him for additional contacts had never crossed my mind. I still believed that *my* personal contacts from *my* past were the key to our success, and I just hadn't got to the right people yet. Maybe if I went back through the Kentucky group one more time, they would see that we were serious and they'd get behind us.

The weather was starting to close in on us. If this new direction was the game plan, we'd better head west. I really wanted to get to Florida, but to go all that way down there for the few churches that would have me was cost prohibitive at the time. Even though I was pretty sure one of them was going to help us. We said our good-byes once again, and pulled out. I had one engagement in Zanesville, Ohio, and one in Cincinnati. These were both very large churches that knew me from past association. If nothing else, they should cover our gas and campground expenses.

I got into the large church in Zanesville because of a guy that had fixed my transmission ten years before. I had witnessed to him at the time and he had received Christ. This was the church where he now worked in the missions department. After the presentation, the pastor invited me to sit awhile with him and some of his men. My personal history, of course, was the subject. When the pastor had heard that I once taught geopolitics, he being one of the few really informed on the subject, decided to test my knowledge. He started by asking me a secret term of a secret organization. Few know this organization from bottom to top. That includes most of those that belong to it. From there he dug deeper and deeper. We amazed each other until we realized that the rest of the men didn't have a clue what we were talking about. I had not maintained those studies since I had quit teaching, and I didn't care to discuss the subject anymore. Why mess with a beehive? He as much as told me that he felt the same way about it. We had fun with the subject anyway, probably for the last time in both of our lives. I sort of thought it would create a rare kind of bond between us, but I never heard from him again.

We went on to our Cincinnati engagement that I think Ron Miller had secured for us. It was actually a church-based college. I can't remember the pastor's name, but he was a Doctor of Divinity from Dallas Theological Seminary. That impressed me; overly impressed me. He put the wife and I up for the night in his own bedroom. The only other Dallas DDs I knew at the time thought they were God's gift, and demanded they be treated like it. This guy was a really great person. But again, we never heard from them, either. Don't get me wrong. Without people like these guys to help us along the way, people like me couldn't last long. At least long enough to finally find the works that God had prepared to work with us.

Some of these guys admitted up front that they would never lead their church to support us. They had just never met a missionary doing it strictly by the New Testament, and if nothing more, they wanted to say that they had helped us along. I think they were just really curious. We are a rare bird today. I thank God for their kindness. They just couldn't bring themselves to seriously examine the possibilities. What they had bought into just might be extra-biblical, but that would be too much to consider. I had all the peace in the world around these guys. No matter how wonderful an outfit they worked with, there was no honest student of the Word that could question my method. I liked never being on the defensive side of the discussions. The more time passed, however, the more I wondered if the right way would work anymore.

We arrived back in Paducah just in time to get in the middle of a standoff between the pastor and two of his deacons. They were two really great men, and had served the church for many years. Ed had put a stop to the country gospel music programs. That cost the church about half of the congregation and half of the budget. Three deacons had supported him in the disciplining of three women that had worked at the distillery. Now he was pressuring the head deacon to take his children out of public school and enroll them in the church school. He had started the school shortly after taking the pastorate. Back in those days, you could still start a private school with no effort. It was taught by his wife and the wife of the only deacon with whom he had no complaints.

I have to admit that no matter how poorly the average church school was run, it was better than a public school. By the early eighties, most of the conservative teachers had been run off. I saw this trend beginning in the early sixties. Our public schools had been turned over to the bureaucracies as far back as the early fifties. The front page of the newspapers was full of the launch of the Russian Sputnik. The rest of the paper was dedicated to the need to let the government take over the schools, or we were going to fall behind the Russians. By the late fifties, any college student failing out was encouraged to transfer to education if they wanted to graduate. By the early eighties, these failures were strongly entrenched in education administration. The agenda had shifted from education to liberal politics. Most Americans would not notice this shift for another ten years. Then it was only because their children couldn't read. We didn't fall behind their communism; but we were rapidly catching up to their socialism.

The pastor asked me to visit the oldest deacon with him; one of the two that were now expressing their discontent. I guess Ed had never visited him. I think we were the last people he expected to knock on his door. He would not have been so quick to yell for us to come in. I'll never forget the look on Ed's face when we walked in. He turned to me and whispered, "Somebody here smokes." That was the last time we ever saw him. Suddenly there was only one deacon to worry about. His name was Tom Nance. I'll never forget that name; it's on my certificate of ordination.

He, too, was a good man. His heart was broken over the state of the church. What had been a full house just a year before was now a mere handful. The bills were barely being made and the future wasn't looking much better. He had a genuine respect for the ministry and that had made it easier for the pastor to beat him down. It broke my heart to look into his eyes. I knew this guy was the only hope for the church to survive. Somehow I had to help him. I had the same problem he had. You have a pastor to deal with, and unless you're just a rebel, that is a very touchy matter. I knew I had to do something, but I was just barely hanging on myself. God was going to have to do something with my ministry or I was out of there.

The pastor from Colorado was in monthly communication with Brother Eddie, who was now in Okinawa. I got a letter that Eddie had sent to my home church. He had a lot of questions. He knew I had gone to Baptist Bible College, but he didn't know if I had joined their organization or remained an independent. He needed to know if my home church was an independent church. I gladly answered his questions. It still never dawned on me that his little group could have a major impact on getting us to the field. I started making my rounds back through the Kentucky group again. I was sure this was going to be our foot in the door, as these guys had contacts nationwide. I had been to a couple of their big missions conferences. They were very nice to us, but we were just not accepted as one of them. It was becoming clear; we were not going to last long enough to make it happen. My preaching offerings were dwindling, and my church was dying on the vine.

It was a tough decision, but one that had to be made sooner or later. It was already almost too late. We couldn't even make it back to Punxsy without raising some travel money. I got another letter from Brother Eddie. He was thrilled that I had decided to pursue the mission field in a New Testament fashion. Being content that we were solid, he asked a pastor from Eastern Kentucky to give my church office a call. I remember the call. "Hey, this is Brother Mike Rodgers. I'm pastor of Mount Hebron Baptist Church. Brother Eddie Sullivan is our mutual Brother, I hear. Can you fit us in your schedule any time soon?" There I sat, wringing my hands, trying to figure out where I was going to preach. I needed to raise enough money to get somewhere.....we couldn't just quit. "Honey, another one of Eddie's churches called today," I told my wife. "His little church is clear on the other side of the state. If I get the average twenty-five to fifty dollar offering, it will only cover the trip out and back. I don't know what to do. The invitation is the only option not leading straight out of the ministry. Let's give it one more shot. I'll take Mark and go. He needs to get away for a day and he'll keep me awake."

I had never gone to speak anywhere with such a heavy heart. This was probably my last service. I just couldn't believe after all God had done to get us this far, that it was over. We got off the highway where the directions told us to, and we took a country road for miles. There it was, a little church, twenty miles from the nearest little town. It was an evening service and already dark. I remember very little about the message. After the service, on the way home, God opened my eyes to what He was doing. After I had spoke, and the people were leaving, someone had yelled, "Wait, we forgot to take up an offering for this brother." About a third of the congregation had already left.

There was this guy, running around frantically collecting what he could get from the rest as they were leaving. By then, I was really down. I figured I wouldn't even get the fifty bucks I was hoping for. As the last of the congregation left the building, this guy came up to the pastor with an envelope and handed to him. It was bulging with cash, clearly more than fifty bucks. The pastor handed it to a man standing beside him and instructed him to go write us a check. The pastor invited us down to his house for a cup of coffee, but it was late and I was depressed. I thanked him, but told him I needed to hit the road. When we got in the truck, I handed the check to Mark. I told him this same thing had happened to me in Ohio a few months ago. After each missionary spoke, the pastor would ask the congregation for a voluntary pledge for the missionary that had just spoke. God gave me a great delivery that day and the pledge had been around two hundred dollars, but when I had left, the pastor gave me a check for twenty-five dollars. I just looked at him. I never said a word. He knew I heard what the people pledged to offer my ministry. He said, "Brother, it's all missions budget; your just one missionary. I have a lot of commitments that have to come out of that budget."

In the negative state I was in, I figured this guy had also just put the offering in the mission fund and wrote me the standard twenty-five or fifty dollar check. After a few miles of driving down the country road in

The Campaign Begins • 189

silence, I asked Mark to open the envelope and see how much they had written the check for. It was dark. He opened it and held the check by the little door handle light and tried to make out the amount. He said "Fifty.....no five zero zero.... no, five hundred......five hundred dollars." I told him he was crazy as I pulled off the road and turned on the interior lights. That was more money than we had seen in months. You think I would have yelled 'Praise the Lord?' You don't know how discouraged I had become. Instead, I said "Man, and I missed a third of the congregation before they took up the offering." We both examined the check again. What kind of church was that? It was a country church, twenty miles from anywhere, with forty families max. Wow! That was everything we needed to make the bills and get back to Punxsy. What a way to go out.

The next day, pastor Rogers from Mount Hebron, where I had preached the night before, called the church office and asked for me. "Hey brother," he said, "Sorry about the mix up last night, but we can make it up to you if you have some time. We have a mission about fifty miles south of here that is currently without a pastor. They would be generous enough to meet your needs. We'd pay you enough extra to help you build up your reserves before you move on. Can you give us a few weeks? You can park your camper at brother Latham's ranch and work out of there. Oh, the men of the church said they want to vote you in as one of our full time missionaries. We'll do that next Sunday. Let me know if you have time to work the mission. I know the guys down south will want to have you speak for them, but pray about it. If you can hang around a few weeks for our annual camp meeting, they'll all be there." Wow again! A lot of churches had allowed me to speak, but I hadn't heard the words 'want me'. Except for a couple of old friends that were too far away to visit at that point, no one else wanted me.

We had stuck it out until we just couldn't go on. Now here was a bunch of guys I had never heard of, that Pastor Rogers believes will all want us to speak. We had only decided to give up because we had starved out. What reason would we have to quit now? For the first time, I was waking up to the fact that Brother Eddie's group might not be as insignificant as I had thought. I knew he only had a handful of churches supporting him, but I never thought it might be because that was all the churches he needed. We had only spoken at one of his churches so far. They had given us ten to twenty times what *my* main contacts had ever given us. They also wanted to support us full time, after only one engagement. It didn't take us long to get our original mind set back on track. I got a new spring in my step. If only I had met these guys a year ago, we would be like most of the missionaries I'd been meeting at the mission conferences. Most of them had about all the support they needed. They were only working on special needs, like travel to the field, and equipment they'd need once on the field.

We were a long way from even thinking about special needs. It was really disheartening to meet a man that had only been on the road for a few months, yet he was halfway home. One night after a conference somewhere in Kentucky, I was sitting on the church steps with one of those guys. I was the only missionary that had spoken that night that wasn't well on his way. In my mind, I was sitting with the competition, but the game was over for them. I hadn't scored with any of the visiting pastors and he knew it. Up until that night, I had looked at all other missionaries on deputation through the eyes of my own situation. I couldn't imagine money in my wallet if there was gas in my tank. He pulled out his wallet and handed me a twenty dollar bill. I couldn't speak. I took it and just looked at him. That was a week's worth of groceries. It wasn't until that moment that I realized we were on the same team. He'll never know how much he encouraged me. Just to think that someday, I might be able to help a fellow missionary, changed my whole perspective. From that day forward, I never looked at my fellow missionaries as competition. No matter what stage of the game they were in.

I couldn't figure out why I had wasted all that time preaching in churches that would never seriously consider supporting us. I know now that I was on a mission right here in the states. I had a message that God wanted preached to that Kentucky group, and every place else we preached. It was right out of Pastor Ed's pamphlet. He had published it when he was president of the college. "What Happens If We Are Not Missionary" was the name of it, and what really happens to a church that does not support missions was the subject. In future chapters, you'll find out exactly what happens to them. At the time, it all seemed to be a big loss of time. I had no idea of the ramifications that would result from that message. Over the next ten years, both pastors and fellow missionaries would inform me that that message had closed about fifty old churches that had forgotten why they had even existed.

Psalms 139:16

Thine eyes did see my substance, yet being unperfect; and in Thy book all my members were written, which in continuance were fashioned, when as yet there was none of them.

Chapter 13
The Race is On

To say that you campaign for office is a misnomer. First, you campaign for your party's nomination as their candidate. Until you win the primary, you're just hoping for a chance to get in the race. I hope you don't think that when God calls a man to a mission field, that he just starts shopping for airline tickets. The competition is fierce. I like to think that only God's chosen ever make it. We had been campaigning for a year. We filed and received all the proper papers, including my ordination, performed by our church in Paducah. Until Brother Eddie contacted Pastor Rodgers with our nomination as the next missionary to Japan, we weren't even in the running. I like to say we were running with the Independent party. It's the smallest and least popular party. There was nothing behind us but the New Testament Church and their sister churches. We now had the party nomination. We were no longer a candidate for the ministry. We were in a race for the field. I had the church make us T-shirts that read 'Japan or Bust'.

If I could go back to any time in my life and do it all over again, this is the time I would choose. For the first time since we had begun, we had the funds to hook up the trailer and hit the trail. For all of us, purpose returned to our life. There was now a light at the end of the tunnel that didn't resemble an oncoming train. The kids were ecstatic to be out of the church school. The pastor's wife had been a wonderful teacher when she had worked for me, but I knew she was not cut out to deal with lower grades. I had kept her in the higher grades for that purpose. Kids drove her nuts, and she returned the favor. Now everything started to make sense. My wife had earned the credentials for home schooling as a part of our preparation. Now it meant something.

I still had a serious problem in my preparation, however. My home church was disintegrating, and I knew nothing was going to change. On the other hand, I personally was doing great guns. Pastor Rodgers had reintroduced us to the Mount Hebron Church. He had requested additional support while we were preaching for their mission. We pulled our home down to where we were instructed to meet the layman that was running the mission. He had taken over when the mission pastor had left for a better offer to preach elsewhere. It was a tire shop and a trucking company combined. We pulled in and parked. I walked to the main building and requested to speak to Mr. Latham. The secretary asked me which Mr. Latham? I didn't know. I told her who I was. She said "Oh, we have been looking for you. I'm married to one of the Latham boys; I'll get the boss." A tall thin guy appeared in the hallway leading away from the show room, and said, "Hey brother, come on back."

He led me to a very nice office at the end of the hall. "Sit down, Brother," he said. "We have a place set up for you to park out on the farm. I'll have my boy Charlie lead you out there and help you get set up." We exchanged pleasantries for a while, mostly about Brother Eddie. He had known him at least as long as I had. This tall man with a deep voice reminded me of Sam Elliot. His character radiated. I felt like after all this time on the road, we had finally found the family we were looking for. I thought it was going to be the Calvert group, but I was dead wrong. God had a definite purpose for us to be working in that group, but it had nothing to do with making it to the field.

We walked out into the large parking lot where I had left my rig, but it wasn't there. Just as I was about to panic, another tall thin guy walked out of the shop. "Charlie, do you know where this brother's rig got to?" he asked. "I put it in the truck bay; it needed tires all-around," was the reply. "Sorry about that, Brother," said the old man. "It won't take them long, and then Charlie will get you settled. You'll have supper with us right? Anything you need just ask Charlie. I'm looking forward to supper with you and meeting your family. Thanks for coming. I'll see you in a couple of hours, Brother." Now I know my wife had not asked for new tires. They weren't even that bad yet. I would have been fretting the expense of eight new heavy duty tires. I looked at this young man with a blank expression, I guess. He said, "I noticed your tires were getting down. I wanted the blessing before anyone beat me to it. I hope you don't mind, Brother. We'll be ready in a few minutes. Anything else you need before we head for the ranch?"

These people were magical. We were not halfway through supper before my youngest was calling them all uncles and aunts. Even the secretary was there for supper. She said she just couldn't wait to meet us. Man, could they cook. For the next six months, my wife was going to be collecting recipes. 'Where did you come from?' 'How did you meet?' 'When did you meet Brother Eddie?' This went on until way after the dishes were done. My wife is a good woman, but she made it clear from the onset that she was not a people person. "You are called; I am called to follow," she told me. "Don't expect me to play the picture missionaries' wife part. I don't speak to the ladies groups. I don't socialize beyond services." That all changed in a hurry. Suddenly she was telling me how to act around these people. "They lost a son to drugs," she told me. "Be careful what you say about this and that........," and on and on she went.

She knew more about these people than I would have learned in a year. God only knows what they suddenly knew about me. After a day or two, Mark asked if he could go to the auction with Charlie. "He has some cattle to sell and he asked me to go with him Dad," he said. "Can I go?" This guy was probably in his early twenties, and Mark was about ten. He came home all excited, and he was wearing a new pair of cowboy boots. "Uncle Charlie said I couldn't go in there without boots," he told me. I had sold veal in cattle auctions when I was in the FFA back in high school. That was just one of many life experiences I thought my son would never have. It was just the beginning of a whirlwind of experiences he couldn't learn in any school.

A southern Kentucky farm is a pretty safe place for kids to be left to roam with minimum supervision. There are no scorpions, rattlesnakes, or wild cats. I let Brandon, my youngest, go in and out of the trailer pretty much as he desired. One morning, he didn't return in his usual five or ten minutes, so I went out to check on him. He was just getting pretty well out of the toddler stage and communicating beyond his years as well. Brother Latham was a busy man with two companies to run. I saw him at supper time and in church, and that was about it. He kept saying he'd like to sit down with me and chat, but even when we had tried it in his office, it didn't work. Here it was about mid-morning on a weekday, so I did not expect to see Ralph leisurely strolling around the grounds hand in hand with my missing boy. Ralph was pointing and talking. Brandon's arm was stretched about as far up as it would go to maintain his grip on this tall lanky gentleman's hand. From that time on, he was Uncle Ralph and Charlie was Bud Bud.

That was a great place to park, and we got generous offerings for just speaking on Sunday mornings. I decided to stay on a little longer than planned. The annual camp meeting was one week away. We were going to take our home with us and head south from there. I decided to use the camp meeting just for introductions, instead of booking meetings as planned. That was the first time in our deputation that we were not living day to day and hand to mouth. We had become that missionary sitting on the back steps of the missions conference, just relaxing. The fact that he was so relaxed had impressed me more than his ability to reach into his wallet and hand me a twenty.

We were now out of the fray. The days of frantically lobbying pastors at the missions conferences were over. Invitations were coming in through Pastor Rodgers to speak in churches all around us. Others came in through Brother Eddie from states as far away as Washington and Oregon. It was more evident every day that no one was in a hurry for us to move on. Cheryl had, for the first time, found sisters she really wanted to spend time with. They loved to take her and the girls shopping. We had been wearing the same clothes we had packed for our maiden voyage. They were probably out of style before we had packed them in the first place. Cheryl was so excited to make me try on something with the tags still on it. No more going through church clothes rooms trying to find anything better than you were wearing. Although we appreciated them at the time, we felt blessed to be back in style. It did wonders for our confidence.

We were floored to hear that Brother Eddie had advanced his furlough date. By the time his letter caught up with us, they were already back in the states. Barring anything unforeseen, we would see them for the first time in nearly fifteen years, at the upcoming camp meeting. The morning we left for the Monticello Camp Grounds, there was a combination of feelings. First of all, we were going camping, but most of all it was a family reunion. We would be with our oldest family in Christ, our new family, and a host of brothers and sisters we had never met. I still refer to this meeting as my 'home run'. Both Eds in our life had done a magnificent job on our behalf. Our pastor Ed had secured a mailing address list from Brother Rodgers. He had sent out an introductory letter featuring us as truly New Testament Missionaries. No one had a better grip on what a New Testament Church missionary was supposed to be. Brother Eddie had sent out his letter indorsing us as the family that they most wanted to join them on the field.

We didn't take our home with us after all. I slept with the men and Cheryl with the women. We only saw each other at meals and evening preaching meetings. She was reunited with Neva, Eddie's wife. Neva was also a favorite with our new friends from the mission in Somerset. My girls had found their counterparts; pastor and missionary daughters from all over the east coast. Brandon was totally immersed in attention from everybody. Mark was spending his time with the pastors and Brother Eddie. These were his professors and older brothers in the work. Mark had made up his mind that he was not just a part of the family; he was a part of the mission. From here on, he was my right hand man in this whole getting to the field thing. By the time we left camp, he was going to know more of those guys than I did.

The last day of camp was the annual softball game. I don't know how long this had been going on. There were now grown children playing positions once held by their fathers. I don't know how they determined what team a new guy like me got assigned to. All I know is when we met for breakfast, I was surrounded by my new team. I was on Garlington's team. He was an older pastor from Louisiana. He asked me if I had a favorite position. I told him I had played first base for a coal company in Pennsylvania. "Ok, you start on first," he said. He said it didn't make any difference because we were going to win this year anyway. Rodgers had brought his brother. He had played college ball and had already been drafted by a semi-pro team. We had him in the outfield. They told me to take first. I guess everybody felt the same way. They played so relaxed that we were down two runs at the bottom of the ninth. I have to admit that I was not paying a lot of attention. I was visiting and didn't even really know what the score was.

To me it was just fun and games at a reunion. Brother Garlington came over and handed me a bat. 'Your up', is all he said. Two men were on base and I was up with two outs. I had to hit a homer or it was over. No one had done that today. For some reason, when I stood in the box,

I remembered how I used to hit the ball. My college karate teacher had taught me how to totally relax before making any move. I had forgotten that. That is how I used to get really good hits when I played for the coal company. I totally relaxed with the bat on my shoulder until the slow pitched ball was right at the edge of the plate. I then swung with a cat-like reflex. It used to work. Holy smokes, it worked again! God had put the icing on the cake.

I didn't even know we had won. Many years later, I'd meet the son of a pastor from Alaska that would address me as the 'slugger of Monticello'. He said, "I was at the camp celebration the year they found your ball." God may have been in the name recognition game at the time. Years later, it gave me the edge I needed to make an impression on this athletic young man. I don't think he would have flown nine thousand miles to visit us on the field had the Garlington team not made such a fuss over finding my ball. He said no one had hit into the woods for four years. When they went in to find the ball some slugger had hit, they had found mine as well. Then they had to start measuring to see who's was the longest slam. I don't remember who won, but they had a big celebration over it. These guys don't get out much. It wouldn't surprise me if that young man went into the ministry.

I ate foods I'd never eaten in my life. Those people could cook, but I paid for it. For the next few days, I suffered from something I named 'Monticello's Revenge'. When I recovered, I began making engagements with churches within a couple hours driving distance from the ranch. Ralph, or another missionary passing through, held evening services for the mission while I spoke elsewhere. One of the churches was special. The pastor had an illness that had taken his voice. He spoke in a whisper that could only be heard over the sound system. Knowing Kentucky preachers, the illness was probably from many years of preaching. Brother Blankenship comes to mind. At a conference in Calvert City, Blankenship ran across the stage and kicked his cowboy boot up over his head. He then ran back across and kicked the other one over his head. Then he ran off the stage and out the door. He ran around the church three times before he passed out. This special church was not like Calvert City. These guys were just different. The pastor owned a chair factory is all I can remember about him, other than his statesmen mannerism.

It was a new world for all of us. I would come home after speaking in these churches and just relax with the family. We would discuss things like how different the people I just mentioned were, compared to the people we had been trying to work with over the last year. They were all good people, but why were we so comfortable with some and felt like intruders with others? What made our group of sister churches like no other group we had ever met? I listened as my girls talked about their new found friends. Tonia was already looking forward to getting to Southern Louisiana. Chris couldn't wait to spend time with Boogie, a pastor's daughter in Northern Louisiana. They were talking about girls they had met at camp.

Except for our home church, they hadn't made a friend since we had hit the road a year before. Suddenly, they were writing letters to friends they had only known for weeks. When we got to some of those churches, we'd find that many of them knew more about our kids than they knew about me. Strange thing is, that for most of them, that's all they really needed to know. The more I learned about this bunch, the more I realized that it was really just all about family. I'd meet people in one church that would tell me their brother or sister or mother or father or aunt or uncle had met us in another church. We knew we were talking about the closest thing to heaven on earth that we would ever find.

One thing about these people stood out above everything else from the eyes of a New Testament missionary. They had no denominational ties, of course, but better yet, there was no collegiate alumni allegiance required. Anyone that graduated from anywhere was welcome to speak for them if they demonstrated basic New Testament values. I love Pastor Cornell; he was my pastor when God called me to the ministry. I met him many years later. He heard that I had left the Baptist Bible Fellowship and he was upset with me about it. I asked him why he was upset. He said I was causing division. These guys just don't get it. It's their devotion to some man-made division of the faith that causes division. God can't send one of *His* men to your church to share *His* ministry with you unless he is associated with your particular division of the faith?

Why do you think God built the New Testament churches with sister-ties to all other New Testament churches? Do you think there is going to be a Bob Jones Division, a Southern Baptist Division, and a BBF division in Glory? Which division do you suppose Jesus is going to be a part of? Don't you know what Paul said about causing divisions among the brethren? I recently offered my services as Chaplain to the Air Force Auxiliary. I can't get in. I don't belong to anything but a New Testament Church. I have been departmentalized out of serving God, because I don't belong to some man-made brotherhood. You better think about it friend. Paul couldn't speak in your church, nor could Jesus. He's not a part of your group. You better drop the independent part from your church's name on your sign. The only thing your independent from is everyone that doesn't belong to your fellowship.

Now that I had this great setup, it was time to do something about the home church. It was in our every prayer. I had no peace about working with any other pastor. It would not have been any problem to find one in our new group of friends, but I had worked for years with Ed. I knew no one with his abilities and devotion to New Testament missions. We agreed that if I could find a new place to build a church, two families were ready to pick up and move. For some reason, I had Houston on my heart. At the time, I just couldn't get way out there to look around. I would have to have a reason beyond the fact that Houston was booming.

As long as the weather was still decent, we would put off our plans to work south. I worked every church within a days driving distance. In the process, I had accumulated many offers that were just out of reach. Several of the Louisiana churches that were waiting for our visit had already voted to support us fulltime. There was no longer a sense of urgency to get down there and sure them up, but we decided to accept the offer from Pastor Russell. Leaving the ranch was tough for the family. We said our good-byes, hooked up, and headed west for Russellville. I now know where they got the idea for the twilight zone. Miss Kentucky or Miss America had come from this place not long before we arrived. She must have been the only one to ever get out of there.

Pastor Russell took me down to a wood-working factory and introduced me to the owner, the manager, and each of the employees. I can't remember their first names, but their last names were all Russell. No one spoke without taking a breath after every one or two words. They moved just about as slow as they talked. Really nice people, but it took you all day to find it out. I figured I could give them a month's worth of messages in one service if I talked at normal speed. The first time I took my wife downtown to a gas station, I pulled in and shut the truck off. I leaned back and started opening the mail that our church had sent to Pastor Russell's house.

They hadn't heard the bell, my wife told me. Self-service hadn't even reached this place. Oh yeah, they did hear the bell.....they were probably just in the middle of a sentence. Relax; they'd be right out in a few minutes. A character trait of a missionary is adaptability. We worked from there for about two weeks. It felt like only a couple of months. I remember the last church I preached in there. The pastor walked out in the middle of the message. I just preached all the harder. I noticed the congregation looking at me, then over at a guy sitting next to the wall on my right. He began to shake his head and say 'amen' when I made a point. The rest of the people remained until I closed. Then, when I would normally turn the service over to the pastor, he was gone. I just closed in prayer. The people started to get up and leave until the guy by the wall stood up and raised his hand. He told the ushers to pass the plate, as he pulled out his wallet. He handed me the offering and shrugged his shoulders. I didn't know what had happened, and I didn't ask. I felt a calmness of spirit. Our mission in the twilight zone was completed.

I believe God sent a last message to a dying group of old country churches. We were done there. I mentioned it to Pastor Russell as we were hooking up to leave. He said he knew it. He told me, "When I heard you give that message at the conference where we met, I knew God was going to bring you to Russellville. That's why I set it all up. I can resign now; I got a job laying block." Wow, I was still a hatchet man. I thought that was all behind me when I had left the campus, but I was wrong. It would be years before I learned the full impact of those side trips. The truth be known, I might not have been as popular as I sometimes thought I was; I was just available. That is another character trait of a missionary....availability. When those side ventures or unexpected opportunities came about, I began to recognize them for what they were. The Holy Spirit made it very clear that those unexpected engagements were not necessarily to advance my program. Every once in awhile, it was an invitation to present His program. I was beginning to believe those off-the-trail engagements were always going to be another trip to the twilight zone. Then he surprised us. He showed us that He could set up the unexpected for more than just a Jonah trip to Nineveh to deliver a final warning.

My pastor was putting out regular letters to all the addresses given to him by our new family of sister churches. Then came the invitation I was looking for. The only church in Eddie's circle of friends that was located in Texas. I figured we would make a loop down through Texas and then jump back on I-10 and winter with our new friends in Louisiana. The girls didn't want to hear that. I had promised them a justifiable long stay with their camp friends if we worked Texas first. So off we went for the Lone Star state. We could make the rather famous conference in Little Rock before heading to Galveston. What a different world it was to set up camp with other missionaries who had progressed beyond the candidate stage. Suddenly we found ourselves talking about where we were going; not where we hoped to be going. That was a really big conference. It was the first time we were scheduled in with veterans that were already on the field. Those guys would even give you a copy of their supporting churches and give you some hints on how to secure an appointment. For the first time at one of these conferences, we were not just promoting our cause. We were helping others to advance theirs.

We pulled out of there with enough meetings scheduled to fill every Sunday and Wednesday service all the way to Galveston. None of those were what I would call an off the trail experience. I think we were done with that appointment. We still had a few weird appointments though. The next weird encounter was at a conference at Independent Bible College, or I.B.C., located north of Dallas. It wasn't like the twilight zone; it was more like an out of body experience. I left the family in the fifth-wheel, parked at a nice church in Dallas where our children were guest students for the week. The college president came out to greet me as soon as I arrived. He told me who was setting up the speakers, but asked if he could schedule me for the college assembly. That meant I was going to get a whole hour. It would not be the usual five or ten minute self-introduction that was allotted to most rookies on deputation.

It was like I had gone back in time. For the last couple years, I had been a little known missionary candidate, speaking anywhere I could. Suddenly, I was on a college campus again. In that field, I was no rookie.

I had attended many years of college seminars with educators from everywhere. Our college was once known as an outstanding example of a ministry of a New Testament Church. There weren't that many of us that had gained national recognition. This school was also a ministry of a New Testament Church. I had been aware of this school for years. It only made sense that he was also aware of ours. "If you don't mind sir, you will share a room in the men's dorm with Professor Milton." I was told. "Please be ready to address the assembly at eleven. I look forward to joining you for lunch in the cafeteria following assembly." I had my orders.

Wow! I was bunking with Doctor Milton. I had heard he was thinking about leaving the BBF. About three years before that, I had received a call from Doctor Drummond. He said he had received a call from a famous theology professor, and he asked me how I'd like having Doctor Milton on my staff. I thought he was kidding, but he assured me they were talking. That's the last I ever heard his name spoken. Suddenly, I was sharing a room with the man. Ten years earlier, it had taken me two years just to get enrolled in his class. In two whole semesters, I had managed to get less than two minutes one-on-one with him. That only came about as I was in the process of ordering his latest book on contemporary religion. I'd only been on campus a few minutes and I'd already got more speaking time than the featured speaker. I was going to spend the evening with a man I held as the leading authority in his field. My head was spinning already, and it had only just begun.

The next day, I addressed the college assembly with many pastors in attendance. I finished right at lunch time, and sat down at the nearest table in the cafeteria. I talked to a lot of people that indicated they would entertain having me speak for them. They told me to give them a call when we got in their area. That is not how you operated once you had obtained the nomination. You didn't have to drive around the country haphazardly, hoping for a break. You got your appointment book out and gave the pastor a date you could be there. This was another group of independents like the first group in Kentucky. They also had a preacher that seemed to be the group leader. When every pastor asked if I knew him, I quickly figured out that they were not going to help me unless he endorsed me. In this particular case, I could say I had known him for

The Race is On • 203

quite some time. His name was Pastor Thomas. He was the same one Ed and I had confronted over his messing with one of our missionaries. I figured the devil had a better chance of getting his endorsement than I did. I knew he would soon learn I was now headed for the mission field, and that would be the end for me in Texas.

I decided that hanging around there any longer would be a waste of time. Then another pastor sat down across from me. He was a short fellow, but stood out in a crowd like a man that was seven foot tall. His dress and demeanor was pure class. He introduced himself and immediately invited me to speak for him Sunday. I figured naturally that he was referring to the evening service. A rookie missionary never got a morning service in a strange church. I was clear on the other side of the state. He said he wanted me to come in Saturday evening and check in at the church so that Sunday morning ran smoothly. He said he would have someone standing by to set us up in a nice room for the night. I told him my family was in our fifth-wheel and we would only need a place to park on or near the property. He drew me a map and stood up to hand it to me with a hand shake. He said he wouldn't see me, but his staff would be there to help me through the services. I asked if he wanted me for morning or evening. He said "Yes." That was the last time we spoke. That would be perfect. From there we could make it to a friend's church that was just across the state line. If I left right away, I would have just enough time to swing through Houston. I'd speak Wednesday evening in Galveston, pick up the family, and head for his church in Pasadena.

"Thank you Lord." My head was spinning. I don't know how I ended up in Sugar Land. I was just looking for a place to start a work near Houston. There I was in Sugar Land; a settlement located right between Stafford and Missouri City. I called Ed and asked him to pray about these three little cities that bordered each other just outside Houston. He was excited and so was I. I wanted to get Ed and his head deacon out of West Paducah Baptist Church, while there still was one. I went on down to Galveston and spoke for a really nice couple that was in fellowship with our new group of churches. I can't remember speaking. I'm not even sure if I did. All I can remember is sitting with the pastor and his wife in their living room, looking at a porcupine quill in a jar. She had ingested it whole at some local restaurant. The thing had to be three inches long. It was removed at the hospital only a few days before. I could see drinking something that long by accident, but how did you eat it and not know it? We put each other on our permanent mailing lists. I went back to the church, picked up the family, and we headed for Pasadena.

It was Saturday afternoon and I followed the map to the 't', but there was no church there. We went around the block twice before I decided to pull in behind a big factory to see if I could find someone. I started to think that maybe the guy wasn't even for real. We parked just inside the large empty parking lot. The place might even be closed, I thought, but I should be able to find a security guard at least. Maybe he could tell me where this church was located. I walked across the huge lot towards a small back door. I knocked, but no one answered. I turned the handle and opened the door. Suddenly, I was backstage, in some kind of production studio. There were curtains, ropes, lights, and electronic stuff. I was definitely backstage. The door was open and the lights were on, so someone had to be around. I yelled something and an office door opened on the other side of the room. "Is that you Brother Jones?" I heard. Holy smokes! This factory was the church. We exchanged pleasantries and decided that where we were parked was just fine. If I didn't need anything else, I was to be right where I was standing in the morning at ten minutes before eleven.

Wow! This was a miracle. Even as a college representative, I seldom ever got in a place that big. Some guy I had never met had invited some guy he had never met to speak in a place like this. Any famous preacher would jump at an opportunity like this. I walked back to the trailer and met my wife standing at the door with a puzzled look on her face. I told her we were parked in the back lot of a very large church, and I was speaking to thousands the next day. All she had to do was find a front door, and I'd meet her back at the trailer after services. I would probably be more nervous today than I was back then. I was riding a wave. I had a burning message, and I couldn't wait to deliver it. I would never have thought it then, but I would soon learn that this was another one of those off-the-trail assignments. It didn't even cross my mind at the time. I thought those days were long gone. I was wrong. How could I have gotten there for a whole day, if the Spirit of God had not put it all together?

In my best suit, I still looked like the poor cousin from the hills next to these people, and I knew it. The only equalizer I had was a powerful message, and that was all I needed. I had learned a hard lesson a while back. I had been speaking for the leader of the first Kentucky group, at the time. He was sitting on the stage as I spoke. It was the worst delivery I'd ever given. I was so intimidated by him that I had softened my points, and my message just fell on the floor. When I shared it with Ed later, he taught me a valuable lesson. He told me God could put anyone in any place at any time. There are places you can't get in, unless God puts you there. When there, you are God's man for the hour. That's the way I approached every meeting from then on. That never happened again, and it wasn't going to happen in Pasadena.

At exactly the appointed time, I opened that steel door on the landing behind the church. The only thing different than the day before was the fact that I walked between hundreds of cars to get there. When I opened the door, I stepped into a production scene in full motion. A real model type took my arm and walked me to a chair where a makeup person was waiting. Bam, Bam, that was over, and she had me by the arm again. This time she walked me over to a painted circle on the floor behind the curtains. She told me when a certain red light came on, I was to step forward to the next circle, and so on. Wow!

I don't remember what I preached that morning, but most likely it was my main message on missions, and what happened if we were not missionary. I remember the evening message very well. It was my second gun; Church membership, the baptism required to obtain it, and the price millions had paid when they had surrendered to it. Invitation time came and I couldn't believe my eyes. The camera lights were so bright that I couldn't see a quarter of the way back into the pews, but when I gave the invitation to surrender for baptism and church membership, the aisles filled with people as far back as I could see. I didn't think anything about it. I figured it was just a continued production. I thought it was like one of Billy Sunday's crusades, where hundreds of workers were assigned to start forward so that others might follow. I turned it over to the song leader when the camera lights went out. As instructed, I turned and walked out the same door, and we were out of the parking lot before any cars had even moved.

A pastor that had a soft spot for the very tough field of Japan invited us to park at his church and use his office and phones anytime we were in the area. We were not due to arrive at my buddy's church for a few days, so we decided to take this guy up on his offer. Back in the days before cell phones, if someone offered you a day or so to catch up on your phone work, you took it. I called Ed and made more plans about our Houston meeting and touched base with our new friends in Louisiana. I was working late when the pastor came in and told me they were holding a special meeting for his college students in the activity room. He said a pretty good speaker was addressing them that night and we were welcome to attend. Out of respect for his offer, we accepted the invitation.

The wife and I were sitting up in the balcony in the dark when the speaker was announced. I don't remember anything about his dissertation, except for one particular illustration. He spoke of the power of the spirit, regardless of who was in the pulpit. I sat there in a daze as he told them about some unknown missionary that had spoken for him last Sunday. Over thirty souls had given their hearts to Christ, and many more had submitted for baptism. Now I use the same illustration, only in reverse. I tell people what can happen when a stranger shows up with a Spirit-given message and presents it to a church full of Spirit-prepared people. My wife had no idea who he was referring to. She had never met him and never would. We went out the back door and he went out the front.

'Wow!' I thought to myself as we headed east. What if that guy had as great a percentage of his T.V. audience prepared for that message as he did in his congregation? I had come out there to find a place to put our pastor and our new church. I believe that was accomplished. I think the whole thing was a sort of personal endorsement. I was only getting Ed and his top man out of Kentucky to save the work in Paducah. I knew Tri-city Baptist Church, as I named it, was only going to serve as the foundation for our mission to Japan. It served just fine. No one could have done a better job for us. But I knew that as good as this man was at what he did, he was not going to win as many souls in all his existence as God had given us in the process of setting it up. Even though the church itself would not incorporate more than another family or two, in this small sense, God had made its coming a bit of a blessing to Texas. Not that Ed did nothing for the state. Even though he didn't build a thriving work, he maintained a faithful hospital ministry that no doubt touched many.

Ed and his deacon established the church in a nice little building that they could rent on Sunday and Wednesday nights. I believe they had use of the office equipment, and Ed put it to very good use. Ed had three hard working boys who began a landscaping company to support the church. Deacon Kirk got a good job as well. With their generosity, the pastor was free to write and publish a pretty nice paper. Through his publications, he became one of the best known pastors in Texas. That sure didn't hurt my work. He was a really good writer and solid on New Testament church and Missions. All I had to do was send him my monthly letter and he would put it out all across the country. His paper got us invited to about every decent missions conference. No one had to wonder what we believed.

Changing your sending church is a real touchy subject among pastors, but Ed handled it perfectly. I don't think we lost any support over our change of address. Ed set up our mission account and took care of everything. He sent us a monthly report and a bank statement along with a big book of checks. We had to worry about nothing more than traveling and preaching. I doubt if any missionary family ever had a better set up.

Acts 1:8

But ye shall receive power, after that the Holy Ghost is come upon you: and ye shall be witnesses unto me both in Jerusalem, and in all Judaea, and in Samaria, and unto the uttermost part of the earth.

Chapter 14
Louisiana and Our Final Sweep

By the time we got to Louisiana, we were rock stars. They loved my pastor, Ed. He'd kept them up on everything through his now popular publication. They also loved Brother Eddie like family. Everyone knew by now that we would be working together in Okinawa. Our kids were in constant communication with the girls they had met at camp. Our arrival was like a home coming. Monroe was our first stop. It was also the first time I ever smelled a paper mill up close. That is an experience you'll never forget. I smelled that smell once in awhile back on Dover Air Force Base, but none of us knew what it was. Since we only smelled it once in awhile, we had decided it was a crematory.

Rock Hill Baptist Church was our destination. The pastor and several of his people were waiting in the parking lot. They were really great people. The pastor, like so many of these guys, worked full time at a secular job. He was a bank manager. His wife was a doll of a stay-at-home mom. She was also a die-hard Saints fan, the only one I ever met. His one girl and two boys could have been models. We set up the fifth-wheel at the church and they took us home for supper. We liked living in our own place and seldom ever accepted accommodations elsewhere. This was different. We didn't want to be anywhere but where they were. There was no question that they wanted you in their home for as long as you would stay. We didn't just like these people or love them in Christ; we just loved these people, period. The pastor's wife was Eddie's wife's best friend. Eddie's wife had been my wife's best friend for two years when we were in mainland Japan. They fit like peas in a pod. Besides being hard headed preacher's wives, they had something else in common. I would not learn about that for many years. Eddie shared it with me after Sue Garlington died.

We were not just missionaries on our way to the field. We had been in the ministry for years. We were way past the stage where you were not sure how you should act or talk around other people in full time service.

The only time we got nervous about that stuff was when a member of their church dropped in for a visit. In that case, we just played off the pastor. If he was really comfortable being his self around them, then we could be as well. Not only do other ministers recognize this, they also know they can relax with you. They can talk with you about things they dare not mention around those they have been called to lead. I had been in this business for years as field rep for the college. It was new to my wife, but she was a natural. She could read any situation and tell me up front whether to be reserved or relaxed. With these people, we could relax for the first time since we had left the ranch in Kentucky.

Eddie and I did not agree on a few things, but we had settled one thing a long time ago. We would never have to worry about each other. Our differences with each other would remain with each other and no one else. As far as I know, it has remained such for forty years. We have been through a few battles; when it would have been beneficial to point fingers at each other. But that never happened. This pastor in Monroe and his wife were another Eddie and Neva. About ten years later, something would happen that puts this preacher out on a limb, all alone until my wife and I would get there. I'd call him one of four people in our lives that I would allow the same access to my soul as has Jesus. What a way to begin our tour of this great state.

We would just sit and talk for hours. He pretty much briefed me on everyone we were going to meet. I guess if this group had any particular preacher that had any more influence than anyone else, this was the guy. He finally got around to asking me about a subject I really wanted to talk about; I just didn't want to be the one to bring it up. I had never heard any teaching on the rapture other than pre-tribulation. I was really shocked when I heard that none of these guys believed in a pre-trib rapture. Eddie had tipped me off when he realized I was going to be preaching for most all of them. He assured me that my accepted interpretation would not cause me any difficulty. That was as long as their interpretation was no big deal to me. I was schooled in pre-trib, and never knew any other possibility. Eddie never taught me, as far as I can remember. Only thing I can think is that he taught me enough to question the normally followed teaching of dispensationalism. My strong point was never escatology, but dispensationalism still never hit home with me. It must have been the solid foundation that Eddie did teach me.

When Leonard Garlington realized I was not as closed-minded as the normal pre-trib preacher, he was thrilled. The funny thing about post-trib philosophy is that it is proven with the exact same scriptures as the pre-trib philosophy. This is not a doctrinal issue. Don't confuse pre-trib with pre-millennium. That is a doctrinal issue. So I opened my mind and decided to begin praying for peace about the matter. The main reason I decided to even review my philosophy was because I was big on history. I learned that pre-trib was never taught or written; you couldn't even find a message on it until after the Scofield Bible was published. It was over this issue that his co-writers had abandoned the project. Leonard gave me everything I needed to begin my study and told me the pastor at Dry Prong, just north of Alexandria, was the best teacher on the subject. We would get down there after we preached for Leonard's brother the following week.

I loved this state. It reminded me of Florida. Our clothes fit the weather I guess. We planned our deputation travels so that we would not have to carry bulky winter stuff. We planned to be in Florida by the heart of winter. We found it hard saying goodbye again, but my girls were excited about it. Chris knew a pastor's daughter in Pollock and Tonia and Mark had new friends in Dry Prong. There were no real highways to either one of these places. We had planned to speak at Pollock Sunday morning and head for Dry Prong for evening services. Bill Belcher was the pastor that would be waiting for us at Pollock. He said there was no way we could miss the place. It was the only building on the road for miles. Sure enough, out in the middle of a deserted stretch of two lane road, there it was.

It was miles from any town. It was just a little building on the right hand side of the highway. There was just enough room to get off the road. I had met Bill at the camp in Kentucky. I really had not formed any opinion of him. He spoke with an accent more common to a Texan than a Louisianan. He was a whole different category of preacher than Brother Leonard, but just as likable. He had married a German girl when he was in the Army. She also was just as different, but Cheryl hit it off with her before lunch was even served. We had to eat and run, but we knew we would be back soon. Our oldest daughter was staying there with her new friend. That was probably her first real friend since we had hit the road. She was ready for some serious girl talk. There was a big weekend outing planned for the end of the month, and we'd be back for that.

The Dry Prong church was an old church of about a hundred and fifty members. This place was like the little town where I grew up. Most kids went elsewhere for jobs after they graduated. These families had been around for generations. We did meet one family about our age, Dennis Korn and his wife Timmi. He was a son of a Deacon. He had come back home after college as a chemical engineer. He could work from almost anywhere, so he had come back home. He set up his office there for very little overhead. Timmi was a die-hard Mormon.

Anytime someone from the outside world came by, Dennis did his best to expose her to them. She was likeable enough, but raised as she was, it was not going to be an easy task to convert her to Christianity. Dennis had the right idea. Don't push her away as long as she is happy living his lifestyle and allowing the children to be raised Christian. After all, she was a Mormon when he had married her. We were very well accepted there as Eddie's new helpers. There was a sad part of our visit, however. We were introduced to a young couple that had put as much time on the mission trail as we had, but had just never made it. There is a real uneasy feeling when you run across people like that. We knew very well how close we came to giving up. We could imagine how they felt.

By then, our son Mark was in the early stages of puberty. The pastor had a daughter at the same stage. We spent the week parked beside their home. We didn't know for years that this would be the location of his first kiss. This was the guy Leonard told me had the best understanding of escatology, and he was right. My conflict with dispensationalism was the point of most of our conversations. I didn't solve my total dilemma with it right away, but he opened doors my prejudiced training had closed for years. Escatology was as clear to him as ecclesiology was to me. He gave me a book called "The Blessed Hope". It was this book that opened my wife's eyes upon the first reading. The puzzle didn't come together that quickly for me. I was determined to keep an open mind and study prayerfully about every aspect of the matter.

It was months before God gave me scriptures that supported the old teachings far more clearly than anything Scofield had interpreted for us.

I couldn't believe how much more sense the rest of prophesies made to me in the light of the old interpretation. What was equally unbelievable to me was how many preachers I had met that had come to the same conclusion. An old preacher told me he used to preach against anything that was not pre-trib. Then he got old and started informing himself on current events. Suddenly he wasn't so sure. I'm hearing it more and more these days. People better just keep an open mind. We can hope there are two separate events; the first being the rapture of the church with the meeting in the air. The second being Christ's return with his saints. But be prepared if it's one and the same. I can only find one event from the Old and New Testament. You'll have to come to your own conclusion. As long as the event is pre-millennial, though, it's doctrinally sound.

We had a really good time with the members of the old church. They had a big barbeque for us the day we were to head back up to Pollock. I can't remember if they voted to support us while we were there or if they were among the several that had already done so. But the cookout was to personally introduce us as their new missionary family. We couldn't help notice when we got to the church for the first time that our mission card and pictures were already in their mission display. Tonia and Mark were in no hurry to leave. They were assured by all, however, of the great time they were going to have camping at Green Lake. Even a couple families at the barbeque had already loaded their campers for the event. They told us they'd already be there waiting for Brother Belcher to bring us down to the lake.

We said our good-byes to the rest of the folks and headed back to the church at Pollock. The church out on the little highway in the middle of nowhere would be a better description. It was miles from the little town of Pollock. As promised, someone was waiting there to lead us to the pastor's home in the country. We followed diligently back miles of dirt roads leading through tall grass and timber lands. Finally, the narrow road ended at the site of a one story ranch home, built of logs. Large pecan trees towered above the home and the surrounding area. French moss hung from the tree tops, swinging gently in the breeze. They parked us under one of the trees nearest the house, and plugged us in. I thought, why set up and level everything? If we're leaving for the lake in the morning, it would be a waste of time. I was soon informed that getting our rig down to the lake was out of the realm of possibilities. What we had envisioned was nothing like we were about to experience. It was not a state park with camping facilities of any kind. The camper they were taking was mounted on an old, but very rugged, four-wheel drive four-door pickup.

Bill and I sat on the porch until after dark getting better acquainted while the women cleaned up the supper dishes and packed coolers for the camp out. We said good-night and retired to our camper. It was so quiet, you could hear yourself breathing. Occasionally a pecan would fall from the tree above us and strike our roof like a gun shot. Just about the time we got used to that, we were again awakened. This time I was sure it was a herd of hogs rooting under our trailer. I was unfamiliar with open range farming. They were hogs that were rounded up once a year. The young were tagged and some were harvested.

First thing in the morning, we awoke to the sound of a truck with loud mufflers. Bill's oldest daughter's boyfriend showed up with his camp rig. It was just as rugged as Bills. This boy was a piece of work. He was raised a Cajun from the south and for the first couple days I couldn't understand anything he said. I knew from what I could hear from Bill that they were worried about my truck making it back up from the lake. They decided I should not take our truck. We should use the old brown suburban that was sitting by one of the out buildings. It didn't have four-wheel drive either, but if they had to push it or pull it, they wouldn't have to be as careful. Our pickup was a late seventies model. As far as I could tell, nothing that new had made its way this deep into the woods yet. I was glad to accept the offer.

They put us in the old Suburban, arranged for us to be between them, and we headed for the lake. There were no signs telling you anything about a lake. We just came to a dirt trail going through the woods and we took it. The trail snaked back and forth between the trees. Some were so close, we had to try a couple times to get through. The farther down we drove, the wetter the road appeared. Finally we were driving through large areas of standing water. I was already thinking of getting back up this hill. I was sliding on the way down. Getting a two-wheel drive back up this crooked little path was going to be an experience.

At last, we reached the bottom. The grass was about knee deep. The trees very large; we were in a swamp. 'Where's the lake?', came to mind. Just when I was convinced that no one else was stupid enough to bring a vehicle down here, we turned into a little opening. It was jam packed with campers. It was the Clampets family reunion. Old trucks with mostly homemade campers on them were parked all around the perimeter of the clearing. Between them were little shelters made of tarps strung between the trees.

A lot of really nice people sauntered over and greeted us. I didn't know these people well enough to joke with them. If I had, I would have asked them where the campground was located. I grew up on an old farm, too poor to raise an umbrella, but at least we had an outhouse. My oldest girl just stood in one little spot. She reminded me of a queen waiting for her bearers to place her on a chair and transport her to someplace safe. Her girlfriend, however, was a true country girl. She came to the rescue and helped her assimilate. She had her walking around in no time. Brandon stuck pretty close to his mother, but Mark was off with the boys as soon as the greetings were complete.

The men were gathered over a large pot near a makeshift table, attached between a couple of trees. Something was cooking, but I couldn't identify it until one of the men said "Lets go get the fish for the gumbo." They headed off into the trees. In about thirty minutes, they reappeared. I wondered where the fish were. They had said they were going fishing when they had left. One of them asked how long they were going to fish. Someone answered "For another hour if the fishing's good." I didn't want to appear any dumber than I must have already appeared. I didn't ask how they were fishing when they were all standing here with me. I had a lot to learn about fishing in the swamps.

I heard a gunshot really close by, but I didn't see anyone. I looked so startled that Brother Bill said "Don't let that bother you. Your boy's getting me a squirrel for the gumbo." He had sent my boy, who had just had his first kiss yesterday, off into the swamp with a shotgun. Without looking too obvious, I slowly headed off in the direction of the shot. I didn't get far when I ran into a very proud little boy. He had a single barrel shot gun in one hand and a nice size Gray Squirrel in the other. His first shot ever, and he was bringing in the game. He handed it to the man that sent him out and requested another shell. I think Bill could tell from Mark's excitement that this was all new to him. He said, "No, I only need this one for now." Then he did something that ruined my appetite. At least for anything that was going to come out of that pot for the rest of the time we were there. I think he gutted the thing, I'm not sure. Then he pulled the hide off and threw it in the pot, head and all. That was it for me. I have eaten a lot of those things, but never with brains and eyeballs.

We sat around the fire and talked until nearly dark. Something out there towards what they called the lake was making a loud grunting sound. Mark asked what it was and someone said it was just an alligator. "Well, we better go see how good we fished before the gators get them," someone said. "Come on Mark, we got room for you and the preacher," as they handed me a lantern. We climbed into the boat and rowed into the dark. "Over here to the right we got one." We rowed over to a dead limb that had a blue plastic gismo attached to it. "Yeah, this one's gone off." He reached over and got the thing and reeled in a catfish. I think they called them jigs. We rowed around for about a half an hour collecting catfish and jigs.

We were almost back to where we launched. I saw a dog in my lantern light just as it jumped in and started swimming for the boat. Mark heard the splash and turned to see something headed for us in the water. He jumped on my lap so fast we nearly capsized that little flat bottom row boat. "Alligator! alligator!" was all he could say. I just held him tighter. I couldn't get enough composure to assure him it was just Bill's dog.

I managed to save a couple of the fish from the brain brewing in the pot. That was my supper. I didn't share what I knew about the gumbo with the rest of the family. They enjoyed it, and accepted the fact that I really just wanted fresh fish tonight. The next day, we let Mark venture off with another single shot, while the rest of us watched Bill catch armadillos. We had a lot of good conversation, coffee, and goodies, but it was time to face facts. We had a good half days work ahead of us. We had to get out of here somehow. I don't even want to describe the events of that adventure. All I'm going to tell you is that there is now a new landmark on that trail. They named it the Jones hole.

We unpacked and played a game of Bible trivia. Then Bill informed me that tomorrow was the day they harvested a couple pigs from the herd that feeds off their land. I guess there's an unwritten agreement. If you permit the herd to graze your land all year and protect them from poachers and such, you may take a couple just before roundup. I said I didn't have a hunting license. Bill told me we weren't hunting; we were just preparing for our fall butchering. "I set this up while you're here because your daughter said you're a meat cutter," he told me. "I usually bring someone in for the job, but she said you would enjoy it." When I got up for breakfast, there was a .22 rifle setting at my door and a note instructing me to shoot only sows, no boars. Just as I walked into the little thicket of what appeared to be crab apples, I heard a shot, followed by another. Then I heard Brother Bill yell that we'd gotten our limit. I walked back to my camper after a hard day in the field and prepared to skin and butcher.

When I was a kid, we would fill a 55 gallon drum half full of water and bring it to a boil. Then we would put the hog in the drum for a few minutes, pull it out, and begin to scrape the hair off the hide. That's not how they do it today. We hung it up and cut one inch strips the length of the hog with a carpet knife. Then we took a pair of pliers and pulled that strip off and put it in a bucket. I don't know what they did with them after that. I know that before I had the butchering done, we were eating fried pork rhines.

Bill's oldest girl was assigned to help me. When I opened the hog to remove the innards, she began to cry. I thought I must have underestimated this girl. I thought she was a real farm girl. Then I saw what she was crying about. She pulled thirteen piglets out one by one. "Oh, my babies, my babies!" she cried. "Another week, and they would have been playing in my yard. Look daddy, she's way out of season." He shook his head and said, "Don't tell your mother." I quartered the hogs and sent them to the outside fridge to cool. I'd butcher tomorrow.

After a full day of cutting and wrapping, we retired to the deck behind the house. There were buckets of pecans still in the shell from the large tree over our head. We learned to open them and dined on nuts and pork rhines until it was time to turn in. The next day we were going to the field for real game. They took me to Pollock to purchase a hunting license, and then we headed out for the fields/swamps for deer. This proved to be much harder and less rewarding than the hog hunt. We traveled in pickups over field after field, looking to get ahead of the main group of hunters from the cities that hunt here every year. We never saw a deer.

This was not Pennsylvania, where there are no less than twenty five deer per cultivated acre. I got bored very soon and just rode in the bed of the truck. The one thing I remember the most was listening to the Cajun boy talking. I couldn't understand most of what he said. He kept saying "my uncle"; it just didn't fit. Finally, I figured out he was talking to Bill's oldest boy, Michael. Yeah, that's his name in Cajun.

At breakfast, Bill asked if I wanted to help him out with a job he lucked into. "We won't have to go into the deep woods," he said. "Today we'll be in a pasture field. A farmer is giving me all his trees just for taking them down. He wants the shade off his pasture. I'll cut and load, you run the skidder." Okay; whatever that is. I can't describe a skidder. It is something made from an old truck with no body. It has a bunch of gears that work the chains that are draped around the fallen tree. I drug them over to the log truck. When we were done, Bill used the boom, mounted on the truck, and loaded them up. About half of the trees weere small, only about eight or nine inches in diameter. We hauled the trees to a rail station in Pollock. Bill said he would take the logs and give me the pulp. I don't know what he got for the logs, but I got over three hundred dollars for the small stuff. Not bad for a days work in those days. It made the bills for the month and gave Mom and I a night out. We needed a night in a motel away from the kids once in awhile.

I was impressed with logging. He said I could go into the big woods with him if I wanted to see the normal routine of logging. I thought we would be in there ourselves, but I was wrong. The entire forest was to be cleared because of a tree killing blight. There were several crews getting ready to go to work when we arrived. The men finished their coffee and all the saws where sharpened and fueled. Then every one just walked to the nearest tree and started falling them as fast as they could. There was so much noise you could not have heard someone yell "timber" if your life depended on it; and it did. I just stood back and watched.

Then about ten o'clock, the noise just stopped. Men came out and got their lunch pails and sat down together on the logs. The subject I heard the most was how well they could lay down a tree. They said they could lay a tree exactly where they wanted it. I remember one guy saying to another, "You sit your lunch bucket anywhere you want, and I'll fall the trunk close enough to open the latches." During the noon break, another conversation broke out concerning one of the guy's vehicles. I heard one guy say, "I had one just like it 'til I falled a tree on it." I must have heard that statement three or four times by the end of the day. I guess this precision tree dropping isn't a hundred percent. But they were pretty good. No one got killed all day. As much as we loved preaching in Louisiana, we knew we had to head south before the weather turned really cold. We had only one contact in Florida that was associated with our new group. I had several old friends from my college days that had considerable influence with the Florida group of independents, however. We could stay busy for the hard part of the winter.

We had some good visits in Florida, and some bad visits. We were asked to leave the church property of one conference we attended because someone saw my girls wearing shorts. Another bad experience happened when we stopped at a church that Dr. Milton had told me to visit. I had called the pastor's office, but he wasn't in. I had told his secretary that we were headed in their direction anyway. I told her we would appreciate it if we could park on the church property, whether the pastor elected to have me speak or not. At least we would have a place to worship Sunday morning. That was before there were cellular phones. I just wanted a place to park for the evening. I told her to tell the pastor I would preach if he wanted me to. If not, no problem. She said okay.

We were on our way to Dr. Milton's home church, as we had a solid preaching date there. The church we were looking to park at was in the middle of nowhere and a safe place to spend the night. We pulled into the drive just after dark. I pulled into the grass out of the way. The next morning, a man came over to the camper and introduced himself as the head deacon. I filled him in on our conversation with the church secretary and told him we would just plan on attending services. He said, "Oh no, I'll make sure the pastor knows that missionaries are here, and we'll have you speak for us, I'm sure". As we were getting dressed, we heard someone pounding on the door. It was the pastor. He was a short stocky guy with fire in his eyes. He blessed me out and told me to get off the property.

I filled him in, just in case he had some misunderstanding. I told him we would be perfectly happy just to attend services. He told us in no uncertain terms that we were not welcome. We were shocked, but we complied. As we pulled out, I noticed he was following us in his car. We concluded that something was going on that we had no idea about. He followed us for miles before he turned around. That was weird.

The rest of our engagements were normal. We finally made it to Miami, which was our main purpose for coming to the state. Brother Hank Hahn was building a very impressive work in a place called the Redlands. He was one of the leaders of the group that had first left the campus back in PA. He was the only one of that group with which we had maintained communication. Actually, it was our daughters that had kept the lines of communication open. He agreed that they had done it all very poorly, and that they should have never gone to the newspapers. He also led his new work to take us on for three hundred dollars a month. That tied them with the Sharps, our old bosses from the Tupperware distributor in Springfield, Missouri. That also put us very close to our final goal and made our current obligations much easier to meet.

He had us park out in an orchard that belonged to one of his members. I remember how cold it got. It was a year that a lot of fruit was lost to frost. There were men working all night with smudge pots to save what they could. Somehow they found time to lay bales of straw all around the bottom of our camper to keep our water from freezing up as well. In the morning, Hank led us to a place we could use for our base of operations for the next month or so.

*I spoke in churches as far north as Orlando. We picked up some offerings that helped out with current expenses, but no additional monthly mission support. We had to spend the coldest of the winter there anyway, and we were with some really wonderful people. Deer season was about to open in Pennsylvania, and it would be my last chance to hunt for at least the next four years. My oldest daughter, Chris, and I decided we would make the drive. A few of the members said they wanted to hunt with us. We drove straight through from Florida to PA. The other members that wanted to hunt with us flew up and met us for opening day. I drove around to some old farms after dark, spotting the fields for a buck. I found an old apple orchard with two buck lying under the trees. Opening day, just before dawn, I put my daughter at the woods line, between the field and the orchard. It was the shortest path from the orchard to cover. I figured it was the most likely path a deer would take at first light. Bob Starks and one other member of Hank's church had joined us. I put them farther back along the woods line. I went back to the dirt road to watch for anything that might cross the road.

It began to rain just about daylight. I was dressed for snow, but it didn't turn to snow for several hours. I had to go down into the woods and find cover under a large pine tree. I no sooner got settled when I heard a single shot, then three more in rapid succession. I couldn't get direction with one shot, but with the following three, I was sure they came from the direction of the orchard. I sat there for about fifteen minutes before I saw someone walking down the road. It was my daughter. She said, "I got a really nice nine point Dad." She had broken its back with one shot. The other three shots were Bob putting it out of its misery. I had taken a lot of deer in my life, but this was the biggest any of my family had ever bagged. I dressed it, we drug it to the road, and loaded it on the pickup. We drove into town to the newspaper office for pictures. My oldest sister was the office manager and she made sure those pictures made the paper. So we had a successful hunt and headed back to the family in the camper parked in the fruit orchard.

Soon the weather was nice enough to travel again. We said our goodbyes and headed north. We backtracked through Louisiana for our final farewells, and then on up to Kentucky for more of the same. When I preached at Mount Hebron, the pastor told the people that this was our last visit before our leaving for the field. It was common practice for them to add an additional thousand dollars to my offering from the mission fund. That church consisted of mostly one main family. It was out in the country, so most were farmers. Eastern Kentucky was the only place in the world where burly tobacco was grown. It was blended into all other tobaccos that were used for making cigarettes. If you've ever smoked a foreign-made cigarette, you know why everyone wants American- made.

Eastern Kentucky was the reason for it. No matter the size of the farm, it was evaluated by the tobacco acreage allotment, which was, in turn, set by the government. Grand Daddy Brogel was the patriarch of this huge family work, and he had been raising tobacco from a child. He had taught the family the value of the crop, and the best methods of production and marketing. He loved tobacco, even though he didn't use it, as far as I know. He had passed this love and care down for generations, and now they were probably the most successful in the business. He also taught them to return their blessings accordingly. Harvest was a big festival each year, ending with their presenting the portion promised to the church for missions. The pastor told me that this small church gave about sixty thousand a year in just mission offerings.

Most people don't know that the three main products of Colonial America were tobacco, whiskey, and slave trade. Lucky for a lot of missionaries, the best tobacco growers in America are Christians. Lucky for all of Black Americans, regardless of the plight of their ancestors, they were not born in the poverty of North Africa, where slavery still exists. Speaking of whiskey, we headed north again to Western Pennsylvania. In the hills west of Pittsburgh lay the heart of corn liquor production. It was barreled and sent down the Allegheny River to the Ohio River, and eventually wound up in French-controlled New Orleans. There it was put on sailing ships that were headed back to Europe. The hill-people that lived west of the Monongahela River had no military protection from the Indians. They also had little say in government. When the US tried to tax their products, we had the famous Whiskey Rebellion. You need to read about it. It was the last time George Washington led an army.

For one final time, the camper was parked in the grass beside the lane on my uncle's farm. Old Uncle Ray was slowing down. His heart wasn't that strong anymore. I walked out of the trailer to find him sitting on the step one time, just watching my door. He said he didn't want to wake me, but he needed to get to the emergency room as fast as I could get him there. The doctor told me he would never be what he once was, but if he took care of himself, he could live awhile longer. I had pretty much lived on that farm since I was eleven years old. It was more of a home to me than my folk's house in town. For the next couple of weeks, however, I'd be spending as much time in town as on the farm. My Dad was almost bed-ridden by then. We would have had to come back here, even if it hadn't already been in our plans.

Old Dad had used the favorite product of those hills really hard most of his life. Other men, older than Dad, had used it just as heavy, but the difference was Dad wouldn't eat. Mom had a hospital bed set up in the living room and an apparatus with a crank on it to lift Dad up so she could put a bed pan under him. Dad had been independent all his life. He couldn't stand a bum. That made this a real hard time for him. It was only a day or two later that Mom called the farm and told me to come to the house. Dad was sleeping with just a sheet over him. She pulled the sheet from over his left leg for me to see that it was solid black and swollen. She told me she was just going to let him die right there, because he didn't like hospitals.

She didn't know what was ahead. A man with a heart as strong as a bull dies slowly, a little at a time. The next day she called me from the hospital. She said she couldn't handle him anymore. He had become delirious, acting as though he were on a train with his crew. He was shouting for them to help him with a train jack, whatever that was. She said she couldn't do anything but call an ambulance. Dad had never heard me preach, so I thought I'd take some tapes and a recorder to his room. Mom said he listened to every one of them. We never got a chance to talk about them. The night he died was really sad. He was in and out of reality. Once he asked me how much money I needed. That hurt, but when I was a young man, he used to ask me that a lot. He had a good heart. I had a better job than he did by the time I was twenty-one, but I guess he never forgot the years when I struggled.

The last time I went into his hospital room, he reached up, grabbed my shirt, and felt my pocket for cigarettes. "Dad, you know I don't smoke," I said. Then he pulled me to his face and said "w-h-i-s-k-e-y". That was the last word he ever spoke to me. Mom was letting him have a bottle in the house the last year of his life. She would have saved a lot of money if she had always let him drink it at home, because at home, she was cutting it with water. She had asked the bar manager at the Eagles Club to do the same there, but he told her that he could go to jail if he got caught. She just didn't want Dad to notice the difference.

Dad never let on that he knew it was watered down. He probably figured whisky and water was better than no whisky when he wasn't able to get to the club anymore. Mom's pastor pulled me aside after the funeral. He said he had talked to Dad about my tapes beside his bed and that Dad had let him lead him in a salvation prayer. He said he had made him pray out loud and he believed he was serious. Dad was always very respectful to ministers that visited the house, but I don't think he would have prayed that prayer out of respect. Shortly after that, I made the final arrangements for our trip to Colorado. I put everything else behind me, where it would stay for many years. I walked into the house to check on Mom the night before we pulled out. When I opened the back door, I heard Dad say, "Is that you son". I almost answered. Many years later, my sister told me the same thing had happened to her. I told her I'd heard him too.

This would be our last trip across the states. We didn't know that at the time, but we did know that it was our best trip yet. We no longer had to have appointments to speak at every service we could just to make expenses. It was almost like going on a year long vacation to tour America. We knew where we were going, and we knew we were invited. That made a world of difference in our attitudes. Living in a thirty-one foot trailer with a family of six requires a good attitude on everyone's part. We had it down to a science by then. Everybody knew their responsibilities. Everyone knew the inconveniences were not in vain. We were going to the mission field; it was fun. We could afford to park in any camp. No more truck stops. We could eat in a restaurant once in awhile. Cheryl and I, when camped in a really safe camp, could spend an occasional night in a motel room.

I didn't have to pace our driving any more. There were no more seven or eight hundred mile days, just to make a mid-week meeting we couldn't afford to miss. We could pick any of the camps along the way, and set up before dark. By the time I had placed the trailer on the pull-through pad, Mark had the water, electric, and sewer hooked up. Chris had the inside ready to start supper. Tonia was off checking out the camp facilities by the time I had the truck cooled and shut down. If Tonia came back and asked me to light the water heater, we knew she did not approve of the showers. If she just came back and put on her bathing suit, we knew the pool was heated.

If she was in a little bit of a hurry, and wasn't getting little Brandon ready to go with her, we knew there were some fellow travelers with not bad looking young sons already at the pool. Once in awhile, she would come back and challenge me to a race. It was then we knew that she had gained the attention of someone near her age. She couldn't beat me, but she was the only one in the family that could make me swim really hard. She had already completed Jr. lifesaving courses, and was definitely an impressive swimmer. I always accommodated her, because I enjoyed showing off her skills. We were home schooling, so that was as close as we got to a competitive sports program with an audience.

Matthew 5:18

For verily I say unto you, till Heaven and earth pass, one jot or one tittle shall in no wise pass from the law, till all be fulfilled.

Dover Air Force Base
Dover, Delaware - 1964.

Cheryl's High School graduation picture.

July 24, 1964
Our wedding reception at Cheryl's parents home in Delaware.

Just kids ....

*Left to Right
Cheryl, her father, her mother,
my mother holding Chris (our oldest), my dad, me
1965.*

Cheryl's parents on left. Mine on right. Around 1969.

My C-130 in Tachikawa, Japan - 1966.

Cheryl' visiting our son Timmy's grave at Gettysburg National Cemetery.

My teammates at my 2nd job after USAF - 1969.

19 years old.

My dad with my airplane - 1975.

Our family while on deputation - a chilly day.

Refueling while on deputation. The 31' trailer was our home for two years while we raised enough support to go to Japan.

Me, Brandon - our youngest boy and Bro. Sullivan - 1982. Okinawa, Japan. We made it!

Preparing for my sermon in my new office in Okinawa

Our English church service in Okinawa - 1983

Our Japanese church in Okinawa around 1983. The only Americans were Cheryl, our four children and Eddys wife and daughter

Baptizing a young Airman, Mike Thornton in a cove in Okinawa

We got many laughs at the Japanese road signs!

One of many trips to other islands with young GI's. Left to right - Brandon (3 years old), Gary, Bro. Ed Sullivan, me, Mike and Mark (13 years old), and Lenny (kneeling). Notice the car door being loaded. Guess they could roll the window down if it got too hot!

Cheryl at 45 just prior to moving to Arizona.

Our retreat in Punxsutawney - Great sign, huh?

My ride on the international Richard Petty tour - 1995.

On the road with Richard Petty's car. Left to right - Lawrence, me, Cheryl and Chucky who passed away 2010.

Me, Mark and Cheryl at Goldfield - 1996. Notice no Church on the Mount yet ... we didn't even know it was coming yet.

Baptizing our youngest son Brandon in Arizona - 1995.

Brandon just out of Coast Gurad boot camp - 1998.

1982 - the plane I was crew chief on for four years in USAF - found it in a graveyard in Tucson, AZ!

Bob Schoose, Mayor of Goldfield and I signing the contract for the Church at the Mount.

The Church at the Mount!

Our Arizona based family - three children and a nephew with their spouses and children. From Goldfield at the base of the Superstitions.

Living Victoriously!

Chapter 15
West for the Cleanup

There was only one more detail to complete before leaving my home town for the west. I had a neighbor when I was in grade school named Bob. We had walked to school together when he was in 6th grade and I was in 4th grade. Then we walked to school together when he was in 6th and I was in 5th; and again when we were both in 6th. The year after that, we were both advanced to junior high. We walked together to that building as well. When we got there, I would go to my home room while he would get on the short bus and go elsewhere. When classes were over, he would be waiting for me on the corner and we would walk home together.

I made many decisions for him and never hurt him. By the time we were young men, we had two separate sets of friends. He was a drummer in a small band and I ran with the FFA (Future Farmers of America) boys. The two groups never socialized together, yet we found time for each other at either his house or mine. At least once a week, we would sit on the porch and talk about nothing. After I got my driver's license, I paid a visit to another old neighbor. He was then a sergeant at the state police barracks. We made a deal. I would teach Bob to drive and he would take care of the drivers test. He knew Bob couldn't read. Our dads had never had cars, and there wasn't anyone else that had offered to help. He told me if I could get him to pass the driving part, he'd get him through the written. Say what you like about small towns. Back in the day, if you were courteous and kept your nose clean, you could be mayor.

Our school buddies went their own ways and I went into the service. Before I met my wife and got stationed overseas, my service buddies would come home with me when we had time off. The base was only about a six hour drive. Bob would see my car and stop in to visit us wherever we were. He never tried to engage in conversation, but it was clear to everyone that we were closer than brothers. No one treated him with disrespect. In return, he made sure no one's glass was ever empty; if anyone needed anything that he could provide, they'd get it.

It was about that time that I met my wife and brought her to Punxsy. There wasn't much to do in the little town for a city girl. The movie houses and the drive-in had all closed. People had to go out of town for any serious shopping. I know they made a movie called Groundhog Day, but it wasn't filmed anywhere near Punxsy. So I decided to create a little entertainment for her. I got a bed sheet from the house and gave it to Bob. I told him I'd bring Cheryl up to the old Grub Cemetery on my bike. I told him to hide down in the middle and wait for us to come up around the drive and park at the top. I made up some story about a ghost. Bob could hear us driving up the long lane. In those days there wasn't a house in sight. It was dark, and on a still moonless night, you could hear yourself breathing. When I turned the bike off, the silence was deafening. We sat on the bike looking down the hill where I had told Bob to appear briefly and then hide again until after we had left. I kept looking but nothing appeared. All of a sudden, she turned and looked up the hill behind us where she had heard a twig snap. She let out a blood curdling scream that scared both Bob and I nearly to death. He stumbled to the ground with a thud. He wasn't supposed to be up there behind us, but then he never was very good with directions. I never even saw him, but I didn't have to act scared. We got out of there with her squeezing the life out of me.

She started the rumor that lasts to this day. Just so she didn't sound like a fool to everyone, I arranged for a few more reenactments. One night my brother-in-law took his new fangled Polaroid with him to see the now-famous ghost. He stood there in the dark lifting the thing to his face every few seconds. My buddy, Mike Ishman, lived on a farm about a mile away. He lugged a heavy log chain all the way to the cemetery. He told me that when he had held it up to rattle it, the weight of the chain had pulled him over the cliff, and he rolled clear to the bottom of Eberhart's hollow. Just before his fall, he appeared through the darkness right in front of my brother-in-law, who had been lifting his camera every other second. He froze with the camera still hanging from his neck. "He saw me," Mike later told me excitedly. I told him the rest of the story. He said it was worth all that work, and we laughed about it every time we met.

I felt so sorry for my brother-in-law that I set up an act he couldn't miss. I got Little Bill Pyles to run through the tombstones about fifty yards from where we would be standing. As he ran through the dark, he pulled the sheet off and tucked it under his dark colored shirt. Just as it was disappearing, Jerry got his shot. All you could see was the reflection of the sheet that appeared as a triangle. I had thirty days before I had to ship out for Japan. Old George McCown always knew when the moon would be out. When I was a kid, he would plan our night horseback rides for moonlit nights. I got him to schedule my moonless evenings for my ghost rides.

Rumors travel fast in a small town. One night, there must have been twenty cars parked along the lane, and that got worse by the week. One night a reporter from Pittsburgh was there with all his fancy gear. I didn't have a ghost lined up that night. I only took Cheryl up there to show her what she had started. Jim Shaffer walked up to me that night and I noticed he had a pistol in his belt. I said, "There's no ghost tonight, Jim, but if you had shot the ghost last night, you would have been trying to kill Bill Pyles." He said he knew it was my prank. He asked me if I remembered where I had hid the original bed sheet. I recalled it was under his mother's porch steps. He assured me he wasn't going to shoot our ghost. I said, "You might not, but this is out of hand, and it's over". Years later, Cheryl told my mother that the ghost had been Bob, but Mom didn't believe her. Mom said, "Everybody knows it was a ghost, and Jerry even has a Polaroid of it." Anyway, that's the legend of the Ghost of Grub Cemetery.

Bob was the first ghost and my wife's first friend in Punxsy. When I shipped out, it was months before she could join me. She lived with my folks for the time being. Bob made sure she got everywhere she wanted to go and was never alone in our strange little town. He knew everyone and everyone knew him. He unintentionally earned his notoriety through the humble and respectable manner he displayed to everyone, from the town drunk to the mayor. Even when people made fun of him, he had a way of dealing with it that garnered even greater respect from decent folk.

Now Cheryl and I were preparing to leave the country again. She went to work contacting the right people and doing the foot work to get him on assistance and into a housing project before we left. We didn't know it at the time, but all the arrangements we made were in vain. Bob was never one to pass up an opportunity to work. One day he jumped on the back of the garbage tuck and helped out every day until they hired him for the summer. He lost everything we had set up for him and was living in his car by the time we would return. At least we left thinking we had done all we could do in return for his constant trust in us.

We had only one preacher associated with Eddies' group between us and Colorado that we had not visited yet. He was also the only one of the group that I had known longer than I'd known Eddie. I call him Deacon Gray. Years ago, when I had set out to find a Christian in my Squadron in Japan, I asked a sergeant if he knew anybody religious. He answered me with the name 'Deacon Gray'. This is the guy that introduced me to Eddie all those years ago. I hadn't seen him since he had left Japan. He was now a pastor in a small town in Kansas, and that became our next target.

We were pretty well equipped by that point. Somehow we managed to get Chris her driver's license. We acquired a little Datsun pickup somewhere with a cab on it. We took about a quarter ton of stuff out of the camper and carried it in the little truck. Having the little truck made it so we didn't have to unhook the fifth-wheel as much. If Mom and I wanted to leave the camp for a short time, we had wheels. And better yet, we could fit the whole family in both trucks, and go somewhere without dragging the house with us. The other kids would ride in the camper most of the time. Remember, they didn't have to as long their school work was done. It was legal to ride in a fifth-wheel camper, as long as you had an intercom system. Chris became the regular driver, and followed us with no problems until we got to Deacon Gray's house.

After driving in Kansas for hours and seeing nothing but corn, I became concerned about running out of gas. We were not on an interstate. I'm not sure if there was one in those days. I can't remember if Dodge City was the first town we stopped in or the last town, but that was the road we were on. We were headed for the western part of the state is all I can remember. Somewhere in the eastern part, I met a Christian and expressed my concern. I remember him leading us to an old garage and digging around a bunch of equipment until he found the answer to my problem. It was a large square steel tank with a hand pump mounted on the top. It fit perfectly behind my cab and in front of the fifth wheel. That gave us at least fifty gallons of reserve fuel. It made the open plains of Kansas, Western Washington, and Northern California a lot friendlier.

Pastor Gray introduced me to his congregation Sunday morning. He told them I was the guy that had beat on his barracks door at three in the morning looking for a Christian to talk to. I had no idea it had been that late, but I'm sure God had him in there just for that moment. We stayed in the pastor's house that night. His house was on a hillside. It might be the only hillside in Kansas for all I know. I was eating breakfast when Chris walked in with her head in her hands. She said, "Dad, I was turning the little truck around and I stalled it. It just ran backwards, and before I could stop it, I ran into the side of the big truck." That turned out to be a real blessing. Our next church was in Canyon City. There was a man in that church that owned a body shop. We would have only spent one day there, but as it turned out, we would spend a couple days locating, replacing, and painting the bed for our one ton.

This guy had a wife that can be put into a very narrow category. She found a kinship with my wife that would last for many years. They invited us to park on their property. They secured us a temporary vehicle and encouraged us to go sightseeing. We visited all the local sights including Pikes' Peak. We stood up there on the exact spot where the lovely lady had penned the words to 'America the Beautiful' from her horse and buggy. The next day they talked us into driving up Phantom Canyon, the original trail to Cripple Creek. That was my first ever gold mining ghost town. That was back before gambling had been approved for Colorado gold mining towns. At the time, almost nothing had changed from the days when the gold had run out and it had become a ghost town.

After miles of dirt road with switch-back after switch-back and forever up hill, we reached the top, over looking the tiny town. There were no trees left, if there had ever been any. We must have been close to the tree line up there. Rolling green hills surrounded the town. They were dotted with dirt mounds where miners had sought for treasure many years ago. We drove down the slight grade to the couple rows of wooden buildings. We shopped the little stores and just basked in reverie. We saw the world's biggest gold nugget; well the first one. We'd find one of them in just about every old ghost town we'd visit after that.

My wife was very comfortable with her new friend. I suggested she just relax a few days while Mark and I toured a couple other old ghost towns. We chose Leadville and Crete. I don't remember much about Leadville except that we visited the old place where some famous women had lived that had owned the lead mine. Face it, lead just isn't that interesting. Can you place some old prospector running out of the hills yelling, "Lead! I struck lead?" I don't know, maybe they did.

Now that I think about it, I can remember one of my first jobs working for John C. Dorsey in Riverdale, Maryland. We were melting lead and molding traps for kitchen sinks. They were to be installed in the new housing development in Toms River, New Jersey. I can also reflect on an old double-wide trailer for which I couldn't acquire a permit to move because its electrical wiring was lead instead of copper. So I guess lead was used for more than fishing sinkers. I always had a misconception about lead. I thought it was heavier and harder than gold. The bartender would put the gold piece to his mouth to test it with a bite. I thought if he could make an indentation in it, then it was gold. It was just the opposite. Gold is harder and heavier than lead. If I had been a bartender in the old west, I would have collected enough lead to open a plumbing and electrical shop.

I was really looking forward to our next stop. I had read about Slumgolian Pass leading up the mountain to Crete. It was named after a stew that the old timers used to make. Everything was just thrown in the pot. It resembled the tangled mess of trees, rocks, and brush that had to be traversed to reach the little town of Crete. Well, thank God there was a nice little dirt road cut out of the ridge running alongside the old pass. We reached the little town about an hour after leaving the hard road.

That place had some real history. We didn't see ten people in the whole town. The few we saw were into their livelihood. They had invested in this old ghost town. They told us it was off season. They said the cattlemen ran their herds up there all summer and had just driven them down the mountain the week before. They told us the famous saying 'The town that never sleeps' was given them over a hundred years ago. They said a handful of them were dedicated to maintaining the legend even through the off season. If we wanted to stay over, the saloon would be open all night. We had money for the first time since we had hit the road, but we still had not adopted the policy of spending it. Besides, the best boarding house in town reminded me of my bedroom at the farm I grew up on.

We had sleeping bags and a camper shell on our pickup. Besides, we still believed the saying that you should not sleep at that altitude if you were not going to spend several days there. We did our sightseeing and camped halfway down the mountain. When that place had been booming, it had become more than just a gold town. It was a real town, with women and children and businesses. The problem was they had had no law enforcement. The cattlemen had been using the mountain grass to graze their herds even before gold had built the town. Cattle were driven down the streets of the growing little town, destroying anything in their way.

The nearest city at the time was Denver. There was a law man there named Bat Masterson. The permanent residents raised enough money to entice him to come to Crete and clean the place up. Unlike Hollywood's portrayal, history tells us that Bat was a short stocky guy that had traveled by buckboard and was armed only with a rifle. His reputation as a lawman in Denver, however, was more than enough to fit the bill. All he had to do was show up and post the orders to respect the streets, the residents, and the businesses. As far as we know, he never fired a shot his whole time in Crete.

I'm not sure, but I think a reformed outlaw named Pat Garret replaced Bat. I read a sign marking the spot where Pat Garret rode off with Billy the Kid the last time Billy was seen alive. They were past friends, but there was no longer a place in Pat's new life for a guy like Billy. I also stood on a rock lying in the grass out in front of an old building that used to be a saloon. That stone marked the spot where Bob Ford was shot to death. They told me the barkeep had shot him with a double barrel shotgun when he had left the bar after bragging about killing Jessie James. I'm so glad we got to visit those places when they were old and run down, but virtually unchanged in time. We returned a little richer in history and having made memories the boy and I still share from time to time.

When we got back, the one ton pickup was finished and looking good. There isn't much rust on things you buy in the Rockies. The truck bed wasn't new, but it was as good as new. We hooked up and headed for Denver. I finally met the church that I had been baptized into on the mission field. We had a good time. They voted to support our mission, and we headed off for western Washington. We were just a little closer to our financial goal. I didn't care much for Denver, but sure was looking forward to seeing the Great Divide and points west.

My fifth-wheel was a northern-built camper and much heavier than the average trailer. It weighed eight-thousand pounds empty, and it sure wasn't empty. The one-ton Dodge with the big engine handled well up those mountains. Down the mountains was another problem we were about to learn about. We were on a big road as we crossed the Divide and started down the west side of the Rockies. I knew we were heavy, I just didn't know how the truck and trailer brakes were going to handle it. I kept the speed down as best I could without going too heavy on the brake pedal. At least that's what I thought, until I saw smoke coming from the wheels. I pulled it into a lower gear, but it was an automatic and that didn't help much. I got it stopped on the roadside and let the brakes cool for awhile before trying it again. I knew enough about these things to know that if they got any hotter, I'd lose them all together.

We tried it again with the same results. I barely got it stopped before I lost them. I was starting to get concerned. I knew the transmission wouldn't hold it back enough if I lost the brakes. We would gather too much speed to make the curves. I couldn't let it out of low and I was still heavy on the brakes. Just when it was looking like I might be days getting off that mountain, a car with emergency lights like a police car pulled us over. It was the mountain patrol. He told me to let it cool for about twenty minutes and he would be back to take us down. I thought he was going to send me a tractor trailer wrecker or something, but he came back in his car. He said, "I'll clear the way. Don't touch the brakes until you see my brake lights come on." He turned on his lights and off we went. He stayed in front of us no matter how fast we went.

We were up to about eighty-five when we came to the first real curve. My brakes were nice and cool after that speed, so I hit them pretty hard as we entered the curve. We had slowed to about fifty or sixty miles an hour when I saw his brake lights go out. It was slow enough apparently; we made the curve and let her go again. We did that about three times before we could see the bottom of the hill about ten miles straight ahead. I don't know how fast we were moving when the road started to level out. I just said thank God for the really good tires our brother had put on for us in Kentucky, and thank God for the Mountain Patrol. Those mountains were beautiful, but I was glad to be off of them. I was also glad there was only one range like them, and we wouldn't be coming back that way.

We had never seen such beautiful country. It made me wonder why anyone lived in places like western Pennsylvania. It's hard to describe the sky we saw out there. I grew up with what they call the lake effect. We had less sun days than Seattle. Well, we didn't have to be anywhere until we got there, so we stopped in many rest areas along the way. That was back in the days when it was safe and there were no prostitutes working them. I remember being parked in one of them when another nice fifth-wheel pulled in beside us. When I came out of the house, my wife was standing there talking to them. The lady was telling her everywhere they'd been and where they were headed. Cheryl said, "Yes, those were nice places. We're from out east ourselves. We wintered in Florida and did Disney World just before we left. We stayed in the same camp you stayed in." There was no question these people were affluent. It didn't take much to see that the lady was becoming annoyed with us.

We were considerably younger than they. To make things worse, her attempt to impress my wife had failed miserably. Finally, the lady could not contain herself any longer. She had been hinting for about five minutes for Cheryl to give her some justification for such liberty to travel. How could someone possibly stay on the road for two years? What about the children's schooling? I spoke up and told her my wife was licensed to home school because we didn't know how long we were going to travel. Then I went back in. "What's your husband doing, is he a writer or something," she asked. "Oh, he writes a little, but were mostly just visiting friends," Cheryl answered. It was clear Cheryl was having way too much fun.

Cheryl came in with a smile like I hadn't seen in awhile. I told her she wasn't being very nice. She said, "I didn't start it. The lady started out telling me we had a nice camper, but let me know hers was brand new. Then she started telling me about their elaborate travels. So I let her dig her own hole. She finally just very rudely demanded to know how we could afford such a life." Cheryl smiled that smile again. She said, "I told her we had a very wealthy Father." Well, she didn't lie, but I don't think I've ever seen that side of her, before or since.

The last place we camped before reaching our next meeting was a camp right on the eastern border of Washington. There was white ash all around the place. I can't remember how long it had been since Mt. Saint Helens had blown. It had been some time, though, and we were clear on the other side of the state. Where was the environmentalist that had let this happen? We contacted the little church that was waiting for us and got the final directions to the pastor's home. He was a big old guy; I think his name was Smith. There are many pastors I can't remember, but the really nice people made lasting impressions. This place was out in the country. I remember how dry it was. There were apple orchards everywhere. They craved fellowship. We caught them up on all the pastors they knew from out east. They wanted to know which churches they were preaching in now. We showed them pictures of their kids and told stories about our visits. They had not seen most of those guys since they had come out west. Some of them weren't even married when they had run together. It was always a fun time.

The few missionaries that worked with this little group of old friends were like the Pony Express. Remember, that was before cell phones and e-mail. People didn't keep up with each other like they do today. Remember long distance calls? You only made them if it was an emergency. I had what we called a long distance phone card. Making a call was a real ordeal. First, you would hook up in the park where you were going to spend the night. Then you would get your book out and see what phone number you had. If you only had the pastor's name, then it was most likely his home number. In that case, you figured out the time difference and waited until supper was over. Then you found the public phone booth and started the process.

First you dialed the main number on the phone card. After you got the connection (you didn't always get it on the first try), you dialed in your twenty or so digit membership code. Then you dialed the number you wanted to call and you prayed that it wasn't busy. There was no call waiting back then. "This is Brother Jones calling from Colorado for pastor so and so," is how it would start. Then you heard something like, "Turn that down mom, its long distance." You were treated sort of special. Even if it was a day call to a church office, no one ever said "can you hold." If I'd get back to the camper in less than fifteen minutes, the wife would automatically assume I couldn't get through. If I'd get back in less than an hour, she would ask if I got through and if everything was alright.

Just like the rest of the bunch, the Smiths wanted us to preach a week of meetings. I had decided early in the game that I was not going to do that. Spend one good evening with the pastor, then give your one best message when you preach. Then there was usually a pot-luck after church. After the meal, a graceful departure worked the best for me. I could easily do a week with men like Brother Garlington or Brother Bill. Don't do it with someone you've never met or at least discussed at length with someone you really trust. Don't give the devil opportunity to set you up. If you talk too much, you're going to hit on something you'll wish had never come up. Besides, people have habits that are perfectly normal for them and those that are close to them. They might be uncomfortable for someone else.

I'll give you a for instance. When I was working with the missionaries at the college, I was called into Fred's office for a chat about a pastor in Kentucky. "What kind of guy is this preacher you hooked Ennis up with?" Fred asked. Ennis was our missionary to South Africa. I told him he was very legalistic. I had never heard him preach without bringing up how women should dress. He had a real hang up about ladies wearing pants. "What's wrong?" I asked. I figured he'd found something out about Ennis that he didn't like and I was being called in for some damage control. It was the other way around.

This old guy had taken a shine to Ennis. He had led his church to support him and even allowed him to park his motor home at his house. Ennis discovered the old guy had a smoking room out back that he would retire to from time to time. Ennis wanted to refuse the support because of it. He asked me what I thought about it. I asked if the guy had cross-dressed while he was smoking. Fred said, "My thoughts exactly."

Make it clear that our relationships are not to be based on self righteousness. See what I mean? We would have sat out there in the smoking room with the old guy, but to Ennis, it was a test of fellowship. Come to think of it, Fred would have sat out there with him if he did cross dress. But at the time I didn't know that.

Our next stop was an interesting place I'd never heard of; Fossil, Oregon. We were still on the dry side of the mountains. This guy was a different sort. He should have been a missionary in northern Alaska. I broke my own rule, and went in too far in advance of my speaking engagement. This place was so far from anywhere that we didn't have any choice. The only thing I remember about that tiny place was that no matter where you looked on the ground, there were layers of seashell fossils. That was entertaining for about five minutes. It might be a little confusing to someone that went to public school and didn't believe in the Great Flood. There we were, thousands of feet above sea level, walking on ocean fish. Our kids were raised with the truth, so this fact was no scientific enigma.

The next morning, the pastor asked me if I wanted to see how he supplemented his income. He took me up in the mountains and we sat for hours looking down into the valley below. I saw a herd of deer cross through. I knew from the gun he was holding that he wasn't looking for deer. It was a very long range varmint rifle. He was waiting for coyotes. Back when sane people ran the wildlife department, they paid you a bounty for turning in their ears. Now we're overrun with the useless game killers. On the way back, he saw a dead porcupine on the road. We pulled over. He said, "I'll bet you didn't know they have valuable fur on them." He was right. I watched him fill a bag with the stuff as he pulled it out from between the quills. His day wasn't a total loss, but my whole trip was. I got a nasty letter from him some time later. I have no idea what he was talking about.

Soon after that, we were going back into Washington and heading for the coast. There was one little church in the Seattle area waiting for us. After that, our Northwest run would be completed. I think the man's name was Ford, but I'm not sure. He was a nice guy though. I can remember sitting in his living room after I preached. He was leaning back in his Lazy Boy and he quietly began to bare his heart. I had preached the message I believe God had sent me to preach to these little old churches. It was titled 'What happens if we're not missionary.' When I left his house, I felt he was just done. He was a really good man that was just heartbroken over the condition of his church. I want to find him in the millennium and take a long ride on our horses together.

I never heard him preach, but that man was a pastor. I never knew anyone for that short of time, yet felt a bond that was almost fatherly. There was something I wanted to say, but I didn't have the liberty of the Spirit. I was not going to give advice to a senior pastor that had just sat through a blistering message on dead and dying old churches. He knew everything I had said better than I did. It felt weird at the time, but it was as if we were sharing grief at the funeral of an old friend.

Well, that finished Washington. We were finally east of the Cascades. Coming down those hills was reminiscent of the Rockies, but we made it. We were back on flat land and looking forward to the ride down the coastline. My wife loves the ocean. She had been so long from the sight of the sea that she was suffering withdrawal. I checked the map and set our sights on two places, Haystack Rock and Tillamook Cheese. I had heard you could drive right out on the beach, like at Daytona. We took the big road until we passed Mt. Saint Helens looming off to our right. We never saw it when it was the majestic picture of the perfect volcano. I found the little coastal road, and we headed for the sea. Have you ever been somewhere before it got famous? Back when it was just a place out in the middle of nowhere? Today, I hear this place is a booming resort. We almost drove past it. It was getting dusk when I spotted this big old rock, just piled out there on the beach. We drove right out to it. There wasn't a car or a building in sight. Now it's in the middle of town. We just camped on the beach, probably right where there's a motel parking lot today.

Do you like cheese? I was never wealthy, but I learned to enjoy some of the things that the wealthy enjoy. The only difference is, I learned to identify the best of the affordable. That was made by the Dutch in Tillamook. The Dutch had bought and settled Manhattan. The English had just elbowed them out and took over without a fuss. But the English loved their cheese, and no one made it like the Dutch. Whenever they wanted some good cheese, they would find a settlement of these people that they had pushed out. The Dutch called these English cheese lovers 'Yon-kees'. That meant John Cheese in Dutch. Now it means Yankee, like in Yankee Doodle. We were a long way from Manhattan, but guess what I found? Call me a Yankee, but I found those Dutch cheese makers. They were only about three thousand miles from where they had started making the stuff.

I was reminded of Louis and Clark. When they had finally got down over the mountains to this place, they had found friendly Indians that fed them the first juicy meat they had eaten in months. After a solid diet of dry wild game, the Indians fed them what Louis called the best meat he had ever eaten. It was dog. If he had waited for the Dutch to get there, he could have had cheese with it. He would have had the worlds first Cheese Dog. We had a dog with us in the camper, but we decided to go Dutch. We were going for the cheese.

I needed that relaxing experience. Our next stop would rattle my cage and leave me with a lesson I'll never forget. Anytime I ever begin to think that I ever was or ever will be someone, I need only to recall this experience. It was another old church out in the country. I can't remember a thing about the meeting. I don't even remember meeting a pastor. The things I would learn later about the history of that church will haunt me for the rest of my life. My memories begin as I was leaving the church. There was an old woman standing at the bottom of the steps just looking at me. She said, "I want to ask you for a favor." I don't remember what I had said when I preached, but I knew this was a special church to me.

I remembered when I had first met Eddie in Japan. I was a young Airman when Brother Gray had led me out in the rice paddies and I had found them literally starving on the field. I didn't know what was going on at the time, but what had happened was his support checks had just quit coming. It was a man in this little church that had discovered that Eddie's checks from the other churches were just lying around the church office. He didn't know Eddie. All he knew was that the man that used to run this office had died a couple months before. It was this man that figured it out and found Eddie and got the checks moving to him again. It was during that void that I had met Eddie and learned what faith was. I probably mentioned that when I spoke for them that day. That must be why that old woman wanted to talk to me. She told me she was one of the few people left in the church that even remembered Eddie. She told me there was only one other member connected to the old days, but he wasn't able to come to church anymore. She told me it would mean the world to him if I could stop by and visit with him for a few minutes.

I was standing in the yard of a run down old log cabin. I followed the simple directions to go about five miles out of town and stop at the first place I came to. I did that, but no one lived there. I didn't even know if I wanted to try those rickety old steps to get up where I could knock on the door. There are times the Spirit of God is more real than we realize at the time. All of the sudden, I had an inordinate interest in why I was there. I wasn't going anywhere until I made sure this place was abandoned. I'm not sure if I knocked or if the door just opened. Either way, I was invited in. I was greeted by one of the most humble old men I have ever met.

I introduced myself, and when I mentioned Japan, the old man's face lit up. I'm not going to try to reconstruct the conversation we had. He told me he had spent most of his youth in Japan as a missionary and he had been a friend of Eddy's for over twenty years. Have you ever been in the presence of greatness and had no idea who you were talking to? If I had any idea who I was talking to, I would have begged his permission to set up the camper out front for a couple of days. I count that as one of the greatest missed opportunities in my life. I thought I was there at the request of an old woman. She just wanted me to let him know that someone still cared about him. That was why I was there, and that was what I did. He was most grateful for the visit, and walked me to the door and hugged me goodbye.

Soon after, we were back on the road and headed for California. I told my wife it was a shame that no one cared enough to take him to church. I told her that he was one of the nicest old men I had ever met. I was glad I could stop and let him know that someone still cared enough to ask me to stop by. I had no idea I had just left one of the four men known as the ones that had opened China to the gospel. How many thousands of Chinese Christians are the result of that man's efforts? Even after the Japanese overran his village, he was able to work out a deal with the Japanese commander to allow him to continue his work. There were two children in that village that had been abandoned by their American father when he had fled from the coming Japanese invasion. Brother Blaylock, whom I had just met, had nurtured those children for years after the invasion.

You have to realize that this all happened just before Pearl Harbor. Brother Blaylock had finally persuaded the Japanese authorities to allow him to take the children to America to obtain their citizenship. That was back when such a thing was valued next to life. On their way home, they made it as far as the Philippines. They were met there by the Japanese army and interned in a concentration camp until the end of the war. The stories of valor he exercised to keep those children alive are beyond description. You think I wouldn't have stayed in that two room cabin and wrote a book for him? Maybe that is why God did not let him reveal his history to me. Instead, he spent the time we had together to encourage me to make it to the mission field. He had fallen between the cracks of human recognition, but he assured me that he was satisfied with the hand that life had dealt him. He had returned to the little church that had first sent him to China, then to Japan, and there he was content to die.

Northeast California should be another state. When I think of California, I think of the land of fruits and nuts. How did Reagan come out of such a place? I couldn't believe we were in California. We were surrounded with normal people. I hadn't met one nut. In fact, they were some of the nicest people you would want to be around. The last church we visited in Oregon was pastored by Brother Wells. He was a descendent of the Wells of Wells Fargo. If I had known Northern California was such a decent place, we wouldn't have hung around with him as long as we did. As it was, I was in no hurry to leave, and the Wells family was in no hurry for us to do so.

He set me up in his office, which is always a treat for a missionary. You can just pick up a telephone and dial the number you want. You can even leave a call back number that will be good for a couple of days. Your mail can even be sent to you from your home church. He went out of his way to make sure I was comfortable at his desk. That was rare. Even when you are lucky enough to get a phone line for a couple of days you still feel awkward sitting a pastor's seat and answering his phone. He made it clear to the congregation that I was taking over his office for a few days, and if anyone needed him they would have to call his home phone. If memory serves, this guy was a missionary's kid and so was his wife. He told me to freely explore his library and help myself to his volumes of old west history. Boy, I had a good time in those old books. After that, I was all caught up with communications and scheduling, not to mention truly refreshed. I was ready to face the fruits and nuts.

What a relief it is to meet really nice people when you don't expect to. Even back then, I knew this state was the proving ground for socialism. What I had overlooked or hadn't learned yet was that socialism is never the desire of the majority. It is the failure of the majority to control their fate. It's our fault. God ordained government. He didn't tell His people to stay out of it. The devil convinced us of that. Voting for freedom or fighting for freedom is not entangling ones self with the affairs of this life. It is preserving and protecting one of God's greatest gifts; the gift that enables us to spread the gospel. At the time, I was just as guilty as most Christians. I blamed our father's and grandfather's generation, while I was just as responsible as were they. A great man once said 'The only necessity for evil to prosper is for good men to do nothing.'

Some of the nice people we met were there to pick plums. Today, they would call that a job that Americans won't do. We were glad to join them and they were all Americans. It was something the whole family could participate in. All you had to do was show up in the orchard. Someone came by with empty baskets and came back to pick them up when they were full. I can't remember how we got paid, but we all left very happy to have spent a week making money we hadn't planned on making. Mom put ours in the proper fund and the kids got some long overdue play money to spend in the campgrounds.

I really appreciate the pastors and friends along the way that understood the little needs I often missed. It was mostly the farmers we visited that did those kinds of things. I think it was Brother Bill that had hired my kids to shell Pecans. I think one farmer had paid them to ride his horse to check the fences. They would have paid him just for the privilege. I don't know how we miss little things like that. When I was about eleven or twelve, a guy came to the farm and asked if he could pick the Elderberries that grew wild along the road. He was related to one of our neighbors, so I helped him fill bushel baskets from our farm and our neighbors place as well.

He asked me and the neighbor kid to go into town with him and help unload them. I don't know what our incentive to help him was, but it wasn't any promise of money. I remember sitting in the old office while the buyer was settling the bill. When we got up to leave, the buyer put something in my hand when no one was looking. "Put it in your pocket, son," is all he said. It was a roll of nickels. Wow, that was a lot of money. I don't know if he did that for my neighbor friend or not. Neither one of us ever opened our mouths about it.

Romans 8:38-39

For I am persuaded, that neither death, nor life, nor angels, nor principalities, nor powers, nor things present, nor things to come, nor height, nor depth, nor any other creature, shall be able to separate us from the love of God, which is in Christ Jesus our Lord.

Chapter 16
77777.7

We had one more appointment in California. It was in San Diego, clear at the bottom of the state. I had an uncle that lived in L.A. That was the middle of the state in my mind. I had never met this man, but his twin brother had lived with us for a short time when I was a young boy. When he had lived with us, he had had something that was relatively new to my generation. He had had an open heart operation. I liked him a lot. He bought a 1953 Chevy and drove it clear out to California to visit this same guy I was going to visit. He has been dead for years now. We were sort of doing this for my mother and a little bit of curiosity on my part. We found them somehow. I don't think we took the fifth-wheel with us, but we camped close enough to make it a day trip.

When I saw him, it was like seeing a man from the grave. He invited us into his garage. We were not welcome in his home. His wife was sure we had come for some alternative motive. I felt so sorry for him. He had been totally separated from his family since the event I mentioned where his brother had driven out to visit him about twenty years before. I shared that experience with him. I told him that trip was the topic of discussion to the day his brother had died. There were not many major highways, and gas stations were far and few between. The stories of crossing the desert had held us spellbound for hours. He told us about check points where he had to verify that he was carrying enough gas and radiator water to make it safely to the next service station.

As we were leaving, under the watchful eye of his wife, he was able to sneak a gun belt and cap pistol to Brandon. I was tempted to ask her why in the world she would think we wanted anything those poor people had. Out of respect for the family, I held my peace. After all, I knew nothing of their affairs. Maybe he had a history of being a little too generous. If so, it didn't run in his family. We once parked in the driveway of another one of his nephews in New York State. While we were there, we painted his house and garage. When we were leaving, they asked us to reimburse them for the beverages we had consumed while we donated our efforts for them. Who knows, maybe living with him all those years had made her like that? Anyway, my mother was thrilled we had stopped to see him.

Our next stop was Brother Bagley's church in San Diego. His son was married to Brother Garlington's daughter. We had met his son when we had first gotten to Louisiana. He was a nut and a lot of fun to be around. He and his wife had flown out just to be there during our visit. We felt and were treated like family. They took us to Tijuana, the first time we had ever visited Mexico. I remember the peso had just been drastically devalued against the dollar. When we got to the little house used for the mission that the church supported, no one was there. The church member that was driving our van was so involved with the work that he had a key and we let ourselves in.

There was nothing in the kitchen but an old refrigerator. Somebody opened it. I wish they hadn't. The only thing in it was a cake pan with a little bit of refried beans in it. The gentlemen that had let us in was visibly embarrassed. He had been telling us how much the church had been helping the Mexican preacher that was living and working out of this little building. We dropped that subject and went shopping. That was funny. In those days, American credit cards and personal checks didn't work down there. Tonia had spent her plumb picking money on some clothes she wanted and she was broke. However, she made it known that she really liked the leather coat she saw in one of the shops. The guy said she could have it for only eight hundred pesos. The guy kept coming down on price 'til she was so embarrassed she walked out the door. He was clear down under a hundred pesos by then. He followed her out into the street and yelled "Hey lady, what you want to pay?" Too bad we had no idea of what was available to us down there; my wife would have had a fund set aside just for that visit.

What had happened to this place? There were only the poor and the rich. The Mexican people are respectable people. They are generally clean, decent, and moral people. They had fought for their independence from Spain as we had done from England. They had won as did we. What happened? They have all the natural resources we have. They even have more oil and minerals than we have. Some people say the industrial revolution never happened south of our border. They never broke free of the religious forces that dominated them. When Martin Luther started the great reformation, almost all of Europe freed themselves of ecclesiastical controls. He made it clear that no man stood between you and Jesus. That was freedom.

For almost fifteen-hundred years of the dark ages, nothing had changed. If you moved something, you moved it on a wheel. If you lit something, you lit it with a candle. All the resources were there; why no industrial revolution? It wasn't until Luther put the ninety-five theses on the door of that church in Germany that men really became free. Suddenly they could produce and possess what they produced as personal property. For the first time in their lives, no man could require their substance or their service in the name of a king or a deity. The Church of England tried to reinstate that ecclesiastical power, but all it did was drive our forefathers to the New World. They paid dearly for their efforts. The rulers of England imprisoned them, and killed and kidnapped their families. They burnt the White House to the ground. Yet they fought for years to give us religious freedom. That never happened in Mexico. Some say they still live in the dark ages.

We spoke for the church and spent some good time in fellowship. We were looking at a long dry spell from where we were to the next place we had been invited to speak. We had to cross the deserts of Arizona and New Mexico to get to West Texas. These states were not only a desert for warm blooded creatures; they were just as dry on engagements for independent New Testament Missionaries. At least we couldn't find anybody in all our travels that knew anybody in either state that would be a contact for us. Thank God we could now afford to miss a week of preaching and still cover our travel expenses and make our bills. We just hadn't got used to it yet. That whole western clean-up trip had been like a wealthy man's vacation.

I'm reminded of the time I picked up our missionary from the Yukon and flew him to Watkins Glen, N.Y. to participate in our church youth camp. We were walking down through a beautiful waterfall when he became overcome with self-imposed guilt. He felt like he was being treated like a movie star. He had spent more time being entertained than working. I remember consoling him with the fact that God is not a slave driver. In His army, we spend time at the front, but a lot of time behind the lines as well. For both assignments, he lavishes us with R&R. (rest and recuperation). This should make us grateful, not guilty.

We climbed over the mountains and out of California into the desert of southern Arizona. I thought I'd seen the desert in our travels, but I had seen nothing like this. We were barely down off the mountains when we saw an altitude marker that read sea level and we were still going down hill. We saw the Salt Flats. They appeared to have no bounds. We saw sand dunes higher than the tallest building in the town where I grew up. I can't remember what the temperature was, but it was the hottest place we'd ever been.

Somewhere east of Yuma, we pulled off the road onto a wide spot between the road and the desert. I put the awning out and sat in a lawn chair just looking at the beautiful tall saguaro cactus. That's what I told the state police officer when he asked me anyway. My wife and daughters were hiding in the camper. I didn't share their embarrassment. The officer told me of a better spot just off the next exit where there was almost no traffic. I took that information as an encouragement to move along. I wanted to make a campground in New Mexico by supper time, anyway.

The west coast clean-up had netted us a couple more churches for sure and a couple maybes. Each month was more encouraging as Pastor Ed would announce a new supporter on the list. At that point, we hadn't considered ending our deputation, but frankly we were reaching the point of diminishing returns. We had only one more church to visit between us and our home church near Houston. Everything just sort of came to an abrupt halt. That was the first time since we had found Eddie's group, well over a year before, that we didn't have a list of appointments. That fact just dawned on me, right there in the middle of the Arizona desert. I wrestled, for the first time ever, with the possibility that we were done. Something was happening. God wouldn't just shut us down.

My mind began going back to the early days when we had found the equipment that had performed so well. I looked down at the odometer to see just how many miles ago that had been. Good heavens, it read seventy-seven thousand, seven hundred and seventy-seven miles. I took my foot off the gas pedal and coasted to the side of the road and stopped, just as the tenths of a mile rolled to seven tenths. Mom asked why we were stopping. "Because we're done," I said. "Get the camera." The kids had come out of the camper to see what was up. Chris was afraid I was going to roll out the awning again. I took a picture of the odometer and everybody looked in the window for themselves. I told them what I had been thinking about when I looked down and saw that we were in stopping distance only of all sevens. Seven is the number of completion.

Twenty-seven years ago, about seventy miles south of where I'm standing right now, I told the family we were done. From that point in Arizona, we were no longer on deputation. We put our minds on preparing to leave for the mission field. Many churches had told us to notify them when this time came. They said they would take up a special offering for our plane tickets and shipping costs. It would be really nice if a couple of the maybes would get on board as well. Now that I had made the decision, I had perfect peace about it. Just saying I was at peace would be an understatement; the whole family was energized.

We set up at camp and I got the typewriter out and got started. With my appointment in San Antonio, I figured we were about a week out of home base at best. I'd put this in the camp mail box and by the time we got to our church, Ed would have the word out. I also told him to notify Eddie and give him a thirty day target date. Cheryl was already in touch with an outfit she had found that promised to help us with flight arrangements. I stopped some time ago to look at some old cars on display. My wife met a lady working at the show. She said all they needed was a date. They would take care of everything through a deal they had with China Airlines. Pull the trigger, Baby, and that would be our date.

I love West Texas. I wish I could describe the rugged beauty of that country. There is nothing out there but rolling hills. There were no major roads yet, at least not the way we went. Campgrounds were few and far between out there as well. We found a place that said 'Camping - two miles'. We turned off the road and up a dirt road for about a mile. There it was on the left. Someone had paved about a quarter mile square of field up next to the tree line. It looked like a really large old tennis court.

There were no facilities and no one in sight, but it said 'Campground'.

I was tired. It was dark already and I was parking. The next morning about daylight, I heard tiny hooves running across the pavement. My poodle started barking at the door. Either Santa Clause had just landed or we were under attack by Indians on their ponies. I opened the door and scared off the largest herd of deer I think I've ever seen. Weirdest thing happened though. The entire herd ran off except one old doe. She ran a small circle and walked back towards me and stopped. I never saw anything like this. I slowly walked towards her with my hand out. She never moved. I put my hand on her neck and looked into her eyes. She was blind as a bat. A voice came from nowhere, "They'll come back and get her after while." A woman had come in and parked on the other side of me. She came down to collect the camp fee from the few of us that had stayed the night. I left Mark pet the deer. I paid her and we headed for San Antonio.

Stonewall Baptist Church was an impressive little place. It was built of stone is all I can remember. The people were great and we knew we had another church. That was one of the few that wasn't associated with Eddie's group. I wanted to see the Alamo before we left. I finally found the little two story building surrounded by big office buildings. I was so disappointed. I let the family go in, but I sat out front in the truck. There wasn't even a parking lot in those days. I was at a parking meter on Main Street.

This is where it had taken the whole Mexican army to kill a group of boyscouts from Tennessee? They should have got into one of the bigger buildings. As we headed for the home church, I thought how good it felt to be introduced as a missionary family in the process of leaving for the field. I think that's why they decided to take us on. Mission money is never so abundant that a church can just vote to help everybody on the spot. It's much easier getting works that don't really know you to partner with you when God has made His calling and provision known. Other churches operate on the same philosophy. Several of the maybes picked us up as soon as they heard we were making arrangements for departure. Thank God they don't all operate that way, but many of them wait 'til they're sure they're betting on a winner.

Four such churches were in Alaska and Hawaii. They didn't just wait until they were sure we were going to the field. They waited until we were en route to the field. The Hawaii group said they would put us up if we would lay over and speak for them. The Alaskan group said they would have the brothers in Hawaii fly me to Alaska if I would give them a week's meetings each. I couldn't pass that up. It sounded like great things to do on the way to the field. We got Brandon's passport and visa while we were in Seattle. Now all of our paperwork was in order. We pulled into the pastor's driveway and dropped the camper for the last time. It had been our home for a long time, but I couldn't wait to hang a for-sale sign on it. Paying it off would be like picking up another supporting church.

Pastor Ed already had his sons building four by eight foot packing crates out of heavy plywood. The women were working hard on making new curtains and reupholstering everything in the camper. When they were done, it looked better than it did when we had bought it. That Elkhart was one of the heaviest fifth-wheels built. It was so well built that nothing else needed repaired. It's a good thing it was, because we off loaded and filled four crates with thousands of pounds and sent them to the shipping docks. Eddie and Neva had supplied us with a detailed list of everything we would need to ship. The list consisted of items either not available in the islands or too costly to obtain. Their twenty years of experience was invaluable.

I had been collecting duffle bags for a year. Brother Bill had given me his old army bag, I had one, and several other people had donated theirs. I had one for everybody, plus suitcases. Western clothing was not hard to find over there, but when you're over six foot tall and wear size thirteen shoes, you're kind of a freak. Eddie told me to go the bank and get as many Eisenhower dollars and Kennedy half dollars as I could afford. That advice opened many doors and provided multiple services over the next four years. The time between loading those crates and packing our bags is a blur. The next thing I remember is lying on those bags in the L.A. airport all night, waiting for our China Airline connection the next morning. We could have gone to a motel, but it was pouring rain and we had so many bags that it was just easier to sleep on them than move them.

We landed in Hawaii and were met by a preacher that took us to a man's home that had prepared rooms for us. He was a really nice little guy, married to a Japanese woman who worked for JAL, a Japanese airline. Everybody knew Eddie and Neva. Some had known them longer than we had. He had brought his wife there over twenty years before. He didn't have enough money to make it all the way to Japan, so he had come here. They lived in a room in the back stage of a church. Eddie had preached and saved enough to continue on to Japan.

Even before I spoke there in Hawaii, one of the pastors, whose brother was a pastor in Alaska, delivered me a ticket to Fairbanks via Seattle. My family was very comfortable there with that generous family, so I flew to Alaska on their schedule. He also gave me something I wasn't accustomed to yet. He gave me a lot of traveling money. He told me airports were expensive, but I had to eat. He told me to have a good meal on them at my layover in Seattle. So I set in my heart to do just that. I found a fine looking restaurant and sat down with great anticipation. I told the young lady I wanted the best seafood meal they had. She returned shortly and placed a glass container with a large mouth on my table. "This comes with your order sir," she said. "What is it," was the last question I can remember asking. I hadn't had wine since I was a kid. I wish I had thought about what had happened that last time.

What happened back then was my father had found a half empty bottle of Thunderbird under the seat of my freshly banged up car. But I was an adult now, and I sure wasn't going to waste a dime of this fantastic setting. The next thing I remember, I was standing in the boarding line for Alaskan Airlines. Some drunk was making fun of my hat because it looked military and had a set of wings on it. They took him out of the line and then turned to me. A young lady said, "Maybe I should see your ID as well sir." I hadn't said a word. Some gentleman spoke up and told her I was not with that loud mouth. She apologized and left me alone. I further reasoned with myself as I boarded the plane....'The disciples may have drank wine.' That's what I was thinking when I first looked at it on my table. I'll bet they never drank it from one of those glass containers with the large mouth at an airport. Boy, I wish I could remember that meal. I didn't want to waste a dime of that meal. In the process, I had wasted it all.

I don't know what the Fairbanks airport looks like today, but back then it was really nice. I love airports that are too small to get lost in. I remember there was a nine-foot bear standing in the middle of the lobby. I flew through Fairbanks a couple times when I was in the USAF, but I had never left the base. The only thing I remember is that is where I quit smoking. I got off the plane and was walking through the terminal when I saw a billboard that said cigarettes caused cancer. I reached in my pocket and pulled out my Pall Mall longs and pitched them into the dumpster. That was the last pack I can ever remember having. That was back in the sixties. I wish that billboard had read that 'disobedience to God causes something worse.' Some things just aren't as easy to pitch.

I was told to stand by the front door and not to go outside until the pastor drove up and opened the car door. When he motioned for me to come out and jump in his car, I realized another thing. I had never been there in the winter. It was getting dark as we left the airport, about fifteen 'til two in the afternoon. I had read about two Eskimos in the Reader's Digest. They had spent their wedding night together, and in the morning she realized she was six months pregnant. Well, we were not that far north, but even here, night fall came several hours before dinner. On the way to his house, we stopped at a grocery store.

He left the car running and told me to sit tight. I can't remember what I decided I needed, but after a few minutes, I turned the car off and ran across the parking lot into the store. As I walked down the aisle, the soles of my shoes began to burn my feet. I pulled one of my dress shoes off. I examined it as if I was going to find I had walked on hot ashes or something. Just about then, the pastor walked up. He was surprised to see me, and asked what I was doing out of the car. He said, "If you wanted to come in, I would have got your gear out of the trunk." I sure had a lot to learn about this country. The soles of my shoes had frozen solid in that short jaunt from the car. Now they were freezing the bottoms of my feet. I handed him the keys and apologized. I assured him I would follow his instructions now that I knew I wasn't in Kansas anymore.

He explained that there was an emergency bag in the trunk that they had put together just for me. If anything happened to him, I was to open it and don its contents before I did anything else. I was starting to get the picture. These people lived there intentionally. If you tried to live there unintentionally, you would die there unintentionally. When we got home, it was dark. As we walked in the door, I noticed a large cloud of vapor going in with us. I have lived in cold country before, where when you opened the door, a little bit of steam was visible for a second. That wasn't the way it worked up there. The cloud came in the door with you, and rolled down the hall before it dissipated. I've seen a little bit of ice form on the inside of the window when it was really cold out. But there, the ice totally covered the window, and spread out a foot or more on the surrounding walls. I asked how cold it was. He got a flashlight and took me to the front door. One of his trucks was parked about five feet away and a temperature gauge was wired to its grill. He put the light on it so I could read it for myself. It read fifty degrees below zero.

I don't know where his wife was; I think she was visiting the lower forty-eight as they often say. The pastor and his son, who I think was a freshman in college, cooked me up a salmon steak. I had never eaten salmon in my life. I don't think it was just hunger that left me with the impression that this stuff was good. Maybe it was the wine. I've since learned that you're supposed to drink the stuff after your meal. I was thinking at the time, that if you drink it before your meal, you can probably eat anything. I have to admit that I have never again enjoyed salmon like I did that night. Just in case, if you bring me salmon, bring one of those glass things with the large mouth first.

We ate and got acquainted until I couldn't keep my eyes open. Yes, it was bedtime. It was after seven already. I don't care what the clock said; when it's dark for hours, it's time to turn in. It was the same thing in the morning. I woke up to dark windows. Finally, I heard noise out there in the house. I was tired of lying there wide awake anyway, so I got up. We drank coffee, watched the news, and made plans for the meetings. We enjoyed breakfast, got out of our morning clothes, and shaved and groomed. We met back in the kitchen just as it began to lighten the windows. I looked outside about ten o'clock and saw a trail of exhaust hanging over the road where a passing vehicle had just left it. There wasn't a breath of air to move it and it didn't go away. You could follow a car ten minutes after it had left the scene if the wind wasn't blowing. I'd been there less than twenty-four hours, and I knew what cabin fever meant.

We had an exciting day planned. The boy was going to take me up to check his traps. Then they were going to let me stand on the three-foot pipe running across the bridge so I could say I had stood on the Alaskan Pipe Line. I had brought a coat with me and a pair of thermal underwear, but at these temperatures, I wouldn't have lasted thirty minutes. I saw a lot of snowmobiles, but wondered why I saw no dog sleds. They told me I wouldn't see any dogs until it warmed up to around twenty or thirty below. They dressed me in a sheepskin coat and a hat trimmed with Martin fur and snow boots. When I stepped outside of the house or the car, my mustache turned solid white with frost at my first breath. We heard on the radio that a man had been found frozen black beside his car. It had broken down a few miles out of town, and he had had no winter gear with him. The interior of the car had been pulled out and burned, along with his tires, but it hadn't been enough.

We passed a young man walking down the road with no hat on. The pastor stopped and told him to get in the car, and we'd take him wherever he was going. He said he was only going about a half a mile up the road, but realized he might lose his ears if we hadn't come along when we did. The guy wasn't too bright. The pastor said it's everyone's job to keep this kind alive. He said no one even locks their hunting cabins this time of the year. They leave wood in the stove and matches beside it in case someone gets lost or their snowmobile breaks down. He said a lot of people leave a two-way radio with a fresh twelve volt battery beside it as well. Someone was telling me about finding his lodge almost stripped of food supplies, as well as the gas can that he kept full to run his generator. Then in the spring, the can showed up on his porch full of gas along with a box of canned goods and a thank-you note. A motorist had run out of gas in a spot along the road where he could see the lodge. He did mention, however, that they used to lock their camps in the summer years ago, because the hippies were moving into them.

We had a full church house every night. Preachers brought van loads of people from their churches. It was standing room only. The last day of the meetings, a pastor asked me to visit a man in the hospital. He said the guy was a missionary and that he wanted to talk to me about something personal. I was curious because I had never heard of him. When I got there, he apologized for not coming to the meetings. He said all his pastor friends had told him he should have been there instead of listening to that new missionary in town. I didn't know anything about it but, Nick, my old missionary to the Yukon, was building a work in Fairbanks. He had heard from one of the pastors that I was coming up to hold meetings for them. He had put out a letter warning pastors not to attend or he would break fellowship with them. The guy said, "I'm the only one I know of that didn't show up to hear you, and now I'm in the hospital." He wanted my forgiveness, just in case. He told me some things that Nick had told him about me, and unfortunately, I told him some things about Nick that only a very close brother would know. I wish I hadn't done that. With the exception of that one guy, I sure wasn't hurt by Nick's warning.

The next day, the pastor was taking me to the other church that had helped pay for my travel. The place was about thirty miles north of town. Up there, that is way out of town. On the way, I asked him if he knew about the warning the new missionary had put out. He said, "That guy is no friend of ours." Someone in the lower forty-eight had sent him a copy of one of Nick's monthly letters. The letter had said he was finding Christians slain and thrown in the ditches everywhere when he had got there. "I didn't want a big fight, so I asked my brother in Hawaii to find out how you felt about Nick," he went on to tell me. "You told him you really respected him, but you just couldn't work with him. That was good enough for us. We decided not to even mention it to you. That guy you saw in the hospital is the only friend he had." "We had good meetings," he said, "And we'll have good meetings up here as well; just forget about it."

There were few homes along the road. Finally he said, "That's it up there on the right about a mile." There was a little more snow up there with only a few snowmobile tracks in the fields and along the woods. When we got close enough, I could see a beautiful log church building, and about a hundred yards beyond it, was a matching little house. 'Where does everybody live?' was my first thought. There was nothing else in sight. We pulled into a circle drive that ran to the house and then on up to the back of the church. We could see both the pastor and his wife standing at the door to greet us. The Fairbanks pastor introduced me to the two of them.

They were probably in their late fifties or early sixties, as I remember.

They were so glad to see us and they gave me a gracious welcome. They were well into cabin fever season, and the meetings would bring a midwinter ray of sunshine. My ride said we had messed around too much on the way up and that he needed to get back before his son started worrying about him. He had already called the pastor, and he was supposed to return the call if we didn't show within the hour. It was already getting dark out. It was a depressing day anyway. It started to get dawn about ten o'clock, but never really lightened up. It turned dusk about noon, and then started to get dark around two. I figured on an early supper. I could already smell a roast in the oven. If these folks were on the same schedule, we'd be turning in around seven, so an early dinner made sense. But those people were like the people we had met out west. I was the Pony Express, and they couldn't wait to see what I had in my saddlebags.

Those wonderful people were so excited to have someone to talk to. They put their little poodle out to do its business and forgot to let it in. In the middle of our conversation, one of them yelled, "The dog!", and they both gasped and ran for the back door. It had only been a few minutes. I couldn't figure out what the fuss was all about. Soon, they had it on the living room floor, examining its paws. "They're not frozen, thank the Lord." They sat back down on the edge of their seats looking at me as if to say 'Please continue'. I wasn't just somebody from the lower forty-eight to these people. I had just made the circuit consisting of about everybody that they held near and dear.

She didn't want to excuse herself and retire to the kitchen alone to prepare the meal. She hinted that we should move the conversation to the kitchen table. You find special people everywhere in the ministry, but the pastors in Alaska and Hawaii are almost close friends as soon as you meet them. They are really missionaries too. They know everything we have been through, plus they put out reports to most of the same people we do. Now that we were this far along, we were fellow missionaries. I needed those meetings to go well, because more people were going to read about them than anywhere else I had preached.

I don't know why food is so much better when it's cold outside and you're sitting at the table nice and warm inside. Boy, that roast was good. They never told me what it was until I had assured them more than once that I really liked it. She told me he had shot it last fall. I asked if it was moose or elk. 'Neither,' was the answer. It was bear. I thought bear was a greasy meat, from what I had been told. That, however, was as good as any beef roast I had ever had. He told me, "You harvest them in the fall when the salmon are not running. I shot this one right over there on that little hill where it was eating blue berries or black berries." He said "That's when they're the best eating." I asked him what he had shot him with. I was finally getting to ask some questions. I was thinking he shot it with something pretty big. Wrong. He had used a .270 with a nine power scope. "That's enough when you're sitting on your porch with plenty of time to place your shot," he said. "But that's not big enough if your fishing," he told me. "When I'm fishing, so are the grizzlies. So you have to have something big enough to knock him down even if you miss. I carry a .450. If I miss him by too much, I just throw it down and climb into the barrel." "Did you ever use that thing?" I asked. He told me he didn't like to, because it killed with one end and crippled with the other.

After a great meal, we chatted a little more, then he walked me out to the church where they had fixed me a bed. On the way out, I saw flashes in the sky. It was the Aurora Borealis or Northern Lights, like I had never seen before. I saw them from Northern Canada once, but nothing like that. After the pastor went back in and I was dressed for bed, I thought I'd take one more look at those beautiful lights. I opened the church door and looked up to see flashing multiple colored streaks of lights jumping back and forth across the sky. All I had on were my thermals. I couldn't look for thirty seconds without shutting the door and warming up for another quick look. The pastor that had brought me up there had left my emergency gear, but I hadn't brought it out to the church with me. I would have gone back to the house and got them, but the house lights were already out. I could have stood out there and watched those things all night. If I ever built a house up there, it would have a heated glass roof in the bedroom. Soon, I figured I'd better get to bed. I didn't know what the morning schedule was, and I hadn't been up that late since I'd gotten there. It must have been nine o'clock.

To tell the truth, I don't remember what morning brought. The next thing I remember was the pastor showing me the greenhouse he had built for his wife. It was light out, so it had to be after ten. The little glass thing was about four feet by four feet at the most, maybe smaller. I think it was heated by electric from the house. He said it wasn't practical to have one, but it was therapeutic for his wife to raise tomatoes. He said she could raise them for about five dollars a pound. I don't know if he was joking or not, but he sounded pretty serious about it.

Across the street, along the side of the road, was a line of dumpsters. I asked what they were doing out there in the middle of nowhere. He told me the state had put them there for the Indians, but they were nothing but trouble. They were the reason that the .450 was sitting behind the door loaded. The garbage drew the bears. I asked if he ever had to use it. He told me just last spring, but he was too late. Two young airmen from the Air base had seen a grizzly getting in one of them and they had stopped. One of the boys had gotten out with a .44 magnum pistol and had started shooting it. By the time the pastor had gotten his gun, the bear had killed the boy. He said, "It saw me coming and yelling, and ran into those woods. After the ambulance left, I took the blood trail and found it about a hundred yards in. I didn't have to use my gun. The boy had killed it, but it cost him his life."

When it got close to time for services, cars and trucks started pulling in and parking everywhere. Everyone had food of some kind, but they all had salmon. They set up in the kitchen in the basement of the church. The smell almost made me ill. I couldn't believe that was the same stuff I had so enjoyed my first night in Fairbanks. I didn't eat it that night, or any night after that for many years. We had good services, and so many people in attendance, that they couldn't all get upstairs into the meeting hall. I can't remember much about the service. I do remember sitting downstairs in the fellowship hall afterwards. Several people had asked the guy I was talking to if he knew why so and so wasn't there. The concern became so apparent that I became concerned. Several men were suiting up for a search when someone yelled, 'They're here, they're here." There was a noticeable collective sigh of relief as the family filed into the fellowship hall. Based on the intenseness of the matter, I was expecting a much more complicated explanation for their tardiness. Turns out, they had had a flat tire a few miles out. I was the only one that appeared confused.

How do you miss a two hour service over a flat tire? Didn't you have a spare? One gentleman took the time to explain it to me. First you have to get your winter gear out of the trunk and get back in the car and get them on. Next, you have to light a torch and heat the jack. Then you have to heat the lug nuts to get them off. Then you have to do the same with the spare. You have to get in and warm your hands between each affair. After the ordeal is over, you get back out of your gear, store them, and go on. Everyone agreed two hours is good time for the job.

We sat there and nibbled and drank coffee until I couldn't stay awake. My body clock told me it had been dark for so long that it must be after midnight. The pastor invited us to his house because people were sitting on my bed. As we were walking to the house, I saw a group of teenagers doing something out in front of the church. I saw a large puff of steam in the air and then they all ran back into the church. As it turned out, one kid had bet another that he could throw a glass full of hot water up in the air and it would vaporize before it hit the ground. He lost. When the cloud cleared, they found several drops had reached the snow.

The next day people started showing up much earlier. I don't know if the flat tire had anything to do with it, or if it was just that I was the only show in town. One guy came so early that he had time to take me back in the woods and show me the cabin he had built for his family. I was thinking a cabin like in Little House on the Prairie. We broke into a clearing and there was a huge, three-story, almost round log cabin. You walked into the front door and found yourself standing in front of a twelve-foot wide staircase that led up to the main floor. At the top of the steps was a large octagon room with a big pot-belly stove in the middle of it. It dawned on me that the guys up there were not welfare people on a fishing trip. Everything up there except what you took out of the woods or the water cost a lot more than it did anywhere else in America. Except for natural resources, about everything was ordered and put on a ship from Seattle. One guy told me the men he worked with had rented a 747 and crew to fly them down to watch the Super Bowl.

All good things come to an end. I had to go back to Hawaii the next day. I went back to Fairbanks with the same preacher that had brought me up. It had warmed up the last few days, and I got to see several sled teams running around. It was still cold enough that your vehicle oil pan heater had to be plugged in. You wouldn't have enough battery to start it if it sat cold for five or six hours. We had to stop at an office on the way home for something. I stayed in the car. As I was waiting in the parking lot, I saw a small fire under a car a few rows ahead of our car. I thought it was rather dangerous to have an open flame under your car, but what did I know. After a few minutes, the car erupted into flames. In my ignorance, I had allowed a car to burn down. There would have been plenty of time to put it out if I had only known it was a short in the heater. It was not just another new device that I had never seen before. Don't tell anybody. I'm not going to.

I don't remember those preacher's names anymore. I've lost all my records over the last twenty-five years. The preacher son's name was Paul. My son remembers him from a later experience. I really liked the kid. He let me keep the hat he made and helped me talk his dad into letting me keep the matching coat. Missionaries are bums by habit. After living hand to mouth like most of us did, it takes years to get it out of your blood. I still have the coat. My dog ate the hat. The next morning, Paul dropped me off at the little terminal with the big bear. He took a picture of me standing between its outstretched arms and five inch claws. It towered a good yard above my head. I thought of the young Airman.

Romans 8:31
What shall we then say to these things?
If God be for us, who can be against us?

Chapter 17
I Can't Read

Hawaii's temperatures are in the seventies year round, I think. I'm not sure, but it's a lot warmer than Alaska's winter, spring, and fall. The sun comes up year round in the morning and doesn't set until it's done a full days work. I woke up way before ten and the window wasn't black like it was when I had got into bed. I also heard something I had never heard before. They were morning doves. I never hear them anymore without thinking of Hawaii. It was also the first time I ever smelled real Japanese food. One evening, our host came home with boxes of it that were left over from a party where he worked. He worked for the same Japanese airline that his wife worked for. He was in maintenance and she worked the counter. We all said "What is that smell?" We were thinking odor as in something that should be on a garbage truck. He said, "I brought it home for my wife. She will love it." Sure enough, as soon as she opened the door, we heard her ask with a heavy Japanese accent, "What smells so delicious?"

I spoke in several churches, missions, whatever. They were churches pastored by missionaries. Most of them were really old works. I couldn't figure out why they hadn't been turned over to native pastors years ago. Instead, they were passed from missionary to missionary, as if that was the way it was supposed to be. I let it go. In the New Testament, the local church is the ultimate authority under God. The missionary is commissioned by the church, and answers to the church. Over the years, the Southern Baptists turned that around; maybe not on the surface, but in practice. The missionary seems to be commissioned by the convention. The churches belong to and answer to the convention, rather than the church.

In the beginning, the churches authorized the convention; now the convention exercises authority over the churches, and uses the missionaries as their regulators. The tail is wagging the dog. For anything to have scriptural authority, it must have a New Testament prototype. There is no other organization in the New Testament other than the local church. This is unanimously accepted by true independent churches in the U.S., but somehow overlooked in foreign countries. I think the fault of this unscriptural practice can be shared by both the foreign mission and the missionary. The missionary uses the foreign work to gender financial support from home-based churches. The foreign works use the missionary for the same purpose.

Hawaii is a really a nice little island, but that is exactly what it is....little. No one needs more than a week to totally explore the place. It's really even smaller to foreigners. When you get out of the tourist areas, unless you're a native, you're not even welcome in Hawaii. At least that's the way we found it. The nice guy we were staying with sent the wife and I to Kauai for a few days. They put us up in a really nice beach house. We spoke for a little church while we were there. Then we just enjoyed ourselves, driving around the island in the car that was also included in the package. That took all of a couple hours.

We pulled into a little overlook where there was nothing parked but a little trailer. We looked down the steep cliff and saw people in a raft that was tied up right in the breakers. We couldn't figure out what was going on until a man stepped out of the little trailer and told us they were making a movie. It was the mayor in Jaws. I don't think we even took a picture. We just said thanks and we drove off.

We just enjoyed being alone together. The place was way out in nowhere country. We could look down over the cliff behind it and view the deserted beach. There was a storm out there somewhere, because we had never seen waves like we saw then. We could hear them before the sun came up. I was sure glad we were high up on the cliff. There is something mesmerizing about the ocean. It's like watching a fire in your fireplace. That was the last break we would get for a long time.

In the old days, missionaries traveled by ship, and they slowly adjusted to their destination. There was no such thing as ship lag. I asked the only missionary / pastor we really had bonded with to take us to the airport. He was married to one of the daughters of the old patriarch of Mount Hebron Baptist Church in Kentucky. He didn't like me the first time we met. He had problems with his Christian school. I had spent a few days showing him how to solve them. He still didn't really like me, but I liked him. He was straight up honest about his feelings, and I admire that in a man. At least you know where you stand with a man like that. The guy that falls all over you but never lifts a finger to help you is less trustworthy when the chips are down.

I trusted him to show up and get us to the right place at the right time. That was a major project. It would take his church van to get us and all our stuff to the same place at the same time. We were dealing through an agent who was dealing with a foreign airline. You couldn't just pick up the phone and change something at the last minute. I had everything set up. We had to show up when our sponsor was there to meet us or we were lost. We weren't going to Kansas.

The most beautiful language I have ever heard is Chinese, when spoken by a woman flight attendant. We couldn't understand a word, but it sounded as though she was singing rather than talking. I could have listened to her for hours, like my wife listens to Italian opera singers. We were really fortunate to be on that flight. That was the largest plane in the world at the time, and it wasn't half full. There were rows of four seats beginning at the windows, then an aisle. There were about eight more seats in the middle. Then there was another aisle and four more seats to the opposite windows. We just raised the arm rests and stretched out across as many seats as we wanted.

Our next stop was Taiwan, where we would change planes for Japan. Someone that spoke perfect English walked us to the proper boarding area and put us in line. It was a really long line. The next flight was not going to be half full. We were about half way back in a line that seemed to be painted on the walls. We stood in the same spot for about ten minutes when a young lady suddenly walked up to us with our boarding passes in her hand. "Come with me please," she said. She took us to a restaurant and told the waitress to serve us. She must have told her to charge her, too, because we never got a bill.

I'm so thankful for living in a time that I call the end of the last American generation. In my day, American politicians, regardless of party, were pro-America. Even Hollywood made pro-America movies. Unlike Europe, almost every Asian country still held Americans in high esteem. We had been pulled out of line because we were the only Americans in line. The lady came back and got us about forty-five minutes later and escorted us back to the boarding area. There was still a short line going through security. That was security like we had never seen in our country. Those people lived in a state of war with main Land China. They profiled at their security checkpoints, and Americans were not on their list to profile. She walked us to the head of the line and right past security. She handed us over to the flight attendant, who took us to our assigned seats. The flight was full. Thank God it was not far from Taiwan to Naha International Airport in Okinawa, Japan. We were right on schedule. Even though it would be well into the night, Eddie should be waiting for our flight to arrive.

Japan is not China. We would soon learn the difference. Taiwan maintains a state of war awareness because of China. Although the U.S. Navy is their only real hope, there are no U.S. personnel stationed in their country. In contrast, this little Japanese island is home to about fifty thousand U.S. military personnel and many of their families. No matter who you were, everyone assumed you were military related. You were received according to their individual feelings concerning the U.S. military presence. That varied mostly with age and political persuasion. Being an amateur World War II historian, I had read a lot about the subject from both sides. Back when I had been stationed in mainland Japan with the U.S.A.F., I had run into demonstrations protesting the war in Vietnam.

One day I was leaving the base and there was a group of protestors at the gate. I saw a Japanese man that I worked with on base. The next day I asked him about it. He told me not to worry about it. He said, "These young socialists stop us as we are leaving the base. It's not honorable to just ignore them. We stand around with them for a few minutes but it means nothing. Most of us that are old enough to remember World War II have great respect for American GIs." He was a commercial pilot hired to fly boomers during the war with China. When the U.S. entered the war and things started going bad for Japan, he had been drafted into the military. He went from making good money to not making enough to keep him in cigarettes. He said, "They treated us so badly, I volunteered to fly kamikaze missions."

How many ex-kamikaze pilots have you ever met? He saw the puzzled look on my face and explained. It had finally come time for his group to fly. They had held their big bonfire celebration and said their goodbyes. The next day, they reported to dispatch and learned that they had run out of airplanes. That same guy told me that the quiet little fellow that worked with us was a fighter pilot. He had been shot down three times. I had much more respect for all the Japanese civilians I worked with from then on. So there I was, fifteen years after that, and I was the civilian. I was standing in front of uniformed Japanese custom officers.

I found myself actually hoping to get one old enough to have fought in the war. No such luck. I got a young stone-faced guy that wound up holding my key ring and acting like it was a bomb. My cousin had made it for me and had put it through an empty 44.mag casing. It didn't take the Chinese officers two seconds to realize it was a harmless ornament. These guys had never even seen a real bullet. Only certain police officers even carried a gun. If they did, it was attached to a cable locked to their body. Barney Fife with his one bullet in his shirt pocket came to mind. Those guys, however, weren't the slightest bit humored.

It was sure nice to see Eddy's smiling face standing on the other side of the glass. I felt a little bit like someone just being released from prison. So many people looked at our paperwork that I was beginning to wonder if something was wrong with it. Eddy explained that such confusion over our paperwork was common. We didn't fit in the box. We were not military-related, nor tourists. There was no standard routine for handling us, and the Japanese are very routine-oriented. "I'll take you down to get your driver's license tomorrow, and you'll see what I mean," Eddy told me. "For now, let's get you home." Soon, I was sitting in Eddy's van, on the side where the steering wheel should be, and relaxed for the first time in days. Wow, we were finally home. I'd lost track of time. Two years must have gone by since I had shared my goal with Nick in my living room in Butler. We were finally there. There was a time when I didn't think we were going to make it.

Japan is not like many other foreign countries, where one can find a considerable amount of English signage. It was getting late, but there was still traffic on the main roads. There were a lot of pretty neon lights above the shops. It seemed like we were moving a lot faster than we really were. The roads were smaller and everything was so compact, that it felt like we were driving about fifty miles an hour. One look at the speedometer, and I thought we were going even faster. The thing was reading sixty, but it wasn't miles per hour; it was kilometers per hour. Finally, we turned off the main road onto a much narrower one.

The street ran down a small hill for about a quarter mile before leveling off. In about twenty more yards, the road ended at the edge of a cliff. I was really excited as Eddy pulled into a short drive and turned the motor off. Everyone was quiet as a mouse. We were just sitting and staring out the open windows. In the quietness, I heard a little sobbing from the back of the van. My first thought was that the emotion of it all had overwhelmed someone. The dome light came on and I could clearly see my little girl with her face in her hands. I said, "Tonia?" She raised her head, and through her tears she sobbed loudly, "I CAN'T READ!"

"Come here honey," I said, as I helped her out of the van. "Come with me a minute." I walked her a few feet back up the street and pointed to the only two lighted signs we could see. "This will be fun, and much easier than you think," I told her. "See the first sign over the little shop on the left? That is written in Romagi. It is used when the word is not Japanese. The first character is pronounced 'TA', the second one 'BA', and the last one is 'KO'; tobacco. See the other sign with the Chinese figure that looks kind of like a spoon in a cup? That represents mixing medicine. That is the only sign you have to remember to know you're looking at a pharmacy. You haven't been here five minutes and you already know where to buy cigarettes and aspirin." She hugged me a little closer and gave my little lesson a smirk followed by a little smile. It was a reassuring sort of 'At least dad knows, so we'll be alright' kind of look. God must have arranged it. They could have just as easily been two signs of which I'd had no clue as to the meaning. From that moment on, she never looked back.

It was dark and we couldn't see much of the outside of the place. We could see that there was a fence that ran along the edge of the street for the length of the property. We could see a lot of greenery in the front yard. We didn't go in the front. We walked into the garage to a door that had a combination padlock hanging on it. I can't tell you the combination though, because it's now the one that opens my son's gun safe. He remembered it from over twenty years ago.

Everything was wood construction. It was an old structure, but it was easy to see that it had been really stylish in its day. I don't remember how Eddy had found it. I think it belonged to some mission-connected outfit up in mainland Japan. It had been built by a missionary right after WWII. Back when it was built, the path down the cliff beside the house did not lead down to the rice paddies, like it did when we got there. It had led down to the South China Sea. Over the years, the ocean was pushed back about a hundred yards. It was held there by what they called a seawall. So this place had originally been built on a jetty of land extending out into the ocean. They must have gone to sleep every night with the sound of waves breaking at the bottom of the cliff. We went to sleep with the sound of a thousand bullfrogs serenading us. There were now flooded rice paddies between us and the sea.

Eddy gave us his phone number and told us to call when we got up. "Neva and I will come over and help you make breakfast and show you where we put everything." That said, he bid us a warm welcome to the islands, and a goodnight. It was warm; really warm. He told us there was a huge old air conditioner in the dining room, but not to turn it on. He said even if it worked, electric on that island was gold. We took his advice. We found three furnished bedrooms in the far end of the place. Two of them had doors and one was just a large opening in the middle of a very long hallway. We put the boys in that one. Their older sisters got rooms with a door. Someone had already decided which one would be the master bedroom. It was the only one with just one bed big enough for two people. Our level of excitement was only matched by our three days of exhaustion. We went to bed without even unpacking a suitcase. Wow, we were finally there.

I don't want to give you the idea that I could communicate. I could read a lot of the characters comprising the easiest alphabet. There are three alphabets used in Japan. I could read a few of the harder ones and none of the hardest one. That phone number Eddy had given us before he left was our lifeline. At that particular time, we could not imagine performing even the most basic function without Eddy present, or on the phone. I remember living off base in mainland Japan, and we had done alright. Oh, I forgot, Eddy had been taking care of all our Japanese communications. I guess you could say we felt secure with that phone number.

We woke up in a whole new world. Maybe because we had lived in Japan before, it wasn't as traumatic as it could have been. We didn't have a grasp on the language yet. We did have an understanding of something that was maybe even more important. We were students of the Japanese culture. We knew the difference between Occidental and Oriental. That is a barrier far greater than language. You could know the language like a native, and yet be totally repulsive and not even know it. On the other hand, you could be very limited in your communication skills, and still be accepted in the community or almost anywhere you went.

People think that the Japanese have become westernized, simply because of the way they dress, the music they listen to, or because of what they drive. That couldn't be further from reality. The Japanese will cut you a lot of slack if you're not Japanese. They know that you don't know you're being very rude. The Japanese language is structured in levels of status. When you address someone, you speak from the level of a superior or from that of a subordinate. All the men carry business cards. If they don't know each other, they exchange cards with a bow before they speak to each other. They then know to speak up, down, or as an equal. Speaking as an equal would be both parties speaking as a subordinate, not using a higher form of speech. The higher level of the language was all we ever studied. We still always prefaced our communications with an apology for not knowing a more respectful way to speak.

The house was great. It was really two houses hooked together. One half was western style. The other half was Japanese style, with tatami mat floors and rice paper walls. A tatami mat is a four by eight piece of rice woven material, about two inches thick. It's hard enough to walk on and soft enough to sleep on. We learned later that it was really two places. The missionaries had lived in the western side, and the Japanese family, which had served as maid and gardener, had lived in the Japanese side. Some of the rice paper was torn and stained with time. Our understanding of Japanese culture paid off right away when it came to the rice paper walls and doors that needed to be replaced. We only had a couple neighbors, but they knew right away that we were not the average American family. We were not military-related, living off base as many Americans did. We never made eye contact with a neighbor without a courteous bow. We made no attempt to rudely communicate without an invitation to do so. They returned the gesture most politely and regarded us as above average American neighbors. They even allowed their little boy to play with our little Brandon.

One of the first things I wanted to do with the nice house was to replace the rice paper that was glued to the sliding wood frame doors. I asked Eddy how to do it. He said he would get me a roll of rice paper and some glue. He said the best way he had found to replace the paper was to take the doors and the paper and lay them in the front yard. Then he said to stand and look at it like you have no idea what you are doing. An old Japanese woman you didn't even know was watching would then come over and do it for you. What a source of wisdom we had in Eddy. Only in my case, it took two days for my neighbor to figure out her part of the equation. Maybe she was shy, but she got the job done without a word spoken.

Eddy gave us a couple days to get settled in after coming over and making breakfast and showing us where all the supplies were located. Our crates where slowly making their way across the Pacific, but Eddy and Neva had us stocked with the essentials. We could walk to the small stores serving our little neighborhood, but we really couldn't go anywhere too far unless we took a bus. Our level of communication wasn't up to a bus trip. I needed a driver's license. We had walked down to the seawall and familiarized ourselves with everything within walking distance. The few times that we had ventured out of our cozy surroundings, we had to pack into Eddy's van. Soon I was comfortable enough that I could handle getting us to the mission and over to Eddy's place on our own if I had a car. What I couldn't do was find the proper office and forms to make that happen. Eddy said he'd pick us up in the morning. We got all our paperwork together and prepared to spend the day in the city.

You have probably been to the DMV in America. Now imagine you couldn't speak or read English, and you didn't have the first clue as to which window to approach or what to say. Now add to that the possibility that you are from Mars. The Japanese are very organized, but if you don't fit into the existing understanding, they are totally lost. When you first enter the building, you get into the line offering the Japanese licenses. When the people behind the counter see you in that line, they make you move over to the counter that processes military-related personnel. When you finally get to that counter, they tell you that you have to go back to the base and get the proper forms. With Eddy's help, they finally figured out that we were not military or military-related. So they put you in the other line. After you have been sent back in and out of both lines about three times, they get together and start going over your papers together. At last, the thing happens that Eddy told us would finally have to happen before we got our license. The manager gets on the phone to Tokyo.

We were eventually taken into a back room with three officers. They studied their books on Pennsylvania licenses for about an hour before they reluctantly gave me a motorcycle endorsement. They just couldn't bring themselves to give me the heavy truck endorsements. Eddie told me they said those endorsements were worth thousands of dollars. When he told them we would be satisfied with just the motorcycle endorsement, they seemed relieved to issue me that much. A couple hours later, we left with Japanese driver's licenses and a motorcycle endorsement. One might think we had just wasted a whole day, but that's not how we felt. We felt more like we had accomplished a monumental task. Everybody was celebrating our great success. It takes a native forty hours of professional instruction before they can even apply to test for their driver's licenses. We did it all in one day and for thousands of dollars less than anyone else in that non-military line. We had had a really good day.

The first thing I noticed from behind the wheel was that the average Japanese had wasted a lot of money on their professional driver's training. The last time I had driven a car in Japan had been up in the mainland in the sixties. There were not nearly as many cars on the roads in those days. The main form of transportation back then was the electric train. The next was the bus and the bicycle. All of those had the natural right of way, so I don't remember being too upset when driving. That was not the case there on the islands this time, but one might think it was. The only thing you could be sure of was that if they could take it, they would. There didn't seem to be a lot of rage about it either. There seemed to be an attitude of amazement. It was like the driver that got cut off was saying 'Boy that was a neat move. I gotta learn that one.' The point I was trying to convince myself of was this: those people hadn't grown up like most Americans in my day. We had been driving farm tractors and pickups and whatever else since we had been able to reach the pedals. It was all new to these guys.

Doing things in an organized manner and doing things in the most efficient manner are two really different things. Why couldn't those people at customs and the government offices figure out how to do what they do on the roads? I had been using the word 'organized', when I should have been using the word 'regimented'. Maybe they had tried driving regimented and found out that it didn't work in traffic. Things changed minute by minute on the road. If you refused to adjust to them, you were going to be in an accident. I figure when they had learned that they could improvise, they took it to the extreme. So I tried keeping my cool by saying 'Hey look, they're thinking for themselves.' That didn't work very long either. You couldn't do most of what they were doing on the road if you were thinking.

That attitude was not going to work. God couldn't bless my relationships with those people if I was upset with them more often than I wasn't. I was the one with the problem. They didn't seem to be upset with each other. I noticed Eddy didn't have any problem. I asked him about it. At first, he only gave me shallow answers. I don't think he realized I really had a problem. Then one day, I included my problem in a prayer meeting. When he heard me sincerely seeking the Lord's help with it, he took me seriously and offered real help. "Tim, I had the same problem back when I first came to this country," he said. I asked him how he dealt with it. "The way you feel is just wrong," he explained. "Outside of their cars or their government positions, the Japanese people are the most courteous people on this earth. In either situation, they seem shocked that you are upset with them. That alone tells me they have absolutely no intention of upsetting you." As I thought, I was the one with the problem.

General McArthur had been put in charge of Japan in 1945. He ran the entire empire until he was put in charge of the Korean War in the early fifties. It seemed to make total sense in those days. I don't know why it doesn't today. We have lost his common sense. After all, it was he that said there is no substitute for victory. Our foreign policy ever since his day has become surrender at any cost. I guess you have to be a politician to understand value in defeat. I gave up on trying to figure that out, but I know history. McArthur was not just a respected victor to the Japanese people of his day. To many, he was the beloved father of their new nation. He had built his governing complex right across the street from the Emperor's Palace. He banned the teaching of the radical religion; the religion that taught that dying for your country gave you a special place in heaven. He never bothered anything else, including Emperor Worshipers. He prosecuted the Japanese military leaders, but he understood the Emperor's anti-military position and respected him for it.

In McArthur's governing facility lived an old Japanese man that had been assigned to the general. It was this man that solved my problem. It solved Eddy's problem with the Japanese of his day and it solved McArthur's. I may not have the right to identify my problem with this great general, but I could apply the solution. The general was one of the highest achievers, along with Patton, to ever graduate West Point. If I was annoyed with this Japanese custom of regimentation, he must have been going out of his mind. The poor old Japanese man must have been pretty stressed himself.

The General supposedly recorded one of their conversations in this manner. The old Japanese fellow told the general the following: "From my personal standpoint, compared to the American occupation forces, I feel like a child. Americans make decisions in realms far beyond what my culture allows me to even consider contemplating. I must be instructed in areas of service that you consider my normal responsibilities." I doubt if this is a reality today. My experience from working with the Japanese back in the sixties tells me it might well have been so in the forties. I don't know where I got this exact figure stuck in my memory, but the general decided to treat the old gentleman as an eleven year old child. By so doing, the stress level between them was normalized. They were no longer frustrated with each other, and even became friends.

This area of thought may not be politically correct today, but it worked for me. I don't subscribe to political correctness anyway. It's just an effort to limit free speech and force you to act as someone else wants you to. When you're dealing with someone limited by those rules, you have no idea who they really are. I just know I got along a whole lot better from that day on. I was a lot clearer when I requested some action or answer. I assumed nothing without a very explicit request or detailed instruction. I might have appeared pretty stupid at times, but all in all, I was treated with considerably more patience as well. What should we expect? There are probably a million people on these Islands. There were only seven families that fit our mold.

The mission was a small cement building that I really don't have any history on. I'm sure it had been handed down to Eddy from a former missionary, sort of like the works in Hawaii. It's funny now, but I never even knew who paid the rent on my house. I don't even know if there was any. I think I was sort of a caretaker for the mission outfit that owned it. My wife would know. It's wrong, but I'm one of those guys that allowed her to manage just about everything she wanted to. All I did was preach, and I didn't even do that for the first couple of months after we got settled. By then my wife was babysitting for a couple of military families who happened to be Christians. We had also met some other service families that Eddy had had some communication with. Before long, we had enough to start an English service. We held this service an hour before Eddy held the Japanese services. It wasn't long before we had five times as many Americans as we had Japanese.

Eddy came to our house every morning and taught Cheryl and I Japanese. Eddy grew increasingly irritated with Cheryl, and she returned the sentiment. After several months, I was relieved when she finally decided to quit participating. I made much better progress one on one with Eddy. That was how he had learned twenty plus years before up in the mainland. He had had a Buddhist monk as a teacher. There are levels of Japanese vocabulary. The old monk had taught him the highest level. Many of the words I learned from Eddy were not even commonly spoken anymore. The older Japanese understood them and felt honored that I would communicate with them on such an honorable level. Employers spoke down to employees, employees spoke up to employers, and friends spoke across or casual. This language is right up there with Navajo. I learned that only the most educated could read all of the daily newspaper. The blue collar, not so much, and the labor class, even less. I was doing so much better than my wife, because I got out everyday and used it.

I met a Marine Chaplain who hooked me up with his commander and I secured an ID to get access to the Marine bases. Not only did this allow me to start a racquetball club, but it gave me access to education programs offered by Maryland University. That is where I really learned to read and write. I didn't need it to make Japanese messages, because I had a bible written in Romagi. That is Japanese written with English letters. All you had to learn was how to pronounce the words. Why I needed to read was to function outside the areas frequented by the military.

The GIs were rather confined once they ventured off base. It is sad to say, but most men stationed on those beautiful islands never got further than walking distance from the base gate. No wonder they couldn't wait for their tour of duty to end. You could get tired of bar street and the souvenir shops in a couple weeks. A few ventured beyond those confines, but most were intimidated by their inability to communicate or adapt to a totally foreign culture. For those few adventurers not impressed with the bars and the small westernized shopping zones, I was their ticket to freedom.

Those islands were the Hawaiian Islands to the Japanese mainlanders. To the average GI, it was a hot inhospitable assignment far from home. I took those lonely and miserably bored young service boys and introduced them to a tropical paradise. I was playing racquetball on base regularly. I would play with anyone that ventured into the gym. It wasn't long before I had several teams. The highlight of their week was to play their match and then come to my house for refreshments.

Our house was a little piece of home. It wasn't military, and it wasn't foreign. It was home-cooked meals and school-aged children that just adored them. The GIs that had their families with them were especially grateful for our fellowship. Their wives could run with our wives. Eddy's wife spoke good Japanese, and my wife was the best barterer on the island. They became fast friends. Few of them ever missed Sunday services. A good work was growing that we had never even planned on building. We had aircraft mechanics, air police, administration, and computer personnel. When I was in the service, I never even met anyone outside my career field, let alone became good friends. Our group contained not only various career fields, but various branches of the military.

One of the Airmen was starting scuba diving lessons. I can't remember how we got involved, but my oldest son Mark and I ended up in his graduation class. Soon, we had weekly diving meets as well as racquetball matches. I landed on that island at about 190 lbs. I'd leave it at 175 Lbs. There was not an ounce of fat on my body. That was really good, because I was living and working with mostly Marines. I was not huge, like most of them, but I could not only keep up with them; I could beat most of them in anything but weight lifting. I was at least ten years older than they were. That generated a great deal of respect. I would really need it for what was about to happen.

My wife's little brother was a Marine. He was preparing to return to his old unit stationed right up the road from us. Though my wife was excited about it, I had some concerns. Peter was enlisted, but after his second enlistment, he had made DI. That was a real accomplishment in the corp. He was very disappointed by how the basic training had changed since he had been a new recruit. He was still all Marine, so he moved on to an even harder program. That was my concern. He was no longer enlisted. We were about to be joined by a WO4, the highest rank a Warrant Officer could attain at the time.

I had a good group of men by then. We had the privilege of winning many of them to Jesus. We baptized several of them and some of their wives as well. We had sergeants and we had corporals. In or out of uniform, our group was a solid first name-basis bunch of buddies and brothers. That was a little touchy at first, but God blessed and it worked out better than Eddy and I had thought possible. Even the wives, who are often worse than the guys, found a level of equality in our group. But we didn't have an officer. Eddy had a neighbor that had become a good friend. He was an Army Warrant Officer. He enjoyed doing things with Eddy's family, and soon with mine, but that's where it ended. His wife didn't even join ours for lunch or shopping unless they were alone. If one or two of the wives of our enlisted men were accompanying them, she had something else to do. We respected that, but we couldn't have two separate English services. Peter was going to bring his friends around and they were going to be officers. How were we going to migrate those guys to sit in the same church pew? They don't even eat or drink together. It was going to take God to work that problem out.

James 5:8
Be ye also patient; stablish your hearts: for the coming of the Lord draweth nigh.

Chapter 18
Sports, Little Children and Memories

Okinawa was really a beautiful place to live. I didn't even realize it at first. The green waters turned to dark blue the further from shore you looked. It is indescribable, really. There were two kinds of military personnel on the island. There were those that couldn't wait to get off of it, and those that couldn't wait to get back to it. Peter fell into the latter category. He had already done one tour there. He didn't play racquetball, but he was a diver. Most men that had learned to dive there seldom dove anywhere else more than once. I have never found another place like it. Pete feels the same way.

There is much better spear fishing off the coast of Florida, but the tranquility is not there. I don't like big fish. When we would go into the water from anywhere on Okinawa, we knew we were inside the third reef. Big fish didn't like it in there. I probably dove those waters more than anyone. If the natives had been into diving, that probably wouldn't be true, but for some reason they weren't. I went through at least four or five tanks a week. At the height of our activities, we made about three day dives and a couple night dives per week. Only a few men in our work did not dive.

Peter shipped his dog over by air a month before he was scheduled to come over. His name was Thor, a very large German Shepherd. The law said this dog would have to go into thirty days quarantine unless there was a non-military household that would keep him for that time period. We said we would keep him. Peter told us to be careful with him around strangers. We *were* strangers. The day came when we had to pick him up at the airport. We had never met this dog, nor did we have a cage to transport him. They just delivered him to our van, and opened their shipping container into our back door.

We were sitting in the front seat with our hands on the door handles. We spoke his name several times and he just layed down. His head was larger than any whole dog we'd ever owned. I had to turn my back to him and slowly drive away. I haven't been that nervous since I accidentally walked in on a bull that I didn't know was in the pasture. I told Cheryl not to take her eyes off him until we got him home. I didn't know what I was going to do then. We figured we would back into our big barn-like garage and close the doors. It was dark. The only light was the doorway into the house. He could get into the area where the servants used to sleep, but he couldn't get into the main house. We decided to keep him there until we fed him a couple times and got to know him a little better.

By the time Peter got there, Thor was my dog. If I went to bed before my wife, she had to sleep on the couch. He layed beside the bed and would allow no one in the room if I was asleep. And sure enough, he cared little for strangers. One day a man snuck into our backyard. The neighbors told me later that he was a peeping tom. They'd been watching him for awhile, but were not able to catch him. The Japanese work together on matters like this. When we had lived up in mainland many years before, I had seen it first hand. I heard an old woman yelling something and then a man ran through my yard and jumped my fence with her right on his heels. A woman on the other side of the fence started yelling the same thing and picked up the chase. I didn't know Japanese in those days. I didn't know they were chasing a thief. Houses were close together and there were no woods to hide in. They eventually ran the guy down and the police awarded them with a certificate of merit for their efforts.

I was one of only two westerners in my island neighborhood. The Japanese had not included us in their watch until I caught the peeping tom. After he had snuck into my yard, a Japanese neighbor stood in front of my garage pointing to my backyard. My daughter yelled that there was a strange man hiding between the block wall and our shed. There was only about three feet between the wall and the shed. I left Thor go in one side and I went around to the other side just in time to tell the dog to stay. That little guy saw Thor behind him and me in front of him. He dropped to his knees and began to pray. I could not keep from laughing. We all started laughing. Even the neighbors which were now gathered in my drive began to laugh.

Our youngest daughter was already a green belt in karate. She was the only one that put on a serious face and approached the guy. She went through one of her training moves, kicking the air and then pointed her finger in his face. The neighbors led him off as they guaranteed him that he would be arrested on sight if he ever returned to the neighborhood. We had two beautiful teenage daughters. That must have drawn this pervert to our yard. However, after watching him wet himself, I was more than satisfied we had seen the last of him.

I was honored that Peter chose to live with us until his family could join him. He could have stayed in the officer's quarters. Staying with us meant he had to walk clear up the street to the main road to catch the bus. I was teaching college in Naha. Cheryl had a license, but she would not drive. Peter's Harley was coming, but still about a month out. He was a lot more of a family person than I remembered. Mark was about twelve then, and he idolized his uncle Pete. It was a two way street. Pete's boy was just a toddler and Mark was big enough to go places with him. He took him to the weight room regularly and even to his office. Mark made fast friends with both the enlisted men that worked for his uncle and Pete's fellow officers. Kids his age were pretty rare on a Marine base. This boy was old enough to be impressed with who they were and also to joke around with them. Some of them became close enough to be invited to a family outing, even though they were enlisted men. After all, we'd go to beaches where you seldom, if ever, saw another American.

I was still looking for a way to include our group with this growing group of Pete's. When members of our group came to my house, they treated Pete with the same stand-offish respect with which they treated their commanding officers. I had to find a way to get them together in a relaxed atmosphere. The guys Peter allowed to join us on weekends were still nothing like my guys. They wouldn't joke with me. Peter was their commanding officer, and I was his brother-in-law. I might as well have been a general. Even the officers that drove Pete home treated me like their superior. They were honored to be invited into our home and they made it very clear, but the only ones that could break the ice were my kids.

I was learning something. In my children's eyes, there was no difference between one of my Air Force sergeants and one of Pete's officer friends. Mark said one night that we needed another racquetball player for the night. "Do you play?" he asked one of Pete's officer friends. "If you'll be my partner, I can play with Mike and Dad." That night, Lieutenant Wade walked into that court with my boy and a low grade Air Force sergeant. The next time it was with two sergeants and me. Then another officer that could play a lot better came to help. Soon we were mixing the teams to make it more balanced. One night an officer asked if he could match up with his enlisted Air Force teammate. The ice was cracking.

One of the men that helped me put it all together, of course, was Eddy. He was twenty years older than all of us. Peter and a couple of his officer friends and their wives were coming to church regularly. My wife was playing the same balancing act with the wives that I'd been playing with their husbands. I was able to win a computer operator that worked for the Navy. He was a Marine sergeant, but to Eddy, he was just Brother Ray. Lieutenant Wade had joined his wife in the Christian faith by then, and we had baptized him. To Eddy, he was just Brother Paul. None of us respected anyone anymore than we did Eddy, and his suffix was Brother. The sir and the sergeant stuff somehow began to fade. I can't remember who called who 'Brother' for the first time, but it was received and respected, as was sister for the wives.

No one abused the privilege. When there was a non-Christian in our presence, whether he was a ranking officer or a subordinate, our men addressed one another in proper military terms. There was however, a softness that conveyed a personal respect for one another. It's not explainable, but it made outsiders comfortable being around us no matter what their branch of service or their rank.

Next I started merging our diving groups. A new man would show up about every other week. He would be introduced by his first name and diving experience. Mostly you were just glad to be included in a group that knew their way around the sport. You don't dive alone and you don't make your first dive anywhere without an experienced guide. About all you judge is the quality of the equipment your fellow divers are donning, and they were looking at yours. Some of our officers were more than happy to be buddied up with our more experienced enlisted men. Other than jokingly, I don't remember ever having an offensive event regarding ones rank. Everyone was on a first name basis or Brother, depending on your relationship. The only one I insisted on being introduced by rank was me. At my age, I would have had to be a ranking officer or something. I wanted it known from the outset that I was a non-military related civilian, these were my guys, and rank was not an issue here. I knew the problem was gone when I watched two of our officer's families stand in the back of the church to make room for visiting enlisted families.

It became rather clear to both Eddy and I that my ministry was to the GIs and their families. We had more baptisms in a year than he had been able to hold in twenty years. He was still solid in his calling to the Japanese. That didn't mean he didn't help me with the American side of the work. The guys really loved being around that old man. He didn't dive or play racquetball, but he could relate to you like your grandfather. These young men are the backbone of our nation, but you would never believe how much they missed their childhood. They were ten thousand miles from home, and leaders in their own right. Nothing reassured them of their decision to serve like spending time with men that were the epitome of why they served. My children were their little brothers and sisters, so what did that make me? That made Eddy grandfather, and he fit the role very well. He had spent most of his life in Japan, and had worked harder than most on American and world history. He could tell a fireside story that transcended age, ethnicity, and gender. When I looked at him, I saw me back when I was the young GI. It was cool to share this with the boys. It gave them a feeling of permanency, like family. They're part of generations of GI and missionary relationships. In that ministry, Eddy and I were an unbeatable team.

More officers were joining our ranks because of Pete. There were a few high ranking NCOs as well. They were comfortable around each other, because they were joint leaders in the command. God used diving, racquetball, and our kids to meld these groups to a very acceptable level at church or beach outings. There was one area that these activities could not transcend. The enlisted men were equally as guilty in the matter. Officers just normally took better care of themselves. Their children were dressed a little better and their wives were often the girl they'd met in college. They got along fine as a group, but one on one, they had very little in common.

The men knew this and were careful not to get themselves invited to a personal gathering where they wouldn't be comfortable. Eddy's family and my family were finding ourselves being invited to places like that more and more. It's not that we'd ever turn down an invitation to anyone's residence. It's just that there was a lot less of us to go around those days. So we decided to do something special for our original bunch. They had been there a lot longer than the officers and therefore had built up a lot more leave time. We put together a two day camping trip to an island; about a five-hour boat ride away.

This chain of islands we lived on had a deadly snake living on them. The Japanese call it a Habu. It is a smaller variety of the Cobra. You could always find a place where tourists would go to watch a match between one of these snakes and a Mongoose. I only went to watch one of them. It's over faster than you can see it; bang and the snake was dead. The story goes that many years before, the Mongoose had been introduced to these islands to rid them of the snake. What they didn't think about was that chickens tasted better than snake and were a lot easier to find than snakes. They soon learned about the only way you could get a Mongoose to kill one of these little cobras was to throw them into the same box together.

Eddy tells a funny little story about an old Japanese fellow he met on a boat coming down from mainland Japan. The old guy had a seriously withered arm. He told Eddy he had been on Okinawa during the war. One of his fellow soldiers woke him up one night and told him not to move. He said he had seen a Habu crawl into his bag. He said he freaked. It's funny to watch Eddy show you how he freaked. But not every island in the chain had Habu living on them. It's strange, but it's only about every other island that didn't have them. We picked one of them for our camping trip. We were going to a place that had no emergency services located on it, either. By the time we could get an airlift, we could die.

I wish it didn't have any Sea Snakes either, but it was still the South China Sea. These islands are still in the same sea. Sea Snakes are air breathers, but they never come out of the water. We'd sleep on the beach. There was no anti-venom for Sea Snakes, no matter where you were. We were all divers except for Lenny. He was the civilian husband of one of our young Marine enlistees. Not counting Mark, he was the youngest and the most fun. Rank meant nothing to him. He was equally belligerent to everyone when his wife was not around. He looked a little bit like Lou Costello, and he got away with almost anything because of it. His wife was a head taller, and looked sort of like a model. He had a cute chubby face with big dimples. There was no question that he had got her with his personality. Mark and Lenny were two peas in a pod. You had to keep a close eye on them both.

The boat pulled up to an old dock. Not many people lived here. A few pigs and some other supplies were off loaded. I remember a truck door being carried off, but I never saw a truck. You can see me standing in front of it with my arms out. I was explaining that we needed one of those. It was so hot....maybe we could put the window down and get some air. We made our way through the light underbrush to the nearest beach. There was no sign of anyone. Japanese tourists aren't really into beaches, and this sure wasn't any place you would find a tourist. There was a little island about a half a mile off to our right. Mark and Lenny snorkeled their way out to it while we set up camp. They came back about an hour later. They said they had found an old lady living out there. They asked for a drink of water but she had given them a beer. They think she was telling them that drinking water was too scarce.

We didn't take any tanks with us; just our wetsuits, snorkel gear, and weight belts. Most of us had been diving long enough to go down about sixty feet and back on a good breath. There wouldn't be anywhere to refill our tanks out there anyway. About thirty days before the invasion of Okinawa, hundreds of ships had sat in those waters. They had shelled everything in preparation for the landing. I found the location where one of them must have anchored. I dove down about twenty feet and found the top of a mountain of empty shells. I wasn't navy, so I don't know for sure what they were. They were about three feet long and six or eight inches around. I said, "Oh Lord, I'm rich." I had never seen a pile of copper like that in my life. How was it that no one had found this? I went up for another breath and back down to try and get one. I grabbed one on the top of the pile and pulled with all I had. It only pulled me into the pile. My dive tool wouldn't even make a scratch on it. Those things had been there for about thirty-five years. They were no longer a pile of individual shells; just one immovable mountain of metal.

I found a small valley of life running along the shallow bottom as I made my way back to shore. I had never seen that kind of life in these islands. I wish I had taken the time to triangulate the location. The current was running pretty swiftly. I thought I could find it again with no trouble. I wanted to show it to everyone. I even saw my first large Moray eel. I crawled my way to the beach until I could stand and remove my fins. As I walked out of the water, I saw Lenny running down the beach holding something on his shoulder. "What have you got, Lenny?" I asked him. "I don't know, but it's pretty old," he said. I got close enough to see what it was and I yelled for him to stop. All I could think was to instruct him to throw it as far into the weeds as possible and hit the deck. He knew by my demeanor that I was dead serious. He complied as requested. The boy had found a Claymore mine. When the powder gets old, it crystallizes if it's not wet. I was praying it was wet. They can be more unstable in that state than they were when they were new. Now I'm thinking maybe those shells were fired on this island.

We never did find that colorful stream of life again. We searched for it until dark. I'm just blessed to have seen it once. Our real bounty was yet to be found. Lenny also made the discovery in the morning. That night, however, is a sight I had never before seen. There was no city on this island and no city this side of the horizon. There was not a single light and there was no moon. The stars ran from the sea behind us to the sea in front of us. Solid stars right down to the ground, or the ocean....either one was right at your feet. Once I flew a guy into a fifteen hundred foot grass airstrip up in the mountains on the border of Pennsylvania and New York. I slept under the stars that night. It was great, but not like this. Besides, I had almost drowned in the dew that fell sometime after I went to sleep. There is no dew in the subtropics, only mosquitoes. I learned how to handle them when I was up in Alaska. I knew the history of the first settlers up there. They were run out by black flies and mosquitoes. I couldn't wait to learn how they controlled them now. When I asked a brother about it, I expected to learn about some super secret formula. He gave it to me. It's conveniently packaged in spray cans. They call it Deep Woods Off. The Japanese had learned this secret as well, and we had bought a can before we left Okinawa.

When camping, I love mornings. There is nothing like breakfast cooked on the campfire. We had gone to sleep by the fire, and now it was just right for cooking. The night before, a moth had been circling the fire. Eddie explained why they did that until they were finally consumed by the fire. He said they navigated by the brightest star. When we built the fire, it became that star. He keeps turning by its light until he finally turns right into it. I told you the old man could tell stories all night. He was running out of them when the moth showed up. Maxwell House made a coffee filter for their electric pot with the coffee sewed up in side of it. It looked like a big cloth donut you just put in your pot. We carried them camping. We would set a pan of water on the fire and bring it to what we call a rolling boil. Then just throw it in the pan and let it boil for another minute. I called them maxi-pads. The first pot of coffee is the best.

I was enjoying my second cup when Lenny walked into camp with a big green glass ball in his hand. "What's this thing?" He was tossing it from hand to hand as Eddy and I jumped up and secured it carefully in our hands. That boy had never been out of the hills of West Virginia, Tennessee, or somewhere; I don't remember. Soon we forgot about breakfast and hit the beach. If one glass ball had washed up, maybe there were more. If you picked one of these up on the beach in Florida, you carried it to the nearest shop and collected one-hundred dollars back then.

This place was virtually uninhabited. We walked the beach for miles picking up glass balls. After about two hours, the last guy walked back into camp carrying his three or four balls. Now we had a problem. We had got off the boat with just about everything we could carry. At best, we might be able to get two apiece back to the dock. That left well over a thousand dollars worth of these collectables that we couldn't carry. We had just enough time to comfortably pack up and make the dock. There was no way we were going to make two trips. I don't want to remember whose idea it was to do what we did next, because it was probably mine. We made a treasure map. Ten feet west from tree marked with an 'X', then five feet north, and so on. We buried our treasure and trusted the map to our trusted leader. We shall return. Luckily for the Filipino people, Macarthur did return, but we never did. Someone probably got rich off the shell casings and built a resort hotel right on top of our buried treasure.

Of all the events that took place on that two day trip, the two real memories of that trip were yet to be made. On the way back, we took another path and came upon a little building. On the door was a symbol of washing hands. That was a thing you almost never saw. The Japanese just didn't waste money on public toilets when a bush would do the job. Even if there wasn't a bush, they still didn't believe in holding their water. One of the first things Eddy taught me was never to pass a toilet, because they are few and far between.

We put down our packs as my twelve-year-old son entered the little building. We thought something was wrong because he came right back out. He walked over to me and said softly, "Dad, I don't know how to use that thing." Eddy heard him and told him to come over to where he was standing. He picked up a stick and began drawing in the dirt. Soon we were all in a circle watching as Eddy outlined the Japanese style toilet and instructed the lad in its proper use. You face this thing. You do not turn around and sit on it. You face it and if you need to sit down, you straddle it. Eddy looked up at us very studiously and said, "Fellows, memories are made of this stuff."

We arrived back at the small dock area just in time to see them loading a few commodities, no people. A man walked up to us with a real serious look on his face and tried to ask us something. He knew from the glass balls we were carrying that we had been on the beach. He was very upset because he had left his wind surfing equipment beside the trail we had gone in on. He must not have had a very good opinion of GIs. He was sure we had tampered with it or destroyed it. It, of course, was a very rare item in the day, and must have cost him a lot to get there. I didn't even know what it was. I thought it was a sail attachment for a small boat when I had seen it. He was really getting frustrated when Eddy finally decided to address him. In crystal clear Japanese, and speaking down to him as a superior, Eddy told him that he and I were American missionaries on a church outing from Okinawa. His equipment was exactly where he had left it. I can't remember hearing that tone from Eddy very often. In essence, this guy was making a serious accusation. Now this fellow knew he had two choices; either apologize, or just shut up and leave. He chose the latter.

I reached in my pack as this was going on and pulled out either an

Eisenhower dollar or a Kennedy half; I don't remember which it was. I was the last guy in line and this fellow would have to walk right past me to leave the area. As he started to pass, I stepped in his path. I'm not as big as Eddy was, but I was younger, and twice the size of this fellow. The guy was in real good shape, but he decided to stop when I asked him to wait a minute. I was using pretty good Japanese by then, not nearly as well as Eddy's, but respectable. It's almost a shocked look they give you when it's coming from the lips of a guy-jean. That is not how 'gai-jin' is spelled, but I wrote it so you could pronounce it plainly. It is a lower form of a word used for a foreigner. That is what he had called us before he knew we could understand everything except his attempt at English. I was using high Japanese, which is about all I knew. I asked him what that thing out there was. He wasn't smiling, but he explained that it was a sail on a surfboard. I said I had never seen one up close. "Did you ever see one of these?" I asked him as I handed him the coin. He looked at it; he had no intention of keeping it. When he tried to hand it back, I told him to keep it for a souvenir, and I bowed.

The guy didn't warm up to me, but by then he probably figured we were culturally savvy. He had offended us already and gotten a good scolding for it. He thought about it for a second and decided not to further offend us by refusing my gift. Not to mention, it was a treasured piece to the Japanese. He told me that nobody ever goes where we had been, so he typically left his expensive gear out there. It's heavy to carry home. He said he was just concerned. He said he didn't know we were teachers. They sometimes confuse the term with missionary. He gave me a nod in respect to my bow and walked off. I'm sure he went straight to the beach. The fact that his gear was safe and he has a collector's item in his pocket was the only witness I could think of at the time.

I had a clear conscience when I got on the boat. Maintaining such a thing will help you a lot when you get into a situation like we were about to get in. I'm not saying every one else had a bad conscience. I'm just telling you what works for me when I'm in a storm. It was a beautiful day as we headed back on our five-hour return to Okinawa. The weather stayed nice, but the seas did not. We were about an hour or less out from Naha Port when we really got into it. Thank God for that. I don't know if our boys could have lasted much longer. It started out with just rougher than normal seas. They were enough to drive Eddy to his Dramamine supply. I was a pilot. I'd only been bothered by motion sickness twice in my life. Once was during an assault takeoff in the service, and the other was when I had got caught in clear air turbulence while flying for the college. Both times I had nearly vomited, and both times were triggered by fear. As the swells rose higher and higher, the men got sicker and sicker. Eddy went below deck; they used to call that under the weather. He managed not to throw up. The rest of the guys were not so fortunate.

I couldn't help it; I had to take pictures of our tough Marines and Airmen. They gathered the large plastic trashcans and tied themselves to the railings. Their heads seldom came out of those barrels. I felt sorry for them, but I knew there was nothing I could do to help them. Mark, my twelve-year-old, kept a close eye on his dad. I knew if I showed any concern, I'd be looking for a barrel for him. Instead I decided to show him the opposite. I walked around the wheelhouse and made my way to the bow. There was a large cargo net stretched across the front of the boat about three or four feet from the nose. I told him that would be a great place to ride this thing out. Mark was right on my heels. We grabbed the net and climbed it high enough to look down over the front railing. I said to my son, "We are in the center of God's will and doing his work; enjoy this experience." We slowly churned up the towering swells, then plunged down into the bottom of the equally deep trough behind them. As we broke over the crest of each on-comer, we yelled like is common at that stage of a rollercoaster ride. We hung there for the duration which lasted until we came within reach of the jetty into the port and the water flattened immediately.

I still believe motion sickness is somehow tied to fear or uncertainty. In seconds, our boys were washing out the barrels with a deck hose. They were worn out, but smiling with relief. After Mark and I had clung to the cargo net and begun to cheer and yell, I looked behind us. About two stories above us was the wheelhouse behind a large glass window. You could clearly see the wheelman and the captain looking down on us. I told my son to look at their faces. Their smiles put any remaining concerns we may have had to rest. We had a ball all the way to the port where Mama was waiting with the van. After pictures were taken of us with our bounty, we piled in the van. "Boy, you guys stink," was her official greeting. "It sure wasn't anything I ate," said one of the poor guys that had spent the last hour with his head in a barrel.

That is the first time I remember her driving. It was Eddy's wife that never drove. I remember Cheryl taking the girls on the Marine base to garage sales. That was when Eddy told me about the last time he had visited the States. He thought things were really getting bad. He said he had seen signs for garage and yard sales for the first time. How do you sell a yard? That reminded me of the first fast food place I took one of my missionaries to after he returned home. You're supposed to empty your tray in the trash bin and lay the tray on top of it. He looked at it, shrugged his shoulders, and threw tray and all into the trash bin.

Suddenly, I was one of those guys. What was changing back home that I knew nothing about? Well, I had a real advantage over most foreign missionaries. I was working with men that were living on American properties. Base facilities maintain current US standards. They broadcast their own TV and radio stations. My brother-in-law could go to the BX and purchase most everything we had shipped over there. Eddy had never had such connections. He also had a slight diversion about such connections. I remember back when I first met him up in mainland Japan. He was the missionary and I was the young military guy that took him on the Air Force Base for his first time ever. He acted like he was doing something wrong.

I didn't know it at the time, but there were American missionaries abusing their base privileges. They would buy mass amounts of commodities and sell them on the Japanese market. Because of them, I could not get permission to enter the Air Force Base there on Okinawa. The Marines gave me a pass for their bases, but no logistical support. That meant I could use the gym and the restaurants and the little convenience stores, but not the BX. Eddie never took advantage of base privileges even back when he could have. I'll never forget when I took him to the A&W on base. I convinced him he was not violating anything as my guest and asked him what he wanted for lunch. He looked at the menu like a kid at a candy store.

In the sixties, Japan had no Westernized businesses like they have now. I just laughed when Eddy said he'd have a root-beer float. It was about the only thing on the menu he could have made at home. He told me it wouldn't be an A&W Root Beer Float if he made it at home. It's not the product you miss, it's the memory. There we were in Okinawa, many years later, and he still felt the same way. I can't remember ever taking him on a base on Okinawa. There wasn't much those days, however, that you couldn't find on the modern Japanese market. It just cost a little more if it was truly an import. The Japanese are great copiers. Anything you can make, they can make it cheaper, and in many cases, better. There was a supermarket called Jimmy's. It would be something like a national chain that we have in the States. They featured foods from all over the world. The founder had copied the best he could find in America, including the name Jim.

My youngest daughter, Tonia, was in a private school that taught in English. It had been started by a mission group many years before. I was on the board of directors from the day I had arrived in country. Their constitution required six or seven in-country missionaries to comprise the board. They were one short when I got there, so I was invited immediately. Tonia came to me one day and asked me to take a walk with her. I knew something was up. She hadn't made that request in years. We used to take walks together from the time she was a little girl. It wasn't much of a secret that she was daddy's favorite. She explained what I already knew.

Her life's goal was to be a wife and mother. She explained that her school was made up of a few missionary kids and the rest were Gobu-Gobus. That meant half and half. Most of them were children sired by Americans and abandoned. "I don't fit, and I don't want to fit," she told me. Mark fit like a native. He already spoke Gobu-Gobu. That's a mixture of the Japanese and English language. She told me that Jimmy's had offered her a job at the supermarket and that she really wanted to take it. I told her I would speak to her mom about it. I had already decided to support her. It was a good decision.

That same little girl that had cried 'I can't read' was making her way around better than any of us. Jimmy put her in his commercials and in all the favorite Japanese magazines. She became more famous than she ever realized. Japanese companies sought her out to model their products. She didn't really know what was happening. If I had been paying real attention, she would have had a manager and really made the most of it. They flew her to other islands for different events. She already had earned a green belt on her own and entered a national cross country competition where she came in second. The only one that beat her was another American. He was a US Marine.

She got a bronze medal for something. I don't remember what it was for. She furnished her own room with a TV, VCR, and anything else she wanted. My only problem was her search for the completion of her life's goal; the one thing she needed most to be a wife and mother. First she brought a young enlisted Marine home that made the mistake of calling her uncle Pete by his first name. That didn't fly. We never saw him again. The effort continued for the duration of her time in country. She was a beautiful young girl, an athlete, and a God-given gift to motherhood. She just had no idea what to look for in a man. The right guy would have found a princess, but anything she kissed turned into a frog.

If ever I could stop time, it would have been right there. The mission was standing room only. We were seeing numerous baptisms and life-changing events. Both enlisted and officers filled my week with activities designed to attract and evangelize others by association. God's first institution was the family. It comes before the school or the church or the government. I believe it was to communicate His love to the world. We never had to witness to a stranger. All we ever had to do was include them. Some ran with us for months before they just had to tell us something. By then we already knew. They had accepted Christ and it was time to make it public. Some we wouldn't learn about until years after they had left the island. I believe every man has his own abilities to minister. Men like Falwell, Hyles, McArthur, Rogers, Olstein, Warren, and several other great pastors have no limit to the numbers they can minister to. I claim no such ability. I seem to max out with the number I can accommodate in my maximum limit of regular activities. I guess most everything we ever did was on a rolling time scale, and time is rolling on. Not only were my men soon facing rotation, Eddy's furlough was fast approaching as well.

Mark 2:17

When Jesus heard it, He saith unto them, They that are whole have no need of the physcian, but they that are sick: I came not to call the righteous, but sinners to repentance.

Chapter 19
Working Without a Net

"I've been performing for years with pretty good success," said the high wire artist. I'd never thought much about it until this point. Starting the next week, I'd be working without a net. Can you imagine your first performance without a net? If you screw up, there is nothing to break your fall. Any situation I couldn't figure out, Eddy was a phone call away. In a few days that phone call would have to be long distance. I would have to take over the Japanese services as well. My world was about to change.

I can't remember if Eddy elected to keep his house and store his stuff until they got back or what. I know they put some large items in my garage / barn and left me some cool camping gear. I wanted the cast iron pot more than anything else. We would dig a hole in the sand and build a charcoal fire in it. We would fill the pot with stew and set it in the hole. Then we would lay the potatoes around the lid which was made like a shallow pan. Then we would fill the hole back up. When we would dig it up, the stew would be cooked and the potatoes would be baked. That way, we didn't have to carry a grill with us. We didn't need a hot fire burning on the beach in the summer time either.

After all the goodbye parties and the final instructions on who to contact for what, the dreaded day came. Eddy's daughter had previously left for college and Neva followed her sometime after. It was just Eddy that I remember taking to the airport. We talked about some important things we had been putting off as long as we could. Personal stuff had developed over about three years working as closely as we had been working. Then there was the one real encouragement I really needed. He said, "You handle the language a lot better than you think you do." Coming from Eddy, those were like words of encouragement coming from your dad. He never mixed words. I knew if he was as concerned as I was, he would have told me so. Instead it was the opposite.

Making a Japanese message was simple, because I could pronounce any Japanese word, especially if it was written in English letters. I had a book that did that. The real test came just days before Eddy's departure. I called it my first performance without a net. Just up the road from us was a three story apartment building. I spent a lot of nights up on its roof to get a little breeze and to pray. There was one GI family that lived in it. They were not very nice people. Several of his friends would show up and get drunk and loud. One day, Lieutenant Wade was standing in my driveway when they started carrying on. He was in uniform and so were they. He commanded them to watch their language. Instead of a proper 'yes sir', they just went into the apartment. Shortly after the incident, the four enlisted Marines walked down the path beside my house. They didn't go on out to the seawall. They hid in a bush at the bottom of the path.

Peter and his officer friend had joined us from in the house. The seawall was off limits to Marines because of a terrible fight down there years before. These officers were concerned for the safety of my family, so they decided to go down and ID them. We walked down the path with the setting sun behind us. Paul spotted them in the bushes and stopped. All they could see were the shadows of very large men looking at them. They filed out of the bushes one at a time and squeezed passed us as they made their way back up the path. I don't know what these idiots had in mind, but luckily for everyone, they thought better of it. Well, on one particular night Paul and the guys were not here, and it was really getting wild. I wasn't going to face a bunch of drunken Marines alone.

I was sure one of the Japanese families would call the police, but maybe they were just too afraid to do so. Then a few minutes later, all hell broke out. I heard the word 'knife' and a woman screaming. This would be my first performance in total Japanese. I called the local police and told them what I had heard and gave them the address. They were there in about two minutes and it was over. Even the drunken idiots knew about the Japanese police. They will beat you unmercifully with their clubs. That's only if they don't intend to hurt you. God had a three part purpose in all this. Number one was that we didn't need drunken GIs anywhere near our teenage daughters. We never saw them again. Within days, a really nice GI family moved in the apartment and became our good friends. Clark was their name, and they had a little girl about the age of our little Brandon, from whom Brandon would get his first kiss before they left the island. Mrs. Clark was a good companion for my wife. It was a real improvement.

Second good thing was that the Japanese neighbors talked to each other. It wasn't long before they figured out which neighbor had to have called the police. Together we got rid of the peeping tom. In turn, we rid them of the only other bad element in our little hood. When the women met my wife or kids in the little neighborhood market from then on, they were greeted with a bow and a smile. I continued to collect large mussels from the reef while diving and placed them on a neighbors step. In turn, fresh cut flowers showed up on ours. We seldom ever spoke. I spoke Japanese and they spoke Ho-gen. It was a very old neighborhood made up of mostly natives to Okinawa. A professor in the college where I was teaching afternoon classes explained it all to me. He had been born on the island. He taught me just enough to really help me in the little stores around the island that were owned by natives. I would use Ho-gen greetings instead of Japanese. Immediately, I would receive special attention.

Thirdly, and most rewarding, was that my call to the police station had received a rapid and precise response. It was even understood well enough that my request for the police not to visit my house was honored. That was the greatest confidence building action that God could have performed for me at the time. Not only did I feel confident, I felt safe. I couldn't call the military police. I didn't live in their jurisdiction, nor was I their responsibility. I had developed what most people call the jungle rot on my left foot. I went to the naval hospital, where I was examined and informed that without immediate attention, I would lose my foot. Then the doctor learned that I was not military related personnel. He told me I'd better find some help in a hurry, and then dismissed himself. God was teaching me the confidence and security that I had observed in Eddy when I first found him in the rice paddies many years before. It's a great feeling to finally accept the fact that God is all you need.

Back when I first met Eddy in mainland Japan, he could have transferred to these islands and been under American jurisdiction. What they call reversion had taken place just eight years before we got there. For some reason, these islands had remained under US Military control from the end of the war until the early seventies. They now belonged to Japan. I don't know the history of it all, I just know what happened when our boys landed. The Okinawan people received us as liberators. To this day, there is a monument on the northern tip of Okinawa that states 'From this point south, we are with America,' or something like that. My fellow professor at Naha University was only about twelve years old when we had defeated the occupying Japanese forces. That's how he put it anyway. He told me of fond memories when the GIs had first come to his little village. They would bring in a truckload of supplies to their store. He would always be waiting for them so he could listen to them as they spoke to one another at the store. They were giants in his eyes, and they had treated him much better than the Japanese soldiers had. He said the Japanese had called the people of his village 'Chinaman crossed with monkeys'. He felt much safer with the GIs. The Japanese took from us, but the Americans gave to us, he had said.

My friend told me he owed his career to those GIs. He had memorized a couple words each time the supplies were delivered. One day he tried using them. Only problem was, he had memorized the words that he had heard the most, and they were not pleasantries. One day he was running after the truck, yelling the words he had learned at the men in the back of the truck. They yelled back to him, "Get the H out of here you little bastard." The next time they returned, he had those words memorized and ready to use. He said he had no idea what he was saying, but he was communicating, he told me with a big smile. Then one day they brought a letter for him written in his language. One of the GIs realized that this kid wanted to learn English. He got a woman that worked for an American missionary to write it. After several exchanges came an invitation to join the woman and learn English. That opened the door that had led to college in the States, where he later got his degree in English.

That guy was truly a friend to me. We ate lunch at the same table in the cafeteria every day. I was the only non-Japanese teacher I ever saw invited to join the Japanese staff for a meal. When you meet a native in a restaurant at a resort, you can enjoy each others company for the length of your stay. They will often give you their business card and invite you to visit them. Don't make the mistake of actually trying to do so. You are not welcome in their home unless you are one of their inner circle. There is a big difference between Occidental and Oriental. We are very independent and outgoing. They are a group culture. This is so serious that they have committed suicide for offending the group. This is one reason that it was almost impossible to win an individual to Christ. They don't make many decisions independent of the group. I don't know if my friend checked it out with his group or not, but when he invited my family to his house for a meal, he meant it. He cooked us the best meat, right on their dining room table. It was really good, but there was a down side. That wasn't all he had prepared for us. He knew that I knew Japanese custom, which meant we were to eat whatever was put in front of us.

A few months after that, we would find ourselves in a place where we would have paid to eat that stuff if we could have only found any of it. I don't know why visas aren't issued for the full term of one's intended stay. You cannot renew them from within the host country, either. This meant that we had to leave the country, and return, for the renewal process to be completed. The nearest non-Japanese island was Taiwan. My children did not need to go through the renewal process, because we could sponsor them for some reason. Cheryl and I, however, had to go, so we decided to make it a vacation. The least expensive way was by boat. I don't remember how I made the arrangements, but we got a round trip in first class for less than one of us could fly one-way. The boat was going to dock at two ports on opposite sides of the island. The first port was a little town on the backside of the mountain that runs down the middle of the island. The other port was the capital city of Taipei. We decided we would get off at the first stop and go over the mountain by land to Taipei. I'd been studying the map for days. I found a train running up the coast to a small town where we could take a bus up over the Sung Moon pass and down to the city. What a plan.

We had already changed our money to Taiwanese, and I had my map. What more could we want? I couldn't speak a word of Chinese, but I had a pocket full of money. I could point at the map and look stupid until someone pointed me in the right direction. That was my plan. We could leave our van at the port in Naha until we got back. All we had to do was find the boat to Taiwan, get on board, find our first class cabin, and go to bed. It was a Japanese boat, so no problem. We found it right away. The Captain looked at my ticket and told me my cabin was at the bow, below deck. He said it was the one on the port side. The boat was no bigger than the inter-island boat we had taken on our camping trip. The only difference was that this one was not a passenger boat. There was not a seat on it. I was thinking everything must be below deck. We walked down the steps, and sure enough, there it was on the port side. There were only two cabins, one on the left side and one on the right. The entire lower deck was covered by rice mats. People and pigs and chickens were laying on them. There was not a chair, or even a bench on this thing.

We just looked at each other and walked to the cabin. At least we had a door. Did we want to open it? Hey, it was definitely first class if there was no pig in there. It was the size of the average walk-in closet, only curved on one side along the bow line. Rice mats covered the floor, and that was our bed. There was a tiny head in the corner, though, and that made all the difference in the world. We could live with this, no pigs and a head. What more could we want? It was a beautiful night, as I remember, going up on deck. The stars were horizon to horizon, and the sea was gentle. For the price we had paid, it was truly first class. The seas stayed good all the way to the little port where we would be processed and directed to a hotel.

We both remember walking from the little office on the dock, looking for anyplace we could find food. There were only two little buildings at the dock. The one that we had just had our passports stamped in, and the little train station we would return to in the morning. Neither one had a restaurant. Our ship captain gave us the train schedule and we left. It was like walking down a country road. Once we left the docks, there were only two structures in sight. There was a rather large building in the distance up on the side of a hill which we figured had to be the hotel. There was nothing else besides one little shack between us and the hotel anywhere in sight. The little shack was an open-front store, about twelve by twelve at the most, with an old woman sitting behind the counter. The shelves behind her had some canned goods setting on them, but there was nothing we recognized. There were chicken feet hanging from the ceiling by string. Where was the chicken, I asked, but she didn't speak English. I made like I was eating with my hand and pointed to the hotel. She shook her head 'no'. I didn't know if that meant no food there, or that she didn't know. From where we were, we could see some huts scattered around the hills, but they had to be family dwellings. "We're in a mess here, Baby," I said. "There's no food anywhere."

We hadn't been hungry since the early days of our effort to get on the field. Even then, we could manage a bag of chips. I'd had given that whole pocket full of money for a bag of chips right then. "Look there," my wife said, pointing to a small tin on the top shelf. "That's peanut butter, and I think that box below it is some kind of crackers." She had scanned every can and box twice when she had finally hit pay dirt. The tin of peanut butter was rusted almost through. The crackers were different, but they were crackers alright. "It's supper, Baby; what a gift from God." Who knows how many years God had made her sit on that high dollar import on the top shelf? No doubt in our minds, it was put there for that very moment. We walked double time to the large old building on the hill. When the shop owner had shaken her head 'no', it had meant there was no food in the hotel. Otherwise we wouldn't have this wonderful memory. We were feasting on crackers and peanut butter in a dark little room in the middle of nowhere.

We had to be at the train station early in the morning. There was no alarm clock, and no phone to call for a wake up. Even if there had been, there wasn't anyone there that could have understood my request. I don't remember seeing any other guests. It must have been off-season. I figured that there must be a season; why else would that old hotel even be there? We managed to make our train in plenty of time. We had plenty of sleep, because after the peanut butter and crackers, there wasn't anything else to do but wash up and go to bed. I think we waited for daylight to see our way back to the port. No continental breakfast by the way; no anything. We hoped the train might have a dining car, but at that point, we weren't betting on anything having to do with food. It would have been a good bet.

Looking out the window of the train, we could see white beach clear up to the road bed that our train was riding on. There was not a soul for miles. There was one rather eerie sight that sticks in my mind. For all those miles, the only thing we saw was uniformed soldiers manning outposts, periodically placed along the coastline. One thing was rather clear; this country was in a state of war.

After hours of empty coastline, we began to see signs of life. We would pass through a little village, and then another one a little bigger. Then they all seemed to run together into one large village resembling something like the outskirts of a large industrial city. There were rail yards, factories, and warehouses, but no city as such. There were just large towns and smaller towns all around the place. The train came to a stop at what I would describe as a large greyhound bus station surrounded by taxi cabs. The cab drivers were lined up between where you got off the train and where you entered the bus station. They were an aggressive bunch, grabbing at our luggage as we disembarked from the train car.

We had not heard English, or any other language we could understand, since we had left Okinawa. All of a sudden, one of the guys grabbing at our luggage asked me, "Where you want go Mister?" I stopped for him. I knew where I wanted to go; I just didn't have any idea how I was going to get there. I told him Taipei. He said, "I take you Taipei."

Just as I was relaxing the death grip on my suitcase, and being pulled towards the man's cab, I heard it again. It wasn't broken English; it was clear and precise. "You want the bus, not a cab," the voice said. "This guy will rip you off." I stopped again, tugging to keep a hold on my luggage as I turned to see who was giving us this advice. Behind us was a little guy and his wife, just standing there as if they were totally invisible to these luggage grabbers. No one was jerking at their stuff. One look at the couple and you knew from their dress to their luggage that you were looking at genuine class. He said "We are going to Sung Moon Lake. You can spend the night there and leave for Taipei in the morning. Follow us; we'll put you on the right bus for a fraction of the cost of this man's cab." The cab driver was so mad that he followed the little guy clear into the bus. I asked the nice gentleman if he was alright, and he told me not to worry.

The bus pulled out into traffic that lasted about twenty minutes, then the road narrowed and the traffic dwindled to nearly nothing. The road was barely wide enough for a car to pass by on the other side of the road. The bus ran like it was on rails. It never slowed down. There was a woman standing to the right of the driver holding a red flag. When we would come upon a motor bike or a bicycle, the driver would blow the air horn and she would wave the flag out the window. There was not enough room for the bus to pass anything if there was any traffic coming the other way. We saw one bike rider after another turn right off the road into the ditch just in the nick of time. Things they had piled on the bike racks would go flying as they crashed at the bottom of the ditch. My wife and I were watching in horror. We knew we were going to kill someone before the ride was over. The lady with the flag also had a two way radio in her other hand. A car could squeeze by us, but no way could two buses pass.

We began the uphill climb through the Sung Moon Pass. You could see the little road winding up the mountain for miles in front of you. Now she was on the radio and in close communication with the driver. All of the sudden, we turned into a pullout just the size of our bus. Seconds later, another bus coming down the pass flew past us. We would take off again just as fast as that big diesel would carry us up the winding road. We would pass another bus in the pullout on his side of the road. After a few miles, we'd be back in a slot on our side. This was a science of radio work. Watching them reminded me of a pilot and co-pilot working a holding pattern at a busy airport. One slip up, and two busloads of passengers would be scattered down over the mountainside. Women were screaming and children were crying. About half the passengers had donned their sick bags from the seat pouch in front of them. I began to wonder if I should be more concerned. No one was talking to each other, or even looking out the windows. They sat with their heads down and a white knuckle grip on their seat railings.

After an hour or two of what could be compared to an airliner caught in severe turbulence, we reached the plateau. The road widened so that two buses could easily pass. The lady put her radio up and stored her flag. Then the dirt road became a paved road. You could hear people talking again. The lady was now collecting the sickness bags and putting them in a large container. We came into a little village and the bus pulled into a station. The gentleman told us we could take a normal bus from there. The suicide crews only worked the pass. Again, he encouraged us to join them at the Sung Moon Palace for the night. The bus we wanted to take to the lake would be leaving in an hour. We agreed to meet at the station.

Cheryl and I had not eaten all day, and we were really hungry. We decided to walk around the little village and see what we could find to eat. The gentleman and his wife sat down with the rest of the passengers and opened their picnic baskets. There are some things you can't learn from a map. One of them is the fact that there are no restaurants on this side of the mountains. We found a little open air place with tables in it and children sitting there eating something. We walked in and sat down. There was a woman standing behind a counter with some kind of machine in front of her. There were two stacks of dinner plates beside her. The only drink labeled in English was Taiwan Beer. We sure weren't going to drink the water, so I ordered a beer. I thought that would be the safest, but I was wrong. I didn't get the runs, but I broke out in a rash that covered my body up to the neck. I thought beer was brewed and the water would have been boiled. I didn't know they didn't do that anymore. I was drinking whatever water they had used to make the stuff, just as if it was right out of the tap.

The thing in front of her was an ice shaver. She would put a block of ice on it and out of the bottom would come slivers of ice. Then the children would point to the color of syrup they wanted her to pour over the ice. She would take a plate from one stack and cover it with ice, pour the syrup over it, and hand it to the child. When the kid would finish eating the colored ice, he would bring the plate back to her. She would take the plate, run water over it, and put it back in the other stack. We sat there the whole time we were waiting on the bus. There was no place else to go. When the first stack of plates would run out, she would pull the dirty stack over and keep serving the ice. I lost my appetite. There wasn't anything to eat anyway. We walked back to the little station just as our bus pulled in. I asked our new friends if there was a restaurant at the palace. He not only confirmed that there was, but he invited us to join them for supper. The wide road didn't last very long after we left the village. It wasn't anything like the ride up the mountain, but you knew you were definitely in the wilderness. Nobody lived up there.

As we started a slight downgrade, a large blue lake came into view. After a few miles you could make out the building on the edge of the lake. The closer we got, the bigger the building appeared. The whole thing resembled a white marble. It reminded me of the capital building in D.C., only it was structured more like a fort. You would have to know a lot more history than they teach in public schools to appreciate where we were about to spend the night. Three Generals had led separate forces against the Japanese for seven years before the US had got involved in the war. Two were communist and one was a God fearing man named Chiang-Kai-Shek. The US was supplying all three in their struggle against Japan. For some reason, we quit helping the one that had determined to defeat communism as soon as the Japanese were handled. This made the two communist generals strong enough to drive Chiang Kai Shek out of China. He took his loyal army to the island of Formosa, which is now Taiwan. This palace had been his residence. I felt like I was walking on sacred ground.

I thanked God for putting us in touch with those nice people. This was truly one of the highlights of my life. God has a way of doing things like that for his servants. There we were in a place not even mentioned on my map. This isn't a Christian country; they only have all the famous Buddha Temples on the map. This place was a secret little museum hid away in the mountains. During supper, our friend told us that he had built this lake many years before. He said they had lived right here for all the years of construction. I said, "Then you are an engineer." He confirmed that he was. He told us he had been educated in America, but he left a lot out. The food, by Japanese standards, was excellent. Eddy always said that any really good food in Japan was Chinese anyway. I don't agree with that; I found several good Japanese dishes over time. After supper, the gentleman helped us secure a room, and they bid us a good evening.

I can't remember what it was that we needed, but I remember what happened that night very well. My friend had gone to bed and we couldn't find anyone that spoke English. That level of frustration must be akin to being deaf and dumb. After trying to communicate with the night desk for about twenty minutes, I burst out with an expression used by the Japanese when the situation is hopeless. "Ya-da-na," I said, and I threw up my hands. With that one word, our world changed a hundred and eighty degrees. The lady behind the desk came back to me in perfect

Japanese. She looked as relieved as I was. She said "Oh, you speak Japanese." It was like a light at the end of the tunnel. I loved this place so much I wanted to stay another day now that I had a lifeline. I asked her if she was working tomorrow. She said she was, so we said to register us for another day. Now I could take my time and see everything hid out here in the mountains.

This was not a resort. I couldn't figure that out. Here was a major piece of history, a really nice place with the bluest water you've ever seen. There was no boat dock, no beach, nothing. I don't think we saw more than twenty people. When I walked through the private little museum with all the General's personal affects, there wasn't even an attendant present. This was the home of the man that had built free Taiwan. It should be a national monument. We went to bed with the feeling that we had found a little heaven in this foreign land. I was looking forward to another day there. The natives might not enjoy the place, but I was sure going to.

At breakfast, a management type walked up to us with a note. It was written in English. It was an invitation to join our engineer friend on what he called the Sung Moon Power Plant yacht. The note said the man delivering the note would escort us to the location where we could board if we accepted the invitation. At supper, I had asked him if there were boats on the lake, and he had told me no boats were allowed on the lake. Now I had an invite to go yachting with him. Of course we were going to take advantage of touring this beautiful lake on the only boat allowed on it. As we boarded, the captain greeted us in Chinese. I figured I had gotten lucky the night before, so why not try it again? I returned his greeting in Japanese, and he restated his in Japanese as well. He explained that we were invited to tour the lake and power plant by the leading nuclear engineer that had built it. He told us the engineer intended to join us, but had run into some problems on his inspection and would not be able to. He said he was still honored to give us the tour. I had the opportunity to inquire how he had learned Japanese. He explained that Japan had occupied about half of China and most of the islands for many years. He had to learn it in school. Anyone over forty could speak it if they wanted to.

We never saw the engineer again, but we were treated like royalty the rest of our stay. After the tour, we ate lunch and Cheryl went to the room or somewhere. I was walking the property alone. I knew I was treading the same marble walkways that the famous General had walked many years before. One of them led me down around the side of the palace to an area that looked almost off-limits. Not a soul was around when I opened the door. I thought it must be a janitor's room, because it was a floor below the main entrance. It was a room with chairs set up like a small chapel that you would find in an airport or a hospital. They were all folding chairs except the first two in the front row. They were big old living room chairs like we had when I was a kid. This was a church. Just as I was about to go and find someone to whom I could inquire about this place, an office door opened, and a middle-aged fellow walked out and welcomed me.

I explained that I was a Baptist missionary, and he explained that he was a Baptist pastor. The General's pastor, up until he had passed away. "Christianity is not popular today," he told me, "but no one will bother this place. That is his chair, and the one beside it is Madame Chiang Kai Shek's chair. You may sit in it if you like." Call me sentimental or whatever, I just couldn't sit in the man's seat. I told him I would be honored to sit in the wife's seat. I was sitting beside a great man that had sat in the chair next to me, and had bowed his heart to my same Jesus. You can't buy that kind of experience. Now I know why I had made the stupid decision to get off the boat at the first stop from Okinawa.

In the millennium, I'll be one of very few that will remember that little room in the basement of this once great palace. I don't know why Christianity didn't gain a real foothold. At least it was enough influence that it allowed faith to be practiced without persecution from the onset. In his homeland, no faith could be practiced without persecution for many years after Communism took over. I stood in the room where the real eternal decisions were made; maybe the very room where the decision had been made to make Taiwan the first free Chinese nation.

The rest of the trip is just a blur. When we arrived on the Taipei side of the island, we were in another world. It was pretty much like Tokyo. About the only thing the wife and I remember is an entire family that drove past us on a motor scooter; there were six on the same seat. The youngest in front of the man that was driving, the wife behind him, and three little ones lined up behind her. We ate at McDonald's, just to say we were back in civilization.

I had to find some souvenirs for the kids. I had already bought about five or six Rolex watches at a flea market type place. They were actually Seikos, and that's not a bad watch. I also found original Yen coins that had been punched at the end of the war. The punch indentation made it useless for monetary exchange. At that time, the exchange rate was about two hundred and seventy yen to the dollar. When this one yen had been minted, it had been equal to one dollar. It was the same size and weight as a silver dollar. I found one that wasn't punched, and I paid dearly for it. This was something you couldn't even find in Japan today. I also found a great decorative sword in a heavy sheath, with a chain to hang it on, for Mark. Now it was time to take our memories and our bounty and head home.

I remember after we passed through Chinese customs that we were walking down the hall towards the docks, and a soldier stopped us. He pointed to my sword, and I handed it to him. He pulled it from its sheaf, swung it across his body and layed it on his outstretched forearm. He looked down the blade, turned it over, and looked down the other side of the blade. He returned it to its sheath and handed it back. He motioned for us to continue on our way.

The next morning we were pulling into the port of Naha and my wife was frantic. She said "Honey, they will never let you back into the country. You are a solid rash from your waist up to your neck." She made me change shirts so I could button up all the way. The rash wasn't the problem. The replica of the Chinese sword, however, would cost us hours. You would think I had a gun. I thought back to a time in mainland Japan in the sixties. Our kerosene delivery man took me to his home and showed me his son's officer sword that he had hidden above the ceiling. He was so proud, but then he became terrified that I might tell his secret. Nothing has changed. I tried to explain to those Japanese customs officers that the Chinese officer had easily and quickly identified my souvenir as a toy. That didn't help.

Now it's an hour later, and we are sitting in a security area watching the security people examining and reexamining my sword. We could see them through the glass. Three years before, I would have just walked out and left my sword like I had left my key chain with the .44 shell on it. I don't know why I was so much braver now. I was even visibly angered. One guy would pick it up, hit it against a steel chair, then hand it to another one so he could abuse it in the same manner. Finally, an officer came out and told me that they were keeping my sword. I told him I wanted to talk to his manager. Finally, his manager came out and told me the same thing. I requested to speak to his superior. There is nothing that rattles Japanese employees like facing their boss. He had to comply with my request; he was afraid not to. I don't know what his boss told him, but about thirty minutes later, we saw two Japanese police officers walk into the room. They handed him my sword. I couldn't hear any of the conversation. The police officer looked at it, handed it back, and walked out. If he spoke to those security guys at all, it was stern and brief.

My wife was getting tired of the routine; she just wanted to go home. When they brought our sword out to us, she was quick to draw it out and point to the dings on the blade. If looks could kill, she would have seriously wounded the guy. These guys are not used to losing. I remembered how fast I had given them my key chain three years before; I should have asked for my key chain back right then. I could have walked out earlier, but somehow I could see that sword hanging in my son's office thirty years later. That is what memories are made of. Without all the drama, it would just be a thing I picked up in Taiwan. It's kind of sad to compare the two ordeals. Just to be there, I would have given them everything I had the day they had taken my key ring. I didn't feel like that now. Eddy was gone. Most of the men we had won to the Lord and baptized were gone. The few Japanese that we still had really needed one of their own for a pastor. The dollar was going down the drain. Several missionaries I knew were giving up and going home or to another field. The only way we could even afford to stay there was due to my job at the college. But I hadn't come to the field to teach in a secular college; maybe I was just tired.

John 1:9-10
That was the true Light, which lighteth every man that cometh into the world. He was in the world, and the world was made by Him, and the world knew Him not.

Chapter 20
The Winds of Change

There was no one left on the island but Mom and the boys. Our oldest girl went back to marry Pastor Garlington's son. On her way, she met up with Brother Robinson's daughter in California, and everything changed. The young man called me and asked what was going on; she had just dumped him. A month later she wrote her mother and told her she was going to marry a Turkish boy she had met. He was in America attending a Christian school. My head was spinning. My second daughter was in love with a young enlisted Marine, and it was getting a little too serious. We sent her home to live with my mother, but she hooked up with the son of the deacon from our sending church and married him. It was the second call I got in the space of a month or so that began with 'Guess what dad? I'm married'. I didn't know what was going on, but the wheels were coming off and there was nothing I could do about it. The work was going down the tubes, and I was afraid I was going with it. I needed a friend.

I was sitting down on the seawall, where the Marines were not allowed to go, and only an occasional fisherman ever came to. I was watching a lone figure working his way up the coastline. The closer he got, the bigger he appeared. It sure wasn't a native. This was a good sized young man. When he came into speaking range, I greeted him and invited him to join me on the seawall. I informed him that he was off limits. I told him I'd be glad to walk him up to my place, which was the furthest place out on the peninsula that a GI was allowed to go. This big fellow was all Marine. He said, "Please help me to the nearest place I'm allowed to be, sir. I've been walking for miles; I have no idea where I am." The weirdest conversation ensued. Almost no one has ever heard of my little home town, except on Groundhog Day. He said, "My Aunt lives in Punxsutawney." He told me his new wife was going to join him when they could afford it, but for now he didn't know a soul on the island. He was a lost sheep. He wasn't even expected to report for duty for another week. All of a sudden, I was the only friend he had. I was his Eddy.

Many years before, Eddy had helped me find a house for my new bride, because I didn't have enough time or grade to live on base. I knew exactly what he needed, right down to meeting his bride at the international airport. We became fast friends, and then in just a few days, he bowed his head in tears and we became brothers in Christ. He wrote his wife about it and scared the heck out of her, just as I had scared mine when I was in his shoes. She followed him though, just as Cheryl had followed me. We baptized him into the now much smaller English mission, but we were good for each other. His wife depended on Cheryl like Cheryl had depended on Neva. Then his wife's brother, who was a Marine, also showed up on the island, and he joined us as well.

I had to get my van inspected on base, because I had a base sticker that my Navy Chaplain had given me. The Air Policeman was confused because I was not military. When he figured out that I was a missionary, he couldn't wait to visit our mission. His family and his fellow Air Police buddy with his family never missed a service after that. It wasn't long and things were almost like they had been when Eddy left. Maybe I was supposed to stay over here after all. Things were running pretty smoothly. I was even picking up a little new support from back in the states.

The Pillar was a first class magazine published in South Carolina. The editor had somehow gotten a hold of one of my monthly reports and published it. It was a letter I had written when I thought that the wheels were coming off, and I had reported it straight up. He was really impressed that I would report it exactly like it was. The editor asked me if I would submit an article, and I did; It was published as well. Then I was invited to co-write an article on Heaven with Dr. Henry Morris, the founder of Science Creation Institute. I became a regular contributor to the absolute best Christian publication in its day.

Remember the church I mentioned I had found in the yellow pages that night we broke down in Mississippi? They never took us on with regular support, but they bought me a Tandy 1000 computer. We got it just in time to meet the regular deadlines for the Pillar. Until then, I was trying to work with an old dos machine. It took more time to make it work than it did to produce any actual work. I can't believe I was entertaining the possibility of closing the English work and looking into another set of islands that was on my heart. I had already begun the process of looking for a native pastor to take over the Japanese services. The only other local church Baptist missionary on the islands lived somewhere up north. For some reason he and Eddy had never got along, so needless to say, I had never met him. I knew the pastor of his sending church, though, so it wasn't hard to get a contact number.

Remember the pastor I was sent to confront about a missionary problem back when I was flying for the college in PA? I'm glad we had mended our relations. We had even become friends. He called me to see if I would support a man he was going to send over to help the work up north. He knew the guy used to be out of the work where I represented the mission programs. My wife had been in charge of handling the money for all our missionaries then. She had informed me of a serious discrepancy with this man's account. I told the pastor I would not lift a finger to intentionally hurt the man, but that's all I could promise at the time. The pastor decided not to send him. I hope I wasn't totally responsible for his decision. Either way, I had already made arrangements to join this old missionary in an off-island outreach. Now that Eddy was temporarily out of the picture, this old guy seemed eager to meet with me.

The old missionary's name was Ed also. We agreed to meet at the Naha airport, where he kept his airplane. He promised to bring a young Japanese preacher with him that I was interested in meeting. That young man and I climbed into the back seat of the plane while Ed and a much younger Okinawan woman took the front seats. I was uncomfortable from the onset. Ed was flying the plane, but the young woman up there with him was not a pilot. In the back seat were not one, but two pilots; that just didn't make sense to me. Old Ed wasn't that proficient a pilot. It was a rather heavy ship for a single engine, and you had to fly it a lot more than once a month to stay proficient. We flew out to a designated island and lined up on one of the old airstrips that had been built during the war. He missed his first approach and set it down way too hot on the second one, but we walked away. That's called a good landing in general aviation.

The whole trip was a waste of time and money, as far I was concerned. The only person that even wanted to talk to us was blown off by the old missionary. He told the fellow to throw away his cigarettes and sake and then we'd talk. What does that have to do with meeting Jesus? Anyway, I met the young Japanese preacher and he impressed me. Japanese Christians are really rare. 'If I ever leave this island before Eddy comes back,' I thought, 'this would be the guy to take over our work.' Maybe now that wouldn't happen, but at least I had found the guy. As for old Ed, I was concerned when he walked back to the plane with his arm around the young lady in a most affectionate manner. I asked him who the lady was. I hoped to hear it was a distant relative by a brother or sister or something. Instead he answered that she was his sister in the Lord, and a whole lot more than just his sister.

I didn't know his history, but soon found out that his wife had left him years before. By Baptist custom, it's believed that you can't remarry and stay in the ministry. This guy was in love with this woman, but had to live in sin with her to prevent being taken off the field. I didn't put this all together until much later. If I had had a full understanding at the time, I would have asked him to allow me to marry them. He did finally do the right thing. He married her, but he resigned his ministry to do so. That was a waste of a ministry, rooted in misunderstood Baptist / Catholic tradition. When a woman or a man leaves you for no reason, they are dead to you. God doesn't expect you to live alone or burn in your lust for one that you love. He didn't have to leave the field, because he owned everything he had. He owned the church, the plane, and his house. Remember the old missionary I had visited in the cabin up on the Washington-Oregon border? He had come back from the Japanese prison camp and instead of returning to China, which was now communist, he had returned to Japan.

The current law right after the war had allowed him to purchase a modest portion of land in the Tokyo area. A foreigner can't do that today, but his deed was legal and clear. When he had returned to the little church where I met the woman that asked me to visit him, he had turned that deed over to them. It was his sending church, and it was the right thing to do. That church should have maintained the mission property, as the group that owned my house did. Instead they gave it to a missionary that wasn't even out of their church. That missionary was Ed. He had sold it and come to Okinawa before reversion, when he could purchase land.

You have to understand what happened. When the old man in the cabin had bought the land, it was worth about what an acre of land would be worth in the middle of the desert back in the forties. When Ed sold it, he sold it by the tatami, which is about six feet by six feet. Now each tatami was worth about what an acre would be worth in downtown New York City. A local church had lost a mission in Tokyo forever, but that wasn't Ed's fault. They had given it to him instead of giving it to his sending church. The sending church would have managed it as a mission property, regardless of the missionary running the mission.

New Testament churches have lost their grasp on ecclesiology. When I left the church campus in Concordville, I lost my house, my plane, and everything I owned. It had been acquired for the work of the ministry. A lot of us had done the same thing. That's the way it works; we all knew that. I don't know what happened to modern Christendom. I think it's because preachers don't come from churches anymore; they come out of colleges. In the beginning, the colleges were owned by the churches, and they understood how it was supposed to work. Today, colleges even own churches. The tail is wagging the dog. These kids, as well as most of the church members, think that's the way it's supposed to work.

My strong point was ecclesiology, from the day I had accepted Christ. I'm not, and never was, interested in religion. The religious crowd killed Jesus. If there is not a prototype in the New Testament for any practice, I'm not interested in practicing it. I will do things like dedicating a baby. It's only allowing the parents to commit to raising the child according to the scriptures. I was way too dogmatic in my approach to New Testament Church practices. I could have led by example instead of dogmatism. It cost me the core of our renewed English mission. The Air police families had finally had all the weekly beatings from me they could take. I don't blame them. My lack of balanced preaching even cost me my oldest girl. I know it was the same reason my sending church had never grown. My pastor was even worse than I was. He eventually ran my younger daughter and her husband off, as well as his own wonderful sons. The devil doesn't care which side of the road you're driving on when he is trying to run you off of it. There is a ditch on both sides.

That was a real blow to the work, and maybe I took it too seriously. I again began questioning myself. There was a lot of money being spent on this mission, not to mention what I was earning as a professor. Then the death blow came. A missionary up in the mainland had retuned to the states on furlough. His support had been dwindling, or at least not increasing to match the devaluation of the US dollar. Just about every church he visited had our mission card on the bulletin board. This was the same man that had told me many years before that I was not qualified for the ministry. He also had a pastor friend in Arkansas who had access to my monthly report. He would send them to this old missionary. He could read of the many souls our ministry was bringing to the Lord. Not to mention, more baptisms in two years than he had enjoyed in twenty years. The sad thing is, that except for his immediate family, I was probably the last one he had ever baptized. That's how I ended up on the roll of a church that I didn't even know about. That problem had almost ended our ministry before it had even got started. Now the same guy that had put me on that roll was threatening our ministry yet again.

The letters started coming from many of our major supporters. There we were, ten thousand miles from home. As far as I knew, I couldn't even get the family home if we lost our regular support. "God, I don't know what to do," I pleaded. "Next week I have to decide if I'm going to teach another semester at the university. I don't know if I can fight this old guy from the field. So far, most of our supporting churches are siding with me, but who knows if that's going to last? I don't even know if I want to fight this guy. I could put out a letter revealing some embarrassing facts about his mission attendance. I know that. He knows I know that. I could destroy this guy. Why is he so bitter?"

The next thing that happened was my pastor called me and told me he had received a certified letter for me. It was from a church up in Washington. That couldn't be good. He wanted to know if he should open it or send it to me. I didn't want him involved, so I told him to mail it to me. He couldn't use a military APO like the Navy Chaplain had set up for me. He had to send it via regular overseas mail, meaning I wouldn't see it for better than a week. You can't imagine life before Fedex.

"God, I need to know what to do," I prayed again. "I've got less than a week to make a decision, and only You know what's in that letter that is coming. I can't lose any support and survive over here. The dollar is in the tank. What am I going to do if I leave the field?" That month I had put out a letter addressing the attacks on my qualifications, but I couldn't bring myself to attack the old missionary that was questioning them. God blessed that decision. Letters started arriving assuring me that most supporting churches were satisfied with my qualifications. They told me that the old man had been able to persuade one major pastor in Arkansas to join him in attacking my ministry. They said so far, no one else had joined him. Only one major pastor? Somehow that wasn't very comforting. I had to evaluate everything, starting with what I was doing there. Was it worth what I was putting the family through? Did God have something else in mind?

Like most people in this world, at one time or another, I had to make a serious decision. That decision would be a final decision, right or wrong. I made it in two parts. I can't remember a lot of things these days, but I can remember these. I can remember the exact spot where I was standing when I made each of them. Standing in the hall of my house, I decided the Japanese part of the mission was as far as it was going. It was fifteen years old or so and had never been this small. When Eddy had it, at its best, there probably weren't twenty in attendance. Then he had made a tough decision. Most of them had a shrine to one of their ancestors in their homes. Ancestor worship is idolatry. Eddy told them to make the choice between God and the shrine. He never had over three women and one man since. They were the same ones I had now, going on four years. It was time to hand this thing over to a native pastor. The American sacrifice could be better used. Part one was over. I had peace about giving it over to them, because that was the right thing to do.

Now, what about the English work? It had been a real blessing to a lot of people. My question then was not about those people; it was about my ministry. Had God called me to Japan to build an American mission? What is the purpose of a mission? It's to build it into a church. How can you build a church out of transients? I had just lost nearly half my people when the air police families had left. Two other families had been restationed as well. Should I rebuild again for the same fate or should I consider reassignment myself?

My friend with ties to my little hometown was even being sent to Korea on temporary duty. About all that was left at that point in time were his family and two others. The two others were short timers. If there was ever a good time to shut it down, it was then. No one would be turned away. They would just all be gone, except my friend and his family. He didn't have any idea what I was running through my mind as he left my house Sunday after church. He shook my hand and said, "Take care of the wife for me, I'll see you in a month or so." We had to take care of the wife; that's the last time we ever saw him. There was a lot of mystery concerning his death. We finally got a report saying that he was packing the radio and had gotten the antenna tangled up with a live wire overhead. I'm not so sure that's how he died. My wife took a beautiful picture of the sun setting into the South China Sea, and I wrote a nice article about it that the Pillar magazine published. There was something about that boy. I had lost more than a friend.

The next decision was made in my classroom at the college. I remember looking out the window between classes. "God, I need some options," I said. "This work here is done." I notified the school that I would not be teaching the upcoming semester. Everything's coming apart, and I'm coming with it. Who knows what's in that letter? I'd had it. I stopped off at a little market and bought a bottle of serious looking red wine. I locked myself up in my office and got drunk. That's what the stuff is good for. It's also good for a headache. You maybe can't get very drunk on one little bottle of wine, but you can get close enough when your not used to drinking it. I woke up the next morning and nothing had changed. There was no note in that bottle.

Maybe there would be something at the post office. I didn't even care about the dreaded letter anymore. I wasn't fighting with anyone about anything. We'd had a very successful term. God had something for me somewhere, but it wasn't there. A fellow asked me to pray about his little country of Tonga. Maybe I was supposed to go there? I was a mess, but I couldn't show it. My family had to think that everything was under control. Bottom line was, I was all they had over there, and they had enough to deal with right now.

I got the package from my church that Ed sent every month. The registered mail would be in it, along with any other personal mail that the church had received. I took it back to my van and opened it. Good heavens, there were two in there that I didn't want to open. I saw the registered letter, but hadn't bothered to read the address yet. I was just as concerned with the one from Hawaii. It was from the pastor / missionary that didn't much care for me. Not only was he a kingpin on his islands, he was married to the daughter of the kingpin in Kentucky. I'd read it first. This guy could be real trouble. I had a short prayer meeting and opened it. I couldn't believe what I was reading. "I've heard it all," he said. "I just want you to know that no one in my realm of influence is going to hang the Joneses out to dry."

He went on to tell me that the preacher in Arkansas that had been bashing me had bit off a little more than he could chew. It turns out that Eddy's wife, Neva, had a pretty big family. It was their church that this preacher was pastoring. I don't pretend to know what happened, but a good guess is a matter of association. It's pretty hard to bash me and not reflect on Eddy. Either way, that guy was looking for a job. Now I was double glad I never took up the fight. I had just given it to the Lord, and He had handled it just fine. I had fought hard for my ministry back at the college, and I had lost. I didn't fight at all for my current ministry, and apparently I was winning. Wow, I needed that. Now I was ready to get to the one that had been testing my faith.

I didn't get it; something wasn't right. The address was a church in Washington, but it wasn't the one I had thought it was. This particular church didn't even support us. In fact, they didn't support anybody. It was from the pastor that I sat with in his living room; the guy that was so broken hearted about his church. I had preached my usual message about 'What happens if we are not missionary.' I opened the letter and found a short note. It read, "You were right; we closed the church and sold the property.... here is your share." The check was for five thousand dollars. That would go a long way towards getting us home. I'd also gotten a little more peace about my decisions. Now it was time to get down to the business of leaving the field. One great thing, thanks to the Marine Chaplain, I could mail what I wanted to take home. We wouldn't have to build shipping crates. We were only charged postage from San Francisco APO to my mother's house in Pennsylvania.

I was still a wreck, but I was busy enough to keep myself together. I had to get the native preacher to take over the work, at least until Eddy returned; even though I personally thought that it was time for a native to take it and keep it. That wasn't my call. Up until that old missionary had broke bad on me, those were the greatest four years of our lives. It was the most beautiful place we had ever lived, and up until now, the closest walk with God I'd ever had. I felt a little like that missionary that had told me he felt so guilty living the missionary life. It's like one long vacation when you're on the field. I never hid that fact in my monthly reports. Who else would pay you to play every day? Yes, you worked hard learning the language and culture. You worked a little bit at keeping the devil out of your work, but that's about it. If you were doing your job successfully, you played so hard that you had to take a vacation once in awhile to rest up.

I thought I was holding up pretty good since things had turned sour, but my wife could see through it. Even though we were nearing the end, she arranged to send me off to Idiomote, another island in the Pacific, for a few days to do nothing. That was the last thing I should have done in my present condition. What I didn't need was time on my hands, particularly off on some distant island where no one knew me. That's a real problem for a legalist Christian that really doesn't have all that much conviction about his lifestyle. Once you break your own rules, you go way overboard. It's like everything is stored up in you, ready to explode. The little hotel I stayed in was right on the docks. At supper, I met a couple Japanese merchant marines. I was the only gai-jin on the whole island, so people treated me differently. If they knew a little English, they wanted to try it out on me. Even if they didn't, they wanted a picture together.

Somehow, I got in an arm wrestling match with these guys. After I beat them, they sent out to the ship for their big guns. While I was beating them, they started feeding me food and drink. These were some strong men, but their arms were too short. They couldn't handle an old arm wrestler in the best condition of my life. We partied until I don't remember. When they couldn't beat me on the table, they tried to put me under the table. If that was their purpose, they probably won. Everything that had been penned up in my flesh came out. I broke all my rules but one. I remember throwing two young girls out of my room. That was a miracle, because I didn't care anymore. I knew I was a wreck, but I didn't know I was in that bad a shape. God has preserved a crystal clear memory of that trip to this day. I could see a lighthouse as I spoke with God. I said, "Father, this is good fun, but I do not desire adultery." I was on my way down, but I wasn't at the bottom yet. I didn't feel like it at the time, but I had some fight left in me. I may lose this spiritual battle I'm in, but not today.

You can take this 'no more fight' policy a little too far. You've got to fight for yourself. I didn't come back refreshed, but I came back resolved. You might destroy my ministry again, but I'm not ready to let you destroy my life. I've learned from twenty-three years as a staunch legalist that you have only two speeds, all ahead full and all back full. If you suppress something that really isn't wrong, when you finally let it bust out, it goes wild and leads to a genuine wrong. The only time I abused anything was when I didn't allow any of it in my life. I love to dance, but I didn't allow it. When I broke that rule, I danced with anyone that would dance, and I danced until I dropped. I think that's what carried me to my room; two young dancing fools. Something terrible could have happened, but for God it didn't.

Well, everything was safely back in their pens and I had a renewed desire to keep them there. I don't know, maybe I needed to loosen up for a couple of days. One thing makes me question that however. I've never loosened up without first being tightened up. I wouldn't have broken all my own rules if I could handle what was going on in my life. I had had no desire to loosen up for almost four years. It's like committing suicide until morning. Some people can't handle their life anymore, so they take it. Some people can't handle their self righteousness either, so they take it as well. Only trouble is, we don't really kill it. It comes back, and the cycle repeats itself until one of the two is finally dead.

Everyday, I was carrying packages up to the base and sending them home. I was holding up ok, but I wasn't really in control. I didn't know what was going on. I made arrangements to leave a couple weeks before the family. I was going to take a look at the Tongan Islands, just in case. I put out my final report with all the plans and set Mark up to run the Japanese work until the native preacher took over for him. I still had no peace about anything except that Japan was over. I was still looking for God in all the uncertainty. I believe that came in my final phone call from the states. It was from a pastor in Florida. He asked if there was any chance I would consider building them an institute. He said he already had enough men surrendered to the ministry to justify the effort. Hank's church was our largest regular supporter at three-hundred dollars a month. Hank himself might be my closest personal friend. He was in the first group that had left the campus back in Pennsylvania, but we had long since settled our differences.

That call took a lot off our shoulders. No matter what happened, we had a sound promise of a secure ministry if we wanted it. Hank said as far as he was concerned, it was a done deal. He had all the peace and assurance he needed, and was ready to send a check at my request. I told him I definitely was interested, but to hold off until I got back from Tonga. He said ok. He also said he would reimburse whatever we spent towards our return from that very phone call on. When I accepted the position, I was to give him the bill.

A double minded man is unstable in all his ways, and I was proving it. I landed in Hawaii and changed planes for American Samoa. I had never seen so many big people in the same place in my life as I found myself with on that airplane. I ended up between two of the largest women I've ever seen. When we landed, just as many big people got on as got off. I asked the flight crew if I could upgrade to first class. He said I sure could, if they'd had one. He said that flight was known as the Samoan Crush. He said I should get some breathing room after Tahiti.

It was a little better after our final stop for the Hawaiian Airlines. I can't remember the name of the Island, but it was the home of the once famous International Date Line Hotel. The shuttle took the few of us that were not heading back to Hawaii to this once famous location. There didn't seem to be much else on this little rock. It was dark, maybe I missed something. We had to wait for the shuttle to return for us when the island hopper arrived to take us on to Tonga. When I walked into that place, I walked into an old Humphrey Bogart movie called Casablanca. Past elegance could be recognized through the dim lighting that made everything appear as black and white. There was no terminal building. This was the only place to go. I walked out the side door after a late dinner onto a boardwalk that overlooked the ocean. I never saw a soul. I walked down the pier to a barricade where there was a construction notice. It informed me that the construction in progress was funded by The Japanese War Reparation Association. I'm glad I wasn't there in the early forties. This must have been one of the many islands once occupied by the Japanese war machine.

I found a little bar with a pool table. I couldn't find any other Americans. In fact, I found no one besides the waiter that spoke English. Two guys were playing pool, so I sat down and watched them. We had hours to kill, but not enough to get a room for the night. They were speaking Spanish or Portuguese, I couldn't tell which. They were having trouble communicating with whatever it was. One of them walked over to me and gestured that I take a stick and join them. He tried some broken English, but it was hopeless. I recognized the word Brazil. I knew the largest population of Japanese outside of Japan was in Brazil, so I took a shot at Japanese. He just looked at me, but the other guy answered in as good of Japanese as I spoke. He was the guy from Brazil. This guy was from some other country in South America. We began playing pool and conversing through the guy from Brazil. None of us spoke the same language, but between the three of us, we worked it out. At least well enough to kill the hours needed for our individual shuttles to pick us up.

My shuttle was the last one to arrive. It took me right out on the tarmac to a small plane waiting for its only passenger. I stepped in, they shut the door, and off we went. They didn't even close the cockpit door. There was only about three others on board and they were sleeping. I suppose this thing could carry about a dozen passengers at the most. We landed on the main island and were taken to town by taxi. I was dropped off in the center of town in front of an old two story building. It was the only one I could see that had lights in the windows.

It was really late, or early I guess, so I went straight to my little room and to bed. In the morning I got a better look around. There was a wash bowl on a stand, but no bathroom. There were towels and wash cloths, so I figured the bathroom couldn't be too far away. I had slept in rather late, so I hoped I could still find some breakfast. I couldn't see anything the night before. We seemed to have driven about ten miles over a narrow but straight deserted road to get here from the airport. When I had come in, there was no one on the streets and nothing open. I couldn't wait to see it during the day.

I walked down the narrow staircase into a tiny lobby with nothing in it but the counter where I had checked in. I could see through the archway into a dimly lit room with a couple tables and a pool table. I walked out the front door onto a boardwalk about six feet wide. It was running along the edge of the main street. It was missing what a lot of main streets usually have on them, like cars, people, and pavement. The only thing different from the night before was the sun in the sky. I found one little stand open where I bought some film. Beside it was a little open-front shop with a jukebox and a pinball machine in it. The feeling came over me that I was standing in an old ghost town. I felt like I was going to see Tarzan swing by at any minute. Then I got it. This was Tombstone, with jungle huts scattered around, but no general store.

I walked back into the hotel and asked the man behind the counter where these people bought their groceries. He said that was over for the day. I asked him what he meant. He said, "You were sleeping. Everyone's pretty much gone home by around six." I asked if he meant in the evening. He said, "In the morning." I asked what time I would have to get up to see it. He told me I would have to be up before dawn. He asked me if I wanted a taxi. I asked for what? He had already told me there was nothing in town. I asked him where I could find some food. He said, "We feed our guests in the dining room any time." "Good, I'll eat and you can call a cab," I said. I can't remember much about anything I ate in that place except for fried bananas. That was a first. There was only one other guy in the little room. He asked if I was an American and then invited me to sit at his table.

"I'm here to introduce Budweiser to Tonga," he said. He went on to say he'd been working on the project for a long time. I told him I was an author working on an article. That wasn't a lie; it was just not the whole truth. I wasn't sure what I was anymore. I know I wasn't happy anymore. I didn't have peace about doing anything. When I get like this, I don't make any plans. I had this idea that I could do anything I chose and God would bless it. I guess I just hadn't chosen the wrong path yet. This big native walked in and sat down with us. He was a government official that had come to invite the Budweiser fellow to a feast of some kind. He said he would pick us up around five o'clock. I started by thanking him and then began to explain that I was not with this gentleman. Before I could get it out, the Bud guy kicked me under the table. He told the big fellow we would be ready. The government official shook our hands and walked out. "You can't pass on this," he explained, 'It's a luau you'll never forget."

He asked me to join him around three for a drink and we'd go on from there. After lunch the taxi driver was standing at the counter waiting for me. He introduced himself and said he would show me around. I said ok, but I needed to be back by three. "I'll take you to the orchard," he said. "You will never forget it." There was a lot going on that day that I'm never going to forget. He was a native and a real source of information. The natives were not white and not black. They had beautiful brown skin like Polynesians. He showed me the king's house. The only difference from it and the others in the little neighborhood was the limo in the driveway. Then we went down along the coastline to a fruit orchard. The treetops completely enclosed the little dirt path we drove down as we headed for the seaside. He stopped the car and stepped out, motioning for me to bring my camera. He pointed up to the branches hovering over the road and asked me if I could see anything. When my eyes adjusted to the dim lighting, I saw them. Flying Foxes, they called them. He said some might call them vampire bats, but they were fruit bats. They were large, fur covered bats with a head that resembled the head of a fox. Then he clapped his hands. What a show.

As we pulled out to the seashore, he told me this part of the coast was famous for its bore holes. I can't remember for sure what kind of holes he called them. He told me to just wait for the next big wave and have my camera ready. I don't know why I'd never seen this on TV. When that wave came, it shot spouts of water up through the holes in the rocks about fifty-feet into the air. It looked like a hundred water fountains starting up where the wave hit, and then running down the coast as far as you could see. I couldn't believe I was the only tourist there. I told him that one day, they would sell tickets to get into this place. I had just got a private showing of a wondrous sight. He said they didn't have much tourism. Most people that came here from the outside went to one of the villages where a family adopted them for a week. They taught them village life and treated them like a special member of the family.

"You should fly up to the northern most island called Vavaue," he said. "There is a resort there and you'll be treated like royalty. If you want to go, I'll make the arrangements for you." I said I'd do it, and that the next day would be great. He dropped me back at the hotel and said he'd see me around seven in the morning. I walked into the little pool room and sat down at a table. There were three or four other white guys in there talking and drinking a New Zealand beer. I can't remember the name, but it's common in the states. The only native was the guy behind the counter, who doubled as a waiter. Then the Budweiser guy walked in and sat down at my table. We had a good conversation. He was a Vietnam vet, Special Forces, kind of a scary sort of guy. He said, "Just follow my lead. The customs and culture here is nothing like you have ever seen before."

We walked out on the boardwalk about five 'til and a pickup truck pulled up. There were about four people in the front and five or six in the bed. The big man was sitting by the passenger window. I stepped down off the boardwalk and started to climb into the bed. No, no, no, everyone said, as they put out there hands as a gesture for me to stop. Then the firm hand of my quiet friend gripped the back of my arm. Moving close to my ear he said, "Don't buck tradition." I couldn't believe my eyes as the government people got out of the front and climbed into the bed of the truck. "Get in the front, I'll drive," he said as he loosened his grip on my arm. There is no way they will sit in front of a white man. The Methodist missionaries from England were the first white men to come to Tonga. They made this culture. They had collected everyone's idols and had taught them to read and write English. Then they had sold the idols for a ton of money. He had some other historical information I won't get into.

We took directions from the people in the back of the truck. We finally found the place way out on the coast past a couple little villages. It was an outdoor stage made of rock and concrete. The native band was fantastic, and the food was out of this world. There were no fried bananas. I was with the elite; the ruling class on these islands. I met the minister of this and the minister of that. After a couple of hours, I started thinking I better not have any more fun. I'd met everybody that was anybody. I'd been promised any papers required to return here at any time for as long as I wanted. God must have arranged this. Maybe I was supposed to think seriously about this place. I collected the business cards just before the party ended abruptly. A wave from hell, or maybe from heaven, I'm still not sure, crashed over the rocks. In a hail of sparks, the band evacuated the stage. The lights went out and it was over.

I had what I needed, anyway. The big man figured out I was not from Budweiser and spent considerable time finding out just who I was. A better description would be that he spent a lot of time just exploring how he might use me. He explained how he could make me very rich if I was interested. He said the organizations like Peace Corp, and a bunch of others from all over the industrialized world needed our help. I thought, is that not backwards? "They need your help?" I asked. He said "Yes. They are running out of places to use as an excuse to raise more money." He said just last week they had given a John Deere tractor to an old villager that didn't even have enough land to turn it around on. We spoke for at least an hour before he got what he really wanted. I told him that motorized hang gliders had just arrived in the islands of Japan. He gave me his card and said if I brought one to Tonga, he would build a factory just for me. If I would teach people how to fly them, he would build them. "Copyrights and patents don't mean shit here," he said. "You take this card, set it up, and I'll make you comfortable in Tonga."

I Corinthians 1:27
But God hath chosen the foolish things of the world to confound the wise; and God hath chosen the weak things of the world to confound the things which are mighty.

Chapter 21
Reunions

When I got on the little twin, I could see an old Piper Apache setting on the other side of the ramp. I was sitting where I could see into the cockpit. I remembered sitting in an Apache in Delaware in seventy-eight. I had just logged my first hundred hours. For the first time since I had flown my solo, I felt a little nervous. It was a really a hazy day, no clouds, but the visibility was as bad as it gets without them. At about three thousand feet, you could only see the ground clearly by looking straight down below you. I don't remember where I was headed, but I decided to land and talk to an instructor about how I was feeling. That was a little strip about ten or so miles north of Dover Air Force Base. I parked on the ramp and walked over to the flight office. I was surprised to see so many young military officers standing around. They already had wings on their chests, so I couldn't figure out what they were doing at a little flight school.

That place was a little beehive. I don't know how, but somehow I ended up talking to the oldest instructor in the whole place. By then, I had twice as many hours as his most accomplished student working on his instrument rating. It was a little hard for him to look at my log book and not see a really experienced pilot by those standards. He handed it back to me and changed his whole demeanor. He smiled and began talking to me like a fellow pilot, rather than an old instructor. "Son, you've flown a lot of places, big places, day and night," he said. "You started out in more of an airplane than most students ever fly. You're a competent pilot, and this will pass. It's called the hundred hour jitters. Let's not waste your money on something you already do as well as I could teach you. Come with me. I'll give you some twin time." We walked out the door and across the ramp to an old Apache. It was even the same color as the one setting here at Vavaue.

Now I was sitting in a state-of-the-art twin turboprop. The only thing I'd ever worry about this thing would be the two kids flying it. There was nothing below us but water. I reassured myself by remembering the young officers at the flight school. They probably had a thousand flying hours. The old instructor had told me that they could see the writing on the wall. They knew the military was cutting back. If they wanted to fly for a living, they had to get their ATP rating. I couldn't believe I hadn't looked at a newspaper or paid any attention to a newscast in years. Far too many Christians were just like me. Oh, we vets knew about that trader Fonda and her crowd. It just hurt too much to think of the wasted sacrifice if these cowards get their way. Well they did, so most of us paid little attention to the news. One or both of those kids in that cockpit had the ratings those Air Force officers were working on. I was in good hands.

About twenty or thirty minutes later, I felt them setting up for a landing. Everything looked the same so far, a lot of water, another island, and then land. We rolled up to a ramp and stopped. I looked out my window and couldn't believe my eyes. There was an old Apache up here too. I didn't know I was looking at the same airplane from a different angle. "We couldn't find Vavaue?" I asked. "Oh, we probably could have," said the young man, "but we decided the safest thing was to return until they get their radio signal working." "Is it an NDB or a VOR?" I asked. I just threw that out there so he'd know I understood there was no reason to worry about the plane. He said, "I have a loran that would get us really close, but I like redundant navs. They'll get it on line in a few minutes. Were going to debark and cap off. We'll be ready to board in about thirty minutes. Sorry for the delay."

We loaded up again. While he did the pre-flight, he strapped in and turned his head to me. He said they had got it working. Someone had gone up and tested it. Then they left the cockpit door open to display their calm assurance to any who might have had a concern. This time I was watching out my window a lot more closely. As we got near the northernmost island, he brought us down to about five-hundred feet. He gave us a look at the most beautiful reef I've ever seen. The deep blue turned to a light powder blue when you crossed the first reef. Then the shallow water appeared a gorgeous green. These were warm waters and crystal clear. I could see sharks swimming around the outside reefs. I made a note not to go out there. The hotel shuttle took me to the resort. It reminded me of an old Howard Johnsons, built on the side of a cliff in a split-level fashion. The beautiful water it overlooked was Cook's bay. Cook's Harbor would be a better definition; a safe harbor found by Captain Cook. This was one place he would sure wish he had remained. He didn't have such luck on the big island of Hawaii. The story goes that they sacrificed him by throwing him into the lava flow.

    I couldn't wait to get on the water. I checked in and went straight down to the dock and found a kayak. There were a couple of sailboats anchored out in the bay. I could see a person moving around on the deck of one of them, so I headed for it. I had read all the sailing books I could find on Okinawa. I read everything from Voss to Norgrove. I had a real respect for these people. I found a guy on Okinawa that had rented a little sailboat for me from the base marina. I was a pilot, a diver, I had driven the biggest trucks, all I hadn't done was sail a boat. I didn't get out of sight of the marina and I was engaged in the battle of my life. I was beaten black and blue from my knees to my elbows. I was trying to tack that thing back to the docks in a ten knot headwind. I remember promising God that if he got me back, I'd never do it again. I'll keep that promise and so would the young Australian I found standing on that boat. She didn't even say hi. She saw me coming and as soon as I was in talking distance she spoke. "Do you want a good deal on a sailboat?" she asked.

    It might still be there. She said it was never leaving that harbor again with her on board. The bay was so still, I just sat there without touching my paddle. She described the horror of single-handling from New Zealand to Cook Bay in thirty days of nonstop hell. I didn't bother to mention my sailing experience or being caught in the death grips of a ten knot breeze off Okinawa. I think right then, it would have been too much for her. She had just endured back to back typhoons. Why add to her trauma? I wished her the best and rowed my white water rig safely back to the dock. At lunch I ran into a white couple, so we introduced ourselves. They were from Florida. They owned a shell shop and supplied it annually from what they collected there on Tonga. When they were comfortable that I was not interested in opening a shop of my own, they told me where to venture at low tide.

    This was probably the last of its kind, or should I say the last of its time. There was no way this place was not going to be discovered. There were a couple backpackers or adventurers to be seen hiking around the island, but no tourist types. I waited until the tide started out and took a little hike of my own. I found indescribable shell life. The only other person I saw was a native with a basket on his shoulder. He had more Trumpet shells in that basket than I had seen in all my years of diving. Of course, I had no desire to put a tank on around there. I'd already seen more sharks from the airplane than I'd seen in all my years of diving as well. This would be the place to fly. I mentioned this to the resort owner at supper. He invited me for a cocktail on the veranda with a few of his other guests. He said, "Boy, we could start a business with one of those." I didn't share with him what I was told by the big government fellow. He knew I was flying up here for a couple of days. He had told me not to get involved with this guy. He said, "We know him well. He has worked many deals over the years, but he is not going to be there for very much longer."

There was one thing I did notice about this place. The place where I had rented the kayak from was owned by a white guy from somewhere. The store I had bought my souvenirs from was also. The resort was owned by a white guy as well. There were no white owned businesses down on the main island that I saw. I had met a white couple at the feast, but they were managers of native owned interests. What I needed to find was someone that had been around there a long time and wasn't afraid to tell me what they knew. I found her sitting on a bench finishing her breakfast. I knew her from the souvenir shop. She was the oldest white person I'd seen on either island. Her husband had passed some years after they had settled in these islands. They had retired to this place. She gave me the impression that this was her last stop. It took a while to win her confidence, and even after that, she made me promise not to mention her name in print. "This is the king's island," she told me. "He has made one thing very clear to all that are listening. We can live here as long as we maintain very shallow roots."

There was still something missing. This place had everything that makes Tahiti, the Bahamas, and a lot of Hawaii what they are. Why was it not being developed? You can't even get a ship into the main island. There was no safe harbor. The product manager I had met at the feast had told me everything was flown in. The Budweiser guy had told me the same thing. That was one of the real problems he was dealing with. You couldn't even run an island cruise ship from the main island. Why was this not the main island? An ocean going cargo ship could rest easily in Cook's Bay. The old gal could detect the bewilderment in my voice. After a few more of her inquisitive moments about my motivations, she opened up. "It's not just us outsiders whose land purchases are limited here," she explained. "Many of the natives have lost property rights here over the years. There is gold on this island; only you don't mine it, you harvest it. Come by the souvenir shop in the morning before you leave. Buy another souvenir, and I'll put something else in your bag."

I woke up to another beautiful day in paradise. This had not been like a visit to a vacation island. This was what I'd call an intriguing island. You didn't visit this place to have a fun filled experience. You had fun just remembering what you experienced. I was going to enjoy the last western style breakfast I was going to get on these islands, then stop by the souvenir shop on my way to board the shuttle for the airstrip. I can't remember what I bought. I still have a carved wooden replica of an ancient Tongan idol. If you could find an original like those that the Methodist missionaries sold to collectors around the world, you would have something. I guess that's why they still make them. They don't worship them anymore. I should have told them I was a missionary. Maybe they would have just surrendered the idol to me. Anyway, she put something in my sack. It was something long and thin. She said, "Vanilla. You are leaving the vanilla capital of the world." I'm not a cook. What did I know? I sat down in the plane and opened the little bag. Whatever it was, it was organic. It was greenish brown, thin, very hard, and about five or six inches long. Maybe it was longer than that, but anyway I got two of them. The woman sitting across from me looked at my puzzled expression and told me they were vanilla beans.

I landed back on the main island a little richer; historically anyway. I wonder how many people had come and gone and never had a clue. I wonder if the shell collectors ever brought back any vanilla. I had to do a lot of research for those two little sticks. I got in the waiting cab. My guy did not forget our Saturday appointment. I was the only one going back to town. I felt like I had my own personal driver. He was also my guide. Now he tells me my best day would be tomorrow. "You will experience the heart of the people of Tonga," he said. "All the village people will be there." At first I thought he meant the street market. It started before dawn. It was like the biggest farmer's market you ever saw. People were milling all around the place. There were piles of vegetables and everything all over the place. They did their shopping for the day and then packed up and left before I normally get out of bed. "No," he said, "There is no market tomorrow. Tomorrow is church day."

He dropped me off in front of the little stand where I had bought film. I needed some more. Beside the stand was the open-front place with the jukebox and pinball machine. It was Saturday night. The place was jumping. There was a crowd around the pinball machine watching the action. There was also a crowd around the jukebox, listening and dancing. I was just standing there when someone asked me if I was an American. I said yes. They pointed to the jukebox and told me that I must know the Jets if I was an American. Well I hadn't done this research. The Jets were a popular rock group in America, but they were all Tongans. I got a history lesson from a bunch of kids standing on a dirt floor and dancing in their sandals or bare feet. They were so proud to have a jukebox and be dancing to the music of their very own people. I listened to them and they had wonderful voices. But I hadn't heard anything yet. Sunday morning was indescribable.

I guess I know where those kids learned to sing. You have never heard anything like I experienced out there in front of the hotel. It was shortly after daylight. I could still see lights coming through the stained glass windows. There was not a soul in sight, but the air was saturated with melody. I could see one church off in the distance. Most of the beautiful sound was emanating from that one, but not all of it. I could also hear at least two other sources of this verbal praise. The Mormon Tabernacle Choir couldn't compare with this. I was standing in surround sound with absolutely no electronics involved. Soon after that, I couldn't hear anything. They must have been listening to a message. I went back into the hotel and ate. I couldn't wait for services to end so they would sing again. I knew every hymn. I felt like I'd been to church.

My driver showed up after church and off we went for another sightseeing tour. I asked him some serious questions concerning the content of the message he had heard that morning. There was no doubt this man was a Christian, and the message as well. It may have been Methodist, but it was old time Methodist. It was from back before modernism had crept in and replaced the blood their founders had preached. They would roll over in their graves if they knew what their organization had become. They're even talking about removing the crosses from their churches for some cultural reason.

My driver, as I had begun to think of him, returned me to town in time for supper and for him to make church. He said he would invite me to church, but they don't use English when they preach. Although they used English more often than not, Tongan was traditional for worship. We made arrangements for my return to the airport and he left. I had supper and returned to the street. For the first time since the morning market scene, people were on the street. They were milling around talking to one another while others were setting up podiums about every thirty yards. They all sat down on the boardwalks on either side of the dirt road. Men in white shirts took their places at the podiums and began to address the crowds. I couldn't understand anything apart from some biblical references. There was no doubt these guys were preaching. I wish I hadn't been so out of it. They probably would have welcomed me to preach. I finally went back into the hotel and sat down with a couple guys from New Zealand and ordered a beer. That was the height of rebellion for me. I'd just been forced off the field that I had once given my life to. My family was in disarray, and I was as bitter as I could be.

A few days before, this setting was so primitive that I didn't know if it would be proper to take my family there. Now I can't remember why I felt that way. It was weird. It's like modern thinking people living in the old west. I could live there if God wanted me to. Only right then, those people could minister to me better than I could minister to them. Not to mention their spiritual lives, those were the most accommodating people I've ever met. I was asking a lady behind the counter if I could get an earlier flight and she told me no. I asked why not and she gave me some reason. I didn't like the reason so I became very stern with her and she changed her answer to yes. I asked her if that meant I could leave on the earlier flight and she said no. I said "What?" rather loudly, and she said yes. I talked this over with my driver and he explained that no meant no, but yes didn't always mean yes. "If you yell at her, you will get the answer you want, but it won't change the results," he said.

I was all ready when my driver showed up. He loaded my bag and then told me he was going to give me a free tour today. I reminded him that I had a plane to catch. He said, "Not until this evening. I'm going to take care of you all day and get you to the proper flight after supper." I asked if he was sure my flight had been changed to the evening. He said he was certain. I knew if I yelled at him I would get a yes, but a yes wouldn't get me a flight. No one was waiting on me anywhere anyway. When I landed in L.A., I was going to rent a car and drive to Ray and Lori's place. They were off on vacation and I had a map to their house. Their neighbor had the house key for me. It didn't matter when I got there. I'd have to change my flight out of Hawaii, though. The worst thing that could happen would be that my airline might have to put me up overnight. Another night in Hawaii never hurt anybody. Not since 1941 anyway.

My wife had been back to the states for a visit, but I hadn't been there in four years. I'd been in eight other countries since I had left, but not one with a culture I had grown up with. I was kind of excited about that. My wife and boys were going to join me in California. I was kind of excited about that too. They were the only stability I seemed to have left. I was still reading my Bible and saying my prayers, but it was only a ritual. It's like I was on leave from reality. Now I know how men that know the truth can function in an alternative religious practice. I was living a life I didn't approve of either, but I was playing the role. I knew how to act and talk acceptably. I could do this, and for some reason, I had the idea that God didn't care. I had the idea that I had done everything the right way, but that way didn't work anymore, and God knew it. He didn't really care how I did His work, or how I lived, as long as I stayed in the business. Isaiah talks about a Christian who is walking in darkness. He tells us that this happens. It's the next thing he tells us that I should have paid more attention to. He said when in darkness, don't try to light your own fire, or you will lay down in sorrows.

The owner of the hotel gave me his card. He said, "If you write a nice article about your stay with us, I guarantee you any papers for an extended visit will be available at your request." He must have been connected. I think I was already beginning to doubt if these people needed any missionaries from anywhere. For then, however, it was my only target that had to do with missions. I was not going to think about anything for at least a month. We spent the day visiting a couple beach resorts. I had no idea these were even there. I saw more westerners than I'd seen all week. You could call these people tourists, but they must never leave the resort. I never saw anyone in town besides the few business guys. Town was probably too primitive for the average tourist. Don't get the idea we're talking about a lot of people. It's just that a dozen or so is a lot more than I expected to find actually vacationing there in Tonga. It was getting dark and my driver told me we better head for the airport.

We were back on the narrow two-lane road and it was really dark. I saw only one car coming toward us. Nothing seemed out of the ordinary until it got almost beside us. The thing was flying, and the right two wheels were off the road. By the time we were side by side, he was already plowing through under brush. We heard a terrible crash. I turned my head for the back window just in time to see the pieces flying as it hit something big enough to stop it dead. My driver started to stop when the lights came on in a little hut just off the road. He looked at me as if he was searching for direction. "If we stop, we could be involved for days," he said. I assured him that no one had lived through that. He hit the gas as if that was what he wanted to hear from me. Maybe the devil wanted to kill us, was all he said. My knees were shaking. I wasn't going to make the call one way or the other. I better trust his decision. He knew more about these things than I did. If the lights hadn't come on in the nearby house, that decision may have haunted me.

What a sober ending I thought, as I looked out at the wing lights flashing in the dark. It was history now. I hoped my driver was ok. I had to get my mind on getting back to the states. When I got there, I'd still have a lot of connections to arrange in order to end me up on the East Coast. I don't remember much more from that moment until I found myself sitting in traffic somewhere near Mission Beach, California. It was a sunny day and the temperature was perfect. I had the windows down, and I was experiencing something I hadn't experienced since I had left this same state four years before. The smell was #2 diesel. You couldn't smell it on the islands, where pollution is zero. Look over there; there was a sign on that building that read 'Mission Motorcycle'. I suddenly got a great idea.

I was sitting in Ray's house watching TV. This TV had more than one channel in English. Every news channel was showing the same thing; it was the reopening of the Statue of Liberty. There was a wild party going on out on the beach. The whole four years I had spent on the islands, we had had a total of four murders. Every one had been committed by Americans. I hadn't been back home twenty-four hours, and that many had been committed right there on that beach. I sure enjoyed the security we had in the islands. My kids could go safely anywhere at any hour as long as they didn't go near one of the American bases. Just before I had come home, two Marines had killed a cab driver just to kill. They got a life sentence. That meant they would live about five years. Americans don't last long in a Japanese run prison. Maybe that's why they don't have much need for them.

Another thing I found. Convenience stores were everywhere. You could buy California wine in a box. What a novel idea. There was more wine in that box than I had drunk in ten years. Maybe it wasn't such a good idea. They gave their gas away, as well. You could buy a whole gallon for less than a buck. What a country; if you just didn't get murdered. I showed up at that motorcycle shop just after breakfast. I was going to reintroduce myself and Mark to America in style. Just before I had left the states, I had visited a Yamaha shop with a friend. They had a brand new bike with a twin engine and chain drive. I wondered if they still made them. I wanted a bike that reminded me of the old bikes. I'd love to have had a Harley, but there's no way I was going to spend that kind of money for a bike that wouldn't even get me to Pennsylvania. There weren't even any dealers out there anymore. Sure enough, they didn't make that model 650 twin anymore. I told him my story about wanting the last of the bikes that still vibrated and sounded a little bit like a motorcycle. He asked me if he could find one still in the crate, would I want it? He said to call him the next day.

Ray and Lori got back from vacation. They were so tired that we decided to go to bed early and enjoy the next day together. We met a little earlier than we planned. We all met in the middle of their living room about three in the morning in our pajamas. I woke up and my bed was bouncing on the floor. It felt like it wasn't going to stop. I ran out of the bedroom and there was everybody else standing there. An earthquake would make a heck of an alarm clock. Not only does it wake you up, it runs you right out of the bed room. We laughed and went back to bed. That afternoon my family was landing, and Lori was picking them up. I remember this because my wife carried her luggage to the car, left it with Lori, and went back for more. When she got back, it was loaded in the trunk and Lori was standing there in amazement. She looked at my wife and said Alan Alda just walked up, loaded your bags, and walked off. There was no fan fair waiting to greet her, but God had her favorite Hollywood personality load her bags for her.

The bike shop told me they had found three and asked if I wanted them to order one in. I told them to get the nearest one and call me when it was ready. Three days later they called and told me my bike was ready. Mark and I said our goodbyes and started our cross-country from the minute we finished the paperwork. Our plan was to meet the rest of our family at the Smith family reunion in Pennsylvania the following Sunday. Our first destination was The Grand Canyon. This was no tour bike. It would run highway speeds, but you had to be in good shape to ride it non-stop for hours. We pulled into our hotel only a block from the canyon. We got settled and grabbed the camera and walked to the canyon. This was back before Clinton cut the park funds, and everything was still free. We walked out on an overlook and there it was. I picked up the camera to take a picture. After about a few seconds I just put it away. There is no way you can take a snap-shot of that. I could put the entire country that we had lived in for the last four years in that hole. You wouldn't even notice the addition.

Thomas Jefferson was out of his mind when he said this new United States could expand clear to the Pacific Ocean. Ninety-nine percent of the population lived east of Pittsburgh, Pennsylvania. Even the biggest dreamers thought maybe we could expand to the Mississippi River. Let Spain keep the rest. I'm so glad that man had such a vision or we'd be paying some Spanish guy for the right to be standing there. If you would have told us that in twenty years we'd probably have to pay some Spanish guy to stand there, we wouldn't have believed you.

We spent the night and headed off to the Petrified Forest. You don't meet any evolutionists there. I wanted to just so I could ask him why these things didn't rot. I love to ask them to explain stratified rock with sea shells in it on the top of a mountain. Today they say it's a pectorial shift. I say ok, then why is it stratified? I just never had the faith it takes to believe in evolution. I won a Navy programmer to Christ just by asking simple little questions like that. If they are truly honest and really intelligent, they do the research. He said, "It takes more faith to believe my college science book than it does to believe the Bible. You can't put any holes in it. For the first time, everything makes sense. If only they had taught me this in school. I wouldn't have had to spend so many years trying to defend the indefensible."

The rest of the trip was dedicated to arriving at the reunion in Pennsylvania before noon on Sunday. When we knew we had it made, we got a motel and rested up for the final ride. Cheryl and Brandon landed in Pittsburgh, ninety miles south of my home town. They rented a car and drove to Punxsy. They met us at the park. I told her to rap up some souvenirs for the auction. The reunion was being held in a park at a little town about three miles from Punxsutawney. Just like clockwork, we showed up about an hour after everyone began to arrive. It was a reunion indeed. We hadn't seen anyone for four years. The last time we saw these people, we were leaving for the field. Somehow it's like you just saw everyone a couple days ago. The average person's life after maturity doesn't change that much. Did you ever notice how everyone ages right along with you? Our hair is gray and we are wearing glasses, but nothing is different. The only thing different is our kids; they're older.

Most of these folks never got any further from Punxsy than southern New York State. The souvenirs we auctioned off made enough to pay for the park that year and the next. My wife's family lives in Delaware, about a five hour drive east. Mark and I decided we might as well take the bike to Rehoboth Beach. It was just an hour's ride beyond Cheryl's family's place. It would complete a coast to coast ride. We went to the farm after the reunion for a private reunion around the fire ring. We sang and carried on 'til after midnight, then retired to Mom's house in town for the night. She had acquired something since we left that she hadn't bothered to share with me when she had visited us in Okinawa. His name was Chuck Kuntz, from Big Run, about three miles from Punxsy.

Big Run is a tiny little town without a single stop light. It has one gas station, which his son owned, and an old grist mill. You could still take your grain in and they'd turn it into flour.

The father of the dentist that I bought my plane from had lost his pilot's license because of health. He had bought a motorized hang glider that didn't require any license in those days. The last time I saw the old man he was landing the thing in a field beside the old mill where I was hunting rabbits. He said he had run out of buckwheat flour and had come into the mill for enough to make breakfast. The only other thing noteworthy about this little place is that Tom Micks was from here. Chuck was a dying breed, a veteran of World War II's Pacific campaign. When I first saw him with his shirt off, I did a double take. He'd been nearly blown in half on a beach in New Guinea. That was bad enough until I saw him with no pants on and saw his wooden leg. Shortly after the war he was driving a dump truck. He told it to me this way: "When you race a train and it's a tie, you lose." He drank whisky, vodka, and beer every night from six until after midnight. I never saw the man drunk. I never heard him slur his words or stagger when he walked.

I may not have the proper degree of self-righteousness required for modern religion. As I said before, I grew up with a lot of old men like this. They didn't use God's name in vain and they were law abiding respectable men. They hated drugs and dishonesty of any kind. Who would ever believe that twenty years after their deaths, drugs and dishonesty would dominate the very elite of our government leaders? The Mayor of the city that was hosting one of our political party's conventions would have to order his police force to suspend drug enforcement until the convention was over. They would roll over in their graves. Maybe that's why I never developed an acceptable level of conviction against their lifestyle. I'd much rather have one of these old guys in the oval office than one that would disgrace it with their lifestyle.

Although Chuck was a disabled vet, he had worked long enough as a union crane operator to retire. He said the only job site he had ever got fired from was where he had set a large pipe in a trench and then went down into it to help out. The pipe rolled and pinned him by the leg to the side of the ditch. He said he didn't notice the job boss was watching as he reached down and un-strapped his leg and hopped out of the ditch.

Chuck said the man was horrified, but when he calmed down, he fired him. The skinny old man didn't play cards much or do any fun stuff. He was a talker. He had a story about anything you might be talking about. Mom loved him so much that it just came natural to the rest of us. He told me that when I got back from Delaware that he wanted to talk to me about an old campground where he had a little trailer. I knew he'd never marry my mother for family reasons on his side. He was still family as far as we were concerned. The only difference was he went home every night.

We took off the next morning for Cheryl's family's place in Delaware. The boy and I would go on to the coast to complete our coast to coast ride. Cheryl's father had been taking experimental medical treatments. He had a condition for which there was no cure. He was even taking dialysis. We blame all that on his being diagnosed with liver cancer just before we returned to the states. They gave him eighteen months if he took chemo. The big man was not much more than a skeleton when we saw him for the first time in four years. He and Mommom were living with Cheryl's oldest sister and her husband, Larry. Larry was a big shot in an insurance company in Wilmington. He hired Dad so he could write policies in his name to help him out.

I'll never forget the day, many years prior, that we were driving somewhere in Poppop's car. He turned around and looked at Cheryl and I in the back seat. He said, "What do I have to do to have what you kids have?" I almost passed out as Cheryl led him to the Lord. I knew it was real when he submitted to baptism within a week. Remembering that event made dealing with his condition much easier for us.

I had sent a thousand dollars to Chris, our oldest daughter, for a car a couple months before. Larry had bought it for her and was smart enough to keep it in his name. She hadn't made any real good decisions since she had come back to the states, and Larry realized it. Sure enough, the police contacted him and informed him that they had found the car abandoned in another state. She had been missing for a month, but showed up about a week ago with some weird girl involved in the occult. At least that's what I believed at the time. We never thought anything like this could happen to us. We always held to the proverb that if you raise a child in Christ, when they are old they will not depart from it. It took us many years to learn that a proverb is not a promise. A proverb means that some action generally practiced will generally give certain results. If you take a proverb as a promise, you will lose your faith.

After she got back to Delaware, Chris and her cousin got an apartment. We went to visit them, but after a few minutes, Cheryl's dad and I left the wives there and took a drive. He wanted to ask me what I thought about cremation. I assured him that it didn't matter what he did with his flesh when he was done with it, as long as it was done honorably. He said he wanted his ashes put in the gulf at St. Petersburg, Florida, where they had lived a few good years before he got sick.

The next day I drove up to an old DuPont mansion that I had found for Dr. Drummond shortly before we had left the college many years before. I mentioned this particular reunion earlier, but so you understand where it fits in chronologically, I mention it again here in its rightful spot. It was located on a little back road near the Pennsylvania line. Just as I did many years before, I pulled off the road onto a deserted looking drive that wound up through the woods along the creek bed. Only this time, when I got to where I could see the garden, the man that walked out of it wasn't a DuPont, it was Fred. I stopped the car and we met with a hug alongside the drive. I don't remember anything we talked about until the next car came in and stopped behind mine. It was the woman that had replaced my wife as his personal secretary. The last time I had seen her, she was running me down to some other newcomer after they had figured out I was leaving the college. She'll never know how much that hurt me. I was one of the original six that had started the original work, and this kid was publicly treating me like dirt.

Fred motioned for her to come over to where we were standing. Fred told her to show me that they held no hard feelings toward me. She began to seduce me on the spot. I had to physically place her out of my way and headed for my car. I was dazed when Fred said, "I think you should know how much it means for her to be able to offer herself to you. You probably don't have any idea how badly you hurt us when you left. When the first group left they went to the papers and did all they could do to hurt us. You left quietly in the dead of night without talking to a soul. Your empty office turned out to be more devastating to the work than anything prior to your leaving." I don't remember if I even replied. That was the last time we laid eyes on each other. It was all like a dream. Not a bad dream; a sad dream. I have made some real bad mistakes in my life, but it was clear to me that leaving there was not one of them. This wasn't a mistake Fred was making. It was a lifestyle he had chosen to live.

After that encounter, I felt like I needed a shower. I drove up to Highway One and pulled onto the old campus. There was a small group of students sitting on the front steps of what used to be the church building. I walked over and asked them if Carl Durham was still around. Only one guy thought he remembered him. He said he thought he was working as a carpenter up in New Jersey. Talk about full circle. The last time I had talked to Carl face to face, I told him this was going to happen. He's a better man than I am. I knew he would have faced the truth sooner or later. I almost felt relieved. That trip sort of put it all behind me. I had to get settled and figure out what we were going to do with our ministry. Were we going to start a campaign for a Tonga mission or take the position Hank offered us before we had left Japan?

First of all, I needed a base of operation. I couldn't live in mom's house. For the last few years before we had left for the field, we had lived in a camper. A camper makes a statement. It says 'I don't know if I'm coming or going, but I'm ready for either one.' The last person that had bought us a van was the Sharpes when they had visited us on the field. Frank Sharpe had since passed away with prostate cancer. Ilene was still honoring his decision to support us each and every month. She was the only person I could think of that could lend me enough for a camper until I figured out what God wanted us to do. Although I was basically in neutral as for directions, I had to take care of the fundamentals. I was going to head for Springfield, Missouri to see if I could bankroll this time of transition. I was either changing fields, or ministries altogether. Either way, it was going to take time and funding.

Of all our supporters, I was headed off to visit the one that was the least connected to our independent ministry. I don't know where I got the figure that I had in my head, but to her it was petty cash. That woman had a heart for missions. As a young girl working on a chicken farm, she must have had the same heart. She had asked God to give her a way to make money to give to missions. A lady showed up one day and offered her a way. When she got involved in Tupperware, the more she made the more she gave. At one time I think it was fifty percent of her income. And as you know, she became the major distributor for three states.

Ephesians 4:30
And grieve not the Holy Spirit of God, whereby ye are sealed unto the day of redemption.

Chapter 22
Round Two

Remember when God had called me into the ministry? I was just a kid, starting my first real career in the insurance business. Thirteen-thousand dollars is what I made in my second year in the insurance business. My father was the top conductor on the B&O Railroad, and I beat him by four thousand dollars that year. I had bought homes for less than that. A lot had changed in thirty years. Thirteen grand was just a figure that even a poor missionary could afford to borrow. Ilene reached in the safe and handed me a book to sign. She looked at it as she handed it to me and said in a soft voice, "This is full of notes I'll never see." She asked me again how much support we were getting. Then she said "You can probably afford five hundred a month, and that's not a bad risk I guess." I said, "It's up to you girl."

I went straight back and started looking for a camper small enough to haul behind my Dodge van and big enough to make do. I wanted the smallest thing they made that had a separate bathroom. In other words, I didn't want a toilet in the shower stall. I also wanted an awning the length of the camper. We spent most of our time outside. We only slept and cooked inside. We were going to put Mark up in my old room at mom's house so he could finish twelfth grade. That left us with just Brandon, so we didn't need a lot of room. I carpeted the entire inside of the van and put a pipe across from side to side. You could open the double side doors and choose your clothing from the rack. My cousin's husband wired the van so I could plug the truck and the trailer in. I made an office that I could access from the back of the van. That gave us more room inside the little seventeen foot trailer.

We plugged in at the farm again and put out our monthly letter telling everyone we were going to take the rest of the month off. I didn't realize how worn out we were. I helped my uncle finish his neighbor's little barn and then I decided to paint the old farm house. I can't remember it ever being painted. The nearest neighbors were about a half a mile off. They said they didn't know if they could ever get used to a large white house sitting on top of the hill. It no longer blended in with the tree line and the apple orchard. You could see it from the top of the five mile hill which was two miles on the other side of town; town was three miles away. I am glad we painted the place. Something very bad was about to happen. Cheryl and I took off for Florida to talk seriously about building Hank's church a Bible institute. He convinced us that everyone was behind the effort and would meet every need. We decided to go back to the farm where we had left the camper and promised him an answer in thirty days. He said take sixty days and relax. He said he'd never seen me so beat up.

When we got back, we saw a horrible sight in front of the newly painted house. A storm had flattened the old barn. No one, including my seventy years plus uncle, could remember it not standing a hundred yards from the house. While we were still on the mission field, a storm had moved one corner off its foundation and twisted the whole structure. A neighbor had come over with his bulldozer and pulled it straight while everyone else secured it by running cables from corner to corner. My uncle told me about the effort and added that when it did come down, his time on this earth would be very short. I remembered that when I saw his face as we just stood there quietly staring at the rubble. Almost twenty years before, I had come home from the service and found the roof in terrible repair, leaking like a sieve. He couldn't afford to replace it and none of his kids offered to help out. I roofed it, but the real damage was forever done. I don't know how it stood this long.

Shortly after, I woke up one morning and found my uncle sitting on the walk in front of my trailer. He was having a tough time breathing. "Take me to the hospital," he said between breaths. "Why didn't you wake me?" I asked him. I took him to the emergency ward. The doctor was very concerned. He told me I could take him home but he would never recover. They gave him something to help him pass the fluid that was suffocating his heart. I barely got him home before he started going out behind the outhouse every five minutes. I knew how scared he really was when he threw his tobacco away. That was the beginning of the end. It wasn't much longer and I was shaving him. He only ever used a straight razor, so I was pretty nervous. I notified Florida and the rest of our supporters that I wouldn't be coming to see them very soon. Almost everyone was understanding and told me to take my time.

The few supporters that were caught up with the old missionary had already dropped us. I didn't really care anymore. I just couldn't imagine putting the family back through anything like we'd just been through. I had to do something different sooner rather than later. The old man held pretty stable for about a month, so we decided to head south. When we got there, the church sent us to Fort Myers Beach for a week to make up our minds. I told Hank we already had, but he insisted we go. That is forever one of my favorite memories. The first couple of days the weather was just perfect. We'd sit on our patio on the second floor and watch the sun set over the Gulf. Then we would go down and sit in the water and dig for sand dollars until after dark. I hadn't enjoyed this kind of peace since I knew we were going to the field many years before. I decided to build that institute and build missions at the same time. I drew up a plan outlining just how it was going to work. I would have six men from day one working the islands as they trained for the ministry. If I could sell it to Hank, I'd present it to my mission supporters. If they wanted to be a part of it, they could keep supporting us. I wouldn't take a salary from the church other than the three hundred they already provided.

Everybody liked the idea of the on the job training program. I gave the choice to my supporters as well. The only hard part would be leaving our home church, but it only made sense that we change home churches. Our church was in Texas, and we'd be working out of Homestead, Florida. Ed was not happy, and I can't blame him. This was tough for all of us. I couldn't build a school for Ed; they didn't have a building or a congregation nearly able to support it. A lot of churches helped a lot, but Hank's church was our largest regular supporter. They had increased it every year that we were on the field. There was a real problem with changing churches that I didn't see coming. The name of the Church was Bible Baptist Church. As it turns out, there was a group that called themselves Bible churches. Hank and I were never a part of any group since we had left the BBF many years before. Getting this across to my old group proved nearly impossible. Hank led the church to cover our losses, plus he promised housing as soon as we got our membership settled.

I had to write some sad letters, but we were so pumped with our new positions that it wasn't really all that bad. The music director was in the fruit business with his dad, plus he owned a large accounting firm. He promised Cheryl a good position in the firm. We were going to be fine. After the fight we had just come through, it was great just to have some real security. We settled our membership and started what we call the honeymoon period. Every night it was supper with another one of the church members. This was the largest New Testament church we had ever been a part of. When we had first met them about five years before, they were renting a little building in an orchard. The last time we had visited them before we had left for the field, they were renting a large Seventh Day Adventist church building. Seventh Day Adventists met on Saturdays, so that worked out great. Now they were in a very large auditorium that I think was owned by the city. They rented church offices in town for the staff. There was a receptionist lobby and three offices. Mine would be the last one still empty.

Cheryl's' dad was in his last days. Hank set the date to start our first semester with this in mind. He expected us to move our camper from Punxsy to Wilmington and remain there until he passed, which is what we did. The day before he died, he called me into his room and asked the others to give us some time. He just wanted to be sure he had done everything he needed to prepare. I assured him he was ready, but I told him I would talk to him again as soon as I got back. I had to take Mark to the high school back in Punxsy to take his SAT tests. Congressmen Starks was one of the first men Hank had led to the Lord, and he was now an elder of the church. He arranged a congressional appointment to Annapolis Naval Academy for Mark, so the SAT tests could not be postponed. We got back to my mother's house just in time to receive the call from the hospital. The last thing dad said to me was that he really wanted to die. He was really suffering, and it was relieving for all of us.

This time while I was at mom's house, it rained. Mom was mopping the kitchen floor when I got up. I said, "Mom, the roof is leaking." She said, "Only when it rains." She wasn't making a joke. She had no idea the damage that was going on. No one had done anything to the place since dad had died. As soon as we got back from the field, I had found the hot water tank rusted to the floor in the basement. My old friend owned a heating and air-conditioning store. I called him and he brought me over a new tank. Cheryl informed me that the washer was also gone. Mom was back to using the old ringer tub in the cellar. So my friend Bill went and got me a washer as well. I called my brother-in-laws and chewed them out. They said they came over every week and mowed the huge lawn, but they never did that on rainy days, and she had never told them the roof was leaking. Junior told me to get what we needed and he'd be there Saturday morning to help us. That would give me time to get back from the funeral. Then I would join her in Delaware for a week or so and we'd pull the camper down to Florida.

Cheryl's mom, we call Mommom, was a weird old gal. Dad had been her total life. She didn't know anything outside of the kitchen. They had been living with Cheryl's oldest sister, Suz. Suz was her peculiar child. I had learned what a peculiar child was, because I was my mother's peculiar child. No matter what you do, if you're that child, you will never win their approval. I had tried all my life, but it was impossible. Suz had done so as well. I read a story about a woman that had been her mother's peculiar child. One day she had picked her mother up and as they drove along she said, "Mom, I've just been diagnosed with cancer." Her mother said nothing for a minute and then said, "You need to try your sisters new dish she served us last week, it's out of this world." When I learned this, my frustrations faded. I realized that I wasn't such a failure after all. I never would have been able to please my mother.

Suz suffered this same torment. Although she had done more than anyone for her mother, she was not appreciated in the slightest. She could live with it while dad was alive. She was his favorite, but with him gone, I knew I had to do something. She was probably closest to dad. At least she would suffer more than most, because her memories are the freshest. The best thing for that time would be to get Mommom out of there. Cheryl was probably the best one for mom to be around then. Problem was, I hadn't got a house yet. Living in the seventeen foot camper would be a little tight. After talking it over, Cheryl agreed; we'd just have to make room for her. The church rented a space for us in a nice little campground not far from the church office. Only thing I didn't realize was that just about everyone in the camp was a foreigner. Most of them were Canadians, but it turned out there were some French as well. Everything went smoothly for a week or so. Then the old Canadians became irritated with little Brandon using their pool. I could handle that, but when I caught a couple of the Frenchmen in the showers, I said "That's it."

We gave up on the house we were waiting on and settled for one a lot farther away than I wanted to live. Tonia had married the son of the deacon of our old church and was living near his family in Houston. With my changing churches, we thought things might get uncomfortable for them, and we were right. They had had all they were going to take; they packed up and moved to Florida. They moved in with us until they could find a place. Someone in the church owned a moving company and hired Mike before they even got to Florida. After a couple of weeks, I was headed up north for a week. As I walked out of the house, I looked over at Mike lying on the couch. "I love you Mike," I said, "but when I get back, don't be here." I was having real problems with my life; the kids didn't need to be around me all the time right then. I was taking the train to Altoona where an old friend was going to pick me up and take me to my mom's house. I really wasn't going there to work as much as I was just running from my problems. The honeymoon was barely over when some really bad things had started to happen. I had not shared anything with my wife yet.

Although we had just got into a house, I'd officially been in my office for over a month by then. There was a young man that worked as a court stenographer. For some reason, he felt as though he had been passed over for my office. At first, I paid little attention to it; the guy wasn't even a minister. Hank may not have been as up front with me as I thought. I ran the institute as the sole administrator, which had been our agreement. What I didn't realize was that Hank had not prepared his men any further than that. I was an ordained elder and Hank took it for granted that his men had understood that when they had chosen me to build the school. Hank and I had no problem with ecclesiology. Bringing me into the work was like bringing in a commissioned officer from another unit in the same army. His elder of music got that fact right off the bat. He was the accountant that hired my wife. He had understood when he had voted to bring me in that I would be at the least his equal. The other two apparently had no clue. Not only were they shocked to hear that my position was a church position; they were offended.

One morning Hank asked me to go out in the hall with my family; he wanted to bring up a vote before the church to increase my support. I was still on the books as a missionary, and he wanted to double the monthly commitment. We had agreed to make the institute a mission of the church. We would use it to reach the islands as part of the training, so it made sense to leave my missionary support as a salary. That would also allow sister churches to help if they felt led to. I had already raised thousands of dollars from donors that were interested in my training program. For some reason, that seemed to scare the other two elders. During the vote, they stood up to protest the church increasing my support. Bob Starks, the Congressman, told the congregation that I should have to work my way up through the ranks before they accepted me as a leader. Hank was flabbergasted, and the church could see it. They followed Hank, and that really did not sit well with the two disgruntled elders. They were not used to being on the losing side of anything.

I could not believe I had put my family right back into this crap. I could have beaten it with ease, but I had no heart for it. I just spiritually quit. I buried myself in Egypt. Every couple weeks, I took a week off and jumped the Amtrak for Altoona. My regular trips to the islands changed from mission work to just getting away. I was teetering on losing it, and I knew it. I had no idea how many really influential people were watching. I could have easily won that conflict, had I known it. The last straw came a few months later. A donor gave ten thousand dollars to the church for the purpose of acquiring a plane for the island work. Bob knew the donor and contacted him. He told the guy if he wanted to give that kind of money to the church, it should go into the building fund. I told Hank that he could work it out; I didn't care anymore. I jumped the train for Altoona. That time when my buddy picked me up, I told him to take me to his brother's place of business. I told him I had a proposition for him.

When we made a deal to work together, I felt as relieved as I had when I had left the mission field. I was done fighting; I'd build my own business. I was out of the ministry. Heck, I'd been out of it since I had left the field. Before we went to the field, I was building a college that would have been one of the nation's best by now. I had convinced enough people that this time I wouldn't fail; we had the right leadership this time. Boy, was I wrong. I got a call that night at my mom's house. It was one of my best students named Brad. He said the pastor was being challenged for misuse of funds. I told him that was bullshit. "Tell me he has a lover, and I'll believe you," I said. His wife hadn't been a wife for as long as I'd known him. Her brain was fried on drugs long before Hank had entered the ministry. He may have put his ministry in jeopardy for love, but not for money, no way. I went straight back to Homestead. The first call I got was from Hank. He said he'd meet me at the restaurant across from the office as soon as my meeting with the elders was over.

The meeting was a farce. Bob told me what I already knew. Hank had been spending way too much time counseling a particular young lady in his office several times a week. They were covering it up by saying that the problem was financial. I was going to handle it, but these two were really in love. I had never seen Hank so happy, and I knew he had never had a home life. So again, I turned a blind eye, and got the same result. They gave me the six hundred dollars the church had voted on. They couldn't muster the fortitude to tell me what they had told Hank. I walked over to the restaurant where Hank was waiting and he told me.

They had closed the institute and confiscated the thousands of dollars I had raised. They weren't going to reimburse me the nine thousand dollars they had promised me either. They had told Hank they were going to give me the six hundred dollars as severance. They did the same to Hank. They owned his house and his car, just as the last college had owned mine. He had no idea what he was going to do. I'd been through all this before. We could have walked right back in there and thrown those guys out on the street. He could have apologized to the church and put his wife in a home where she belonged. Then he could have made an honest woman out of the lady that loved him more than life. That's what King David did.

That's life. If you're going to serve God, you need to deal with it. The only thing that could have gone wrong was that we could have split the church. I doubt it, but like Hank thought, it wasn't worth the risk. I was already gone. I gave him my wife's car and told him to take me home to pack my camper. I hope you get this picture. We're not talking about a little country church. Hank was on the verge of building one of the largest churches in South Florida. The institute was already slated for a successful enterprise.

Hank and I just trashed it all over a cup of coffee. For that, I would suffer four years of hell, and Hank may never recover. I began my four year sentence by heading for Egypt; that's Punxsy for me and my family. We had left Mark there to complete twelfth grade. I didn't even clean out my office. All my transcripts from colleges that didn't even exist anymore were in my files. Somewhere in the back of my mind, I thought I could later recover them. My daughter and her husband still lived and worked there. Maybe I didn't even care. When we pulled out of there, I said 'This is the end of over twenty years of ministry. I don't care if the whole valley floods over.'

I have said that most of my life; 'I don't care if the whole valley floods over.' I don't even know where I got it. This time, I wish I hadn't said it. Before we even got settled back in Punxsy, we got word that all of Homestead had been devastated by the worst hurricane in history. My daughter's family followed close behind us to Punxsy. She called me one morning before I had even turned the TV on. She told me her friend had just called her from Florida and told her she had been awakened by a bathtub that had landed in her bedroom. Her friend told her our old house and my office were history. Wow, the whole valley really had flooded over. I forgot to ask my daughter to clean out my office. It was like God cleaned up my whole past in one fell swoop. Twenty years......gone.

At the same time, my return to Punxsy was as never before in my history. It was the first time I could not just pull into the lane at the farm and plug in. The month before, when I had stopped by to see Uncle Ray, he was having a really bad day. "Boy, I'm glad you showed up," my Aunt said. "I need to get him to the hospital." I took him there for the last time. Aunt Fay called me the next day and told me she didn't expect me to return from Florida since I had just been there. She said he wasn't going to last the night. Forty years..... gone. I lost my uncle before I lost my college, but it didn't hit home until I had come back. Now both losses were setting in at the same time. I ran into the little brother of my best friend that I had lost in Vietnam. He told me he had a house out in the country if I needed it. I told him, "Great, I'll take it."

That place was in the middle of nowhere. There were three roads out of Punxsy. One went south to Indiana, PA, one went north to Brookville, and one went east to Dubois. No matter which one you took, a couple miles out of town, there was a sign pointing to Knoxdale. Even if you followed the sign, you wouldn't know if you found it. There were only three houses left. There were no stores or gas stations. You just came to a place where three little roads intersected. One of them was a dirt road which led to a little seventeen acre plot, mostly woodlands. The house sat at the north end of the property, right on that little intersection. Our road was the only one that had a stop sign. We were right downtown. That was my new hideout. From there we would build a little business. We would work all three of the towns at the end of whichever road we took out of our driveway. In a year, we would be passing through those towns for the big cities like Pittsburgh, Erie, and State College. In another year, we would be passing through those to the neighboring states and beyond.

We started our business by painting our neighbor's house. Within a few months, you couldn't get us unless you were recommended by some judge's wife or one of her rich friends. We didn't know what we were doing; we were not businessmen. We didn't know how to purchase wisely or how to price jobs correctly, and we knew nothing of HR. We hired people that we later ended up traveling to other states to bail out of jail. I did some plumbing as well. I didn't know how the two different professions were going to work together into one major profession, but it did. All we were doing was making the payroll; buying equipment, doing bigger jobs, and buying bigger equipment. Mark went off to Penn State because he was one week too young for Annapolis Naval Academy. With him gone, I stopped taking the small construction jobs that he and Mike had been doing. I don't know; maybe God had been blessing in the beginning, but Satan was about to take over the job. I can remember asking God every morning for work, but work that I could do. I had already done jobs way beyond my abilities.

Somehow people got the idea that we could do most anything. Local big shots were hiring me for insurance jobs that were way over my head. I did personal work for the biggest machine-shop owners in the country. I was constantly calling in consultants. But the truth is, it was not fun any more. I think God was saying "This is what you wanted." You have to remember, I was only there because I was running in the first place. I didn't need that pressure. I decided to finish up everything I had pending and started refusing everything else. I told an old classmate that I would pour a concrete floor for him. That was going to be a really big job; about fifty yards of concrete at least. I went out to the little county airport where I had learned to fly and met up with Mike Lelock. He had just rented a large hangar where he intended to build a helicopter. I hadn't seen Mike since grade school. He had been a real nerd as a kid, but I kind of liked him now. We could talk general aviation very well and basic military aviation. That had been his life up until Carter had gotten in office and started cutting all of our military programs.

Mike was the only engineer still living of the four that had designed the B-1 Bomber. Now with all the budget cuts, he had come back to Punxsy. Like me, he didn't know where his life was going. Money wasn't a problem, though. He handed me a couple thousand to get the job started. He said he'd labor for me, but he couldn't finish concrete or build the drain work that he wanted in the floor. I got him started on the simple forms and went looking for a carpenter to build the big floor drain. Since I was already out there in the country, I drove over to the old farm to see if the neighbor, Don Evans, would do the work I needed. He had been doing construction down by Pittsburgh, but he too had been laid off. He was glad to help, especially when I handed him a couple hundred bucks and told him to lay it out and I'd plumb it in. I lined up Bob Clark to work the shoot and do the come-along when we poured.

The only thing I wasn't too sure about was the motorized float. It's called a helicopter, because of the rotating finishing blades. Mike said not to worry about it; between the two of us, we'd figure it out. He just needed me because I could read the concrete and supervise. After a really grueling day, the last truck cleaned up his shoot and pulled off into the sunset. We were just sitting there waiting for it to set up enough to hold the heavy float when a plane landed. Mr. Hock parked his 172 and walked over to see what we were doing. He was still in his Civil Air Patrol flight suit, so I could see that he was a Lieutenant Colonel now. I remembered back when I was thirteen years old. I was with the guys that had recruited him as a radio man. "Did you ever run one of these things," I asked? "Sure have," he said, as he walked over to it and started the motor.

My wife never cared much for small towns, but I liked knowing just about everybody I ran into. No matter what I needed to get done, I knew someone that could help me. So I knew he was a union carpenter. He was really impressed with the work we had done. He didn't think a scab could handle fifty plus yards of concrete in one pour. He said, "My friend is building a body shop. My brother is going to plumb it, but we don't have anyone to do the concrete." He said it was a joint effort. The guy was a really good body man, but he didn't have much money. He said he wanted me to meet these guys and see if we could work something out. I was looking for another line of work anyway, so I agreed to meet them at the job site. I found it behind the guy's house the next day. I introduced myself to the guy and told him Don had sent me to look at the floor. He ran into the house and came out with a couple cold ones. I said, "It's kind of early isn't it?" "Not around here," he said. "How much concrete do you think I'll need?" I thought it probably wouldn't take much more concrete to pour it than it would take beer to finish it. By that point, if you didn't know me, you'd never figure I was a minister. About the only difference between me and these guys was the fact that my curse words didn't contain any deities.

He told me Don's brother Bob was bringing in the last of the plumbing for the air lines that night. As soon as we plumbed them in, we could start figuring on the floor. "If you're going to team up with the Evans' boys, you'll have equal use of the shop," he said. I'm not a mechanic; I had no idea what I'd use it for. After we talked awhile, he got the idea that I wasn't looking for anything permanent or complicated. "I'll teach you how to detail," he said. "My brother's car lot will keep you busy." So I told him, "Alright, I'll come back this evening and help get the plumbing done." I knew this guy's family. His father was an evangelist and his brother had Rebuck's Garage on the other side of town. It was a pretty big operation. If he was all that good, I wondered why he wasn't working with his brother. The beer and the language might have been a good guess for starters. I had been trained a religious legalist. When you're brought up that way, you're either walking the line or living the opposite lifestyle. I know, because that's pretty much where I was.

Bob Evans was one of the most unique individuals I'd ever met. We started on the plumbing right after supper and worked well into the night. He is one of the only people I know that understands cryogenics and isn't a pilot. He was impressed with my basic understanding. Not to mention the fact that I had assembled and installed the cryogenic valves that are still lying on the moon. By the time we were finished, we were fast friends. I didn't know this was going anywhere. I detailed one car before he approached me with a contract to work with his company. He said they would pay me to drive out to Canton, Ohio and talk with his boss. I didn't think so.

I didn't know how far gone I was. I kept thinking God was going to open a door any day, and I'd be off somewhere working in some ministry. Bob didn't let up. One night, having a beer together at the shop, he said he had to go out to Canton and pick up a new truck. He said, "Just ride out with me, keep me company, and I'll give you a tour of the air plant." That did it. You can't just get in an air plant. They don't even teach the stuff in college. Bob had learned it in the military, as had the rest of the few people I had ever met in the industry. "You bet I'll go," I told him.

We got there just in time for lunch. Bob's boss and the plant manager were waiting to take us out. During lunch they explained that they needed a man with my basic knowledge to paint Cryogenic tanks. You couldn't just call in a painter to work around this kind of equipment. If you broke a line on a tank at a hospital, you could kill somebody. They didn't really care how well I could paint, as long as I could put their decals on straight and not break anything. The tour of the plant was interesting.....ear splitting, but interesting. The first thing that liquefies is just air. Liquid air had powered all of White Beach Naval Station in Okinawa back in the forties. You can power anything with it, with zero pollution, but that's all top secret now. The next thing that comes off is nitrogen. Liquid nitrogen is really cheap. It is used in industry, vacuum packing and such. They blow most of it back into the atmosphere. Next comes oxygen, and they keep all of this for medical use. Next off is specialty gases; nitrous oxide, argon, and such. It comes off in much smaller quantities, but at a good profit.

"Okay, you're really nice people, so I'll give it whirl," I said. The tanks were all different sizes. Most of them were about forty feet tall. I painted one, under the watchful eyes of hospital security, and all went well. I made more for painting one tank than I had made for painting a whole house. All of the sudden, I had enough tanks to keep me busy for a year. One thing was sure; I wasn't painting any more of them from a ladder. Before the large insolvent banks had bought up all the little solvent banks, we still had a little family bank in town. All you had to do was walk in and ask for your loan officer by his first name. This was the same guy my father had introduced me to when I was in high school. He simply asked, "How much do you need, Tim?" "Eight-grand for a lift," I said. "Tell Betty I said to extend your line of credit by eight-thousand. How's your mom? Blah-blah, thanks, have a great day."

When Bob saw me pulling my lift behind my van, a light came on. "That thing would pick up my evac fins and set them over the fence," he said. "How about helping me with new installations?" That was the gist of our next conversation. "You can already run plumbing. I'll teach you how to silver solder and you can work with me. You can paint tanks between jobs, or let Cheryl and Mark paint them." Mark was on break from Penn State and needed the money. I would hire them a helper or two, and send them out in my camper. I'd let them paint two or three and see how it went. I gave them some tanks way out there, where I didn't like to go anyway. I intentionally picked out a few liquid nitrogen tanks at first. That way, if they broke anything, nobody would die from lack of oxygen. I told Bob I'd work with him. Just like me, he determined we'd handle a nitrogen installation first. He had to switch out a tank at a factory in Clearfield. "You won't need the lift for this one," he said. "I'll just teach you silver soldering and regulators. Pick you up in the morning."

Man, was that fun. All our copper tubing was cleaned and capped. Every solder joint was made with silver, not lead. The normal head you use to solder won't even begin to melt the silver. We used what we called a star head. It puts out about five times the flame. The joints aren't ready to be soldered until both the fitting and the pipe are cherry red. You had to learn a delicate balance; one second too much heat, and the joints would melt before you could apply the solder. You wreck three or four joints learning, and then you get it. When the manifold is built and everything is connected, you pressure test it. This set up was used to line the walls of a furnace with nitrogen so the fire wouldn't burn through the steel walls. You would have to know nitrogen to understand the process. For you engineers, you know if there's nitrogen, there's no air, and that means no flame. As you know, a liquid tank is nothing more than a big thermos bottle. You set the regulators to allow expansion. This stuff expands about fifteen hundred to one when it reaches ambient temperature. It supplies its own pressure if you set everything just right.

What I really liked about doing an installation were the inspectors. You know, the guys in the white hard hats? They did everything by the checklist they carried on their clipboards. Only problem was, there wasn't anything on their checklists concerning cryogenics, but they'd try. "Did you blow out that tubing before you installed it?" they would ask. "No sir, it's cleaned and capped by a federally regulated process at the manufacturer. We wouldn't use anything blown out with unfiltered air and not tested for purity," was our answer. "Did you use solder that is certified at eighty-seven percent purity or above?" they would ask. "No sir, if you use that junk on our equipment, we'll pull it out. We only use pure silver." That was usually about the end of their attempts to use their checklists.

Once at Children's Hospital in Pittsburgh, where we did a really big job, an inspector reached a little further. He stopped me during a set up and asked if a certified union installer had signed off on my procedure. I knew there was no such thing as a cryogenic union, but I also knew this guy had no clue. I wasn't the one to straighten him out. This was a multi-million dollar installation, and had been contracted by experts more informed in these procedures than both of us put together. I could try to explain this to him, but it would result in a work stoppage, and it would be my fault. The safest thing I could say was the truth. "No," I said. I had finally run into one of these guys that I couldn't handle with a smart-ass response. "I'm just a contractor sir," I said. "You'll have to consult the company rep." I laid down my torch and walked out of the installation. I knew Bob would be back within the hour. I also knew he wouldn't be able to handle this any better than I could.

We just sat in the motel until Bob's pager went off. The union Super wanted to speak with him at the installation. Bob called Corporate and they said the rep was on site….just stay put. The union explained that no work would be done on that site that was not done by them or an affiliate union. They demanded all installation instructions be submitted to their steamfitters. Everything corporate had was then faxed to the site. We went home. The next day Bob was called to meet with the Super as they had originally requested. He called me and asked me to hang loose. He didn't know what was going on. About four o'clock, I got another call. "Can you come down in the morning?" he asked. "We got it all settled and need to finish the job." The union had called the rep and said they couldn't figure out the instructions. They needed Bob to assist their steamfitters. They would make a special exemption for a non-union employee in this matter. Bob explained every connection; he even provided certified material that was foreign to them. They couldn't get one connection to pass pressure testing.

I showed up on site in the morning, and no one was in the installation except Bob. He filled me in. He said he had showed them everything. They didn't understand a single thing about it, but they made the connections. "Seeing how they were union certified steamfitters, I didn't think it was my place to teach them to silver solder," he said. "They gave up after a few hours and called the inspector in for a pow-wow. After another hour, they asked us if we'd finish the installation, so I called you. I think they'll stay out of the way." I knew I was involved in high-tech stuff. I just didn't realize how exclusive it was. The best the union had could not silver solder, let alone plumb in a cryogenic manifold to the hospital supply lines. I was feeling pretty cocky the next time the inspector walked in to the installation. I was setting the regulators. He asked me when we would be ready to charge the system. I never turned around. I just asked, "Isn't this where we left off last time we spoke?" I never saw him again.

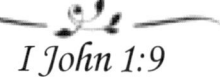

I John 1:9

If we confess our sins, He is faithful and just to forgive us our sins, and to cleanse us from all unrighteousness.

Chapter 23
Finding the Way Back

The money was good, but the relationships were gutter type. I was getting tired of myself. I think God knew I would eventually come to myself. He just put me in front of one low-life after another. I think he went out of his way to find them. In Bob's field, most of the people are impeccable. Bob was too.........it's just those that surrounded him off the job weren't. When you're a leader, followers gravitate to you. Even before I first met Bob, it was clear that he was their idol. As bad off as I was, I think I was a breath of fresh air to him. I didn't make a dirty joke about everything. He was the first guy I had had an intelligent conversation with in a long time. I mean with someone that I really liked being around. Mike Lelock was far more intelligent than I, but he was so intelligent that he wasn't the most fun guy to be around. I think that's why Bob and I bonded so quickly. He really wanted to work me into his career, and it was very tempting.

There is almost no competition in the field. A lot of people know a lot about their particular division of this career field, but almost no one knows it all. With the knowledge these guys possess, you could make a little air plant small enough to fit in a pickup truck. It might not take off oxygen, maybe not even nitrogen, but it would liquefy air. If you knew how to use it, you could run a large enough generator to power a large house. With some real engineering, you could power the truck as well. The only thing that would go back into the air is air. This is why I know there is no serious effort to free us from oil dependency. I won't be surprised if someday, a would-be publisher calls me to say this part has to go. Maybe not. I've seen one of these things on TV with a marketing promise; what happened to it?

At any rate, my knowledge level in the field had way surpassed painting the tanks. I was putting in a manifold at a university hospital in Kentucky when some engineer told me I was not plumbing it properly. He produced a diagram that he had requested from the people I worked for. One look at it and I could see that the regulators had no backup. I tried to explain it to him, but he insisted I copy the diagram. I wasn't going to try and convince him that the manifold that had been made in Bob's dad's garage was state of the art, and this thing was antiquated. I had only ever met two other technicians besides Bob and both of them had asked me the same question. They wanted to know where they could get a manifold like mine. Bob's family might not have been high on morals, but they sure weren't lacking on brains.

I was in that little garage behind Bob's dad's house when two engineers had tracked the old man down. They said they'd been hired to remove a boiler from an old building that was being made into a railroad museum. They couldn't figure out how to get it out without harming the old structure. After a lot of investigation, they found that he was the man that had installed it. They figured if he could tell them how he got it in, then they could figure out how to get it out. You would think that the most sophisticated piece of equipment installed in the largest hospitals in our country probably came from NASA. This old man built them in his garage.

The world is not as depicted on TV. Do you know the first person that ever attempted to build the very first boot that set foot on the moon? Dr. Luff walked into my little room in retrofit where I was working on a space suit and asked me to do it. I was a young punk fresh out of the Air Force. "Why don't you ask one of those kids fresh out of college?" I asked. "Because they only know two things son; America sucks and vote democrat," was his answer. Man, it was fun working on America's greatest accomplishment with some of the greatest Americans. They say if we wanted to go back to the moon today, it would take five years to get back to where we were when we did it the last time. I'm not so sure. We have the technology, but we did it on American ingenuity. We still have some leading ingenuity, but I think we're a little short on Americans.

Sorry for slipping off into reality. Let's get back to the hospital in Kentucky. This deal at the hospital was the same sort of thing. I called Bob and told him I wasn't going to finish the job. He sent the area rep down from Pittsburgh, but he didn't have any affect on the situation either. Finally, they had to send the old man that had drawn the diagram down from Ohio. He explained that he had drawn it up shortly after he had gotten out of the service; the industry had made a lot of improvements since then. The engineer couldn't believe there wasn't a government approved installation manual somewhere. He tried all his friends in academia and couldn't find a single professor in the field. He finally found his counterpart in a major medical engineering outfit in Pittsburgh. He gave him the personal phone number of whom he said was the leading technician in the industry. When Bob answered his mobile phone, which was mounted in his service truck, the guy started to get the picture.

By the time I was finally trusted enough to work on my own, I had already decided to quit. If Bob had called, I wouldn't have taken the job, but this particular call came from his boss. He said that it was just impossible for Bob to get there at the time the job was needed. When I turned him down, he promised me the moon if I ever wanted it. Bob had told him there wasn't anyone else in the state he would trust to do it. I felt that maybe I owed them one last job. I felt I owed Bob that much, as well. He really wasn't a bad person; he just hung with the wrong type. It was a holiday of some kind, because Mark was home from Penn State. I asked him if he wanted to make a hundred bucks for a three hour job; one hour down to Pittsburgh, one hour of work, and one hour back. He asked what we had to do and I told him I'd fill him in on the way down. I was afraid if I told him up front, he might not go. I knew when I told him, he would get antsy, but I had an answer prepared.

Bob had dropped the equipment off at the site a couple days before. We had to put in a six-pack; that's six large portable oxygen bottles. They were already setting in the basement of the hospital when we got there. All we had to do was manifold them together and put in a regulator and a backup. They were doing construction on the road outside the hospital between the large tanks and the hospital. They needed to cut the main supply and re-route it. We would hook our rig into the main supply so they could turn it on while they did their work. After we had it all hooked up, Mark asked what would happen if this didn't work. I told him that everyone in the hospital relying on oxygen to stay alive would die. Mark looked at me like a calf at a new gate. "Isn't there anyone that can come down here and make sure we did it right?" he asked. I said, "There's no one this side of Ohio that I know of." He said he was really nervous. That is what I was waiting for. I said, "Remember when I asked you what you wanted to do with your life? You told me you wanted to be like Red Adair. Anytime there was an oil well fire anywhere in the world, they called him because he was the only guy that could handle the job. Well, you're that guy today."

What a way to end my fledgling career in cryogenics. It worked or I'm sure I would have heard about it. Now what was I going to do? This was a great career opportunity, but I had to get away from these people. I had found a little country church a couple weeks before. The pastor managed the biggest machine-shop in town, plus one in Alabama. He had grown up as a missionary's kid in Brazil. He asked me the week before if I'd speak for him every other week for awhile. I had just decided to trash everything I had going for me. What did I get for it? The first offer I'd had to preach since I had left the ministry. This might be the beginning of my way back.

Chuck, my mom's guy friend, asked me to meet him at the Army Navy Club for a drink a couple months earlier. He wanted to present something to me. He said, "You have a camper, and I have a camp. The CB club bought it from the Groundhog Club for a dollar about ten years ago. They lost interest in it and let it run down. We cleaned it up and fixed the pavilion and used it for an annual camp out to meet the expenses. The problem is, the same thing has happened to us that happened to the Groundhog Club. Except for the annual camp out, only I and one other guy use it. When your mom and I were kids, it was called Allaho Park. I used to be in charge of lighting the gas lights every weekend. You're kind of a smart fellow, I mean from what I've heard. You might be able to help us."

I don't know why I said I'd look at it. I guess I just liked the old guy. He told me it was about three miles from town on the back road to Big Run. It sits down in the river bottom across from Big Run. I always thought the road to Big Run was the back road out of town. Well there's a back back road I had forgotten about. I found the place the second time I drove past it. From the little road in the woods, you could see a dirt road going down the hill toward the river bottom. You could just make out a gate, made out of a large pipe, closing off the road. He had given me the combination, and told me no one was down there this time of the year. I backed up and pulled off the road onto the lane leading down the hill to the gate. This was in the middle of the woods. The trees were tall old oaks, beach, maple, and pine. The underbrush wasn't bad, because not much sunlight could reach through the cover to the ground. The road really dropped off from there. I could see the bottom, but nothing more from where I stood. I swung the pipe from across the road and headed for the bottom.

At the bottom of the hill I came into a small, but overgrown clearing, about the size of a football field, in the middle of the forest. I followed the lane for about thirty yards where it came to a "Y". I stopped the van and got out. It was so quiet you could hear a fly, let alone the birds. To my left, about ten yards off the lane was a breathtaking sight. Walden's pound......I had found it. It ran longer than wider, with no defined edges to speak of. The far end was swallowed up by the forest. You couldn't tell if it had an ending or not. A large fish topped the water. The splash brought me back to the reason I was there. I left the van sit, and began to walk the lane that forked off to the right. The only structure you could see was at the far end of the clearing; it looked like a large wooden umbrella. A huge old oak was reaching out of the forest. It covered the half of it that snuggled up to the forest. I felt the same feeling I had when I had found that old Confederate mansion in the middle of the cornfield in Virginia many years before.

The whole old building was a big circle, made of large beams like you'd find in an old barn. You walked up about six steps on a wide-railed stairway to reach the wood planked floor. One large pole ran from the floor up through the open rafters to the peak of the pavilion. The roof was shingled with about ten different colors of shingles. No one had put any money into this place, but at least they had pieced enough together to keep the rain and snow off the old plank floor. Wow. Jubilant voices and the noise of dancing feet filled the silence. My own mother had rode a long-gone trolley car from her little town, down through Big Run, and danced right here on these very boards. This place did not just happen. That's what it must be like for those people that believe in the big bang theory. This was a concerted effort, grown from the dream of one long-forgotten soul. How can this place be lost in the woods? Where are the rest of the kids whose mothers danced here before they had even met their fathers?

I walked back to the van and looked up the other fork in the lane. There was a little iron fence that fenced in an area about six foot square. Inside were two small tombstones. There was another stone that informed you that you were looking at the graves of Phil and Phyllis. It said they'd been executed by the state of California. No last name. My mind ran several scenarios. How did they end up here? They sound like brother and sister. No last name and they end up in the middle of nowhere. Maybe I had found a Pennsylvania version of Bonnie and Clyde. They were buried out here on a secluded piece of real-estate that eventually would be developed by the elite group called The Punxsutawney Groundhog Club.

'What's that big black limo doing down here?' I thought as it saw it coming towards me. It was coming right over to me. This was really weird. I was standing at a grave and a hearse had showed up. The driver stepped out and the passenger followed. They were dressed to kill. They introduced themselves as next of kin to the guy in the back of the hearse. They explained that Mr. Margiotti had lived in Pittsburgh when he died, but had several last wishes before his internment. One was a final visit to this old camp and the gravesite of the two groundhogs that he had sent to a zoo in California.

Wait a minute......Groundhog Club.......Punxsutawney Phil; it was starting to come together. After further consideration, I found these two groundhogs to be victims. They had been given to a zoo in a state that didn't know they could dig. They had dug their way to freedom only to be tracked down and executed by the state. They had said they didn't need any new rodents. Anyway, across the dirt lane from the groundhogs was a perfect spot for my camper. There was a dry streambed running between the small opening and the woods. As long as I didn't let anyone use the toilet, I could run my gray water out when it rained. I followed the streambed back into the woods where it just dissipated into nothing. This was the perfect place to turn my life around; I knew it from the day I had found it. I was going to move my trailer to this little camp. I was not going to do any more cryogenic work. My rent and utilities were my biggest monthly expense. I could isolate myself out here. I could paint a couple houses for food money, preach for that independent church, and let God show me what was next.

It worked like a charm. All you have to do when you find yourself in any bad situation is get away from the evil influences and start preaching. It works every time. The darkest days of my life were over. I can't believe I had let myself sink to the depths I had sunk to. I'd lost the confidence of everyone that meant anything to me. I can't believe my wife stuck with me. I'd have left my sorry butt six months after I had left the ministry. I put her through a couple years of hell, and she was still there. I forgot......this wasn't the first time she had stuck by me. I can't believe anyone can care so little for their life. I should have died; I knew it and I didn't even care.

Oh, there were a few that had tried to help me. A pastor from South Carolina had called me. I don't know how he found me, but he took the time. He said he had been following my life ever since the break-up of the first college I had worked for. He told me that when we had lost the second college down in Florida, and they had thrown the pastor out, that they had called him down to help them find a new pastor. He said he talked to a lot of people, and had come to the conclusion that I had been through more serious battles than anyone he had ever known to survive. He offered me a position on his staff, and promised he'd stand by me. He said, "You really need some healing time, my Brother." He didn't know that I had not survived.

I might have stepped out of the fire, but it was going to take a lot to recover. We decided to try and pick up somewhere in the general area of where we had left off. We had been missionaries for about six years before we had accepted the call to Florida. It was really Florida where we had left everything we cared about. We decided to pick up there and see what happens. I called the pastor that had got canned when we did, and he said to come on down. He was working for an insurance company in Deland. We put all our equipment in storage, hooked up, and headed south.

We had no real income anymore, but great credit, along with a bunch of plastic to prove it. We parked in Hank's backyard just beside the pool. It was really a weird visit. His wife's family (they used to be really close to us) never even came out of the house to say hello. His wife was cold as we might expect; we had supported Hank after his affair. The reason we had was twofold. His wife had never been what we called a wife for as long as we'd known her. Secondly, I do not believe you can return to your mate if you have defiled the relationship. I don't mean because you committed an act of adultery. I mean if you left your mate and lived in adultery with another person. The Bible says to return after that is an abomination. That was exactly my counsel when he had told me he was going back to his wife. In the depths of my depravity, by the grace of God, that never happened to me. I separated with the jewel of my life once, but I never played house in my life. I never even slept with my wife until we were married. Even as a lost person, I had refused to sleep with her until we were married.

Something strange happened the night before we pulled into Homestead. Something happened that had never happened before or since. I had decided not to complete my intended journey down to Homestead. I had been sitting alone by the pool at the campground where we had parked that night. There was a little floating ring, the kind you would throw like a Frisbee. I had a little ball, like one you would use to play pool volleyball. The ring was floating about three feet from the edge of the pool, where I was sitting. I had been contemplating the possibility of never having a ministry ever again. I sat there praying and mindlessly attempting to roll the ball into the floating ring for over an hour. It was impossible. I even fished it out of the pool to see if the ball would fit in the ring. It fit just fine.

I was reading my Bible regularly, and I don't believe in signs, since we have a completed Bible. For some reason, with all the seriousness in the world, I asked God to show me if I had any future in the ministry. Gideon got away with it twice. I said I would be satisfied with just once. Out of total frustration, I reminded the Lord of what He had done for Gideon. I knew He had done it for him because Gideon was really scared about the ministry God had just chosen for him. I, too, was scared. I was about to put it all behind forever. I said, "If you want me in the ministry in any form, put this ball in the ring." From only three feet away, I still couldn't do it. I said, "God forgive me for seeking a sign," and I went into the camper for my nightly reading.

My scriptures that evening were David on his deathbed, commissioning Solomon to take over. He told him he would have the heritage of the heathen coming to him from all over the world. That was a little much for me. I had never even considered the remote possibility of ever pastoring. I put my book down and walked out for my final evening prayer. When I was done, I turned to walk back into the camper, and there was the ball lying right in front of me. I just picked it up and threw it the length of the pool, not aiming at anything. I opened the door, and put my foot on the step to go in. For some reason, I felt impressed to turn and look at the ball I had just tossed to the other end of the pool.

The little ring had floated down to the far end of the pool and was floating just inside the "L" shaped portion at the end that was made for the little children. When I turned around, the ball had somehow skipped into the little "L" clear at the other end of the pool. As I watched the ball, it appeared to stop. Then it started to move 90 degrees into the entrance of the shallow enclave. Unbelievable as it was, it crawled right over to the little ring, and right up into the center of it, and stopped. I had not been able to do that from three feet away, no matter how I had tried.

God had done physical miracles for me over the years, but only to save my life. Never before had He done it at my request. God was not done. That was just to get my attention. The clarification part would take place much later, and more spiritually. I was invigorated, to say the least. I headed for the church in Homestead with high expectations. We got almost there when it got too late to proceed. We found a campground and settled in for the night. I was sitting on the picnic table doing my nightly reading when God gave me some confusing scriptures. It was Paul talking about a pastor that was an overlord. It said he loved to lord over his people.

I didn't even know who was pastoring the work. I was in touch with the head elder that my wife used to work for. We were supposed to meet at his house in the morning. Paul's last words to me that night were not to let anyone put me down. I can't remember the words, but that was clearly the message. When we got to the head elder's house, he called the new pastor and told him I was in town. He said he wanted to bring me down to his office. The new pastor was the same young man I had voted to deny a pastorate many years before, because he was a novice. I had asked him to let me train him for at least a few months. They gave him the mission anyway, and as I predicted, he lost it. It may not have been his fault; I have no idea. But one thing was for sure, he had never forgotten my input.

When we got to his office, he was ready. He thought I had abandoned the work back when I had lost the institute. He didn't know the elders had asked me to leave. The head elder didn't even know. He wasn't at the meeting, and they didn't share it with him. They just told him I had resigned. I left him rant for about ten minutes, then I remembered what the scriptures had instructed me not to do. I informed him that I was asked to leave. He stammered around a little bit. He said he had no idea I hadn't resigned. He said, "You probably think I'm still a novice compared to you, and I may be but......" I stood up and told him respectfully that he was out of bounds, and he knew it. I was warned, but I had let him do it anyway. What I didn't realize at the time was God was not restoring anything.....He was finalizing it. The final chapter of our old ministry was closed forever. Too much had gone down here, and I'd never get the blood off my hands. I maybe didn't stay and finish the fight. I could have perhaps come out on top. Maybe God was using this kid to say just that. Either way, what God had showed me back at the pool had nothing to do with Homestead.

I don't know how I hooked up with an old friend from the church, but we did. He offered me a thirty-day contract working some construction at the Orlando International Airport. We found a camp a few miles from the airport, and settled in 'til the job was done. Cheryl got a job as a maid at the motel in front of the camp. Brandon waxed campers. We were out of funds and living on plastic when George asked if I needed any money besides what he was paying me for the work at the airport. He said he had about four-thousand in his mission fund, and I was welcome to it. I thought it was a gift, right up to the day my wife collected the check from his wife. She informed Cheryl that it was a loan. I should have turned it down right then, but I really needed it. I told him I'd sell some equipment when I got back up north and pay him back. That would have been a simple thing to do if he wasn't so far down on the list of people I owed by the time I sold out. I told the work at Homestead that owed me nine-thousand dollars to pay him back and forget the balance. I don't know if they did or not. I'll find him one day and make it right if they didn't. George Hale is his name, if you happen to know him.

I came back from the airport when we were finishing up. My wife yelled for me to come in and look at the TV. CNN was live on the battlefield. Gulf I was underway. For the remaining week of our stay, I'd come home from the job and watch CNN until dark. Then I'd walk through the park until bedtime. It was there, in that park on my nightly walks, that our new mission was born. I don't know why I was so overwhelmed with the idea that the faith was going to come under a vicious attack at any moment. It was so real, I dedicated the rest of my life to preserving the faith. It may have had something to do with my recent visit to Homestead. I didn't even recognize the place. You couldn't even stop for gas if you only spoke English. Nevertheless, Faith Preservation Ministries got its name right there in that little park just outside Orlando. The timing is sealed with the start of Gulf I. Just down the road, the Bills were losing the Super Bowl to the Giants.

We decided to spend the rest of the winter with Cheryl's mother. She was staying on the beach in lower Delaware. I thought I'd start putting things together. I had a lot of ideas. While I was there, I visited my old boss from the insurance business. When I stepped out of my van, he ran over and greeted me like an old lost relative. "You need to write a book," were the first words that came out of his mouth. "I've been keeping up with you over the years through Bobby Walls. He knows some people from his old church connections that tell him where you are from time to time."

I wondered who in the world would want to read it if I wrote it? I haven't accomplished anything worth writing about. I just hadn't realized how mundane a life most responsible people live. I hadn't set foot on his place in ten years, and absolutely nothing had changed. The garden, the fish cleaning area, the boat.......it could have been yesterday that I last saw this place. There's virtue in that, however. It speaks of stability and satisfaction. His wife had beaten cancer before I had even left the company, and she was still doing fine. I drove off thinking that maybe old Mac should write a book; share a little stability with the rest of us.

I contacted a bunch of organizations and visited some churches, but nothing was developing as I had envisioned. I planned to go back to

Punxsy when we got a break in the weather, where I could find some land, figuring I'd get things rolling. Well, we went back, but nothing rolled. All I got was one great idea after another that went nowhere. I put the next six months into designing my Christian Cemetery program. I never worked so hard.....but nothing. One thing was missing. I'm still old school. No ministry is truly authorized without a local church. I couldn't believe I'd put that much time and effort and had even borrowed money into this idea. It was almost Christmas. That meant nearly a year had gone by with nothing to show for it. The night I put it all away, I got a scripture from Romans. It assured me that putting it away was the right thing to do for the present, but not to give it up for good. Maybe it was not all a waste. Maybe God has a plan sometime in the future. At least until there was a church to authorize the effort, I would put it down. I'm not sure what the purpose was. Maybe the dream kept me going or maybe it was to finish something else. I think a part of me sort of died with it. Maybe that part of me had to go before God could begin doing other things with me. Now what?

The next day, Mark came home from Penn State and wanted to plan a holiday party. Somehow my niece and her husband showed up for it; we never ran with those kids. My sister must have invited them. Pat was the boy's name. He remembered when we had had Jones and Sons, and that I had done some plumbing work. I had even helped him finish up a small job once. He told me that Crescent Supply, an old name in wholesale plumbing and heating, was looking for a salesman. He thought that I'd be perfect for the job. If he had not been there that night, I don't know what I would have done. We were bankrupt. We had sold everything. I couldn't even have started over on my own. His idea felt good from the second I heard it. I showed up at the Punxsy branch Monday morning. I must have said the right things; they set me up for an interview at the home office in Pittsburgh. I showed up on key and sat down with the young owner. Presenting myself as a salesperson is no problem. I love to sell anything I can believe in. I'd love to sell for a company whose name I'd known since I was a kid. The company was second or third generation.

I hadn't worked directly for anybody since I'd been in college. A resume was quite flexible with my background. I could slant everything in the direction of the goal I hoped to obtain. I had him from the onset. The only major problem I had was lack of experience with boilers. It seemed that since the former salesman had left, they hadn't moved one percent of their boiler stock company-wide. The bottom line came down to one question. "Can you sell a hot water heating system?" I danced around the question, but he kept bringing me back to the same qualifying question. Finally, he asked me straight up; could I install a boiler? Now the question to me was clear: did I want the job or not? One thing I'd discovered during the dance we'd been doing for the past hour was that he knew no more about how a boiler worked than I did. "Is that all that's bothering you?" I said. "Of course I can."

'Then you're our man,' was the answer to that stretch of the imagination. The rest of the day was spent outlining my territory. It was the largest territory in all three divisions of the company. I had never worked for a wholesale outfit before. There were no Home Depots in the day, at least not in the backwoods of northwest Pennsylvania. When I was running Jones and Sons, I'd had a real hard time getting a deal from these outfits. The only way you could get an account with one was to have a really known contracting outfit. I was really on the outside, along with a bunch of other little guys struggling to make a living. I was about to change all of that. All of the sudden, I was the guy for the whole northwestern state that decided if you could buy wholesale. If you were a home owner, or if you owned an apartment or two, you were not considered a contractor. If you didn't at least have a little ad, or a name on your truck, then you were not considered a contractor. In my eyes, you deserved the same advantage as the big guy. It sure didn't take long for that to get out. I was getting calls from all the little Jones and Son's outfits in every little town clear up to the New York line.

I found contractors that were glad to let me work with them. They taught me everything there was to know about a hot water system. I learned the engineering part on my own. I went to all the schools our vendors offered. I could size the job and make an entire estimate before the contractor ever placed an order. It seemed no one else was taking the time to do this. I would work every evening, well into the night, designing systems. All the contractor had to do was get the job and call me to design it and price it. The only problem was, I didn't have any low end equipment. I sold Burnham, the best in the industry. It became known that you could go over to my competitor and buy cheap stuff, but he wouldn't design anything for you. Even if it was a particularly big job, he wouldn't go with you. He wouldn't help you present the equipment and go over the installation with you. I spent three years in this field. The first year, I traveled all over my territory every week just signing up contractors. The second year, I couldn't keep up with the business. I worked by phone, answering questions and taking orders. I only went out on the really big jobs.

The third year was almost funny. The kid that ran the company figured I was making too much money, I guess. He cut my expense account twice, and finally cut off my oversized territory gas allowance. I said fine. By that time, I was working the phones morning and night. I just decided I wouldn't travel at all, and I didn't. I spent the mid-days at camp, fishing. Sometimes I went home and took calls, and sometimes I just spent the night. I had two big operations now that were dealing only in my equipment. One was up in Saint Marys, and the other in Punxsy. They were the two biggest operations going. I got them because I was the only wholesale outfit that would stock their shop on consignment. They knew they could drive into camp and get me to go open the warehouse for them day or night or Sundays. If they needed me to work out an HVAC formula for them, I could do it almost by memory. It was almost getting boring. The only thing I really cared about was preaching, and that was going away because the pastor was not traveling anymore.

I had gone as far in this work as I possibly could. I was playing half a day every day, either at camp or in the pool room at the Elks. My young owner could have made me a manager, and let me train a couple guys to handle my territory. This would have allowed me to expand. Instead, he tried to set it up so my customers could bypass me and work directly with the local office. That backfired. These guys were not buying my equipment; they were buying me. Even if I didn't see them anymore for weeks at a time, they could always call me. They would get an answer the office couldn't begin to provide. A rift began to open with me and the local office. I was moving their entire inventory, but didn't even bother to show up anymore. The local manager and his secretary were just paper pushers. They hired another salesman. They were all excited. They wanted me to meet him for breakfast at the Grubb motel. The company owner from Pittsburgh would be there, so they were sure I'd show up.

I was late. The owner stood up and welcomed me to the table. I hadn't seen him since the award ceremony in Pittsburgh a couple months before. They were giving this new guy a territory east of mine that ran over to the State College unit. He was a special guy, ready to handle anything. He came into the office everyday. They wanted him to ride with me for a couple weeks. I think they thought maybe he could rein me back into the fold. I hadn't been in the office for over a month. Now I was even making them do my orders. I'd design the system, list the parts, price it out, and fax it in. They weren't used to that. That was the salesman's job. They were the managing staff. I got tired of that right away. They didn't have a job if I wasn't giving them paperwork to do. I decided to let them pull my orders and make the paperwork in the first place. I guess they figured they better do it, or they wouldn't have any thing worth processing. But now, there was this new fellow. Here was someone that just might be glad to take over any orders I didn't want to process. It would be his right to do so. I was sending half my people straight in to the shop by then. Surely, if there was another salesman around that could process their order, then I wouldn't send them in.

The introductions were made. The guy was a class act. I thought about the problems he might give me if he was in the office. This had been my place now for several years. Heck, I had guys coming into the shop that had never met me other than by phone. If I wasn't there, this new guy could process them. I'd lose some business. I sat down and they motioned for the waitress. This little thing came over and took our order. When she walked away, the new guy said, "You might think she's a hot little girl, but believe it or not, she's a mother with kids." "No, that's not possible," we said. "Oh yeah, I've known her for years," he said. "She lives with some guy, but I don't think they're married."

There we were out in the country, and this guy knew everybody. That's the impression I got. Several other exchanges and evaluations concerning his revelation were mentioned, and then we began small talk. The owner finally spoke directly to me. "What do you think about opening a territory east and taking some off your hands?" he asked. Just then, the little bit showed up with our order. Now their eyes were going right through her. She couldn't have been over thirteen. I looked up and asked her how Joey was doing. She answered, "He's good, Uncle Tim. He's really excited about the heating tubes you're putting in our floors."

I liked that impression better. Not only did I know these people out here, they were my customers. I went on to ask them some basic HVAC questions. I was kind, because I remembered how little I had known just three years before. I described the three-way system I was working on. It was so complex that the rep from Burnham was working on it with me. I confessed that I hadn't known all that much when I had started. I recommended the same man that had taught me, but the new guy wasn't interested. He said 'This is the nineties', whatever that meant. The office loved him anyway. He would go into the office and do his own paperwork. The only time I ever went in was late at night with my wife to use one of the hot tubs in the display room. I always liked to have a big order to leave on the boss' desk. Then I wouldn't call in for a couple of days, so I'd be sure he had to get it done in time for delivery.

The only guy I liked in the whole place was an older guy that they would bring in whenever we would get really busy. He used to work full time in the office until he had trained his son as his helper. Once he had got him trained, they kept the boy, and let old Albert go. I wish I hadn't been in the office the day that boy got a call from home. He turned white and ran out the door. The boss came in and told me that his dad had just come home from the doctor's office. He learned he had cancer. I thought that was bad, until he told me the rest. The boy's mother had found his dad sitting out behind the barn. He had laid his arms open with a box knife.

When they had let Al go, that meant he had no insurance. The old guy thought he was saving the farm for the family. He had no idea how glad his family would have been to trade the farm for another day with him. I never realized how selfish suicide was until I saw that boy's face. Well, the company got out of paying anything by making him part time. I met the old man that had started the company. He was a really nice guy. His young son and his son-in-law had taken over the company. They treated him like a maid. When we'd visit the main office in Pittsburgh, they would let him serve the snacks. These two young men are what gave the Jewish businessmen a bad name.

Mark called me one morning after that from Phoenix. He asked me if I'd come out and play some golf with him. He waited until we had a bad snowstorm before he called. I told him I didn't think I could get away. The very next day, my phone rang. It was the young boss in Pittsburgh. That was the day they had decided to take away my gas allowance. I said, "Fine, have a nice day." I called my son, and told him I'd come out. He said he'd already bought the tickets. I spent my last week telling my customers I was leaving the company. I wasn't surprised that many of my regular customers were upset. I was shocked though when one of my biggest builders up in Saint Marys, a guy I'd spent a lot of time tracking down for payment, tracked me down. He was hurt when he heard I was leaving. He ran over to my car and said, "What am I going to do? Who is going to design my systems?" I remembered the many months it had taken me to get his business. When I saw how serious he was, I had to get serious. I had to give him the name of my best competitor. I knew no one in my outfit would do it. No one in my outfit could do it.

I earned my people. When I'd finally get a shot at an estimate, I'd sit up late into the night, figuring the entire job right down to the smallest part. When I'd finally get one of the jobs, they would say "Just send the unit, no parts." The next time I'd do the same thing. Then one day they'd give me back the estimate with most of the parts scratched off. Next time, there'd be less scratched off. Then finally, they'd say just send it all to the job site. The smart builders figured out that they didn't have to keep an inventory, period. It was a lot of work for no pay, but when I finally got their whole business, my sales per job doubled. I'd keep copies of each job, and it would get easier each time. By that point, I could build a job in my head, right down to the smallest copper fittings.

Once you got a contractor that far, you had him for good. They'd just call in and say, "There's a house framed up at such and such, my foreman will call you when he's ready for delivery." That also took the foreman out of the buying loop. That took most of your competition out of the loop. It was easy to find a foreman, but it was hard to find the owner. When a foreman would give me a chance at a job, I'd track down the owner and give him a copy as well. I'd take the address from the first check and send copies of everything to his office. Foremen came and went.....owners were forever.

Oh, I would still visit the foreman, and give him hats and other trinkets. The owners were all pretty similar; they would only call me once in a blue moon. They'd tell me how bad I was ripping them off. Then they'd ask for a favor. They would have some weird customer that wanted a really complex system, and they'd ask me to meet with them and try to keep them on budget. Of course they'd take a minute every time we talked to remind me of just how much money they were spending with me. They did this to feel better about not shopping around. I would always remind them that, unlike my competitors, I didn't work on commission, and that my bonus was based on total sales, not profit.....they always forgot that. I'd assure them that nobody could buy from me as cheaply as they could. I'd send them a coupon to a nice restaurant with their next bill. I'd inform them that if they'd pay on time that month, I could get them another two percent. I didn't push that too much, though. They liked me because they knew I wouldn't shut them off. They knew I'd chase them down at the last minute. They'd bitch, but they'd pay. I was the best partner they'd ever had.

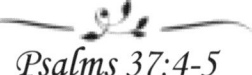

Psalms 37:4-5

Delight thyself also in the Lord: and He shall give thee the desires of thine heart. Commit thy way unto the Lord; trust also in Him; and He shall bring it to pass.

Chapter 24
Laying Foundations

It was going on four years since my life had turned around. I'd given up on ever going back into the ministry. I was just very glad to be living an honorable life again. You know, that's not really true. I mean the again part. I had never lived like this before. Even when I had been in full time Christian service, I had been a lot weaker under temptations than I was at this point. I'd screw up every five or six months back then and put myself through a couple months of pain and penance. Just when I'd get back to feeling pretty good about myself, I'd screw up again. For the last four years, though, I just hadn't felt an overwhelming desire to do anything I'd be sorry for.

The major reason for this is I had finally relaxed about ninety percent of the self-imposed restraints that I used to live under. Suddenly, if a customer bought me a beer, I didn't feel like I used to. I used to say, "Well, I blew it; I might as well get drunk." As you know, when you get drunk, it's just the first step in doing other things you wouldn't normally do. It's unbelievable, but for the first time since I'd become a Christian, I was happy with myself. I think the word normal fits pretty well. Normal Christian Living fits me really well. I like it. I wish I'd tried it a long time ago.

My few friends thought I was nuts for giving up what I'd built, but I was really excited about it. I felt like I was climbing out of a bottomless rut. The best future I could envision by staying in PA was working another twenty years and then retiring to live in the home I was born in. I saw my dad pretty much do that. The only thing that really kept me going was that old camp. I had pretty much rebuilt it. I got the club to sell off about sixteen thousand dollars of timber, and had used the money to rebuild the old pavilion. I felt like we had saved a valuable old landmark. I had my family members in all the officer positions. There wasn't anymore I could do here. I was just living in the past anyway. I was tired of hearing some old man tell another old man about me. 'He's been half way around the world and done about everything,' they would say. I'd been looking back for too long. All of the sudden, everything changed. All this wasn't something I'd built for a comfortable end after all. It had just been a three year furlough. Besides, I could do what I was doing then just about anywhere in the country.

I hadn't seen my boy but one day since we had spent Christmas with him in Minneapolis the year before. He was moving so fast, I couldn't keep up with him. It seemed like just the other day he had finished college. I had found an old Camaro, had the body fixed up, and had a fancy paint job put on it. I had a small block 350 bored out to a 355 and built it up. I gave it to him for graduation. He took it to Daytona, brought it back, and parked it in my backyard. He said he was leaving for Wyoming with a friend for awhile. The frame rotted in half. I had the motor pulled out and junked the car. He got a job out there working as a waiter and bartender in a men's club. One day he called me and told me one of the guys he worked with had just been offered a restaurant to manage in Arizona. He told me the guy had come back in just before leaving for Arizona and had asked him if he wanted to go with him. He told him all he had to do was show up in Casa Grande, AZ and he'd guarantee him a manager's position in the biggest restaurant in town. Mark told him he didn't have a car. The guy threw a set of keys on the bar and said "You have my number. Call me when you get into town."

A couple months later he called to tell me he had completed his training and was an assistant manager at the Flying J Restaurant. He said the only problem was that everyone that worked for him was Mexican. He said he could probably handle that, but the fact that they were all related made it almost impossible. I told him to come home and work with me. That was way back when I was contracting. He went to his boss and gave notice that he would be leaving. The boss told him to do him a favor before he quit. "Go to the home office in Salt Lake and talk to them," he said. "I'll fly you up and back. If you don't like what they offer you, I'll help you get wherever you want to go." They offered him a new position as a fuel sales representative. They were starting a new division designed to work with trucking companies. They would coordinate fuel purchases from Flying J Truckstops nationwide. There would be a dozen of them on the team; he would be based in Minneapolis. That's why we had spent Christmas in Minneapolis.

Shortly after that visit, he called me for some advice. He said Mobil Oil had offered him a position on a new team that they were building. He would be working with truckstops, introducing a new Mobil program. "They want me to go to Washington for a meeting next week. I don't know what to do. I have it pretty good with Flying J," he said. "I can go almost anywhere in the country, and there's an executive suite waiting for me," he said. I asked what kind of compensation they were offering. He told me twelve K more to start. I said, "Son, you can do the math. You do whatever you feel led to do." A week later he called me from Washington. "Pop, my whole team is here, all but one, and I just called him," he said. "He's going to join us too. Because of my experience in the west, they want to relocate me to Arizona. I'll stop on my way back if I can." That's the last time we had seen him for a day. Now he was working out of an apartment somewhere in Tempe, AZ. I couldn't wait to see him.

The first day, he took me golfing in Scottsdale. That was the nicest course I'd ever played on. A couple other guys played with us. Everyone treated Mark like a super part of their work. They treated me very well just for being his father. I didn't know what the boy had gotten into, but it was a very honorable position, whatever it was. I know first class people when I meet them, and these guys were top notch characters. They all said they were looking forward to spending the weekend with me. I didn't have any idea what they were talking about, but I was ready to participate in whatever they had planned. It was a NASCAR event. We all met the next morning along with several other equally solid people. I really felt honored just to be in their company. I also noticed that my son fit perfectly.

I had left him to live with my mother and complete his twelfth year of school. What I had noticed most was his choice of friends. He joined the football team, even though local politics wouldn't let him participate in much more than daily practice. The team really respected him and knew if he had been allowed to play, he could have really enhanced the team. I went to one game and heard the team yelling for the coach to put Mark in the game. They had the game won, so the coach put him in. All the guys were cheering for him and he performed like they knew he would. Small school politics hurt a lot deeper than just sports. When we enrolled Mark into twelfth grade, he was already a National Honor Student. The administration had to really fight to get their personal choice elevated above him. Mark asked us not to fight the system. He said it didn't matter to him if they made him king. He'd feel little honor to be chosen as their very best. They were a bunch of meaningless people. He was two years younger than his classmates because he had skipped two grades, but he could still see right through them. This kid could read a phony from twenty fathoms.

You'd never believe I practiced basketball in that little school under coach Chuck Daly, the future coach of the Olympic dream team, but I did. He got out of the place, too. Mark's own cousin was in school with him, but Mark wouldn't associate with him. I asked him why that was, and he told me they really had nothing in common outside of being related. The only boy he ran with was a solid Christian kid that went on to become a medical doctor. Now I could see his standards were paying off. After the race, we went out to eat with some of the guys from the Mobil team. I was really impressed. It'd been years since I had worked with lowlife, but I'll never forget the emptiness I felt. Even when I was exalted as one of their leaders, it was empty. You just can't replace real character. I'd be proud to work in the lowest capacity available in this industry, just to be in their company. When the boy and I got back to the apartment that night I shared this feeling with him. He said "Dad, I think I know someone that could make it happen. Let me make a phone call in the morning."

"You're Mark's dad? Can you drive a tractor trailer?" was how it started. I said, "I haven't for years, but I sure can." "We'd sure be glad to have you on our team," they said. "Get your CDL and call me. We'll get you started with us as soon as you're ready." Boy that was hard. I asked Mark, "Do you think your mother would want to move to Arizona?" He said, "Yes, dad, she's already packing. You're tired of what you're doing and my little brother needs to get out of there." I asked him what he was talking about. Brandon had just been named the most recognized player in his last football game against Altoona. He said, "I hate to be the one to tell you, Pop, but he's just been suspended from the team for drinking. He's fallen in with the wrong crowd. You need to get out here as soon as you can. It will be great being together again. I need someone to share my life with, Pop. God's really blessing. I'm not sure I'm ready for all that's happening. Sometimes I feel out of my league. Sometimes I don't even know who I can talk to. Let's go down to Gallaghers and have some wings. They're about the only people that know my name in this town."

Commercial drivers licenses were something new to me. They didn't have such a thing when we had left for the mission field. I made some calls and found out where to pick up the paperwork and a study book. The next day, I went down and took my test. They told me I'd have to hire a third party testing agent for my road test. I found one out on Buckeye road. He was impressed with the score on my written exam, which is always a good thing. Whether it's a road test or a flight test, it sets the pre-prejudices for the examiner. They'll cut you a lot more slack if you show up with a better than average score on the written. We did a quick run around the block and I had my CDL. Hoyt Starr answered his cell. He talked like we'd known each other for years. He said he was meeting my boy for dinner at the truck show in Kentucky. He said he was really looking forward to meeting me. He told me to call him as soon as I got the family moved and he'd come down for a weekend. "You're already on the payroll, so don't be worrying about a job," he said. I really didn't come down here thinking I'd go back with a job. I figured I'd bring Mom and the boy down and then find something in the HVAC field.

I called Mom and brought her up to speed. She asked me what I'd be doing. I told her I didn't know. She asked me how much I was getting paid. I told her I didn't know. Now that she was all caught up, I figured I'd take care of the next most important matter. I didn't want my boy on the bench for his whole twelfth grade season. I started calling coaches in every local high school. Most of them admitted they were bound to the politics and he probably wouldn't get a fair trial, no matter how good he was. One of them, I can't remember which one, told me to contact Coach Jones at Red Mountain in East Mesa.

Red Mountain was the newest public school in the valley and was already leading the rest of them in almost every field except sports. I contacted him and learned he was serious about building a winning team.

I told him about the drinking incident and guaranteed him it was a one time fluke that had never happened before and never would again. I gave him the name of Brandon's coach and asked him to give him a call before he made his decision. He asked me where Punxsy High was located. I told him North Western Pennsylvania. He said if we'd move into his school district by spring training, he'd start him first string.

Brandon was really excited about a second chance. It would have been a real political battle to get back on the team in Punxsy. I spoke with his old coach who explained it to me. The parents of the kid that would start in Brandon's slot next year were already lobbying the administration for the position. He said the whole thing was an unfortunate mess caused by the father of the kid my boy had spent the afternoon with. Someone smelled beer and Brandon had confessed. He told me he was just glad the kid will play. He told me he was going to call Coach Jones and firm things up for him. It was these two that got the boys records transferred when the administration refused to release them. They wanted disciplinary action of some kind. These little people were upset that an outsider had somehow slipped by them in the first place. He was making the papers and the radio every week, and no one that was anyone even knew him. What really bugged them was no one had kissed their asses for the privilege to excel. They wanted to meet with me. This was get even time.

I know a little bit about education, and the bureaucracy that has taken it over. I told Coach Jones I was going to enroll my boy into a private school that would accept him on the evaluation placement. Then I'd transfer him into Red Mountain. He sold the idea to his administration. They agreed to accept him on a temporary registration so he could start practice. Only in Arizona could you pull off something like that, the last Bastille of American freedom. Of course that was back when the republicans ran the state. Since all the liberals moved in from California and took over our government, you wouldn't be able to get away with it today. While I was back in Pennsylvania loading up for the move, I called the school and made an appointment to meet with them. When I got there, no one was there but a secretary. She informed me that she had been told to transfer the records. I told her to give them to me. She said this had to be done by proper school protocol or Brandon would just be dropped from the legitimate education process. I wasn't going to beat up on her. It was evident that she had got stuck with meeting with the guy nobody had met, and now didn't want to. Their coach had already informed them that Red Mountain High was starting Brandon this semester, with or without his records. Thanks guys.

What a drive from Pennsylvania to Arizona in a truck, loaded with everything you own, and pulling a car behind you. As we unloaded and carried everything up to the boy's second story apartment, I had to share something with him that might have been better left until later. "Son, we have to do all this again in a month," I said. "You live in Tempe. We have to find a place in East Mesa. We have to live no further west than Recker Rd. for your brother to attend Red Mountain High." I think I spoiled his plans for organizing everything as he had planned. He was excited though. He wanted to see his brother start for Red Mountain as much as I did. I didn't know the half of it. We decided we might as well not wait. We started looking for a place right away. Since Recker Rd. was as far west as we could live, we started there. We wanted to be as close to the school as possible so we started looking at the north end of Recker. That was about as far east as civilization went at the time. A half block east of there was Power Rd., where the school was. There was nothing beyond the school grounds except desert to the east and mountains to the north. Phoenix was the fastest growing city in the country. It had spread east into Tempe, and farther east into Mesa. We were at the far east of Mesa, and the end of the line.

Out in the middle of nowhere, we could see what looked to be a lone group of new apartment buildings. They were apartments, but they were filling up fast. The only thing available was on the top floor, three stories up. As we unloaded the truck, I came upon several large file boxes I'd been moving from place to place since college. I looked up the three flights of stairs that ran up the outside of the building. Between me and those stairs, about thirty feet away, sat a large dumpster. That was the last nail in the coffin that contained the faded hopes of ever returning to the ministry. I'd have to find a church around there somewhere. First I needed to meet with Hoyt and find out what my job was. We were meeting with him the next week. He told me his favorite restaurant down here was a place called the Ford on Mill Avenue in Tempe. It sits right on the Salt River, which has been dry now for about a hundred years. It's hard to believe the famous founder of the Lost Dutchman Mine had died there as a result of that river flooding its banks. But I had a lot to learn about that Lost Dutchman. For now, I had to figure out another old guy.

Hoyt was a wiry little guy for seventy years of age. His Texas accent added to his charm. Almost everyone I'd met from Mobil knew him and spoke well of him. He owned and operated Mobil Oil's nationally known show truck. He had made a deal with Ford Motor Company to provide him with a brand new tractor. He had made a deal with Featherweight Trailers to provide him with another show trailer. It was great advertisement for them. His plan was not to retire his old rig, but to assign it to me. When Hoyt found out that Mobil had begun a truckstop program, he realized he could keep another show truck busy. What a deal for both of us. My son represented the program for the west coast, and his dad would run the shows. Hoyt couldn't lose. My boy would set everything up for him. I would do that work and Hoyt would keep operating the major annual shows. Mark really liked Hoyt. They had tremendous respect for each other. Mark was building a great program that a show truck would fit right into. On the other hand, Hoyt was on a first name basis with most all of Mark's bosses, and often their bosses.

Things were really looking good. Brandon was now a solid part of the Red Mountain football team. You could find the star players sitting on our balcony most every weekend. They already called me and Cheryl 'Mom and Dad'. They loved Mark and often sought his counsel. Ford hadn't built us another truck yet, but continually assured us that it was coming. Hoyt didn't want to lose the 'Mark and his Dad' setup. He continually assured me that paying me to sit and wait was just fine with him. He said he was sending me a ticket to join him at the national truck show in Louisville, Kentucky. I don't know if Hoyt already knew what he was going to tell me when I got there or not. If he did, it was a classy way to do it. He met me at the airport and took me to the show. That was the first time I saw the truck other than on calendars and ad material. It was beautiful jet black with Mobil Delvac in gold lettering. His office was in a second story built in the nose of the show trailer.

Hoyt sat down behind his desk and got a check book out. He said,

"I'm paying you a little extra, because I have some bad news. I just got word that Ford is not providing us with the promised equipment." He wrote me a nice check, the most I ever made for not doing anything. He said, "Lets go get something to eat and talk about some plans I'm working on for next year. You might be interested." He bought me a nice meal and while we were enjoying our coffee, several guys sat down at the table next to us. They all said 'hi' to Hoyt as they sat down. You could tell they had noticeable respect for him. I also respected the man for flying me all the way across the country just to pay me for nothing and give me the bad news in person. One of the men at the next table said, "Excuse me Hoyt, but I've got a real problem you might be able to help me with. I lost a driver this morning. Do you know a team that might lend me one of their extras until I can find a replacement?"

Hoyt motioned for the guy to wait a minute, and then leaned over to me and spoke softly. "Do you want to help this guy out for a season? If you do, I'll have things worked out with Ford, and we'll be in business by next season." I said lets talk to him. Hoyt turned back to the guy and said, "I might have you a guy right here." The guy came over and sat down. Hoyt introduced me as an old friend in the business that might be available for a season. The guy was desperate. You don't advertise for a driver for a show truck. You have to find a showman that you can trust with millions of dollars worth of clients. The fact that he can handle a couple hundred thousand dollars worth of equipment is secondary in this business. "What will I be doing?" I asked. "You will be one of my four International test drivers, contracted to Navistar, and assigned to Richard Petty," he said. "If you could even give me a few weeks, I'll fly you anywhere you need to go." Hoyt said, "Excuse me, we were here today planning his season; he's not an extra. Do you need him or not?"

I don't know what it is about these guys. They none talked about money. The guy said, "You're hired. You'll be on regular team salary for the season." Hoyt told him where he had me put up for the night. The guy said he'd take care of it, and have me picked up in the morning. Hoyt seemed pleased. He said, "We're still partners; just give me a little more time." I called Cheryl from my room and told her the news. I told her how much we had made for not working and she asked me how much we were making now. I told her we were making the same as the other three test drivers. Over time, I found out the reason a paycheck was not an issue. There was a multitude of qualified drivers that would have volunteered their services just for the opportunity to break into the industry. I was once offered a hundred dollars by a driver if I would let him run along and help me with just one show.

It is a phenomenal industry. Every manufacture is looking for the best exposure. The team I was assigned to was given four tractors a year to pull Richard Petty race cars. The model of trucks we got from the factory would not be available to the public until the following year. No one else is trusted with equipment that has never been driven. About the only thing required is a clean record, because you're going to be arrested at least a couple times a week. The law says you must stop at every scale house. The law also says that every truck must be registered and display the name of the company that owns the truck. Well, these trucks had never been sold. No company owned them. When the officer runs your record and finds no moving violations, he has to think about it. 'You pay fines at every scale, in every state, and here you are at mine. I would be the odd ball if I pulled you off the highway or impounded your equipment'. What a good show company needed was four well groomed drivers with clean driving records. That was necessary so they could stand in the scale house, in clean pressed uniforms, with their wallets in their hands, smiling at the arresting officer.

About fifty percent of the time, it became a light hearted affair. Usually, when they directed you off the scale to the holding lot, they would send a guy in coveralls out to inspect your rig. When they looked at four of the nicest rigs they'd ever seen (so new, they had next years manufacture date on them), that guy seldom came out. Once, a guy did come out. After a few minutes, he came over and asked me if I'd explain some of the equipment he had found on my truck. I had a couple of experimental devices installed. One was a steering trim system and the other was an electric oil cleaning system. The guy was so enamored, he told the other guys to come out and see the rigs. We opened the supply trailer and gave them each a hat and a T-shirt. We still had to pay for the state sticker, but they didn't give us any more problems. We knew they'd stop us on our way back for not displaying the stickers, and we'd do it all over again.

Since I was the new guy on the team, I would get the last choice of the show tractors. Cab-over is what you call the flat nosed tractor. Conventional means it has a hood out in front covering the engine. In the cab-over, the engine is below the cab. There was always what you call a dog box between the seats. You had to crawl over it to get in the bunk. In the conventional, you could walk between the seats into a little office area and your bunk. No one wanted the cab-over, so naturally it was mine. What they didn't know at the time was that that cab-over was the first of its kind. It would be the most popular of the four trucks we had that year. All the dealers were excited to see the first flat-floor cab-over. There was no dog box to crawl over. When we would set up for a show, the engineers would come out of the woodwork to see it. No one could figure out how they had built it. For the first several months, I was not allowed to raise the cab for anyone that didn't have a corporate ID. Once they got into production, the security lightened up.

We drove way too fast, and always much too close, but that was part of the show. Most trucks are governed from the factory so that they can't run much over the speed limit. Ours were wide open. Except for a few owner-operators, no one could run with us. Once in awhile, someone would challenge us. We ran with some pretty fast guys in the western states, but no one ever ran away from us. The only way we could tell how fast we had gone was to have an engineer check our satellite boxes and print out a record. My speedometer pegged out at ninety, but I could run over a hundred in a controlled run. We really trusted each other or we couldn't have performed a lot of our eye-grabbing feats. On a night run, we would turn our show lights on. They were soft blue lights, mounted under our cabs. From across the median, we looked almost mystical. The idea was to get the word out that we would be showing at some location in a few days, and any driver could test drive our equipment. It's amazing how many drivers set their schedules to be there. We were the greatest show on the road.

We were so good at what we did that offers started coming in from other manufacturers to perform for them. I think our boss began to worry about it. There were five of us on the team. One of us was always on a weeks leave at home. I didn't always fly home, because they would fly my wife to me. They learned that when she was running with us, they had an extra hand on the job. She fit in so well they even started to pay her for the time she spent with us. The crew so much appreciated her, that when the tour ended, we voted to give her Richard's personal jacket. Ripples began to accrue when a strange driver showed up instead of our regular guy that was due to rejoin us for the Canadian run. We accepted him because he told us that our regular guy was having problems with Canadian customs. This guy was not a team player. Something was amiss, but we couldn't put our finger on it. He had no pride in his appearance; he was not a showman in any way. But when the boss showed up, the two of them were inseparable. We figured it out.

The '96 season ended. I was requested to deliver my tractor to the test track in Chicago rather than back to the factory. Road King wanted to do an article on my test drive of the new flat floor. That thing was really popular in the industry. I had requests from dealers all across the country to show up at their places, and they'd take good care of me for my troubles. Once, while up in Canada, a dealership owner offered me his beautiful sales manager if I would let the other trucks go on to the next show and stay an extra day at his place. I stayed, but I settled for a nice jacket. By 1996, a lot of the moral standards had been neutralized in Canada. The twenty-year fight between the conservatives and the socialists was over. The socialists had won. The New Testament churches were closing. They were being fined if they preached anything concerning homosexuality. My old college friend was a missionary up there, but he was run out. He said there was a five-thousand dollar fine for passing out literature if it contained most anything from the book of Romans. What a shock. Canada had become ancient Rome incarnate.

I hadn't been home for a week when Western Star called with a sixty-day contract offer. Their new tractors were ready for show, and they needed four showmen to make the rounds from dealership to dealership. We would be starting in Canada and ending up in the southern US, two months later. It was a great truck, but had the same problem it always had. It was too heavy. The heavier the tractor, the less payload you can carry. When I went to pick up my tractor, a very proud engineer was waiting to climb aboard with me. The designers, like this guy, have the impression that us test drivers are the epitome of the industry. We represent the most accomplished of their customers. We didn't bother to explain that that wasn't always true. Most of us had come from another division of the industry. Most of us were never truck buyers. We had come from the show side and some of us had got there with very poor credentials beyond license and availability. Nevertheless, we were the ones they wanted to most impress.

I climbed into the rig and must admit, I was very impressed with the new design. The only problem was that I had a cup of coffee in my hand. I just looked at him. He finally noticed I was paying little attention to the introduction of his latest creation. He was talking about the added space, ease of access to the sleeper, and on and on. Then he just stopped and looked at me. He said, "What?" I held up my cup of coffee and looked at him in the eyes. After a considerable silence, he said, "Oh shit. How could I have missed something so basic?" He reached out and took my cup. He said, "I guess we have to put an engineer in each tractor just to hold the driver's coffee." I eased his embarrassment with one simple statement. "Don't feel privileged; you're not the first engineer to hold my coffee when I entered their new design," I told him. The now famous Flat Floor International was the latest one. The now fiberglass extrusion from the dash was originally a plywood addition, hastily designed for my convenience.

Western Star didn't go that far. They didn't build me a temporary holder like International. They just asked me to inform all others that the addition would be included in the production model. I spilled a lot of coffee over the next couple months. They even replaced the carpet once. Working the tour for Western Star, I was never offered a beautiful woman as I was in Calgary, but I was offered something far more repulsive. Terry, the Western Star distribution manager for the southern US states, took a real liking to me. One night, he took me on a cruise across some bay to a great seafood restaurant. He had already gone out of his way to introduce me to people in the industry that were way above my level of introduction. I didn't know what was going on until he made his pitch. He was KKK and wanted to recruit me in his chapter. All those big shots I was invited to party with were likewise.

The funny side of that tour happened when I was running with the Western Star Company Representative for the Southern region. Don't confuse him with the representative of the distributors. I was driving, and his phone rang. After a short conversation with someone, he turned as white as snow. He said, "That was my wife. She wanted to know what the large crate in my driveway was." The story goes like this. He had spent some time recently with NFL coach Jerry Glanville, who had talked him into ordering a new Harley. Jerry had said, "Don't worry about it; you won't get it for a least six months. By then you can have it sold for more than you paid for it." He said, "That's good. I'll have to have it sold before my wife finds out, or I'll be in real trouble." So he ordered one. But as a gesture of kindness, Jerry had called the factory and talked them into moving him up on the list. That was funny, but what happened next wasn't.

I was home waiting to be notified of when my next International show truck would be ready. I got the call, but it wasn't from Magic. Magic was the black guy that was our team leader. This call was from that rep that had bought the Harley. Not only was he going to be on the tour, but he was the new leader. I asked what had happened to Magic. He told me he hadn't been invited back. As soon as I hung up, I called Hoyt and told him I quit the tour. He told me to sit tight and he'd get back to me with another show truck as soon as it was delivered. Just like the last time he told me to sit tight, I was on the clock. Once again, Ford had promised him they would deliver this time.

I had a lot of time on my hands, so I did what I always did, I explored. To the east of us was a little town called Apache Junction, at the base of the beautiful Superstition Mountains. One day, I took Mark for a drive and showed him places we could easily purchase for the rent we were paying. He kept telling me it was too far from the airport that he used almost daily. One day we were playing golf on the newest housing development being built on Power Road. That was as far east as you could go without going into the desert, where I was trying to get him to consider shopping for land. He said, "Dad, they're expanding this development; lets see what they have available."

Two months later, they finished the house we picked out. Mom and I were sitting on the front porch watching a rare lightning show one night, shortly after we had moved in, when the phone rang. It was Hoyt. He said Ford was never going to build another tractor, but he still didn't want me to take another job. "I'm putting something together for us, so sit tight," he said. "I'll put another check in the mail." Mom and I had done a short gig for Caterpillar down at their proving grounds, south of Tucson. There was an old copper mine up in the Sonora's, but you'd think it was an active mine. When you saw all the heavy equipment Cat makes, working all over the hills, you'd think it was for real. They put on a great show. We also did a farm show in the mid-west for a few days, but that's about all we did. I was ready for most anything. But I sat more than anything. I sat and watched every phase of the building of the pool. I started to feel like the old men in the neighborhood I had grown up in. If I painted a house, they would stand and watch me all day. If I poured a sidewalk, here they'd come again with their lawn chairs. I determined many years before that that I would never retire.

Our youngest son, Brandon, had graduated high school and was playing football for Quincy University in Iowa. Only problem was, his major, party 101, usually ends up graduating you into some branch of the military if you're worth your salt. My boy chose the Coast Guard. We went to the academy in Jersey for his graduation. The only branch of the service that is at war during peace time is the Coast Guard. I didn't know that. The kid saw more action than I did. They don't just risk their lives saving people; they are the police of the sea in the Navy's stead. If we're not at war, even when the Navy stops a ship, they have to call the Coast Guard in before they can board it. That's what Brandon did. I told him not to even think when a situation turned bad; just shoot. I'd rather him face some legal trouble than let some drug dealer get the drop on him.

The illusive call finally came. I got the Mobil Show Truck. How cool is that. At all the shows, my boy and his superiors would set up on my display location. We showed all over the country and Canada. My wife was really good at helping me get ready for a show. She would crawl into the engine and make that chrome shine like you couldn't believe. Since we were in charge of the central Mobil display, we were accepted as part of the company. We enjoyed the best year of our life since we had returned from the mission field, but all good things come to an end. Hoyt was really old. Even though we were in the process of forming a new show company, it didn't happen fast enough. He couldn't run the show without us, and we weren't experienced enough to run it without him. On the shelf in our church office is a model of the Mobil show truck.

Laying the Foundation • 415

Lying on the trailer of that model are all the actual keys to run that equipment. Mobil decided to retire it, simply by cutting off the annual three-hundred-thousand dollars it cost us to run it. It was a fun ride, but it was over.

I figured since we were going to be home, we had better find a church. I found a good one, East Mesa Baptist Church. I told the pastor I was a former missionary and my wife was an experienced church secretary. He hired both of us on the spot. I went home and told Cheryl that I had found a church, and "By the way," I said, "You're the secretary." I was working with the food bank. We were providing about three-hundred meals worth of groceries a week. We collected about five ton a day and distributed it on Wednesdays and Sundays right after the evening services. My wife fit right into the office just like old times. Things were going quite well.

One day Mark and I found a sports bar where we could watch the Steelers play football. Because they are an East coast team, we couldn't get the games on local channels except for playoffs. The place had three major rooms; one for the Green Bay fans, one for the Pittsburgh fans, and one for all the rest of them. Our waitress was a girl about Mark's age, and she knew how to work a table. She also knew how to dress for the best results. The first time she served us, Mark made some kind of a remark after she left the table. I asked Mark what she looked like. He answered that he didn't know; he had never looked at her face. I always encouraged my boys not to consider marriage until they had their bars on their shoulders. That was assuming they went into the service. Either way, it meant they ought to establish their career before they took on a responsibility like a family. Mark had followed that advice to the tee. He had had some serious offers while in college, but had avoided them effectively. Sometimes I had to answer the phone when a date started to get too serious. He would just disappear. The one I remember best was a Princess of Guam that he had met on an airplane. She called everyday for about a month before she got the message.

Mark had been working the truckstop program in the west for Mobil, but the program was run on a contractor basis. Since then, Mobil had hired a couple of them into corporate positions. He was one of them. Since then, he had advanced to running accounts on the west coast from

California to Alaska. One of the accounts was Grease Monkey, a large chain of quick lube facilities. The manager in charge of those stations on the west coast was also a single guy about Mark's age. They really hit it off. He lived on a beach in California. He was a weightlifter like Mark. He was even in competition and had even been crowned Mr. Washington one time. JT was a great guy to be around, but he had a real short fuse. I think JT liked running with Mark because Mark could handle his temper. After a few beers, Mark could keep him out of trouble. But it was mutual respect, and decency in work and play that bonded them like brothers. They lived high on the hog on their expense accounts if it was company business, and on their own cards if it wasn't. But the high life was getting old for the both of them. Things were about to change for all of us.

Proverbs 3:6
In all thy ways acknowledge Him, and He shall direct thy paths.

Chapter 25
And Then There Were Two

Mom and I had become Mom and Pop, not only to JT, but to Brandon's Red Mountain football teammates as well. Brandon had learned his lesson on choosing friends. Living in the same house with his big brother was a real help for him as well. Brandon's closest friends looked to Mark as their big brother too. He became their mentor. They played cards, went to events together, even joined us on some family outings. On weekends, it was one big happy family. Even after Brandon graduated and went off to college with Blake, one of his high school football teammates, the rest still frequented our home if Mark was in town. JT on the other hand, would show up even if Mark wasn't in town. He'd take me golfing just as Mark would. The food bank wasn't much more than a living. The wife's pay went for our pool payment. If it wasn't for the generosity of Mark and Jeff, I wouldn't have gotten out much.

Mark is a mature and generous man. I didn't live in fear of his eventually going in a separate direction. Whatever happened would be done decently and in order. But I wasn't ready for what was about to happen. Mark met a woman up in Washington at one of his accounts. I don't think he'd seen her more than a couple of times when he called me and asked me to set something up out at Saddle Mountain Pass. He said I would find a box in his room with a bottle of wine and a couple of glasses in it. I was to find a way to put it on the trail where he would find it. He was going to put a ring in her glass. I had never even met her. This was not the way I had pictured adding to the family, but what could I say. I got Brandon to drive me out to the saddle just after dark. I dressed in an old leather Aussie hat and a full length duster. I sat on the box at the side of the trail. Brandon dropped me off and parked down the road a ways. As soon as I got settled in the dark, a pack of coyotes moved through on each side of me. That was equally scary.

Later that evening, Mark introduced the family to his new fiancé. She had the weirdest story about this old Indian they had bumped into out on the trail sitting on a box. She told the Indian they'd go somewhere else. He said no bother. She said, "You forgot your box." He said, "You keep it. You need it more than I do." She told us we would never believe what was in it. The next day Mark told me she owned a home in Washington that they would probably live in after they got married. He told me we'd work something out with the house we'd been sharing. He figured we'd probably sell it, and find something Mom and I could afford. Something wasn't right. I'd know it if it was, but I had no peace in the matter. He told me he was taking her to a company function in Reno for a few days and when they got back, we'd make our plans. I felt no leadership or direction, no matter how hard I tried. Something just wasn't right. "Don't be worried, dear," I told my wife; "Things will clear up."

Mark was not at peace with the whole thing, either. I know when he's sure of what he is doing. Nothing was final yet. Sure enough, I got a phone call from Colorado in a couple of days. "Dad, don't make any plans," he said. "There's something wrong. I just spent an hour with my closest friend in this company and he asked me if I was sure about this woman. She has made such a fool of herself, some of my friends think she is not mentally stable. There is something really wrong with her. She's not just jealous, she's nuts. God was in me bringing her up here. I almost decided against it, but I'm so glad I did. I'm going to fly her straight home from here. We'll talk about it, but I don't think there's much to talk about." I could have told him I knew something was wrong, but he had enough on his mind.

That was close. I think it turned him off of the whole marriage thing. I was concerned enough that I tried to get in touch with a really nice girl he had dated back in Delaware while on college break. After Mark had disappeared from her life, she had driven clear up from Delaware to meet privately with me. She said, "I don't want him to know we talked but I really love him. He is just not ready for a serious relationship. I just want you to care enough about me to give me a second chance. Promise me you will get a hold of me when you think he is serious about settling down." I promised her and she walked out of our lives forever. That was ancient history now.

Things went back to normal. JT, Mark, Mom, and I made the races and the oldies concerts, and enjoyed good family times. We had to break up the occasional confrontation between JT and whoever was dumb enough to look at him crossways, but he was worth the trouble. But it wasn't always one way. I think of the night JT had Brandon by one arm and Mark had him by the other. They were pulling him backwards as they ran for the US border with a whole bar full of Mexicans chasing them. Brandon was still calling out challenges as they crossed to safety. I was cursed with three big boys afraid of nothing. I was also blessed with three big hearts that loved Jesus.

When Mark and I walked out of that sports bar where we had watched the Steelers game, he said, "Dad I'm coming back here." I felt ok about it. I had found the place because I knew the guy that owned it. Mom and I used to stop into his old place once in awhile. It was friendly, and close to home, but it wasn't very classy. Mark only patronized the classy places. Now we had a friendly family place to watch the games. The next weekend, Mom was with us. We had the same waitress, and she was more than friendly. She stole my hat and replaced it with a Dallas Cowboys hat. I don't know how she knew that they were the team I despised the most at that time. Mark shared with me that she was only a part-time waitress and bartender. Her full time job was with a copier company. She was a single mom and had to work two jobs. Now how did he know all of that? Well he had said he was coming back. He didn't say he was coming right back, but that's what he meant.

"I want to move her into the house, Dad," Mark told me. "She really can't afford the apartment she's living in. I'm going to live with her here or there for the rest of my life. We might not have started out right, but she's right, I know it." He brought her home and moved her into his room. They wanted to have a big wedding, so I married them that night and we didn't tell anyone about it. We didn't want to dampen the big ceremony they were planning to have later. What I liked about her was her outgoing personality. Her family lived on a ranch about four hours south of us, down below Tombstone. Our first visit down there was a blast. The place was out in the middle of nowhere. There was a long dirt lane into the place. You could see a very tall windmill in the middle of the property. Her parents lived in a little camper trailer between two metal buildings. One was a tool shed, and the other a large workshop.

Behind the shop were piles of boards and other building materials. Her dad was waiting for us by the shop. He was older than me, about the same height, but thin as a rail. He fit the rugged surrounding right down to the gun on his belt. I liked him from the moment I met him.

He had built a large, round thatch pavilion, with nothing in it but a picnic table for card games, and a beer fridge. He also put up a big old army tent with a wood stove in it for the guys to sleep. The girls slept in grandma's trailer. The whole family plan was to collect building supplies by tearing down old buildings. They would stockpile it, and then build a large house. The other buildings had been built for that purpose. What a great idea.....no mortgage. Her little brother was a tall thin guy also that was working as a prison guard. Her mother was less outgoing, but she was very congenial. I got the impression they felt their daughter had done okay by hooking up with Mark. Kind of the way my family felt when I had brought Cheryl home for the first time. Keo's first husband hadn't really fit in and had apparently given them the impression they were all low class people compared to him. He was ashamed when Keo would come to the ranch and lend a hand in menial tasks like building and repair. Oran, Keo's dad, had daughters that were better mechanics than most men will ever be.

Keo went to church with us as expected of her husband, and he ministered to her continually. One day she asked if I would baptize her. Mark said he thought the request was genuine. I asked pastor Hughes if I could perform a baptism, and he granted my wish. Everything was going pretty well until Pastor Hughes told me he was going to join the church to the Baptist Bible Fellowship. They had been wining and dining him for some time. I wrote him one of my famous poison pen letters, telling him what I thought about joining a New Testament Church to anything not in the Bible. He was a very hard man. He reminded me of Nick Bickish. I respected him very much, but I was not going through that again. I'd already lost one church to the BBF. He couldn't argue with the scriptural evidence I had provided, but he really wanted the recognition that came with joining the fellowship. He called to ask if I had shared my opinion with my wife. I lied; I told him I had not. He told me he was sorry to lose us, but my wife could remain his secretary. She knew my feelings, and shared them, but she decided to serve him faithfully.

God gave me peace about my decision. The family still attended Sunday morning services out of respect for his retaining my wife, but I was looking for another job. I tried selling home pages on the internet with my daughter's help, but I sold only a few. Out of desperation, I started working for a bonded carrier outfit, delivering documents between government agencies. The only people that worked there were either retired or otherwise unskilled and couldn't find a real job. I had reached bottom. It wasn't really that long before, when I was driving the show truck, that some people had even asked me for my autograph. Now I was asking for autographs just to confirm that I had delivered their documents. I couldn't believe I'd sunk so low. The fact is I needed it. I thought way too much of myself. Mark, on the other hand, was going the other direction. A head hunter had found him and was making him all kinds of potential job offers. These people find successful employees, and then sell them to other employers that are looking for talent. Mark wasn't taking her too seriously until one day she got a real hit.

Exxon was looking for an oil man with a genuine background in Japanese language and culture. Mark had been the leading Japanese language student in his last year at Penn State. They had sent him to a college in Japan as an exchange student. Therefore Mark also had a degree from a very affluent Japanese College. They wanted a representative to manage one of their biggest accounts, Toyota USA. Suddenly, he started taking her serious. At first, we talked about Mom and I keeping the house if he took the offer. That was out of the question. I told him I would find something we could afford in a trailer park somewhere. He said bullshit; there was nothing holding us there, we were all going. "They're flying us to Cincinnati to find a place," he said. "I'll find something to accommodate all of us."

On the surface, it sounded like a neat idea. We had got along pretty well so far. As far as my job was concerned, there was no way but up. They let us help decide on the options for our new home that they had found. Finally, they found one with everything they wanted, and it had a finished basement, carpet and all. We made the move, and I liked it just fine. I decided to look for a job driving. The first call hired me. I wondered why I hadn't done that back in Arizona. I hired on to an outfit that was leasing two tractors and crews to Watkins Transportation. I was a team driver. We ran coast to coast pulling doubles. I would drive for five hours and sleep for five hours. You could keep this up for seven to ten days, only stopping to eat and shower before you ran out of log time. Then you had to be home for three or four days to allow your log book to recover. Then you could run another forty hours. I could write another book on just the eleven months that I did that. Like the time I ran into black ice up in New York State, when my back trailer tried to pass my front trailer. Only a miracle saved me from that career-ending event.

I was co-driving with a Polish immigrant for the first six months. That was cool, because if you got caught at a scale house, and you were overweight on one of your axles, he would let on that he didn't speak English well enough to understand what they were saying. They would get so frustrated trying to talk to him that they would finally just turn on the green light and tell us to go on. The only problem was that this young man had a terrible temper. Once I was talking to two other Polish drivers, and I told them my co-driver was a Polock. When he walked in, they told him what I had said. I thought he was going to beat them to death before I got him stopped. I later asked him what had set him off. He told me that when I called him a Polock, it was not offensive. When another Polish person called him a Polock, however, they knew they were offending him. I never called him a Polock again. One run, after being out about seven days, I got really sick. I slept through a drop and re-hook. He lost it when I finally woke up. He scared me so bad that I called the owner and quit.

I got a new partner, a sixty-two year old black guy with real class. He dressed so well, he was often mistaken for a bus driver, and they wouldn't let him pay for his meals at the truckstops. One day I got a call from the owner, who told me the old man had gotten a ticket while driving his car and he hadn't reported it. Watkins disqualified him to drive for them. They told me I would be driving with a young guy they had just hired. On our first run, we made a drop in Texas and went to the motel. After I went to sleep, he took the tractor to a bar, picked up a girl, and took her to another motel. When he brought the truck back in the morning, my fridge and my radio had been stolen. When I got home, I told Cheryl I was done with that outfit. She told me she had just read an ad in the paper looking for local drivers. Miller Brewing had just opened a plant ten miles from us and needed fifty drivers.

I made one of those few calls you make in life that you never forget. The largest publicly owned trucking firm in the country was JB Hunt. Throughout my entire trucking career, we had made jokes about them. Their trucks were the slowest trucks on the road. Their drivers were mostly older men, and they drove a very unpopular style of tractor. It was the flat floor cab-over. I had test driven the first one ever built. It wasn't that popular anymore. The ad did not say to call JB Hunt, but when the lady answered, she answered JB Hunt. I laughed, but it didn't seem to surprise her. She won me over with pure kindness. I told her I'd check it out just for her. I sure liked the idea of driving single and being home every night. Besides, I had never met an old Hunt driver that I didn't like. I couldn't figure them out though. They wore nice uniform shirts and seemed to be very proud of their jobs, even though they were the blunt of every trucking joke. It was as though their attitude was more of a pity for me.

We had been living in the house with the boy for about a year by then. A lot had happened since the night we had moved in. The moving van owner had built Mom and me a walk-in closet. I was not used to such professionalism, but such was my boy's world....only the best. Shortly after we moved in, a neighbor from across the street invited us over for a Bible study. Before we could respond to the invitation, they saw Mark having a beer while mowing the lawn. They made things real clear when their kids were not allowed to come near our place from that day forth.

Keo had delivered their second child already. The first was born before we left Arizona. If my wife had written this, you would have known all about that long before now. You know men. Until they're big enough to take hunting, we are hardly aware of short people living in the same house. He was born, like his daddy, with a head full of red hair. We all thought our second one was a boy as well. Even the doctor told us it was a boy. What a wonderful surprise when the nurse held her up for them to see it was not another boy.

Keo was working for an armored car manufacturer and Mom was in her glory, keeping our two little red heads. The guy straight across from us was an insurance man of some kind. His place was also off limits to the neighbors for the same reason ours was. He was in the middle of a divorce, and his world was changing. When you have been married nearly twenty years, and then part company, who gets the friends? She must have gotten them, because all we saw was a pretty lonely guy. Mark set out to change that when he walked across the street, handed him a beer, and introduced himself. Tim was very high class, and rather reserved at that time in his life. Mark was all the more determined to befriend him. He was sort of a man's man, and easy to respect from your first introduction. The feeling was mutual; it wasn't long after that, he walked over to the patio with a six pack of fancy brew. That became a weekend habit, and soon he warmed up to all of us. We became his new best friends. He was about our only friend in Ohio at that time.

I showed up at the new brewery, which had a whole wing dedicated to JB Hunt offices. I was impressed with the organization from day one. Until then, Watkins was the most professional trucking outfit I'd been associated with. At Watkins however, there was always a glass between you and them. You were just the driver. Not so with Hunt; you were the star player in that office. Every driver knew it, and carried himself accordingly. Except for the top management people, the driver also knew he was the highest paid in about every office in the company. The only glass that ever confronts him is at one of the eight national terminals. The terminal manager and the safety manager were about the only two people he held somewhere between his equal, or slightly superior to himself. Neither one of them were at this location. The project manager and his assistant were about it, and they were always on a first name basis with a driver.

For the first time in trucking, I wasn't looking for a job. I was being offered a position with a company. I found out how JB Hunt had gotten the bad rap. Years before, they'd had a training program, and had had a lot of young inexperienced drivers on the road. Not only had they long since canned that effort, they had become maybe the hardest outfit to get into. If you had a speeding ticket in the past three years, or a DUI in the past five years, you need not apply. God began dealing with me much closer than he had for a long time. I felt it almost immediately. I really wanted the job, and I knew I didn't qualify. I turned in my application and went home knowing I'd never get a call. I talked with God about it all the way home. It wasn't possible, I figured, but if I got called, there would be no question it was God.

Tim, our neighbor and new friend, met a girl at the office, and brought her over to meet us. Mark and Keo started going out with them about every weekend. Our daughter Tonia had recovered from her brain tumor operation. We moved her into a trailer park not far from us. I didn't tell you about it, because the whole ordeal is just too sad. I had put it out of my mind. Now she was living just down the road with her two boys. Her husband, the deacon's son, and one of our best friends, was living in California with a woman he met on the internet. That girl could write her own book when it comes to men. Now that she was close by, however, Mom and I were being included in some of the weekly outings. We'd been around the world, and had enjoyed some of the nicest places on earth, but it'd been years since Mom and I could afford much more than fast food. For the first time, I had a whole other attitude about nice places. I know I didn't deserve that lifestyle, and I was humbled by it.

You could have knocked me over with a feather. I got home from job hunting one day, and Mom told me Hunt had called me with an offer. It would be some time later, and way too late to matter when I found out what God had done for me. The person confirming my background had made a mistake. Watkins had confirmed my eleven months safe driving employment with them, but Hunt or Watkins had confirmed eleven years. I was enlisted as a senior safe driver, and well up on the assignment roster. When I reported the following week, I had no idea the assistant would have given me one of the new conventional tractors if I had asked for one. Several months into my employment, I casually mentioned that I'd like to have one. I was one of the top ten on the monthly performance list. I figured they might give me one by then. Ken, the assistant, said he had no idea I'd wanted one. He gave me the brand new one he had just received. He further humbled me by telling me that of the fifty drivers he scheduled daily, I was always one of the four he assigned first.

I would leave the yard by four-thirty, five at the latest, every morning. I would make my delivery, mostly somewhere around Detroit, and I was back in the yard by three-thirty or four that afternoon. I read my truck computer, recorded my day, and received my run for the next day. I would then find my assigned load, hook up, and go home. What a joy to be home every night early enough to mow some grass and have a beer before supper. Life couldn't get any better, or so I thought. I was always out of the yard before daylight. I never saw the bulk of the drivers coming in later to pick up their shorter runs. I had no idea there was a daily fiasco going on. Someone would drop a trailer on the ground or do some other stupid thing. Things were about to change.

I got a message on my truck computer that we had a required meeting Sunday morning in a restaurant downtown. No one ran on Sunday, so all fifty drivers had to attend. I had never met these people. Four of us would leave the yard about the same time each day, a blonde girl and two other guys. I seldom saw anyone else. Now we were all sitting in the same banquet hall. We were greeted by a big guy, about thirty-some years old, named Carl. He had just arrived at our project from a logging project on the west coast. He had been sent out west to clean up the logging outfit that was having way too many incidents and accidents. Now he had been sent here for the same reason. Over coffee and donuts, he said he wanted us to elect a safety committee right then. In front of us was a pencil and paper. "You're whole job today," he said, "which I'm paying you for of course, is to give me four names you want on this committee." I only knew three drivers, and I didn't know their names. I asked their names, and only submitted those three. He gave us a little of his background, told us he was our new manager, and let us go.

Nobody had asked me my name. I never gave the ordeal another thought. After I made my Monday morning delivery, and was headed home, my computer notified me to stop and call the office. "You have been selected for our safety committee," they said. "Will you accept it?" I said 'yes', if for no other reason than to find out why. One day Mark was in a train station in DC, and he had seen a leather Australian hat that he just had to have. He soon realized it was far too ugly to wear in public, and let me have it. I wanted it for a rain hat, but I got in the habit of wearing it, even if it wasn't raining. I decided to wear it all the time after an incident that had happened in an elevator in Phoenix. I was at the lowest ebb in my life back then. I was delivering packages for the carrier outfit. It was raining that day, so I had worn it. In the elevator of that fancy place was a woman of high society. She looked at my hat and asked if I had another one like it. I knew what she meant; one to crap in and one to cover it up. She left it go, because I answered her as nicely as one could about the rain. I decided, however, not to leave home without it from that point on.

Tim's divorce settlement was final. He had to sell out and move to an apartment downtown. We still got together regularly, but we couldn't walk across the street and have a beer on the porch after work. He and I had become friends as well. His age put him just about exactly between Marks and mine. He was like a connection of our two generations. He was impressed, as are most people, at the fact that my son and I chose to dwell together. His place sold in a couple weeks and we had new neighbors. A nice couple with two girls and a spoiled little boy moved in. After the neighbors invited them to Bible study and then put them off limits to their children for the common reason, we made our visit. We invited them to a barbeque. We ate good, enjoyed a couple of beers, and became instant friends. Only this time, Satan wasn't going to sit back and let us win another neighbor without a fight.

I was always out of driving hours by Thursday. Ken told me I couldn't drive Friday, but Carl would pay me to attend a safety committee meeting Friday morning. "Ken, how did I get chosen for this?" I asked. "You, and I don't remember the young blonde's name, were the top two chosen, hands down," he said. "Every other ballet I counted either said the blonde, or the guy in the Australian hat. There was the black guy in the Air force cap as well." Carl wanted to meet with us individually. It was a good meeting. I just had to figure out how I could help with the problem. I was about to learn that just trying to find ways to help, helps. When the effort's afoot, somehow it gets traction beyond your imagination. The boss had safety committee hats made up for us. Just talking to other drivers from under that hat inspired them to focus a little more on their activities. It was like someone cared about their work and they didn't want to disappoint.

Keo and our new neighbor were like two peas in a pod. At first, I thought it was great. Then I saw a real problem developing. I can't explain what happened, because I don't know what happened. All I know is, the bottom dropped out of our happy home. I've been told there are two sides of the story, but I only know the one I saw. I was always told two women can't live in the same house. Will you tell me how the Mormons did it? No, I'll tell you. You can't be wife number two, or even number one, and have an ounce of self pride left. The Bible says 'from pride cometh all contention'. You can't put two proud women in the same house.

There are places in China with six and seven family couples dwelling together peaceably. However, you have to understand the oriental culture. The elders are the most honored in the household, yet they are the most humble of the household. The eldest son, when of age, is expected to manage things. When you get this mix figured out, peace will be maintained. A neighbor, although a brother or sister in Christ, is not family. The Bible says 'withdraw thy foot from thy neighbor's house'. That doesn't mean don't visit the house. It means stay out of their home. The new neighbor started attending our living room services and got her life right. I guess you could say we all did. There will always be emotional scars from that battle. However, real victories often leave scars.

The following Friday's safety meeting was interesting. Carl said, "I want you to vote on a committee chairman." He said he was the fifth and final vote. In other words, 'If you all vote for yourself, I'll decide'. "Plus, my initial vote counts, regardless of my deciding vote," he said. "For example, I'm voting for Tim. If Tim votes for Tim, and you each vote for one of you, it will be a tie. I will then break that tie with my deciding vote, and Tim will be the chairman." He continued, "I have a big job ahead of me, and I intend to do it with the best people I determine to be available to me. Do you get my drift?" We understood the directions and voted for me. All because of an old hat and a screwed up background check.

I encouraged my fellow committee members to stop their trucks when leaving the yard or returning to it, and talk to the drivers. Take a minute and ask their help in reducing accidents. Ask them to ask their friends to take an extra minute and rethink what they're doing. That's all it took. We just gave them a reason to break routine. Give them a flashlight. Say, 'Here are a couple new ones you can give to your friends'. Encourage them to make sure the pin latch was closed when they hooked up. Incidental yard accidents dropped remarkably in just a couple weeks. We were heroes to every level of management, but we didn't even know it.

About six more months went by with business as usual. I was making more money than I'd ever made in my life. We gave up on searching for a church that didn't beat us up three times a week. God was really blessing our jobs and things had really turned around with the family. Mark had led the new neighbor to Christ. That really helped things with the girl's relationships. I was not going to enjoy God's blessings and not return the worship He so deserved from us. We decided to begin Sunday services in our home; no longer just Bible studies. Tim and his girl, the new neighbors, and our three families with all the kids, gave us a house full. But God was doing something else in my life. I was more than satisfied with my life. I remained in the top ten producers, had a great relationship with management, and really enjoyed my evenings and weekends at home.

Every afternoon as I returned to the yard, I felt more impressed to trust God for even more. I didn't know what that might be, but I had real peace about it. Each day as I turned back into the yard, I would say, "Ok, Father, I'm ready for the next level, whatever it may be." I felt almost ashamed of myself. Since we had left Arizona, I had come from life's bottom to what most professional drivers would call the top. Yet I came to believe that God wanted me to trust Him for something even better than what He had already given me. Shortly after I had begun this practice, I was notified to report to the Project Manager at my earliest convenience. We had done meetings like this from time to time concerning safety matters, so I wasn't expecting anything out of the ordinary. When I reported to the main office, I was told that Carl was waiting to talk to me in his private office. I had never been in there.

"Have a seat on the sofa and I'll order us drinks," he said. I just sat there dumbfounded, until he pulled his chair from behind his desk and sat right in front of me, eye to eye. "Tim, I'm going to shoot myself in the foot," he said. "There are nineteen area risk managers in the company nationwide. They answer to the project managers, but they oversee the safety programs put out by the eight national terminal safety managers. Our area risk manager works out of the Louisville terminal. This district has rejected his services, and he has been reassigned. My boss and I have requested corporate to give you his position. That means it's pretty much a done deal if you want it." I didn't know what to say. "You're offering me a corporate position?" was about all I could get out.

"I'll talk to my boss and get back to you," he said. He shook my hand and thanked me for coming in.

Wow, but nothing happened. Fall turned to winter, and no one said anything more about it. One day, I walked into the new field office we had located out in the yard. A driver was giving the assistant manager a hard time about something. I wasn't paying a lot of attention until Ken told the guy to ask me about it. The guy said, "Who is he?" Ken said, "He's like me. He used to be a driver but now he's corporate." The argument was about inter-company advancement of drivers. He used me as an example. When the guy left, I asked Ken what he was talking about. I told him I had never heard anymore concerning the offer Carl had made me. I didn't even know he knew anything about it. "Oh, don't worry about it," he said. "Carl's boss said no one else is getting the job. He's like number two in the territory. He and Carl are going to corporate next week for meetings. Your position is probably on the agenda."

It was, but they didn't bring it up. Corporate safety brought it up. One of the Corporate Safety Managers said that they needed to find these guys a risk manager. Carl said, "We already found one." "Well, we don't know him; besides, the man you replaced didn't give him a very good recommendation," was the response. This came to Carl as a surprise. He thought the man he replaced had left the company long ago. It turned out that the guy was at corporate finalizing some issues, the same day Carl had submitted my name for the job. Carl said, "Oh, that explains the hold up. The man with a major safety problem didn't approve of the man we chose. We chose him because he helped me turn it all around in just a matter of weeks." Carl pointed to his boss and said, "I know you respect this man, and I think you probably hold some respect for me. We both interviewed this man and he is our choice." The corporate safety manager stood his ground. He said, "You are the top project managers in the country, but no one from corporate has talked to him."

Out of the blue, God brings in a real player on my behalf. Carl and his boss were really respected project builders and managers, but they weren't in the same league as the terminal managers. There were only eight of them in the country. The two closest terminals to my project were Detroit and Louisville. No matter who was hired as area risk manager in my territory, he would answer to the Louisville terminal safety manager. The Louisville terminal safety manager's boss, the Louisville terminal manager spoke up. "I'll interview him," he said. Now I'm just an old truck driver. I didn't understand any of this, but something had just happened that had never happened in the long history of that great company. The most powerful people in the field had just challenged the top level of corporate safety. Man, I wish I could have been there after I learned how things worked. I would have watched the very first corporate safety man ever, get hired from the field. Do you know what that meant? It meant I didn't have a friend in corporate, and if hired, I would work for corporate.

Matthew 16:18-19

And I say also unto thee, That thou art Peter, and upon this rock I will build my church; and the gates of hell shall not prevail against it. And I will give unto to thee the keys of the kingdom of Heaven: and whatsoever thou shalt bind on earth shall be bound in Heaven: and whatsoever thou shalt loose on earth shall be loosed in Heaven.

Chapter 26
What a Ride

For the first time in JB Hunt history, corporate safety had been challenged by the highest management in the field. Now you have to remember that just eighteen months earlier, I was pushing packages around Phoenix with a bunch of retired guys. Most of those guys had just been working for something to do. Now I was scheduled to meet with one of the eight national terminal managers of the largest transportation company in America. I have been recognized in the Christian school movement. I was one of the few independent missionaries that had made it to the field. But all that was ancient history now. There were no earthly dividends for once being involved in God's work. I talked to a few of the pastors I had worked with in the old days. They were no better off than I was. Several of them were too old to preach anymore. Like me, they had no insurance to help them now that their work was over. I began to look at myself as one of the lucky ones. I was able to bring an old profession up to date. I was able to get my class "A" driver's license. Now God was using them to restore my life.

Carl messaged me with the time and directions for my appointment in Louisville. That's when it began to dawn on me that this was real. The hand of God had not been this clear since I was working my way to the mission field many years before. I had almost forgotten what it was like. From the day I stepped onto JB Hunt turf, God had been pulling strings. I wouldn't even qualify to drive for them if the lady that was verifying my time with Watkins hadn't recorded eleven years instead of eleven months. That was God. I wouldn't be recognized or even considered for this job if I hadn't been the chairman of the safety committee. That was God. If I hadn't worn that stupid leather hat, none of this would be happening. Carl said they would negotiate my salary, so he told me to figure out the least I could accept before even talking with them. I was on track to make $48,000 as a driver, but he told me not to expect to start in management anywhere near that. Mom and Mark and I sat down the night before the meeting and came up with a minimum of $42,000.

This was supposed to be an interview, like the one I had had with Carl's boss several months earlier. Carl had me a little nervous, because he seemed to be a little bit scared of this guy. When I arrived, a receptionist seated me in a waiting room, and told me she'd come for me when the terminal manager was free. I sat there and got prayed up in anticipation of questions that I probably wouldn't know the answers to. She never did come back. He walked out of his office, told his secretary to tell the safety manager to meet us for lunch, and off we went. He never asked me anything except how my drive down had been. We pulled up to a pretty nice restaurant and waited in the parking lot for the safety manager to arrive. I had never laid eyes on any of these people before, but they all treated me like an old friend. "This is your new man," he said to the safety manager and his secretary as they climbed out of their car. That was my interview.

We had lunch, talked about everything except the job, and then returned to the terminal to discuss my pay. We went back to the safety office where he offered me $38,000, a car, a phone, and a laptop. I can't remember what I said, but it must have been pretty clear that I wasn't going to take the job. As I was driving home, wondering why God had let things go this far, my phone rang. Carl called me and told me that if I would take the job, he would get me the minimum $42,000 I had requested. Well that was it. Carl gave me the terminal manager's number and told me to call him and accept the position. When I talked to him, he told me to keep driving for the rest of the month and be ready to start the first of the year. I told him that I had real reservations about getting back in a truck. It would be like a carrier pilot's last mission every time I got in my truck. He said, "You're right; park it, and report to our safety office Monday."

He told me to pack for a few days and they'd put me up in a motel. He told me I should bring my wife with me if I could, and that we should be ready to join them for the staff Christmas party. There was a tone of seriousness to his voice. I took it as my first corporate level assignment, and told him we'd see him Monday. I couldn't get over the way they treated me in the whole terminal safety department. Everyone treated me like a superior, except the terminal and safety managers, and they treated me as an equal. There were no private meetings with the rest of the management staff. They held them, but they held them right in my presence. About the second day, I asked the manager something about how he wanted me to run something. He replied "I'm not your boss." I said, "You're not?" He said, "No, your boss in an asshole in corporate. I can't stand the guy; but his boss is a vice-president and a really good guy." He said, "I deal directly with him or his secretary if I have to deal with corporate." He told me he just couldn't deal with my boss. Then he told me that it was his immediate boss that had hired me last week.

I had had one short conversation with the man that he was referring to, but I didn't know that he was my boss. I didn't like him either, and it was plain that he didn't like me. He was the guy that hadn't wanted me hired. I had a long talk with God about him, and I got another miracle. The next day the safety manager told me that corporate wanted me to work directly under him until further notice. "Ok boss", I said, "I like that just fine." My son had his Exxon office in our home and I shared it with him. With the safety manager's help, I was set up with a phone, a computer, and everything I needed to run an office. It was great. He did all of the corporate stuff for me, and even assigned me his secretary for most of my paperwork. Since we needed to work most Saturdays, he asked me to pick another day of the week to take off. He said he didn't want me working more than five days a week. He meant it, too. I chose Monday, and one Monday shortly after, he called me just to ask me what I was doing answering my phone.

Suddenly, Miller Brewery became just another one of my many projects. I had drivers everywhere. I was in charge of making sure they remained compliant with all the regulations, both federal and state. The project managers loved it when I showed up in person. Carl once told me that those guys would be my bosses, but it didn't take long to learn that it was the other way around. They called me for approval on just about everything they did. Their boss was the first man that had interviewed me. Then along with Carl, they had insisted that corporate hire me. I didn't know it, but it was his power and influence alone that had gotten me this job. The terminal manager's offer to interview me had been the icing on the cake, but these project managers didn't work for him. Their boss was Carl's boss, and he worked directly for the VP of

East Coast Operations. I can't remember his name, but he often walked into a project to find me going through the driver's records. I was bringing them up to speed with some new regulation. He was so grateful for the personal attention, that one day on a conference call, he made me his number two man. This was most impressive; his boss up in Detroit was on the call as well. Now I had a vice-president of operations throwing my name around. He invited me up to his office to meet with him. I had no idea what was going on at the time, but my whole position was the subject of a spitting contest between North Central Operations and Corporate Safety. I was the only one of nineteen national area risk managers that wasn't even on the Corporate Safety's conference calls. I think they just wished I'd go away, but that wasn't happening. My name was appearing on a lot of stuff by then, and suddenly a VP of Ops was asking for me on his conference calls.

God made me my own little slot in a very big company. I didn't care about any of this; I had a job to do. I was building duplicate records for all my drivers. Carl was impressed with what he had created to the point that he assigned me one of his office people as my assistant. Now, I'll never completely understand what happened next. One day, while at a meeting down in Louisville, my manager came over to me with a very serious look on his face. "Your new boss at corporate is on the phone and he wants to talk to you," he said. "He's done chewing my ass." I figured he was either calling to fire me or hire me. By that time, I think I must have been the only one that still thought I worked for corporate safety. The voice was reserved. "I'm Chuck Conklin, Corporate Safety'" he said. "I just traded territories with Dan." Dan was the guy that had never accepted me as one of his. It would be a couple years before I would find out that God had destructed a corporate entity for little old me.

I sent up a flare prayer and answered before he could say whatever he was going to say. "Boy, is it good hearing from you, Sir'" I said. "I've been working for you for months, and I sure could use some guidance out here." I figured this was all or nothing. The silence was deafening. In the same quiet voice, he said, "Well, I hear you're doing a fine job for us." I think he was shocked to hear me say that I worked for him. The conversation lightened and I liked the guy from that moment on. God had done it again. The terminal safety manager couldn't believe it when I told him that he and I and our wives had been invited to have dinner on him anywhere we chose. I could have knocked him down with a feather. I said, "He told me to put it on my expense report, and from now on, send them to him instead of you. He said you and I had built the best level of cooperation with operations in the company."

I never had so much fun. One day, I read that a new terminal was being opened in Phoenix. Keo's boys lived in Mesa with their dad and spent their short summer vacations with us in Cincinnati. I also knew Mark's job with Exxon's Toyota account was really becoming stressful. That night I asked Mark and Keo how they would like going back to Arizona. When they realized I was serious, they started to pray about it. It wasn't long after that discussion that ExxonMobil informed Mark about an available position in Phoenix. It would basically be a lateral move for him from a career perspective, but his management knew it was on file that he would like to return to AZ if the opportunity presented itself, due to the fact that Keo's boys were there. He accepted the position and he told me to pursue the Arizona thing. I asked Chuck about it. We had become the best of friends over the last year or so. He liked my wife even more than he liked me, but not in a bad way. Once she takes a liking to you, and that's rare, she makes it a real pressure to be in her company. Chuck was one of the privileged few. He said he'd set up a meeting with his counterpart over the Western region and start things moving.

A couple weeks later, he called me and said to meet him at corporate. He introduced me to the guy in charge of the West. That night at a barbeque at Chuck's house, we really hit it off. He was a big black fellow and he was having problems with operations in his territory. Since operations paid the bills, they would have to ok the transfer, and he didn't think they'd do anything he requested. I asked him if he would hire me if I could get ops to accept me. He told me that he would, but he still didn't think it could happen. I made one call to the VP of Ops in his office in Detroit. He made a call to his counterpart in the West. My very surprised new boss called me and said, "I don't know how you did it, but they'll take you. They won't move you, but they'll pay your expenses to move yourself. You start in two weeks."

Several years before, God had told me from his word that he was going to send me in power to a wide land. The first time we moved to AZ was not the fulfillment of that impression. This time it was. I worked out of the Phoenix terminal for months until the terminal manager resigned. When the new manager came in from California, he chose the old assistant as his safety manager, and gave me a week to move my office. I moved to one of my projects and worked out of there for several months. Then I got a call from Chuck asking me to meet him at the terminal. I didn't have a clue what was up. We met in the terminal manager's office. Chuck told me my boss had been let go. He was in charge of training his replacement when he had met the Phoenix terminal manager and had a powwow with him. Now the manager wanted to talk to me in Chuck's presence. Chuck said, "He wants to hire you from us. I don't want to lose you from corporate, but he has an offer for you."

"Operations wants to hire you from us, and they'll make you an offer today if you'll consider it," Chuck said, in front of the terminal manager. I looked at the terminal manager and said, "You asked me to clear out of here when you took over; what happened?" He said, "You were on corporate's payroll, and I didn't know what I know now. I need your skill, and I'm ready to pay for it." Chuck broke in and said, "He's offering you an increase of three grand and the position of one of their eight national terminal safety managers. It's a pretty good offer Tim." "What are you going to do with the guy that the old manager chose, and that you hired?" I asked. "We're putting him, or the assistant that you hired, back on a truck; your call which," was the answer. I said, "I want Bill." He said, "Okay, nobody else wants him." Nobody could seem to handle him. I assured them both that Bill was well worth the special handling. I had never had a faster study in any field I had ever worked. I would go on to prove that beyond any doubt.

What a ride. I went from an area risk manager that corporate wouldn't even acknowledge existed, to a manager of one of their eight national terminals. When that showed up on the computer, the calls started coming in. There were several risk managers that had never even heard of me, and several more that had treated me as an outsider as well. Now everything they did West of Colorado had to have my stamp of approval. Well, not so much my approval, but my support. My main job was hiring and training drivers. Secondly, it was my responsibility to make sure that every driver in the West remained current. I was the balance between corporate and operations. Operations would push a driver out of his compliance just to get their obligations met. It was the risk manager's job to make sure that didn't happen with the projects, but they had no say in national operations. The terminal had charge of the over-the-road drivers. Their GPS was monitored from corporate, and any time the unit ran beyond compliance, it showed up on my screen. We eight terminal managers also managed all the drug tests in the nation.

Every week, we'd start out with about sixty people in orientation. If we had a good week, we would get about half of them qualified and hired. We were then one of the hardest companies to hire into. But we could offer fifty-thousand dollars a year if we hired them. I think we had the best drivers in the country. Wal-Mart may have been a little harder than us, but they didn't need near the quantity of drivers we needed. When your goal is to make a penny a mile, you've got to have a lot of drivers racking up the miles. If you can make five dollars a day per truck after all expenses, you can do well. That's running five hundred miles per day per truck. Take that times eight-thousand trucks and you've got about forty-grand a day. So where does all the pressure come in? If you had five hundred of those tractors parked against the fence, you were in trouble. Keeping drivers in those trucks and keeping them qualified was one of the hardest jobs I've ever had.

I'm going to sum up the next three years in a few paragraphs. God. I guess I could have done it in one word. God blessed everything we did. The first month that corporate set up a monthly terminal evaluation that monitored men hired, men fired, and safe performance, we were number one. Chicago had eight safety personnel on their staff. We had me, one assistant, and a half of a secretary. We beat their performance the first month. God gave me the heart of everyone that was anyone in the whole company, except one. He was a VP and just happened to be the head of safety. Everyone he had hired to work in corporate safety that had ended up as my boss, had become one of my close friends. Even his personal secretary and I were on a first name basis. One of his closest friends was the VP of AIG, our insurance company; he didn't like me either. Wait 'til you here how we ended up.

They hired a young man to replace the big black guy that I liked so well. The young man came out to Phoenix and told me that Chuck had said he better learn terminal affairs from me. He had told him that I would be the friendliest of the Ops safety managers. "If you can win Tim and Cheryl as friends," he had said, "You will never have a problem in Eleven West. If you can get Tim to speak well of you to Danny, the head of California, then that's your whole territory." I thought the kid had guts to tell me this, but as we worked together over the next year, I realized he had more than guts. He was an intelligent leader. It takes a lot to win the confidence of men that know more about what you're doing than you do. That takes character, self respect, and just the right amount of humility.

Joel was the kid's name. I took him to meet the project managers in our immediate area. They all knew me from back when I had been their risk manager, their equal at best. Now I was the man from ops that hired and fired their guys. To them, I was still the guy from back when we had worked together just to stay out of trouble with the guy that is now me. By that night, Joel was convinced that Chuck had led him in the right direction. He became one of my family's favorites.

Starting right here, I could write a whole book on running a safety department. How to maintain a proper balance between management, compliance and safety, and the best team of drivers ever assembled, is valuable knowledge. There are probably not a hundred people in the world, though, that would appreciate the value of such knowledge. I talked to a guy in California that about summed it up. He said, "Once you reach this level in the transportation field, you find that it's a very small world. We're like a bunch of NFL linemen. We know what each other do and how hard it is just to keep up. No matter what team we're on, we have the same obstacles. We have government regulations on one side and company objectives on the other. The better we do our job, the happier both sides are to see us go away. We are just necessary evils to both sides."

Joel was advanced to head up the claims department. He called my office one day and said he had an unbelievable story to tell me. "You know that VP of AIG?" he asked. Of course I did. I said, "He was a personal friend of my VP in corporate safety and no fan of mine." "Listen to this," Joel said. "He heard they were closing your terminal. He heard you refused to take over the L.A. terminal because you won't move to California. I couldn't believe what I saw at the cafeteria," he said. "I heard a loud conversation where the safety department people were sitting. The next thing I saw was the VP of AIG stand up and point his finger in Greer's face, the VP of safety. He yelled 'We'd be better off if Jones would take over the whole Western Region. Let him work it from Phoenix,' and he stormed out. What do you make of that?"

The kid was now the head of a much larger department than mine, and yet he took the time to pass that on. To this day, I reflect on it. I had already agreed on a severance package. Yet our top insurance advisor, who was no friend of mine, was advising my boss's boss to promote me to the top safety position in the West. What a send off. I didn't go away unnoticed. The whole management cafeteria was thinking about me one last time. Carl, the man that had recommended me for risk manager years before, was now the head of the Wal-Mart distribution. He was also having lunch with his department and witnessed this rare outburst. He called and offered me the best he ever had in my area, but it was a real stretch for both of us. He was a good Christian man and understood when I told him that we would be pushing on doors that God just wasn't opening for us. God was doing something. We just had to accept and follow. Carl said that I had made him proud over the years. I made it clear how grateful I was to have crossed paths with him. That's the last we spoke.

About a year before this, my sister and her husband, along with my uncle and aunt, had come down from PA for a visit. It was September 10th 2001, when I picked them up at the airport. In the morning, we were planning to go to the Grand Canyon for a couple of days. I was awakened the next morning by a call from my son, Brandon. He was still serving in the Coast Guard at the time. Mom handed the phone over to my side of the bed. She said, "He wants to tell you about some plane accident in NY." I told him that was unfortunate, and I handed the phone back to Mom and rolled over and went back to sleep. The phone rang again. "Dad, you've got to get up and turn on the TV," he said. "What I thought earlier was a little plane accident was a lot more." Soon, we were all sitting in front of the TV watching the prelude to the falling of the twin towers.

We had been planning to spend the next day up at the Grand Canyon, but we heard all national parks had been closed. We decided to take a drive out past Apache Junction and visit the Goldfield Ghost Town. I'll never forget that day, not only because of 9/11, but the memories of that little ghost town. I remembered all the undeveloped land around the town. We were holding Sunday services in Mark's living room in Gilbert. I told the four or five families that my options had been to move to L.A. or go back on the road for awhile. They asked me to try and find something local for now, and we'd pray about what to do next. There are not many openings for top-level management, I soon learned. I did get a tip from a manager of another trucking company about a consulting firm they often used. At my interview, they told me they had not hired anyone since the four of them had started the firm many years before. "You are, however, at the right level for us to train to do what we do," he said. "We turn down a lot of work you could do. Come back next week and meet the president."

The guy was eighty-one, the founder, and a master mind. After we spoke for awhile, he told me that I would be required to work court cases for lawyers. "We represent people or companies involved in suits for or against their professional drivers," he said. He said he would start me out at $110K, then instructed one of the girls to cut me an advance. I started training, but in a few weeks realized that this was what I call the devil's alternative. I was required to be in court everyday of the trial, no matter what state in which it was being held. Unless the case was being tried locally, I'd be on a plane most every Sunday, in preparation for Monday morning sessions. I held in for awhile, working smaller local jobs that none of them wanted. The big money wasn't in them, but I was home on Sundays.

One night Mark and Brandon came over and asked me to go for a walk with them. They wanted to talk to me about going full time as a pastor and getting a building somewhere. I sat down on a bench on the pavilion. I owned a place in an adult park, fifty-five years and over. We were the only ones around that late. I told the boys that they had no idea what they were asking. I couldn't go through it again. They kept pressuring me, and I kept telling them I'd never go through another ministry. By then I was in tears, and they wouldn't stop. That went on for an hour or more when I finally said I'd do it on one condition. I'd preach, but they'd run it. I was done with the fights and the phony lifestyles. I was at total peace with God. I wouldn't go back to living with self-induced convictions. "If we do build a work, it will be built out of people that are satisfied with living a normal moral life, and worshiping with the same," I said. They said, "Amen, find a place."

Find a place. That brought me back to 9/11. There was all that undeveloped land out behind the ghost town in the shadow of the beautiful Superstition Mountains. I contacted a real-estate agent and we started visiting available locations in the area. I kept seeing the ghost town up on the hill. I wondered who owned all that vacant land behind the town. I decided to go to the saloon in the ghost town and see if anyone knew who owned it. The barmaid told me that the mayor of the town was in his office up in the bordello across the street. The bordello is a museum of the ladies of the old mining towns. I use the word 'ladies' loosely. I crossed the dirt street and climbed the spiral metal stairs up to the porch of the bordello and knocked on the door. "We're closed," said a deep raspy voice from within. "I was told I could find you here," I said. "I have a question I'd like to ask you if you'll give me a minute." The door opened. "You got a minute," the voice said.

Behind the desk sat a broad-shouldered, heavy-set guy, with a head of mostly gray hair, and a full beard to match. "What can I do for you?" he asked. "I want to build a church in the shadow of your old town," I said. "I just wondered if you could tell me who owns the land out there behind you." "You want to build a church, build it right here," he said. "I'll help you build it." You don't meet many real men that don't have to tell you that they're real men. My life's gone full circle. I was looking back through time when Eddie Sullivan had stepped out of his door many years before in Japan. The same heavy voice had said, "The gates open, what can I do for you?" I just stood there in front of his desk and looked at him. He could tell the wheels were turning. He stood up and stretched out his hand. With a big smile, he said, "I'm Bob Schoose." That was the beginning of a relationship I would learn to treasure.

I tried to keep working, but it was clear God was not in it. Part of what I was given to do was building compliance records for large local farming operations. There probably weren't more than a dozen people in the state that knew the federal regulations any better than I did. The problem was that most of them were to be ignored when dealing with the Arizona agriculture business. How do you document a driver when the driver isn't documented?

It finally came down to just one job I would do for the firm. I held three hours of driver's orientation every Thursday for Knight Trucking. It was the best training program I'd ever seen in my entire career. I would get more attention than in any other safety class I ever taught. At one point I would explain the fact that they were holding the wheel of one of the most dangerous weapons licensed for public use. At that point, I would pull out a .357 magnum. I had their full attention. I would say, "I'd rather you shoot at me from the back of the room with this gun, because you might miss me, or only wound me. However, if you lose control of your tractor and run through that back wall at only thirty miles an hour, I'm dead. At thirty miles an hour, you're traveling forty-four feet per second, and your bullet is eight feet wide." Then I would start acting carelessly with the revolver as though I was talking on a cell phone or something. I had a live shell in the chamber, but there was no bullet in it. I would pull the trigger as if by accident. Some people would dive under their desks. "Hey, you're holding a whole lot more dangerous weapon than this little thing," I'd say. "When you drive by me while on your cell phone, should I dive under something?" They got the message, but some of them still had to go to the restroom.

Mark put his house up for sale, as did I. The idea was to sell our places and find a place near the ghost town, so we could get started with the church building. Nothing we tried worked. We'd find really good deals out East, but our places just wouldn't move. The housing market really started heating up. Every house in the neighborhood that was for sale would sell in a matter of days. We didn't get a bite. I finally had to rent mine and move in with Mark. My wife got a real good job working in the beauty salon in the new Apache Junction Wal-Mart. My renters moved out, so we moved back into our place. Month after month went by, and nothing. Finally one day Mark and I were driving somewhere and I said, "I think I know what's wrong. I got a scripture that said 'Seek ye first the kingdom of God, and all these things will be added unto you'," I said. Mark said he had gotten the same scripture; "Let's do it."

We didn't have any money. I had used my severance to pay off my car, and Mark was still paying off his old debts. We didn't have any money, but we had good credit. Let's build on credit and sink or swim. We met with Bob in the saloon and signed the contract. He said he didn't have enough money to pay for the block and the re-bar to build the retaining wall behind the spot we had chose to build the church. He said he would buy the block if we would buy the re-bar. So we spent our first two grand. Keo got on the net and started finding pictures of 1860 churches. I can't remember who gave me a picture of an old church building in western Colorado, but it was perfect. It was sitting out in a field, but you could see it from the country road on which they were driving. It had long been abandoned, but it was in good condition. Bob introduced me to the architect he had been using for many years. The old guy took one look at the picture and said he'd handle it, and we'd like it.

It took a couple weeks and few hundred bucks before we saw the first draft. After our first meeting in his office, we were excited about what he'd put together. Just to have the plans in our hands began to turn the dream into reality. Finally, the retaining wall was complete, and the location prepared for the foundation to be built. Bob introduced me to Mike, the mechanic he chose to do the framing. We could have him for just ten dollars an hour, but first the platform had to be built. By then, it was getting hot. You couldn't even touch your tools by ten o'clock in the morning. Bob said if I was ready to start building the platform, we should start around three in the morning. I said I could help everyday, but didn't think I could get too many others on that schedule. He said more than one or two would just get in the way at that point. He said the most important job was to get the super structure right. He would bring in the best guy to help us get it right.

It was July 23rd at three in the morning when my grandson Derek and I pulled up to the job site. It was a beautiful night, as are most of our nights out here in the desert. From up there at the top of the town, you could overlook the valley from Florence to Phoenix. There was just dark desert for about three or four miles between us and the first lights that started at Apache Junction. Behind us was the dark outline of the five-thousand foot high Superstition Mountain sitting in a backdrop blanket of stars. A couple of guys were setting up light stands, and running cords to the nearest available power outlets. Derek says he remembers, after being given the tools and the instructions, driving the first nail. All I remember is Bob, and this guy he called in, working their lines and levels. I could not appreciate their celebration that followed the mornings work. From what I could gather, this turned out to be one of their masterpieces. I heard statements like 'Can you believe that?' or 'It's perfect at every point,' and 'I never had one come together like that.'

I was impressed from the first. Everything Bob did had to be perfect, or we did it over. Bob's son, Jacob, was only fourteen or fifteen, but he could fabricate metal like a pro. He was building the steel braces that now appear as perfect crosses at the top of every truss. Bob took a short vacation to Colorado while Mike and I worked on the framing. One night, I got a call from him. He said, "I got it. It just came to me." This was when he put his son to building the braces. He said, "I found a saw mill up here, and they make just the rough cuts we need." He called his older son to meet him with a trailer and asked me to put together some help to unload it. Weeks had turned to months. We made it through what we call the monsoons of July and August. We call it monsoons because the humidity leaves our comfortable eleven or so percent, and doubles or triples until about mid-September. As soon as it broke, we started working days. With the humidity back down, a hundred and ten degrees was nothing, as long as you stayed hydrated.

I'll never forget the day he started telling me that in a week or so, we were going to need a crew. All those months, the most help he'd seen from us was my two grandsons. I could tell he was concerned. I assured him we had a crew waiting and ready. I still don't think he believed me. He got very firm as the weekend neared. "I hope you have the help were going to need starting Saturday," he said. I could tell he was still concerned as we cleaned up Friday night. He was almost begging me to tell him to hire some backup. The steel had been delivered and tomorrow we would start covering the roof. It weighed hundreds of pounds per sheet. In the morning, I introduced him to my sons and grandsons. They were all big boys, and their wives were ready to do anything as well. As he met each one, his smile got broader, and his spirit got lighter. The only thing he ever said about the crew after that was, "We won't need that many again until I tell you." He was comfortable knowing that when we needed them, they'd be available.

I never missed a day of construction until someone found us the oldest pews available on the west coast. There were some older ones available way out on the east coast, but that was way too far for our budget. Up on the Washington-Oregon border, a church was pulling them out of the old section of their building, and replacing them with the modern chair type used today. While we were pulling them up and loading them on my trailer, I spotted what is now the oldest thing in the church. It was a wooden pulpit setting in the hall in the basement. I had to have it. I didn't have any more money, but I just knew that thing was mine. Finally, I got a hold of the right guy, and he told me we could have it if we would display it for what it was. The famous Hammond Theater in Washington had donated their original organ to them in 1931. Years later, the church updated from the old pipe organ to a more modern version. The famous old relic sat in the basement for years. Then one day, some genius had cut it up and built this pulpit. Finally, the church outdated the relic, and it had ended up in the basement. They provided me with paperwork, declaring my pulpit as the remnant of maybe the oldest Hammond organ in America.

Soon, there was nothing left but the porches. Mike had just started the front porch when he cut his finger off. Bob was busily catching up on all the maintenance around town that he had neglected for several months while putting the finishing touches on the church. It looked like we were going to have to wait for weeks for Mike to heal up and finish the job. A young man showed up out of nowhere, and said he could finish the porches. The kid was good. He finished in just days, and then he was gone. Bob asked me if I knew of that famous church in New Mexico where the nuns had held a nine-day prayer vigil praying for a carpenter. They had needed someone to build them a staircase up to their loft. A stranger had showed up with a roll of copper on his jackass and built the now-famous free-standing spiral staircase, and then disappeared. You can find the story on the net. Bob said he was going to give me a bill for the guys work, but now he thinks it was the same guy that had showed up for the nuns. He said he called his phone number to tell him he had a check for him. The person on the phone said the guy was gone. He had said, "I'm done here; I'm going back to New Mexico."

Well, what could I say? I'd been looking for our electrician ever since he'd finished his job. We owed him hundreds of dollars. He kept saying he'd bill us when he was done. Now he was done and the inspector had approved his work and we were ready to open. We've never heard from him since. Maybe he went back to New Mexico, too. My daughter-in-law and her sister finished the drywall. The family and some of our closest friends from all over the country helped us finish the oak flooring. That was the toughest, but one of the most impressive accomplishments Bob had laid out for us to perform. The final inspector walked through with his clipboard. I was on pins and needles. He just walked over to the occupancy permit and signed it. "I've already seen what I need to see here," he said. "I've been watching Bob build for many years. He builds so far above code that if he made a mistake that I missed, it'd still be better than code." With that said, off he went. We can open. That was the beginning. You already know THE END.

II Chronicles 7:14
If my people, which are called by my name, shall humble themselves, and pray, and seek my face, and turn from their wicked ways; then will I hear from Heaven, and will forgive their sin, and will heal their land.

Chapter 27
Final Words

Friday, Nov. 20th 2009 was a very interesting day. A wise man once said that you really don't know that the Lord's leading by looking over the horizon. You know it by looking back over your shoulder and saying, hither to has the Lord led. For this reason I advise everyone to write an autobiography, even if they have no intentions of publishing it. You will understand more clearly where you are and how you got there. God has shown me many things concerning my future as well. He did so in such a manner that I could not have recognized without looking into the past. Remember the footsteps in the sand? You don't see them in advance but it was so reassuring to find that you were really never alone. His indelible footprints are right there beside yours. You might think you have been places Jesus would never go. I used to believe that. I don't anymore. If he had not been there with me, I never would have gotten out.

Until yesterday, I was beginning to doubt the validity of my encouraging words. I was even contemplating removing them from the previous chapter of this book. I have been telling the congregation not to live in a spirit of fear. As bad as things look now, they will, at least one more time, improve. Everyday, however, things get worse. We have always had evil in high places, but never as blatant as at the present time. Never before was it said openly that if the government cannot accomplish what they want with the power of persuasion, then they will use the persuasion of power. This is from the same guy that dedicated his book to Lucifer. I don't care who you are, that statement should make you wonder what country you're living in.

Forget about politics. Time has gone beyond them. Changing leaders will not change hearts. If that were possible, it would have shown during the Reagan years; but it only got worse. People talk about rebellion. There is no scriptural authority for rebellion. You might say we rebelled against England; no we didn't. We ran from religious persecution, but never fought her until we had our own government that we could scripturally protect. Corrupt leaders are most afraid of Christians, but a true Christian is their least threat. Even Saddam Hussein knew that. I was told he parked a police car in front of their meeting places for their protection. The only way they could even band together to protect themselves was if he would have authorized them to do so. The constitution once gave us that authority, but that has been changed forever. There is no loophole unless it would be legally revised. Even with a Christian in office, I don't think such a thing could be accomplished.

I don't even believe you can fight against the government on the authority of your state government. If such a thing were truly legitimate, God's will might have been done for the Confederate States. I'm not sure of the real reason for that war in the first place. I really don't know if God could have stood with them or not. What I am sure about is Bible prophesy. We have seen more of it come true in our lifetime than any time since the birth of Jesus. Just me talking, but I believe there is space in that prophesy for one last God-sent revival. I said there is space for it; I didn't say it was a given.

I know we are running desperately thin on Bible time. Once Israel returned for the third and final time, nearly a generation ago, we ran out of further generations this side of Christ's return. The next clear prophesy fulfillment will be the Mid-East war on Israel. At that time, God said He will send fire on Magog and the isles that dwell carelessly. Magog is Moscow, and if we fit anywhere in end time prophesy, we fit in those isles that dwell carelessly. If you live in Washington DC, or any major city for that matter, I would encourage you to pray about moving. All the rest of the pre-war prophesies came true. It's a little late to start betting against this one. Remember when those that dwelt in Jerusalem were clearly warned to get out? Those that did not had their blood run down the streets like water after a rain.

I want to say one last thing to the Christian that is not dwelling carelessly. If you know what is going on, then you are already listening. If you are paying no attention, because you think God is going to tell Scotty to beam you up at the slightest sign of trouble, then good luck. You've been reading Scofield's notes, not the Bible. You will go up before God's wrath, but if you get out before then, Scofield owes an apology to the millions that died under the wrath of the dark ages.

God did not tell us to clear out. He didn't tell us to find a sheepskin and head for the desert yet. Anti-Christ is not in charge of America yet. We are a God-instituted people living in the only Christian nation ever founded. We are the children of the children of Israel. When God told Abraham or Jacob that his seed would be like the sands of the sea, it included us and every soul born of faith. We are spiritual Jews. God used us in modern times in ways that parallel in many respects the way He used Israel in Old Testament times. He used us to free the Jews and help them return the third and final time to Israel. We also evangelized the world, or tried to anyway. When we slack up on our Christian civic responsibilities, we end up with an oppressive leader. When we wake up and cry out to Him, we get a Reagan. 2 Chronicles 7:14 may well apply to us. (^{14}If my people, which are called by my name, shall humble themselves, and pray, and seek my face, and turn from their wicked ways; then will I hear from heaven, and will forgive their sin, and will heal their land.)

Don't get me wrong; I know the devil has big plans for this nation. I believe he desires to destroy it and build a socialist world government on the ashes of our capitalistic freedom. Satan, however, has never faced a nation like ours since the Israel of old. We are not pre-Hitler Germany, pre-Stalin Russia, or pre-Mao China. We are spiritual Israel. I ask God continually to give me, from His word, a clear picture of our place in my time. I can't continue to encourage people if I should instead be warning them. He gave me Esther chapter eight. I'm in my 60's, and I've only had two events in my entire ministry that were as clearly from the finger of God as what He gave me. I'd be concerned if I was reading this from a man that thinks he has such events every other day. You just read my life history. This is number three.

An order was once put out to persecute the Jews throughout the kingdom. It has been that way with us for some time. No religion is openly persecuted in this country except Christianity. More laws are passed against us than any other faith in America. Esther turned the heart of the King and allowed Mordecai to reverse that order. The Jews were ordered by their government to defend themselves. Mordecai went so far as to tell them to be aggressive in their defense. Many became Jews out of the fear of the Jews. I believe God is going to send us an Esther.

I don't mean generically, but someone called for such a time. Many older preachers are starting to question the fact that we won't be here when these things come to be. They are even thinking that maybe such an end times revival could be the catalyst to usher in the man of sin. This corresponds with what Paul told the churches that thought they had missed the rapture. He said none of these things will come to pass until the man of sin be revealed. Yes, we are to look up, because our redemption draweth nigh. You can't do that with your head under a rock, waiting for the sound of the trumpet. Don't believe the lie, which I believe is the great lie in the scriptures. You were not born out of season. Wake up and be a part of the time for which you were born.

1John 4 ¹Beloved, believe not every spirit, but try the spirits whether they are of God: because many false prophets are gone out into the world. ²Hereby know ye the Spirit of God: Every spirit that confesseth that Jesus Christ is come in the flesh is of God: ³And every spirit that confesseth not that Jesus Christ is come in the flesh is not of God: and this is that *spirit* of antichrist, whereof ye have heard that it should come; and even now already is it in the world.

John is talking about Christmas. If you want to put it in plain English, you could say that everyone and everything that does not support the Christian understanding of Christmas is of the spirit of Anti-Christ. Did your jaw drop? It is not politically correct to even say Christmas anymore. Then that philosophy is likewise Anti-Christ. Are you getting the picture that John is presenting? There are only two Spirits in this world. One is of Christ and one is of Anti-Christ. I heard about an old lady that asked everyone she met if they believed in Christmas. She had it figured out long before I did. If you believe that the son of God, co-equal and co-eternal with God the Father, took on flesh at Bethlehem, then you are of the Spirit of Christ. If you do not believe it, you are of the spirit of Anti-Christ. How much more simple could John make it? He did not begin at Bethlehem; he took on flesh at Bethlehem.

Some people have a problem with the virgin birth. The Bible says that by Christ was everything made, and without Him was nothing made. I missed that for most of my ministry as well. This means that he created life in the first place. How much of a problem would the creator of life have with a virgin birth? Every other philosophy of the beginning of life begins with an uncaused first cause. No matter how far back you want to take it. Therefore they are of the spirit of Anti-Christ. Louis Pasteur's proof of the fact that life cannot come from non-life has never been broken. The president of Harvard science department has reportedly said he cannot even put a dent in it. Yet he said that he has chosen to embrace the impossible, because he will not accept the alternative. You either believe in Christmas or you don't. You are either of the spirit of Christ or the spirit of Anti-Christ. You can't have it both ways.

So let's move back towards my original point on the future of our nation. Can we expect tyranny or revival; destruction or healing? The prophesy concerning us has not been written. Our future has not been revealed. We know what is going to befall almost every other nation. We know what is going to happen to Russia, to all the Mid-East, and the revised Roman Empire clear out to West Africa. What about us? God already knows because of his foreknowledge written by Paul in Ephesians. Eph. 2: [10]For we are his workmanship, created in Christ Jesus unto good works, which God hath before ordained that we should walk in them. We are part of a plan. God already knows what choice we will make individually and as a nation. The only problem is we don't know because we have not made our choice yet, and He has not told us in advance what we chose. We know what China, and Russia, and most of the rest of the world chose.

We have the nation created in Judaism and we know everything that is going to happen to it. Now we have the only Christian nation ever established, but only a few very thin shadows of possibilities for us. As a nation of peoples, we are the most prophetically informed. We know what is going to happen to almost every other country except ours. God's foreknowledge is not causative. Don't get the idea you can just sit back and hope for the best just because God already knows the end. It is still up to us to make the choice. I believe that choice will be which spirit you choose to follow and support. According to the scripture, the spirit of Anti-Christ will be increased in these last days. I believe it will be present almost everywhere in your life. It will be present in almost every decision you face. You are going to have to make a conscious decision as to which spirit you are going to support.

Let's just take the source of our daily information for example. Does your chosen source believe in Christmas? It is common knowledge that most every media outlet does not permit a Christian to be employed. The largest one doesn't even allow their people to wear a US flag lapel pin. So witch spirits are you listening to? There is one major cable news broadcast that does hire Christians. They are under attack from all the rest. Is that why you don't tune them in? These are spirit choices you will be held accountable for making. Ask yourself this: does the person I'm reading or listening to believe in Christmas? In the field of journalism, the answer is ninety out of a hundred do not. You call yourself a Christian? Why do you not seek a source that is led by the spirit of Christ? I have met people that say they believe in Christmas, yet they follow those that do not, rather than those that do.

Ok, all I wanted to do was set the tone for my final words. I managed to write this whole book without preaching to you. I just had to leave you with something that will last beyond the closing of the covers; something to look forward to that was formulated from the ashes of my past. I have been so long writing this thing and the editor has been so long getting it to the publisher that I feel like I have been in a race with global warming. My grandfather used to say "sure as Christmas". I didn't know where he got it, but I found it in Jeremiah. God said all the universe and the earth will do as He appointed them to do just as sure as He will use David's seed. Without his seed you don't end up with Mary and Josephus. So, just as sure as Christmas, God has not lost control of creation.

I've had a lot of time to think about the vastness of creation, therefore the gravity of his control. Think about the speed of light, 180,286 miles per second. Pretend you can ride on that light beam. In the time it takes to clap your hands twice, we are on the moon. However, to reach the nearest star, would take us four years. To go to the edge of the known universe, it would take us over ten million years. The same clown that told us he invented the internet is now telling us that God is out of control. We are all going to die if we don't send him more money.....Global warming is coming. The same God that is controlling it now said it will happen at the end of the millennium. I am hopeful they can get this book published before that happens, but I'm not as sure as Christmas.

I just started a great read; 'Quiet Strength', about the life of Tony

Dungy. I was amazed at the small army of people that participated in the production of that book. To date, only two people had anything to do with this one. I'm not putting my talent on the same plane as those guys, but I'm not feeling quite as badly about my editor. He is really busy with his day job. Their contract with GM was up at the end of last year. It is his responsibility to get it renewed. He is flying back and forth between Phoenix and Detroit a lot more than normal plus maintaining his other duties. He hasn't had much time as late to work on my book. I was surprised last week when he asked me to write one final chapter. He said he was almost ready to send it on to wherever it goes next. Tony's book also reminded me that I need to write acknowledgments. Tony has a couple pages of them. Mine is going to be pretty short. I've got an army of one working on mine. I doubt that Denzel Washington will be writing my foreword either, as he did for Tony. If you didn't get anything else out of this writing, but it caused you to think about reading "Quiet Strength", then we both won.

Instead of writing a foreword, I should have written an afterword. There are probably several pages of people that would like to comment on the book now that it is published. There are just as many that would credit me for leaving their names out. There are two other people not in that category that I left out. Not just their names, but our entire relationships. One was just a speed bump that God used to make sure I ended up in the Air force. If that would not have happened, I would not have found Cheryl, and I would have no life worth writing about. The other one is as close to blood as you can get. The first twenty years of our relationship is no doubt why she is a New York Times Bestselling author. Come on, I put her in the college newspaper office when she was just a kid. She watched my publishing relations with papers and magazines for years. I'm the reason she writes, but I'll trade all credit in return for no credit for any other ideology she embraces. My exclusion was not merciful nor offensive, just convenient to our individual purpose.

One name I would have on a credits list, if I had one, would be Bob Schoose, the Mayor of Goldfield, of course. My family and brother Sullivan are my beginning and my constant, but Mayor Bob is most likely one of the final stamps on my life's passport. He called the other day and said we better get together and sign a new contract. We met at the Saloon where we signed the first one over six years ago. The first one was only for three years. We really haven't had a contract for over three years, but we none worried about it. Our business relations are based on trust in character, not ink. We are both getting older though, and we both want our business relationship to outlive us. The new contract is for five years with a five year option. Our goal is to live long enough to take the option. At least it is a guide to those that will follow us if we don't. I just missed a good chance to die and if this current administration gets their wish, my VA health care may go away at my age. It might be better if I don't get really old.

If I started naming our members and our regular winter visitors, I'd forget somebody. We had 119 a couple weeks ago, and we don't even count the nursery. That matched our all time high. This year we have been over a hundred every week since winter. Keep in mind, a lot are first time visitors just passing through. A woman talked to me after services last week. She said for 50 years she had wanted a horse and for 50 years she had needed Jesus. She said Jesus had used that horse to bring her to the ghost town and come to the church where she found Him. She is now most likely a seasonal regular. A young couple came a couple months ago to arrange a wedding. They have not missed a Sunday ever since. I was just told they want to join. They are the third or fourth fulltime couple that we have gained this summer. That is about equal to the fulltime couples we have lost. They have moved on to a full service church with Sunday schools and teen programs and all the extras. That is fine with us. It takes spiritually strong, self-sustaining Christians to become what we call our permanent people.

I have been in this business long enough to know that we have the cream of the crop. We have dozens of solid people that need zero maintenance. When I said fulltime couples we have lost, I was not including the numerous souls that got saved and moved on in less than a year. I include them with what I call our home missions successes. I just realized something that I never thought about until right now. The permanent people are people that are growing old together. When I think about our deacon Gene Smith and his wife Jan for instance; they told me after their first service that they were not going anywhere else ever again. They meant it. We had no idea he was going to be a deacon or that she would be our ladies Bible study teacher and counselor. Now that I think about it, he was only my age when they told me that. He has gone from his early 60's to his late 60's. I have gone from my mid 50's to my early 60's. Young people don't think like this but we are probably going to bury one another.

I have preached many of our regulars their last message. I just preached a funeral for a wonderful man named Bob Argent. He and his wife showed up about four or five years ago and started taking notes. They would go home and look up the scriptures. When his son spoke at the funeral, he said only his dad could go out into the desert and find God. I can't believe how good of friends we were. I'm looking at his picture right now setting on my mantle. We did this by only seeing each other an average of once a week. That's what I mean by zero maintenance. Every Saturday evening, he made sure the church was ready for services. He always kept the filters changed in our A/C and heating system. Someone already took that job over, but I don't even know who it is yet. A great fact of this work is that no one wants anything from anyone.

We never even had a building program. We built everything on our personal credit. I think in October of last year we finally paid off the building. I know the treasurer asked me for the address of another missionary because we had some money left. That is fantastic. Now we can focus on building our fellowship hall and nursery. I'd also like to help our sound people, Gary and Cathy, get us up to broadcast quality. Then there is my original dream of a youth camp down by the RR tracks behind the church. I'd like to partner with some area churches in that effort. There is no better location to bring our youth back to historic values. I know what you're thinking. A minute ago I was talking about giving or hearing our last message. I haven't lost that thought, but we are not all my age. I have three young dedicated sons standing in the wings. The mayor's boys are young as well. Our partnership with church and town is still in the hand of our main partner, and it's not over until Jesus says it's over. If old Bob Argent was the only one to find God out here in the desert, all our labor would have been well worth it. However, all the victories we have seen, souls saved and lives changed, may only be the foundation of one of the last great works. I thank God that it is with this work that I have been blessed enough to be Forced to Pastor.

I Peter 4:17
For the time has come that judgement must begin at the house of God: and if it first begin at us, what shall the end be of them that obey not the Gospel of God?

Epilogue
Final Words ... One Year Later

I wrote this last chapter as sort of a bonus chapter. Not a bonus to you, but to me. I haven't written anything but sermons for about a year now, since the last time my Son asked me to write a final chapter, and I miss it. I got a sermon ahead last week, so I had a couple of days to kill. I still couldn't go outside because the medication was still in my system. That's another reason I wrote this; I was pretty sure my time on earth was over. You'll read about that horrible experience about halfway through this chapter. You'll see that I rambled on for a few pages before things started coming together again. Anyway, I hope you liked the book.

I want to say one more thing, then you can finish the book again. I told you earlier about the one supernatural event that I'd experienced in my life. When I finished this book, I was not sure if our outreach here was the fulfillment of that event, or if that end was yet to come. That was the only time in my life that I have ever experienced anything visually that went beyond the law of probabilities. Romans 1:20 says the invisible attributes of God are clearly seen. I'm not talking of these; I see them as normal. What I saw was not normal, nor was what I heard shortly after I completed this book normal. I always tell people that if you hear God audibly, then you are eating too many onions on your late night pizza. I don't think I heard the voice of God, but I heard something that stood my hair on end.

It was election night and I was sitting out back by the fire. For weeks I had been very uneasy. I didn't care to watch the returns on TV. After it was plain enough as to who was going to become our new president, I walked into the main house headed for my room. As I passed through the TV room, I could hear nothing but a clamor of voices, all talking loudly at the same time. The room was full of company, and with my hearing disability, it is almost impossible to make out any single voice if there is any background noise. I walked past the confusion towards my door. Just as I reached my door, one voice spoke out with crystal clarity. In the midst of all the hoopla, I heard the words "Isaiah 47". Even if someone in the room had said it, I never would have made sense of it over all the racket.

I ran for a Bible and read the first verse of Isaiah 47. It said 'come down and sit in the dust because there is no throne'. I thought something must be going to happen to our new leaders before they ever got in office. That didn't happen. The rest of the chapter spoke of the sudden destruction of a nation that turned on Israel. What's it all mean? I'm not sure. I know it happened and I know it's real. I knew from the time I read it. When I closed my Bible, a peace came over me that I haven't experienced since the day I knew I was forever forgiven. I have an unexplainable confidence that God can bless His people in the midst of the unthinkable.

The last place in prophesy where I can clearly find this nation is WWII when the Leopard, the Lion, and the Bear were joined in allegiance. That's the US, England, and Russia. I believe our part was not written for a purpose. If the Apostle John saw our end when he received the book of Revelation, then it was incorporated in the part that the Angel told him not to write. When the Anti-Christ is chasing the 144,000, and it says they are saved by the Eagle, I hope that is referring to our 6th fleet sitting out there in the Mediterranean, but who knows. We know the final disposition of most of Europe and the Middle East. Do you think the greatest nation that has ever existed on planet earth has no part to play?

Through the foreknowledge of God, I'm sure our fate is known, but that fate may have been determined by decisions we have yet to make. II Chronicles 7:14 says "If my people that are called by my name", that's you Christian, 'will humble their selves'. That's the part that scares me. God is not going to deliver us from a position of arrogance and strength; it will be from a position of humility and weakness, or not at all. There is room in prophesy for one last revival. The stage is also set for no divine deliverance and no revival that we have anything to do with. All it says is the gospel of the kingdom will be heard around the world and then the end will come. We have pretty much done this already via satellite. Are we done?

The sun is still shining. It's about 109 degrees outside right now, not quite as hot as it's been the last couple of weeks. It's going to get clear down to 90 in Phoenix tonight. That means up here on my hill, it will be way down in the mid 80s by midnight. I only saw one rattler this year. My grandson ran into it down by the mailbox. The neighbor kid dispatched it with a few well placed rounds from his air rifle. It had two of the most beautiful black rings just forward of the rattlers. Now I know that what Keo killed last year on the porch was not a Ring Tail. I'm afraid it was a Mohave, the only protected snake in this state. I'm not sure, and there is no way of knowing now. Shortly after it suffered reptile dysfunction, something carried it off. I'm glad, because I was told that you would have a better chance of staying out of jail in this state if you killed a person than if you killed one of those things. A couple months ago, they found a woman hiker on a trail just north of here. Her knife was still sticking through the Mojave's head. They would have arrested her, but it had already killed her. I love this state, but I don't care much for its politics. Protecting a snake, but not an unborn child, doesn't make any sense to this old cowboy.

When I finished the last chapter the last time, you could tell that I was not sure if my course had been run or if there was more for me to do here. We built the church out here in the desert and saw five wonderful years. I was satisfied with that and still am. We saw more people come to Christ than most churches ten times our size. That's paramount, of course, but it's still the little things that are so encouraging. Another young couple found Christ and finally learned enough to realize that they needed to get married so we could baptize them. He was a builder so our economy here was a dead end for them. They didn't want to leave the church, but had little choice. He kept putting his move off week after week. With each right decision they'd make, he'd find another weeks worth of work. Then everything came together. A land owner up in Idaho offered him full time employment with a house waiting for him. A year ago, he would have been on the first plane. Instead, he said he wasn't going anywhere until we married them and baptized them. The next Sunday we married them after services and went straight to the pool and baptized them. They left with their lives a little more complete. Just another couple that can say they found the water of life in the barren desert of Arizona.

Another of our young couples lives in Holland. They come to Arizona to buy old cars. His employees make them like new and then he sells them all over Europe. If you think you might have something he would like, you can find him on the web. They are seldom in America on a Sunday that they are not in the little church in the desert Ghost Town. How did that happen? I don't know. One Sunday they brought Arizona Joe with them. He is a pretty famous restaurateur in these parts. Joe showed up last week and brought another couple with him. I am beginning to recognize another set of regulars besides those we typically enjoy every week. These are those that don't attend anywhere regularly. Many of them work on Sundays, but when they can get away, they worship with us. That's been our attendance program from the beginning. God can send who He wills, when He wills, and for what He wills.

A few months ago, the Goldfield Mayor's wife blessed us with a visit. She wanted to take one of our ladies horseback riding. She told her husband she was going to church first and invited him to come along. We love to have him, but I understood his answer. He said "Honey, you don't understand; it's standing room only." He may be really well known, but he's not much for crowds. We are just happy that people are comfortable with us once a week or once in a while, and for whatever reason. They know when they do visit us, they are going to hear the Word of God. They come anyway, though, and that's all that really matters.

God sent a couple, Gary and Cathy, which eventually felt it was their calling to put a microphone on me on Sunday mornings and make CDs of the sermons. Although not advertised, his CDs are requested in four or five states already. Whatever cost they recover for their efforts, they give to the church. Don't get me wrong, they don't do anything without informing the church, but it's clearly their ministry. We have a sound man that is, without question, sent by God.

The same thing is true with our music people. Lee and his wife are a dying breed. There are no real professional cowboy singers anymore that I know of. There may be a few old guys left out there, but most of the pros have passed away. We lost our wonderfully talented music girl that appeared in our lane on the back of a motorcycle. We lost her pretty much like we lost the one before her. We left them get a little too close. They were like family, and you know what they say about family; you can choose your pastor, but you can't choose your family. Since we gave up organized religion, we have become comfortable with who we are. What you see is what you get. Some really good people just need a little more than what they can see.

Lee was singing over at the saloon. He is such a personable guy that I felt comfortable asking him if he would help us until I found someone. After a couple Sundays, he told me not to look too hard. That fits us right down to the ground. We haven't talked much on a personal level, but from all indications, he has tried the religious life. If I'm right or wrong, he still seems quite content just being around normal, moral living people that love the Lord. They decided to find some horse property closer to the Ghost Town, which is no easy task. That is about all he has ever asked me to pray about. I was thrilled to do it. It turns out that our young friend from Holland owns some property out there as well. Not long after Lee told me he had found a nice place close by, my Dutch friend said, "Guess who moved in on the property next to mine?" Small world isn't it?

It's 114 degrees on the other side of those doors leading out of my "A" frame. My cats will not go out until the sun is completely down. The dog will only go out because she would walk into hell with me. I typically stand when I write. My wife got tired of the ugly thing that I used as a portable desk over the years, so she bought me a fancy fold up desk which I'm working from right now. I love standing, but my legs are tired this afternoon. My Son called me out of bed early this morning. He was at the Phoenix Airport, just about ready to board his plane, when he discovered his passport was missing from his briefcase. I checked the safe and his office to no avail. The last he saw it was the last time he had pulled it out of it's hiding spot to travel out of the country months before. We're afraid it has been stolen from his hotel room. Anyway, I'm about three hours short on sleep.

I just went to his office, since he is home, and asked him to get me a number for Michael Blake. He is the author of Marching to Valhalla, and lives on a ranch somewhere south of us. I just finished his book and I want to tell him how much I enjoyed it. He enlisted in the same branch of service as me, just months after I entered, when the war started to get serious. You know from my book what I was doing with my time in the service. Michael was learning to write. I wasn't aware of any of his work until Dances with Wolves, but I bet he'll bring me up to speed.

I'm still not sure where we are going; I'm just very glad to be a part of it. Around six months ago, my doctor scheduled me for a colonoscopy. She told me I needed one every ten years. She told me to get it and forget it. After it was over, they told me I would get a letter if anything was wrong. That letter came a couple weeks later. It told me I had six polyps removed and they were all benign. I thought that was nice; I was glad that's over. About a week later, another letter came to inform me that I was scheduled for another scoping in three months. I remember thinking 'What happened to the ten year thing?' After that was over, I got another letter telling me they removed several more polyps and found them to also be benign. Well that was more good news, I thought, until I received another letter scheduling me for another scoping. This time I didn't get a letter, though; I got a phone call. "The doctor would like to meet with you on Thursday at ten o'clock", was the message they delivered.

The wife and I showed up, not sure what was going on. The caller wouldn't tell me anything except that it was not as bad as I may be thinking. So this was our mind set when we arrived for the meeting. He pulled up all these pictures of my colon from the scoping. He went on to tell us that he was not concerned with the bulk of the polyps he had removed from my left colon. He was able to get them out intact, and was sure we didn't have to worry about them. Then he moved to my right colon and started showing concern. He got to the last couple and showed us they were flat. He explained that they were the really high risk type for cancer. He explained that he was not able to get them out in one piece. Then he dropped the bomb. Pathology reported a cancer cell in one of those polyps that he couldn't get out in one piece. He told us that he may have gotten all of it, for all he knew, but there was no way he could tell what was between the walls of my colon.

He told us nothing had spread to the veins or the lymph nodes, though. One option was to just watch it real close. It wasn't like he had found a bloody polyp that he couldn't even get the scope through. He explained that we were way ahead of the game, but still advised we talk with a surgeon. Cheryl asked him what he would advise if I was his father. Because I was only 62 and fairly strong, he would probably recommend removing the right colon. It has a track record for growing the bad stuff. He scheduled me for another scoping for three weeks later and suggested we talk to the surgeon in the meantime. If we opted for surgery after speaking with the surgeon, we could simply call and cancel the next appointment.

I dislike going to hospitals. I tell people to avoid them except to go there to die. I try to find a couple members from the church, that feel led and comfortable, to make the hospital calls. I advise young preachers to do the same. It is time consuming, if done correctly, and it requires an understanding individual with the right heart. The Phoenix VA hospital, however, makes me feel differently. I don't feel like I'm going to catch something just by walking through the doors. I have been in and out of it now for the last five years, and not once because I was sick. I realize that the hundreds of vets walking the same corridors are probably not sick either. Most of us have been sent there by our local VA clinic for a test of some kind. It doesn't matter your walk of life, when you're in those halls, there is a sense of camaraderie, no matter what your age. A man feels privileged; not proud or humbled, just a healthy mix of the two.

When I woke up this morning, I thought I was dead. For a few minutes, nothing hurt. You have to understand that I have been fighting infection ever since I got home from the hospital. This is the first week in over a month that I'm not on medication. The first round of antibiotics didn't work, but left my skin hurting, no matter what was touching it. Now, at least it doesn't hurt to lay in bed. The second round was 14 days of really bad stuff that hurt to move my wrists and elbows. One of the several pages of side effects described how it can cripple me for up to two months after I stop taking them. What choice did I have? I had to get that tube out somehow.

I still need to get out and walk but it's 114 out there right now. I have only been off my pills for a couple days, and I'm still not supposed to be in the sun. I'd feel like a vampire if my place wasn't so open. The top half of the front of our "A" frame is glass. That's great in the winter, but works the a/c pretty good in the summer. You'll never get cabin fever in my place. I can see further than a man could ride in a day, if he was riding hard. Of course, this time of year you'd kill a horse if you tried that in the daytime. My surgeon told my wife to take me to the mall for exercise. She informed him that it would be a cold day in you know where before I agreed to go to the mall. I haven't had any real exercise since our last visit to the hospital. I always manage to park somewhere on the wrong end of that massive complex. Even when one of the volunteer vets pick you up in a golf cart and take you to the nearest door, you soon find that the door is still about a mile from where you need to be.

About all I could suffer through out there today would be a round of golf, but I'm not allowed to do that for a couple more months. I have been turned back over to my personal doctor to get me through the recovery period. We have become rather close over the years. She tries to watch her tongue, because she knows I'm a preacher, but sometimes she slips. The first time I saw her after my surgery, she was really upset with me. She gave me a disgusted look and said, "You were one of my healthiest men." We are both pilots and both golfers. She said she didn't want to catch me out behind my house messing around with even a short iron until the fall. She told me, "I don't want you to get a stinking hernia; I want you back on your feet." I know she wouldn't shed a tear if she found out that I didn't make it, but I can see her bitching me out for having the audacity to make her my x-doctor.

I had to turn the tables on her. I told her, "It's your damn fault. You have been insisting on this scoping for years." Even when I told her that I'd had no cancer in my family, she parted with the fact that it didn't really matter these days. She said, "It's everywhere; you have a damn shower curtain, don't you?" I think that was the statement that did the trick. I told her to go ahead and schedule me. I am glad I did it. I got rid of thirteen polyps that I didn't need. I am not sure, however, about the surgery. If I had had any idea what I was going to experience, I would never have done it. They tell me now that I probably would have been fine for at least five more years, even if I hadn't gone through with the surgery. I would have taken that in a heartbeat, but somehow I missed that offer until after the surgery. Bottom line, the decision was mine, but with heavy persuasion from the wife and family. Mark said he would think about my concerns and probably support me if I chose to put it off. Cheryl, however, would concede nothing to consideration. Her mind was made up from the onset.

Just over two weeks after Cheryl and I first met with the doctor who set up the meeting with the surgeon, we got a phone call. For years now I have been dealing with these nice people by mail. Now this was the second personal call. There are thousands of us veterans in this system, but somehow they made me feel like I was talking to a person who thought I was the only veteran in Arizona. As though I was the only person she was going to talk to from that moment on, until this was all over with. She didn't even ask me for my number. Even the guys I'd been working with at the clinic for years asked me for my number. She had confused me with somebody special. Nobody else I dealt with at this place even knew my first name until they had asked me for my last name and number. Then and only then, except for my personal physician, has anyone called me George.

Well everything is back to normal. We're sitting in a large waiting room at the Special Surgical office. It's now two hours past our appointment time. The lady at the check-in announced that due to an emergency surgery, everything was running late. Those waiting to meet with a surgeon were asked to please be patient. A guy that had come in on the bus from way up in Snowflake told me he had been there from the time the door had opened that morning, and by then it was late afternoon. The 'special' treatment had gone away and things had slipped back to what I was used to. "What's your number? Sit down please." Finally, I saw some guys in scrubs through the window. They were apparently back, but another forty-five minutes went by and my name had not yet been called. This was the most impersonal treatment the VA had ever given to me. I don't mind waiting if I am waiting there to talk to a foot specialist, but I was waiting to talk about my life. I was just about to get up and leave when a lady from behind the check-in counter called my name. She didn't just push a button to open the door like they do when I'm there to see my foot guy or for lab work. She takes us back the hall a ways and stops. She turned around to face my wife, two sons and myself. She said softly, "I held you guys over because I wanted you to have the most experienced people we have, and they just got back into their offices." I felt like a fool. If this were anywhere else, who would have cared if I had left? The whole family looked at me with a blank look as if to say "Does she know you, Dad?"

In the public sector, it would have taken a minimum of six weeks to get that meeting, and yet she was apologizing for it being delayed a few hours. She led us to an office where she had told us there was a really good lady surgeon, but she wasn't there. She then led us to another office and opened the door and looked in. I heard her say to another doctor that the doctor she was looking for was not in, and she asked him if he would like to handle this meeting with the Jones family? He must have said yes because she turned to us and said softly again, "This is the Chief Surgeon; I am giving you to the best there is." How stupid of me; she did know me. She had calmed my fears and expressed genuine compassion. She was not a receptionist; she was the voice on the phone.

I had to lower the a/c down to 80 this morning. It must be really muggy out there. I was talking to a guy down at the water station last night. He said he had lost his electric during the storms the other night. We had also, but only for about a half an hour. He lost his for eight hours. He said he saw the storms building and dropped his a/c to 78 in preparation. He said his house is so tight that they made it through the night. That wouldn't work with our old house. The last time we lost power for that long, the electric company showed up at the bottom of the hill with truckloads of ice. That saves your food, but doesn't do much for the people and the animals. Cats pant just like dogs when it's over 100. It's no wonder we never see a mountain lion in the summer.

The only difference between life in the desert today and life here a hundred years ago is an electric wire. Medically, you might add penicillin. My wife would have been just as dead as the Old Dutchman from pneumonia without it. How blessed we are. I'm standing in a facility that is as large as the entire city of Phoenix was when the old man died in the little shack not far from here. Now I'm sitting in the little office introducing my family to a man with more medical knowledge than the old man's world possessed. He had the same pictures up on his computer that we had seen two weeks before. He was explaining that the VA system is the only one in the world that can do this. He has everything on the screen in front of him that has happened to me since my first visit to the clinic five years ago. He showed us where the last doctor had tattooed the inside of my colon. He explained how much easier it made things for his staff.

The doctor explained that I was in no immediate danger. He said we could just watch this problem for a while if I didn't really want to go through with the surgery right away. My wife wouldn't hear of it. She wanted him to get his knife out while I was still sitting on his table. I think he could see the concern on my face. He explained it to my wife. He explained that we were talking about major surgery. I just sat there and listened while the four of them made up my mind. He started pulling up every test I had ever had. He was explaining how they determined if one qualified for this big an operation. He went through every aspect of my health, right down to my body fat. He seemed almost surprised. He said just about all the good numbers were because I hadn't smoked in over forty years. He explained how he had to turn a woman down for the same surgery just that morning, based on her age and history of smoking.

The decision was made, and I don't think I ever opened my mouth. He said, "Do you know what this looks like?" He said this as if he had not expected it or experienced it very often. "This looks like we are going for a cure." I didn't know it at the time, but this type of surgery was usually just the first step to a cure. An old friend of the family came to see me after I got home from the hospital. He had had the same operation as mine, but I remember how surprised he was that I did not need to go through chemo as he had. We all stood up to leave when the doctor put his hand on my shoulder. He looked to be about my age, so I understood what he was saying. "You are young and healthier than average; I think you will do just fine."

He walked us to the nurses' station and introduced us to a very pleasant lady. He told us this would be my surgical nurse. He asked her for her personal business card and assured me that she would take my call anytime concerning my planned procedure. I never called her, but she called me to go over some preparations she wanted to make certain I understood. I had it wrong, sure enough, and she walked me through everything I needed to do. She wanted to make sure I made my appointment with the pre-surgery department and told me the easiest way to find it. I found the offices on the second floor by using a staff entrance that I didn't even know anything about before then. I was questioned by a couple staff people about my presence in their area. When they discovered what offices I was looking for, their whole demeanor changed. One of them even flagged down a subordinate to take me where I needed to go.

I had been in this system for five years by then. In their normal routine, they are some of the nicest people you will ever meet; busy but still congenial. Suddenly, I was somehow out of the mainstream. The offices I went to at this point were not crowded. There was fresh coffee waiting for you, and offered as if they had made just for you. The hurry was gone. Even the doctors greeted you with, "Mister Jones, my name is Sue. Do you mind if I call you George?" I didn't even know my personal physician's first name, yet I met five doctors that morning, if you include the guy that was going to put me to sleep. When I left those meetings, I was sure of one thing; nothing ahead of me was going to be treated as routine. It was going to be an individual effort, performed for an individual they knew.

For a while, back in the mid-sixties, I rubbed shoulders with men that were in combat the week before and were planning to be back in combat the next week. I know what it is to be congenial, but not personal. I knew that the next time I was that close to them, they may be in a black bag on the floor of my aircraft. I was not being treated congenial, however; I was being treated personal. It was as if somehow they knew that I was going to make it just fine. I was just not that sure. I had reason to believe that maybe my time here was over. I sure didn't get that feeling from anyone else. I could write another chapter on the last few weeks before surgery. I lived three weeks in a world that most of us will never know until it's our time. Cancer sufferers live in a different world. The people around me made it a special world that I will never forget. If I would have died, I would have died happy.

The afternoon before my surgery I received one more call. She said, "I just want to go over everything with you one more time." These people are good. I was not sure if I was going to show up or not. I was thinking that maybe I would just put everything off for a few months. That's the last thing I remember. I don't know how I got to the hospital or who went with me. I don't remember anything but waking up in captivity. I don't remember my plane going down. I don't even remember being captured, but there I was constrained to a metal box in a small bamboo cage. It was hazy and smoke-filled, but I had clear visions of pajama-clad figures in control of my fate. They would poke me and get in my face, then leave. This went on night after night for I don't know how long. I had visions of family fade in and out, but I was sure there was no hope of rescue. The torture was unbearable. I never felt such pain. Death would have been a welcome friend.

All my life, I have had a misconception about drugs. When a dear saint, by the name of Dale, was dying of cancer, he still never missed church. The last time we spoke, I asked him how he was doing. He told me that modern drugs were great. You see, I thought they were too. I can get high on an aspirin. I thought this whole ordeal was going to be like a night in the opium den. I was looking for a week in the desert on a horse with no name. If there was a horse, it was standing on me. I was sure I was going to die, and then it got worse; I was afraid I might not. I don't even want to think about what I remember about the next few days. I would have given everything I ever had if I could have had my cancer back in trade for however many years I would have had without this pain. I don't know what they were giving Dale, but I didn't get any.

Even now when I look back on this whole experience, it's hard to come up with a bright side. Maybe I would have got really sick as early as three years from now. With what is going on with our healthcare today, maybe I would have been left to die an agonizing death. If I lived in the UK, I would not even be eligible for this operation at my age. I don't know what is going to happen with our veterans. Maybe the Lord wanted me ready to live longer than I ever thought I would. If this is not the case, the only other upside is still a really good one. My new outlook on my marriage relationship is a breath of fresh air. We just forgot how much we needed each other around. I could never have gotten through these weeks of complications without her. They would have put me in the VA home, and I would have been glad to be there. I can't stand to be dependent. She made me feel like I was worth some special care. I think she made everyone feel that way.

My friend and neighbor has a brain tumor. I have watched him over the last few years. He could do less and less each year. He did some remodeling for us until he was not able to use a ladder. Then last year he lost his driving privileges. He was a really good carpenter. He built a really nice home. Now that he is on full disability, I figured he would enjoy the retirement he deserved. Last week his sister brought him over to see me one last time. His wife had thrown him out and he was going up north to live with his brother. She said she couldn't put up with his disabled condition. I said, "God forgive me; what a wonderful woman you gave me."

It's three in the morning. That wonderful woman just came into the dark bedroom, stumbled over my dog and crumpled to the floor. I've been in bed since eight, so I'm really awake now. She is flying out to Delaware in the morning to visit her sister. They went down to visit her brother last night, but I was feeling really tired. She said I looked tired, so I went to bed when they left. I took a pretty good fall in the office today. I don't know if that had anything to do with it. It's the first real shock I've had since they opened me up. I seem to be alright now. I wouldn't tell her if I wasn't, because she needs to get away and relax for a while. She has been at my beck and call now for over a month.

This is the first time I've been up before dawn since I got home. At least it's the first time that I wasn't sick or tending to some other ill. I had forgotten how beautiful the valley is at night. In the summer, the sea of lights twinkles like a million Christmas trees. The whole landscape seems to be moving and waving with the escaping heat. I can't wait for dawn now. The sun will soon begin to rise over the mountains to the east. Because our place sets in the shadow of the same mountain, the valley to the west will get the sun first. It's a wonderful process to watch it move across the valley below and creep up the hill towards us. It's an awesome part of life; you can't hurry it, and you can't stop it. Then it clears the ridge behind us, and the oven doors are opened for another glorious day in the desert. It's Saturday August 1st 2009. I wonder what it will bring with it today?

Revelations 22:18-19

For I testify unto every man that heareth the words of the prophecy of this book. If any man shall add unto these things, God shall add unto him the plagues that are written in this book: And if any man shall take away from the words of the book of this prophecy, God shall take away his part out of the book of life, and out of the holy city, and from the things which are written in this book.